# The Christian Life Series

# The Christian Life Series

## NORMAN H. JAMES

Whitaker House

# THE CHRISTIAN LIFE SERIES

Norman H. James
Association of New Testament Ministries
3831 Washington Pike
Bridgeville, PA 15017  USA


ISBN: 0-88368-367-9
Printed in the United States of America
Copyright © 1995 by Association of New Testament Ministries


Whitaker House
580 Pittsburgh Street
Springdale, PA 15144

1 2 3 4 5 6 7 8 9 10 11 12 13 14 15 / 08 07 06 05  04 03 02 01 00 99 98 97 96 95

## DEDICATION

I would like to dedicate this book to my wife Rebecca and my three sons, Norman, David, and Eric, who have been such an encouragement and support to me during the many years this book was being formulated.

## PART ONE

## BEGINNING THE CHRISTIAN LIFE

**Chapter**

# PART TWO

## PERFECTING THE CHRISTIAN LIFE

### Chapter

# PART THREE

## UNDERSTANDING THE CHRISTIAN LIFE

### Chapter

# PART FOUR

# LIVING THE CHRISTIAN LIFE

## Chapter

# PREFACE

Years ago, I began to realize that there are many Christians who had accepted Jesus Christ in a fervency of new-found faith and had begun to walk with Him, but they soon either became tired of the rigors of that walk or else became discouraged, not knowing how to adequately fight the enemy and protect themselves from his various attacks. These are those spoken of by Jesus in Matthew 13:20,21:

> *"And the one on whom seed was sown on the rocky places, this is the man who hears the word, and immediately receives it with joy; yet he has **no firm root in himself**, but is only temporary, and when affliction or persecution arises because of the word, immediately he falls away."*

Another unfortunate phenomenon that I have also observed is the kind of Christian described in Hebrews 5:12:

> *For though by this time you ought to be teachers, you have need again for someone to teach you the elementary principles of the oracles of God, and you have come to need milk and not solid food.*

In other words, we have here described for us the Christian who, although he believes, doesn't know a lot about **what** he believes, and because of this lack, he is not able to explain his faith to others. It is altogether remarkable that an individual can be trained to perform satisfactorily in a new job in a relatively short period of time, whereas some have been Christians for years and are still not proficient in the Word, even as it concerns the most basic elements of their faith.

A third condition which is all too prevalent among Christians today, especially among charismatic Christians, is the subjective outlook which is based upon experience more than upon the Word of God. This leads many to accept their own private understandings and interpretations as being the rule. These people are very hard to teach, and it is extremely difficult to lead them into deeper truth because they have already accepted their own standards as being final. Jesus commissioned us to "go . . . and **make disciples** of all the nations" (Matt. 28:19). The very word *disciple* implies the discipline involved in the process of learning about our new Master and becoming more and more like Him. It is a discipline which includes a systematic impartation of truth as well as a day-to-day sharing of life from one believer to another. The mature, experienced ones are the teachers; the young and inexperienced are the ones who must learn. It is dangerous for any believer to feel that he does not need to be a part of this learning process.

Although all of these conditions exist side by side in the church, they should not be considered as being normal to the Christian walk. The normal progression of development may be found in Colossians 2:6-8:

> *As you therefore have received Christ Jesus the Lord, so walk in Him, having been **firmly rooted** and now **being built up** in Him and **established in your faith,** just as **you were instructed,** and overflowing with gratitude. See to it that no one takes you captive through philosophy and empty deception, according to the tradition of men, according to the elementary principles of the world, rather than according to Christ.*

You see, it is not enough merely to receive Christ Jesus. New believers must begin to walk in their faith, allowing themselves to be instructed so that they may be (1) firmly rooted, (2) built up in Him, and (3) established in the faith. When believers have given themselves faithfully to this process of discipleship, they will be able to share their faith adequately with others and, at the same time, keep themselves free from the deceptive philosophies of this world.

This day-to-day sharing of life can only be accomplished within the framework of the fellowship of believers—the local church. The systematic teaching of the truths of our salvation should also be presented within that framework if they are ever to be meaningful and more than mere exercises in learning. This book was not written to be read and studied in the privacy of one's home; rather, it is meant to be taught by pastors to their people within the context of the local church (refer to *The Teacher's Guide to The Christian Life Series*).

The purpose of this book, therefore, is to provide new believers especially with a consistent and practical presentation of the basic truths of the Christian faith in such a way that they will know that they are building on a sound foundation, will also have the assurance that what they are building will stand the tests of both time and the enemy, and will endure through the ages to come. We believe that the advantage of these truths being taught within the framework of the local church is that a background of reality and integrity is thereby provided against which the new believer, in particular, may gauge his progress.

Part One of this book is entitled **Beginning the Christian Life** and is based upon that body of truth which we refer to as the "foundation stones" of our Christian experience. Our approach is certainly not an original one—many Bible teachers today recognize the importance of beginning with a sound foundation of truth and experience. Furthermore, Jesus had much to say about foundations, and the apostles, especially Paul, wrote of their necessity. It is here that we will discuss such things as sin and re-demption, faith and healing, and water baptism, as well as the baptism of the Holy Spirit.

Part Two is entitled **Perfecting the Christian Life** and is concerned with those truths which are relative to the church as a whole. Just as Part One addresses itself to the need for the individual believer to lay a proper foundation, so also Part Two concerns itself with the need for Christians to be built together corporately (that is, those who are "in a body") on a proper foundation. It is in this section that we will discuss such things as the church itself, the gifts of the Spirit, the ministries within the church, church discipline, the ministry of giving, and discipleship and commitment.

Part Three is entitled **Understanding the Christian Life** and covers such basics of our faith as the nature of the Godhead, the attributes of

God, the creation of the world, the fall of Adam, the government of God, and the manifestation of His kingdom. Part Four is entitled **Living the Christian Life** and contains teaching relative to the ordinances of the church.

The amount of benefit which you will personally receive from this course of study will depend primarily upon the amount of **time** and **energy** you are willing to put into it. I learned long ago that little, if anything, in this life comes to us automatically. This is especially true as it pertains to the things of God. There is a price to be paid for truth; Proverbs 23:23 says, "Buy truth, and do not sell it." You will learn little by simply attending classes; much of what you ultimately gain will depend upon your studying at home. It will certainly take time, but it will be time well invested in your own salvation and in the kingdom of our Lord Jesus Christ.

*Be diligent to present yourself approved to God as a workman who does not need to be ashamed, handling accurately the word of truth.*                                        2 Tim. 2:15

Norman H. James

# FOREWORD

*Do not fear, O land, rejoice and be glad,*
*For the Lord has done great things.*
*Do not fear, beasts of the field,*
*For the pastures of the wilderness have turned green,*
*For the tree has borne its fruit,*
*The fig tree and the vine have yielded in full.*
*So rejoice, O sons of Zion,*
*And be glad in the Lord your God;*
*For He has given you the early rain for your vindication.*
*And He has poured down for you the rain,*
*The early and latter rain as before.*
*And the threshing floors will be full of grain,*
*And the vats will overflow with the new wine and oil.*
***"Then I will make up to you for the years***
*That the swarming locust has eaten,*
*The creeping locust, the stripping locust,*
*     and the gnawing locust,*
*My great army which I sent among you.*
*And you shall have plenty to eat and be satisfied,*
*And praise the name of the Lord your God,*
*Who has dealt wondrously with you;*
*Then My people will never be put to shame.*
*Thus you will know that I am in the midst of Israel,*
*And that I am the Lord your God*
*And there is no other;*
*And My people will never be put to shame.*
*And it will come about after this*
*That I will pour out My Spirit on all mankind;*
*And your sons and daughters will prophesy,*
*Your old men will dream dreams,*
*Your young men will see visions.*
*And even on the male and female servants*
*I will pour out My Spirit in those days."*

Joel 2:21-29

These verses from the book of Joel speak to us of restoration. Restoration is more than revival; it is a returning of things to their first estate—things as they were originally intended to be. As used here, it contains the Lord's promise that in the day of His visitation He will restore the church to its original state of integrity and power. The swarming locust, which is the enemy of all that has ever been planted by the Lord, has indeed stripped away much of that which is true and meaningful in the church. To many, however, this impoverished state has not been as evident as it should have been because man has artfully attempted to make up for the lack of "rain," "new wine," and "oil" (the active presence of the Holy Spirit) by the substitution of his own religious productivity. Regardless of the motives and events which have been responsible for this development, it remains that Christianity has for many become a mere religion rather than The Way to Life. In order to understand this process more fully, we need to go back to the early days of the church and trace its progress through the ages right up to our day.

The history of the church of the Lord Jesus Christ from about A.D. 300 to the early sixteenth century was frequently characterized by moral and spiritual impoverishment. The New Testament Scriptures themselves speak plainly of this very thing, beginning with Jesus' own testimony of the coming false prophets, "who come to you in sheep's clothing, but inwardly are ravenous wolves" (Matt. 7:15-23 q.v.), and ending with the warning against the "deeds" and "teachings" of the Nicolaitans (Rev. 2:6,15). Also read Acts 20:28-31; 2 Corinthians 11:1-4; Galatians 1:6-9; Ephesians 4:11-15; Philippians 1:12-17; 2 Thessalonians 2:3-7; 2 Timothy 1:13-15; Jude 1-3.

The Lord, as He had promised through His prophets of old, began to restore spiritual truth and health to His church with the Protestant Reformation, which had its beginnings in the sixteenth century. To many, this restoration of truth ended with the Reformation period. There are churches today whose main tenets of faith were formed during that time and have remained virtually unchanged to this present day. Fortunately for us, however, the Lord did not consider the restoration as having been completed. There have been sprinklings of renewing rains down through the years, resulting in the various denominations. The Pentecostal Movement was born in an outpouring of the Holy Spirit at the beginning of this century, and in 1948 the Lord moved in still another restoration of

# MAJOR DENOMINATIONS
# IN AMERICA TODAY

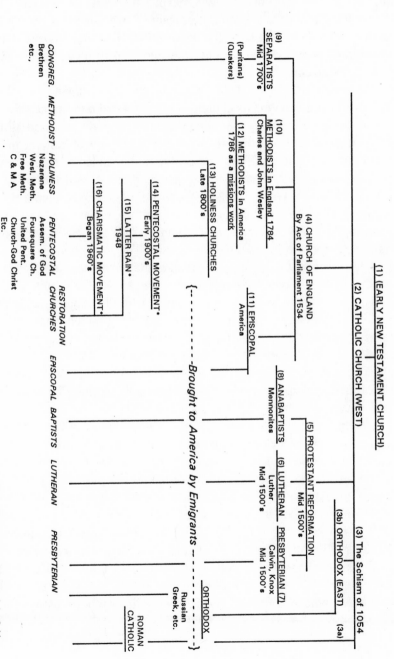

spiritual truth and life. This mighty move of God, with reverberations felt around the world, was termed Latter Rain. Sad to say, many of God's people who were swept up and transformed by that great movement of restoration soon began to consider the fulness of truth as having been restored to the church.

My friends, once again God is moving in the earth, bringing refreshing rains of life and truth to His church. Let us not make the same mistake that others have made by assuming that we now have received all the truth. It is more than obvious that the denominational system, under which the church has suffered for centuries, has failed to fulfill Jesus' prayer to the Father, "that they may all be one . . . that they may be perfected in unity" (Jn. 17:21-23). There are those who believe that this present move of the Holy Spirit, referred to as the Charismatic Movement (from the Greek word *charisma,* meaning a "gift of grace"), will bring about a "corporate renewal"—ecumenism. The Lord, however, is not going to renew and perpetuate this man-made system that has fractured Christianity for so long, whatever form it may eventually assume.

Then there are those to whom the Charismatic Movement is an end in itself. They view this present outpouring as being merely another new dimension to be added to their Christian experience—and that is all. There are also those to whom the Charismatic Movement is a threat. The baptism of the Holy Spirit and the accompanying gifts have never been a part of their tradition. They therefore oppose these things because they don't understand them.

Finally, there are those who are of the conviction that the Lord is at long last completing the healing and renewing of His body, the church, by calling His people out from their various religious backgrounds and loyalties and building them into one new man in the Spirit (Eph. 4:11-16). I share in that conviction. I believe that this people will be God's people—His "chosen race, a royal priesthood, a holy nation, a people for God's own possession" (1 Pet. 2:9). They will not be known as Catholics, Methodists, Baptists, Presbyterians, Pentecostals, or Charismatics, but simply as Christians. In the early days of the church, the word Christian was a term of derision applied to the followers of Jesus by the unbelievers—those who were **not** following. It may be so again in our day.

*Be patient, therefore, brethren, until the coming of the Lord.*
*Behold, the farmer waits for the precious produce of the soil,*
*being patient about it, until it gets the early and late rains.* ***You***
***too be patient; strengthen your hearts, for the coming of the***
***Lord is at hand.***                                              Jas. 5:7,8

Yes, be patient, brethren, for the rains are here! The new wine and oil of the Holy Spirit have been restored to us and His coming is at hand. You and I may very well be living in the day when we shall see the Lord our God gather to Himself all things, ruling and reigning in the earth from the midst of His people, and we must do our part to hasten that day! These are not days to be idle "on beds of ivory" in Zion (Amos 6:4). These are days for caring for the ever-increasing flocks of the Lord as well as for toiling in the harvest fields of this world, praying fervently all the while to the Lord of the harvest that He will enlist more and more laborers for His service (read Matthew 9:36-38).

I believe that in order to fulfill this task as well as the mandate of the Great Commission of Matthew 28:19, "Go therefore and **make disciples** of all the nations, baptizing them . . . [and] teaching them to observe all that I commanded you," we shall have to have a strong sense of identity and purpose. We shall need to be "taught of the Lord" (Isa. 54:13; Jn. 6:45) and "strengthened with power through His Spirit in the inner man" (Eph. 3:16).

This book, which was written to aid God's people in the attainment of these goals and was undertaken in an effort to present the old truths of the Christian experience in the new light of restoration, would not have been possible without the labors of others. I am indebted to those who have been used by the Lord over the years in ministering solid foundational truths to me, especially Mrs. Patricia Gruits and Pastor James Lee Beall of Bethesda Christian Church in Detroit, Michigan. I also want to thank Lisa Felty and Janet Hunger who have worked so tirelessly with me in the actual typing, proofreading, and printing of this work. Additionally, I would like to give a special thanks to the artists, John Margeson and Ernest White, who produced the excellent illustrations which add so much to this teaching.

Finally, I am most grateful to the Holy Spirit for His leading and enabling. Please be assured that any errors in this book, whether in writing or in the presentation of truth, are the result of the author being able to comprehend with mere human abilities the magnitude of that which the Lord is doing. This book is therefore presented to the churches of the Lord Jesus Christ with the prayer that it will help them to be rooted and built up in Him and established in the faith (Col. 2:7).

Norman H. James

# Part One

## Beginning the Christian Life

# OUR FOUNDATION

**Chapter 1**

Having a solid, well-built foundation is essential in building anything that is meant to last. If the foundation is not solid, the superstructure that is built upon it, regardless of its sturdy appearance, will soon crumble and eventually come down. At the least, it will fall into such disrepair that it will no longer be fit for habitation. This is a principle of construction that is recognized by men of all cultures and societies where buildings are erected. Because all men understand this principle of the necessity for a sound foundation, the Lord has used it to instruct us concerning the proper building of our lives as well as that of our corporate life which is the church.

The Bible speaks of our lives as being buildings (2 Cor. 5:1) and describes for us the kind of foundation upon which they must be built. The Bible also refers to the church as being a building (Eph. 2:19-22), and there, too, describes for us the foundation upon which it must be built. Part Two of this book deals with the church. In this first part, we will study the proper laying of our personal foundations.

## 1. WHAT DID JESUS TEACH ABOUT OUR PERSONAL FOUN-DATIONS?

In teaching us concerning our personal foundations, Jesus gave us the parable of the two houses. This parable is recorded for us in two places, first in Matthew 7:24-27:

> *"Therefore everyone who hears these words of Mine, and acts upon them, may be compared to a wise man, who built his house upon the rock. And the rain descended, and the floods came, and the winds blew, and burst against that*

*house; and yet it did not fall, for it had been founded upon the rock. And everyone who hears these words of Mine, and does not act upon them, will be like a foolish man, who built his house upon the sand. And the rain descended, and the floods came, and the winds blew, and burst against that house; and it fell, and great was its fall."*

and secondly in Luke 6:47-49:

*"Everyone who comes to Me, and hears My words, and acts upon them, I will show you whom he is like: he is like a man building a house, who dug deep and laid a foundation upon the rock; and when a flood rose, the torrent burst against that house and could not shake it, because it had been well built. But the one who has heard, and has not acted accordingly, is like a man who built a house upon the ground without any foundation; and the torrent burst against it and immediately it collapsed, and the ruin of that house was great."*

What does this parable teach us?

°   First of all, if we want to build our lives in a sound manner, we must not rely upon our own judgment nor follow our own way. We must (1) come to the Lord, (2) hear His sayings, and (3) do them.

> *"Everyone who comes to Me, and hears My words, and acts upon them, I will show you whom he is like."*
>
> Lk. 6:47

°   Just as it is possible to come to the Lord and yet not really hear what He is saying, so also it is possible to come **and** hear but go away without doing either.

> *"And why do you call Me, 'Lord, Lord,' and **do not do what I say?"***
>
> Lk. 6:46

2

*But prove yourselves doers of the word, and not merely hearers who delude themselves. For if anyone is a hearer of the word and not a doer, he is like a man who looks at his natural face in a mirror; for once he has looked at himself and gone away, he has immediately forgotten what kind of person he was.*

Jas. 1:22-24

° A man who both **hears** and **does** the word is like a man who built his house by digging deep and removing everything between himself and the rock in order to assure a solid foundation.

*"He is like a man building a house, who dug deep and laid a foundation upon the rock."* Lk. 6:48a

° A house must be built upon a rock because storms **will** come; it is the nature of life. A house without a proper foundation will not be able to outlast the storms, and sooner or later it will fall. God uses the trials of this life to perfect us and make us ready for the life that is to come. We must all face the judgment seat of Christ, and if we meet the Lord in these times of shaking now, there will be fewer useless and fleshly things to answer for then.

*See to it that you do not refuse Him who is speaking. For if those did not escape when they refused him who warned them on earth, much less shall we escape who turn away from Him who warns from heaven. And His voice shook the earth then, but now He has promised, saying, "Yet once more I will shake not only the earth, but also the heaven." And this expression, "Yet once more," denotes the removing of those things which can be shaken, as of created things, in order that those things which cannot be shaken may remain. Therefore, since we receive a kingdom which cannot be shaken, let us show gratitude, by which we may offer to God an acceptable service with reverence and awe; for **our God is a consuming fire.***

Heb. 12:25-29

3

He that comes        . . .hears        . . .and does. . .

 =

° Every man is building something, and every man's building is
someday going to be judged (1 Cor. 3:10-15; 2 Cor. 5:10; Rom.
14:10). If we want our building to be judged and accepted by the
Lord, then we must do two things:

a. Dig down deep and find the rock—not sand or soil. Sand is
the same material and substance as rock, only loose and dis-
connected. Many Christians are building their lives upon a
loose arrangement of Scriptures and experiences. This may
stand for a while (just as sand at the seashore remains firm
under foot until the waves begin to wash it out), but sooner or
later, it is going to begin to crumble. We cannot afford to be
building our lives upon a lot of notions and head knowledge

and a loose collection of "Christian ethics"—we **must** have a personal encounter with Jesus Christ Himself, who is the sure and steady Rock for the believer (the marginal note for Matthew 16:18 states that Jesus used a word here that actually means "bedrock"). When we then gather all our personal experiences together and relate them to God's Word on the basis of the Lordship of Jesus Christ, we have a solid foundation—and not just a backyard full of sand.

b. Once we have found that Rock, we must begin to build a solid foundation **in order** and **according to God's word.** We must not attempt to construct our foundation with a loose collection of experiences, nor must we attempt to assemble it with "untempered mortar," that is, with no real cohesion or order (Isa. 28:9-13).

° When buffeted by the storm, the house which had been built upon the rock remained firm.

*"And when a flood rose, the torrent burst against that house and **could not shake it,** because it had been well built."*  Lk. 6:48b

He that comes  . . .hears  . . .and doesn't do. . .

° Of course, the house which had been built without a foundation fell under the attack of the storm.

> "But the one who has heard, and has not acted accordingly, is like a man who built a house upon the ground without any foundation; and the torrent burst against it and immediately it collapsed, and the ruin of that house was great." Lk. 6:49

## 2. WHAT DID THE APOSTLES TEACH ABOUT OUR PERSONAL FOUNDATION?

Paul states the absolute necessity of the foundation in 1 Corinthians 3:10-15:

> *According to the grace of God which was given to me, as a wise master builder I laid a foundation, and another is building upon it. But let each man be careful how he builds upon it.* **For no man can lay a foundation other than the one which is laid, which is Jesus Christ.** *Now if any man builds upon the foundation with gold, silver, precious stones, wood, hay, straw, each man's work will become evident; for the day will show it, because it is to be revealed with fire; and the fire itself will test the quality of each man's work. If any man's work which he has built upon it remains, he shall receive a reward. If any man's work is burned up, he shall suffer loss; but he himself shall be saved, yet so as through fire.*

There is a difference between the foundation, which is our appropriation of the total redemptive work of Jesus Christ, and our works—that which are those things which we build upon our foundation. In the day of judgment, our foundation will not be tested, but our works will. If our works remain, we will receive our reward accordingly. This "reward" does not refer to our salvation because that is a gift of grace by faith, which is not given to us on the basis of

6

works (Eph. 2:8,9). If our works are burned up in the consuming fire of God's holy judgment, we ourselves will yet be saved because we have built upon the solid foundation of Jesus Christ—and that will remain!

The Apostle Peter also wrote of the Rock which has become our foundation:

*And coming to Him as to a living stone, rejected by men, but choice and precious in the sight of God, you also, as living stones, are being built up as a spiritual house for a holy priesthood, to offer up spiritual sacrifices acceptable to God through Jesus Christ. For this is contained in Scripture: "Behold I lay in Zion a choice stone, a precious corner stone, and he who believes in Him shall not be disappointed." This precious value, then, is for you who believe. But for those who disbelieve, "The stone which the builders rejected, this became the very corner stone," and, "A stone of stumbling and a rock of offense"; for they stumble because they are disobedient to the word, and to this doom they were also appointed.*     1 Pet. 2:4-8*

Paul again speaks of our foundation in his letter to the church at Ephesus:

*So then you are no longer strangers and aliens, but you are fellow citizens with the saints, and are of God's household, having been built upon the foundation of the apostles and prophets, Christ Jesus Himself being the corner stone, in whom the whole building, being fitted together is growing into a holy temple in the Lord; in whom you also are being built together into a dwelling of God in the Spirit.*
*Eph. 2:19-22*

7

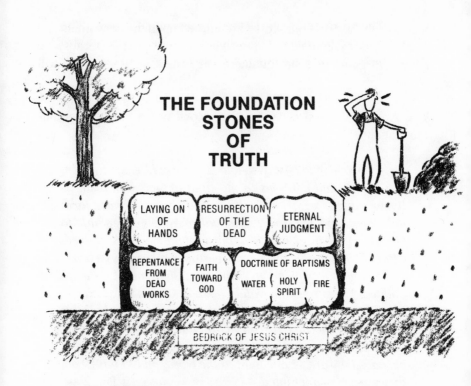

THE FOUNDATION
STONES
OF
TRUTH

| LAYING ON OF HANDS | RESURRECTION OF THE DEAD | ETERNAL JUDGMENT |

| REPENTANCE FROM DEAD WORKS | FAITH TOWARD GOD | DOCTRINE OF BAPTISMS |
| | | WATER ( HOLY SPIRIT ) FIRE |

BEDROCK OF JESUS CHRIST

## 3. DOES THE BIBLE SPEAK MORE SPECIFICALLY ABOUT OUR FOUNDATION?

Yes, the writer of Hebrews describes the foundation even further in Hebrews 5:11-14 and 6:1,2:

> *Concerning Him* [Jesus] *we have much to say, and it is hard to explain, since you have become dull of hearing. For though by this time you ought to be teachers, you have need again for someone to teach you the elementary principles* [literally, "elements of the beginning"] *of the oracles of God, and you have come to need milk and not solid food. For everyone who partakes only of milk is not accustomed to the word of righteousness, for he is a babe. But solid food is for the mature, who because of practice have their senses trained to discern good and evil.*

8

*Therefore* leaving the elementary teaching [literally, "the word of the beginning"] *about the Christ, let us press on to maturity, not laying again a **foundation** of. . .*

1. *Repentance from dead works*
2. *Faith toward God*
3. *Instruction about washings* ["baptisms," KJV]
4. *Laying on of hands*
5. *Resurrection of the dead*
6. *Eternal judgment.*

Remember, these are **foundation** stones of truth, the very beginnings of truth—the milk of our salvation. Believers will never understand the meat of the word until they have comprehended these basic truths.

## HOME STUDY QUESTIONS: CHAPTER 1

1. Briefly define the word *foundation,* and then in your own words explain why it is an important concept to you spiritually.

2. List the six foundation stones, or principles, of Christ in their scriptural order.

3. Using a concordance or other similar reference tool, locate and list at least three other places in Scripture where the term *foundation* is used, other than those referred to in this chapter.

4. If you were to meet a Christian who was of the opinion that an understanding of doctrine is not necessary to living a successful Christian life (that is, successful in God's terms), what would you tell him?

5. Using your own Bible, look up all the Scripture references used in this chapter, and read them in context. It is important for you to see and read these verses in your Bible and not just as part of the lesson in this book.

# SIN

**Chapter 2**

Before we can truly understand the meaning and working of the first foundation stone, repentance from dead works, we must define for ourselves that from which we are to repent.

This chapter was not undertaken with the purpose of presenting a profound theological statement concerning sin; quite the contrary. Its purpose is to set forth that which the Bible teaches concerning sin and its basic working in our lives in a language that is forthright and uncomplicated.

## 1.  WHAT IS SIN?

The Bible defines sin for us as the "transgression [willful breaking] of the law" (1 Jn. 3:4 KJV). Although there are many kinds of sin, we will discuss them under two categories: iniquity and dead works.  A careful study of the various New Testament Greek words which are relative to sin, and the passages in which they are found, tells us that sin is "transgression," an overstepping of the line which God has fixed between good and evil, right and wrong.  It is "error," a departure from the path of that which is right.  It is "trespass," an intrusion of self-will into the sphere of God's authority.  It is "lawlessness," moral and spiritual rebellion against the established laws of God.  To sum it all up, sin may be correctly defined as **any violation of, or lack of conformity to, the will of God.**

## 2. WHAT IS INIQUITY?

Iniquity, also called lawlessness, is that sin which we inherit when we are born into the world. The Bible also refers to it as the "law of sin" (Rom. 7:23; 8:2). This inherited sin or iniquity causes us to come into this world being **"by nature** children of wrath" (Eph. 2:3) and in desperate need of being born again. The basic element of iniquity is **self**ishness—the love of and for self as opposed to love for God.

> *Behold, I was brought forth in iniquity, and in sin my mother conceived me.*　　　　　　　　　　　　　Ps. 51:5

> *Strip yourselves of your former nature—put off and discard your old unrenewed self—which characterized your previous manner of life and becomes corrupt through lusts and desires that spring from delusion.*
> 　　　　　　　　　　　　　　　　　　　Eph. 4:22 AMP

> *And you were dead in your trespasses and sins, in which you formerly walked according to the course of this world, according to the prince of the power of the air, of the spirit that is now working in the sons of disobedience. Among them we too **all** formerly lived in the lusts of our flesh, indulging the desires of the flesh **and** of the mind, and were **by nature children of wrath,** even as the rest.*　　　Eph. 2:1-3

Contrary to what is often thought, we are not sinners because we **do** sinful things. If this were true, then its opposite would also be true: that those of us who do not seem to do wrong things are not in need of salvation. The Bible teaches that we are all born into sin and that there is "none righteous, not even one" (Rom. 3:10) and that "all have sinned and fall short of the glory of God" (Rom. 3:23).

## 3. WHAT ARE DEAD WORKS?

Dead works are the things we do as well as the attitudes we have (Eph. 2:3) which are unacceptable to God and contrary to His Law. These dead works, which may be anything from merely attempting to establish our own righteousness to committing gross sin, are the results of the inherited iniquity within us, which in turn causes us to want our own way and to live our lives apart from the direct government of God.

> *All of us like sheep have gone astray, each of us has turned to **his own way**; but the Lord has caused the **iniquity** of us all to fall on Him.* Isa. 53:6

> *"For **out of the heart** come evil thoughts, murders, adulteries, fornications, thefts, false witness, slanders."* Matt. 15:19

> *But each one is tempted when he is carried away and enticed **by his own lust.*** Jas. 1:14

All of the examples of sin mentioned above are rather obvious and easy to identify when seen in operation. The most prevalent manifestation of iniquity, however, and the one most difficult to detect, is the inborn hostility in each one of us to the things of God. This hostility manifests itself in our lives most apparently during the time the Holy Spirit initially convicts us of sin and begins to draw us toward reconciliation with God. Some of us resisted a long time before yielding to Him. Moreover, this resistance continues to work in us, in some measure, even after conversion and on through most of our Christian lives. We frequently respond with such difficulty to the recreating and perfecting work of the Holy Spirit within us. (Read Genesis 6:5; 8:21; Romans 5:10; 7:18; 8:7; 1 Corinthians 2:14.)

13

## 4. HOW CAN WE KNOW THAT INIQUITY IS INHERITED?

The Bible tells us that God created man in His own image and likeness. Basically, this means two things:

° Man alone, of all that was created, is a reflection of the personality and character of God in that he is a rational, intelligent being and capable of love, compassion, etc. In his original state, man was innocent, that is, not only sinless, but also completely unaware of even the possibility of sin.

° Secondly, man is composed of body, soul, and **spirit** (1 Thess. 5:23; Rom. 8:10,16; 1 Cor. 2:11; Heb. 4:12). It is primarily in this way that man is a reflection of the nature of God and is not merely an extension of animal life.

After the creation had been completed, God told Adam that he could partake of all that was in the garden of Eden with the exception of the tree of the knowledge of good and evil and warned him that, if he disobeyed, he would die (Gen. 2:16,17). Adam disobeyed God's command, thereby sinning and losing his innocency and, eventually, dying. Hereby we know that sin is inherited: (1) **every man** sins (Rom. 3:23), and (2) **every man** dies (Rom. 5:12-14,17-19).

## 5. BY WHOM WAS SIN BROUGHT INTO THIS WORLD?

This is an extremely important question, and it is of the utmost importance that we do not take the answer for granted. God is **not** responsible for sin. Sin was brought into the world by not only the devil, who once was a holy angel, but who sinned against God and lost his heavenly estate (Ezk. 28:12-17; Isa. 14:12-14), but also by man who, of his **own free will,** yielded to the temptation of the devil.

*The one who practices sin is of the devil; for the devil has sinned from the beginning.* 1 Jn. 3:8

14

*Be of sober spirit, be on the alert. Your adversary, **the devil,** prowls about like a roaring lion, seeking someone to devour.* 1 Pet. 5:8

*For it was Adam who was first created, and then Eve. And it was not Adam who was deceived* [in other words, he fell because of a willful and knowing decision]*, but the woman being quite deceived, fell into transgression.*
1 Tim. 2:13,14

*Therefore, just as through one man* [Adam] *sin entered into the world, and death through sin, and so death spread to all men, because all sinned.* Rom. 5:12

## 6. IS THERE A MEANS OF DELIVERANCE FROM THE CURSE OF SIN?

Even before we have begun to understand the origin and nature of sin, we long to be free from its evil influence upon our lives and to know that it has been vanquished once and for all. Is this possible? Yes!

Concerning the nature of this deliverance from sin, Paul said:

*I see a different law in the members of my body, waging war against the law of my mind, and making me a prisoner of the law of sin which is in my members. Wretched man that I am! Who will set me free from the body of this death?*
Rom. 7:23,24

*There is therefore now no condemnation for those who are in Christ Jesus. For the law of the Spirit of life in Christ Jesus has set you free from the law of sin and of death.*
Rom. 8:1,2

John the Baptist testified:

> *"Behold, the Lamb of God who takes away the sin of the world!"*  Jn. 1:29

Isaiah wrote:

> *Surely our griefs He Himself bore, and our sorrows He carried.*
>
> *But He was pierced through for our transgressions, He was crushed for our iniquities; the chastening for our well-being fell upon Him, and by His scourging we are healed.*
>
> *He was oppressed and He was afflicted, yet He did not open His mouth; like a lamb that is led to slaughter, and like a sheep that is silent before its shearers, so He did not open His mouth.*
>
> *But the Lord was pleased to crush Him, putting Him to grief; if He would render Himself as a guilt offering.*
>
> *As a result of the anguish of His soul, He will see it and be satisfied; by His knowledge the Righteous One, My Servant, will justify the many, as He will bear their iniquities.*  Isa. 53:4a,5,7,10a,11

Jesus Himself said:

> *"For God so loved the world, that He gave His only begotten Son, that whoever believes in Him should not perish, but have eternal life."*  Jn. 3:16

Once again, Paul, in writing to the Corinthian church, says:

> *For the love of Christ controls us, having concluded this, that one died for all, therefore all died; and He **died for all,** that they who live should no longer live for themselves, but for Him who died and rose again on their behalf.*
>
> *Therefore if any man is in Christ, he is a new creature; the old things passed away; behold, new things have come.*

16

*Now all these things are from God, who reconciled us to Himself through Christ, and gave us the ministry of reconciliation, namely, that God was in Christ reconciling the world to Himself, not counting their trespasses against them, and He has committed to us the word of reconciliation.*

*Therefore, we are ambassadors for Christ, as though God were entreating through us; we beg you on behalf of Christ, be reconciled to God. He made Him who knew no sin to be sin on our behalf, that we might become the righteousness of God in Him.*                    2 Cor. 5:14,15,17-21

And finally:

*For if while we were enemies, we were reconciled to God through the death of His Son, much more, having been reconciled, we shall be saved by His life.*          Rom. 5:10

## 7. HOW CAN WE CLAIM THIS DELIVERANCE FROM SIN FOR OURSELVES?

We can claim this deliverance for ourselves and find forgiveness from sin by accepting Jesus Christ as Savior.

°   Romans 3:23 says, **"All** have sinned . . . ."

°   Romans 6:23 says, "The wages of sin is death." This is not merely death sometime far off in the future. Every sinner is in a living death **now** because of trespasses and sins brought about by being by nature children of wrath (Eph. 2:1-5).

°   Romans 5:8 tells us, that even though we are sinners and worthy of death, God demonstrates His own love toward us in that, while we were yet sinners, Christ died for us. Jesus, who knew no sin, became sin for us and died on the cross for us, bearing all the sin and iniquity of the world upon Himself.

17

° The atoning sacrifice of Jesus Christ must be personally understood and accepted by each one of us. "As many as received Him, to them He gave the right ["power," KJV] to become children of God" (Jn. 1:12).

° Salvation is a free gift from God (Rom. 6:23), but this free gift must be personally claimed and received. How do we receive Jesus? Here is how:

a. Romans 10:13 says, "Whoever will call upon the name of the Lord will be saved." We must honestly and openly come to Jesus, repenting of our sinfulness and asking Him to accept us. We also have this promise, "the one who comes to Me I will certainly not cast out" (Jn. 6:37).

b. We must confess our sins. First John 1:9 says, "If we confess our sins, He is faithful and righteous ["just," KJV] to forgive us our sins." And we can read in 1 John 1:7 that "the blood of Jesus His Son cleanses us from all sin."

c. We should then confess Him as Lord and Savior before others. "If you confess with your mouth Jesus as Lord, and believe in your heart that God raised Him from the dead, you shall be saved; for with the heart man believes, resulting in righteousness, and with the mouth he confesses, resulting in salvation" (Rom. 10:9,10).

Our "born-again" experience is then made complete as we obediently enter the waters of baptism and are indwelt by the Holy Spirit.

> *If we confess our sins, He is faithful and righteous to forgive us our sins and to cleanse us from all unrighteousness.*                                    1 Jn. 1:9

*Jesus answered, "Truly, truly, I say to you, unless one is born of water and the Spirit, he cannot enter into the kingdom of God."*                    Jn. 3:5

*"Brethren, what shall we do [to be saved]?" And Peter said to them, "Repent, and let each of you be baptized in the name of Jesus Christ for the forgiveness of your sins; and you shall receive the gift of the Holy Spirit."*                    Acts 2:37b,38

*"Repent therefore and return, that your sins may be wiped away."*                    Acts 3:19a

*For by grace you have been saved through faith; and that not of yourselves, it is the gift of God; not as a result of works, that no one should boast.*
Eph. 2:8,9

## 8.  IS IT POSSIBLE FOR A CHRISTIAN TO SIN?

Yes, it is possible for a Christian to sin, but there is a difference between outright, intended (that is, willful) sin and those things which we may classify as mistakes and faults (remember, we are not intending to apply theological terms to these things!).

°   We have already discussed in this chapter that kind of sin which is the willful breaking of God's law, whether it is something we have overtly done or merely a sinful attitude we have allowed to remain.

°   A mistake is something that we should not have done but which we did because of weakness, immaturity, or error in judgment. A lot of misunderstanding about sin in the life of a Christian can be cleared up simply by acknowledging this difference between sin and faults or weaknesses. Not every wrong thing that a Christian does is sin. There is a great difference between momentary falling through weakness and out-and-out sin, which is the purposeful breaking of God's laws. Think of a child, for instance. Many times a child will display behavior that is not acceptable and may actually do things that are wrong, not because he is rebellious and wanting to misbehave, but because he is a child and needs to be trained to maturity.

It is possible, however, that a weakness or fault may in time become sin if it is not dealt with as the Holy Spirit brings both conviction and the ability to overcome.

° A fault is something that is within us and must be overcome because it is not acceptable to the Father. Some are able to overcome so easily, while others seem to make very little progress. God is merciful to those who are weak (1 Cor. 9:22; 1 Thess. 5:14), but we must not take advantage of His patience. First Corinthians 4:5 applies to such situations: "Therefore do not go on passing judgment before the time, but wait until the Lord comes who will both bring to light the things hidden in the darkness and disclose the motives of men's hearts; and then each man's praise will come to him from God."

° It is also important to learn the difference between freedom and using that freedom as an occasion to the flesh (Gal. 5:1,13; Rom. 14; 15:1). What may be sin to you may not be sin to another. (Remember, we are not talking about those things which the Bible declares to be sinful for everyone.)

° We must also consider those things about which the Lord may not yet have convicted us. For example, the Lord seemed to overlook the many wives of Jacob although His pattern from the beginning was one man, one woman. Why? Probably because that was not one of the principles of truth He was ready to require of His people. What was overlooked in Jacob, however, became Solomon's downfall because he knew better.

Another prominent example is that of the high places. The Lord forbade from the beginning the use of high places for worship by His people Israel. (See Leviticus 17:3-5; Deuteronomy 12:13,14.) The Lord not only seemed to overlook this for a time, but He even blessed Samuel who made the circuit of the high places to offer sacrifice. Once the temple had been built, however, the Lord God placed His Name there, and the people were forbidden to worship elsewhere (1 Ki. 3:2; 2 Chr. 7:11-16). When they continued to frequent their high places, the practice became gross sin and idolatry to them.

There are, no doubt, many areas in all our lives where the Lord has not yet brought conviction. This does not mean that those things are not sin; it just means that the Lord is patient, not willing that any should perish.

## 9. WHAT HAPPENS WHEN A CHRISTIAN SINS?

When a Christian sins, he must repent and ask for forgiveness from the Lord. The unregenerate man is not a sinner because he commits sin, but because he was born into sin. Man comes into this world as a sinner. An unsaved individual may live an outwardly righteous life, but he is still a sinner because he has not been cleansed by the blood of Jesus Christ and born anew according to the Gospel.

The Christian, on the other hand, has been reborn into a newness of life and has died to sin through the work of the Holy Spirit (Rom. 6). This new birth brings him into the family of God, and the Lord will never look upon him again as a sinner. When a Christian sins, this does not cause him to be regarded as an outsider, but as a disobedient son. The parable of the prodigal son is especially helpful in the understanding of this difference. The young man took his inheritance, left home, spent all he had, and finally found himself in the pig pen, but he was still the son of his father. All he had to do was repent and go home. Notice that, although he did not regard himself as being worthy of sonship any longer and was willing to work as a slave in his father's household, his father not only welcomed him **as a son,** but rejoiced greatly in doing so.

> *If we say that we have no sin, we are deceiving ourselves, and the truth is not in us. If we confess our sins, He is faithful and righteous to forgive us our sins and to cleanse us from all unrighteousness.* 1 Jn. 1:8,9

> *My little children, I am writing these things to you that you may not sin. And if anyone sins, we have an Advocate with the Father, Jesus Christ the righteous; and He Himself is the propitiation* [satisfaction] *for our sins; and not for ours only, but also for those of the whole world.*
>
> 1 Jn. 2:1,2

## 10.   WHAT DOES SIN DO TO US?

a.   Sin breaks our communication with God.

> *But your iniquities have made a separation between you and your God, and your sins have hidden His face from you, so that He does not hear.* Isa. 59:2

b.   Sin robs us of both our self-esteem (our feelings about ourselves) and our self-confidence (our feelings concerning how others feel about us). This is especially true in our relationship to God.

> *Be gracious to me, O God, according to Thy lovingkindness; according to the greatness of Thy compassion blot out my transgressions.*
>
> *Wash me thoroughly from my iniquity, and cleanse me from my sin.*
>
> *For I know my transgressions, and my sin is ever before me.*

*Against Thee, Thee only, I have sinned, and done what is evil in Thy sight, so that Thou art justified when Thou dost speak, and blameless when Thou dost judge.*

*Behold, I was brought forth in iniquity, and in sin my mother conceived me.*

*Behold, Thou dost desire truth in the innermost being, and in the hidden part Thou wilt make me know wisdom.*

*Purify me with hyssop, and I shall be clean; wash me, and I shall be whiter than snow.*

*Make me to hear joy and gladness, let the bones which Thou hast broken rejoice.*

*Hide Thy face from my sins, and blot out all my iniquities.*

*Create in me a clean heart, O God, and renew a steadfast spirit within me.*

*Do not cast me away from Thy presence, and do not take Thy Holy Spirit from me.*                    Ps. 51:1-11

c.  Sin produces guilt.

Our conscience was designed by God to act as an inner compass to keep us pointed in the direction of righteousness and holiness. When we sin, this inner compass indicates to our inner man that we have veered off course, resulting in the feelings of guilt.

*. . . in whatever our heart condemns us; for God is greater than our heart, and knows all things. Beloved, if our heart does not condemn us, we have confidence before God.*                    1 Jn. 3:20,21

d.  Sin becomes a bad habit.

If we refuse to listen and respond to the convicting voice of the Holy Spirit, sin will continue to increase in our lives until we are no longer aware of our sin—having our consciences seared and our hearts dulled.

23

1. Sin cuts communication with God.

2. Sin causes us to lose our sense of self.

3. Sin produces guilt.

4. Sin becomes a habit.

*"If you have sinned, what do you accomplish against Him? And if your transgressions are many, what do you do to Him?"* Job 35:6

*. . . by means of the hypocrisy of liars seared in their own conscience as with a branding iron . . . .* 1 Tim. 4:2

*To the pure, all things are pure; but to those who are defiled and unbelieving, nothing is pure, but both their mind and their conscience are defiled.* Tit. 1:15

## 11. IS THERE SUCH A THING AS AN UNFORGIVABLE SIN?

Yes, the Scriptures refer to blasphemy against the Holy Spirit as an unforgivable sin (Matt. 12:31; Mk. 3:29; 1 Jn. 5:16). Blasphemy (from the Greek *blasphemeo* meaning "to speak evil of God"), as used in the Gospels, appears to have consisted of attributing to the power of Satan those miracles which Jesus so evidently wrought by the power of the Holy Spirit.

Apostasy, the falling away from and denial of the truths of salvation which have been both professed and experienced, is also an unforgivable sin.

*For in the case of those who have once been enlightened and have tasted of the heavenly gift and have been made partakers of the Holy Spirit, and have tasted the good word of God and the powers of the age to come, and then have fallen away, it is impossible to renew them again to repentance, since they again crucify to themselves the Son of God, and put Him to open shame.* Heb. 6:4-6

*For if we go on sinning willfully after receiving the knowledge of the truth, there no longer remains a sacrifice for sins, but a certain terrifying expectation of judgment, and the fury of a fire which will consume the adversaries. Anyone who has set aside the Law of Moses dies without mercy on the testimony of two or three witnesses. How much severer punishment do you think he will deserve who has trampled under foot the Son of God, and has regarded as unclean the blood of the covenant by which he was sanctified, and has insulted the Spirit of grace? For we know Him who said, "Vengeance is Mine, I will repay." And again, "The Lord will judge His people." It is a terrifying thing to fall into the hands of the living God.* Heb. 10:26-31

There is, however, a kind of blasphemy which can be forgiven, provided it is repented of, and that is blasphemy which is committed out of ignorance. Paul himself was guilty of this sin before his conversion.

*Even though I was formerly a blasphemer and a persecutor and a violent aggressor. And yet I was shown mercy, **because I acted ignorantly in unbelief.***
1 Tim. 1:13

We will have to answer for any sin that we have refused to repent of when we appear before the judgment seat of Christ. In that sense, it is unforgivable.

## HOME STUDY QUESTIONS: CHAPTER 2

1. Define sin in your own words.

2. What is iniquity, and how does it differ from dead works?

3. How would you explain to a nonbeliever the process by which he can find forgiveness and release from his sins?

4. Where Scripture references only are given in this chapter rather than the whole verse, look them up in your Bible, and read the passages in their entirety.

# REPENTANCE FROM DEAD WORKS

**Chapter 3**

## 1. WHAT IS REPENTANCE?

Repentance is that work of God in our hearts which causes us to have a complete change of **mind** and **actions** in respect to our relationship to God through Christ. It is not mere sorrow for sin or remorse, though sorrow for sin may lead to repentance. Repentance is the necessary prelude to the operation of saving faith.

> *I now rejoice, not that you were made sorrowful, but that you were made sorrowful to the point of repentance; for you were made sorrowful according to the will of God, in order that you might not suffer loss in anything through us. For the sorrow that is according to the will of God produces a repentance without regret, leading to salvation; but the sorrow of the world produces death. For behold what earnestness this very thing, this godly sorrow, has produced in you: what vindication of yourselves, what indignation, what fear, what longing, what zeal, what avenging of wrong! In everything you demonstrated yourselves to be innocent in the matter.* 2 Cor. 7:9-11

Old Testament repentance was mainly a sorrow accompanied by the desire or the purpose to change. Generally speaking, however, the Law was not capable of bringing about a permanent change of heart. Repentance includes a **turning away** from that which is wrong and a **turning towards** that which is right. Conversion is the experience that results from the combining of these two elements.

A New Testament example of repentance is the parable of the prodigal son, found in Luke 15:11-32.

## 2. WHERE DOES REPENTANCE ORIGINATE?

Repentance cannot be brought about by man's own effort. It originates with God and is a gift to us by the agency of the Holy Spirit.

> *"If God therefore gave to them the same gift as He gave to us also after believing in the Lord Jesus Christ, who was I that I could stand in God's way?" And when they heard this, they quieted down, and glorified God, saying, "Well then, God has granted to the Gentiles also the repentance that leads to life."*
> Acts 11:17,18

> *And the Lord's bond-servant must not be quarrelsome, but be kind to all, able to teach, patient when wronged, with gentleness correcting those who are in opposition, if perhaps God may grant them repentance leading to the knowledge of the truth.*
> 2 Tim. 2:24,25

## 3. IS IT POSSIBLE TO DENY REPENTANCE?

Yes, it is possible to deny repentance. As a matter of fact, repentance is refused much more frequently than it is received.

> *See to it that no one comes short of the grace of God; that no root of bitterness springing up causes trouble, and by it many be defiled; that there be no immoral or godless person like Esau, who sold his own birthright for a single meal. For you know that even afterwards, when he desired to inherit the blessing, he was rejected, **for he found no place for repentance, though he sought for it with tears.***
> Heb. 12:15-17

There is a time and a season for everything in God, including a time for repentance (2 Cor. 6:2). For this reason, we must not put God off when we know that He is dealing with us. If we do not accept repentance when the Lord is granting it, we may not have another opportunity.

What happens when repentance is refused by man? If the man is unsaved, it may be the last time he will ever have repentance held forth to him by the Lord. If the man is a Christian to whom the Lord has granted a season for repentance (Rev. 2:20,21), he may have another chance or he may not. If not, because the Lord will not always strive with man (Gen. 6:3), he may seek repentance but not find it, or else be completely hardened toward his need for it (1 Tim. 4:2).

Hebrews 10:26-31 describes the case of those who continue to sin **"willfully** after receiving the knowledge of the truth." Because they are not repentant, they cannot obtain forgiveness. They will thus have to bear their sin before the judgment seat of Christ.

## 4. HOW DOES REPENTANCE COME ABOUT?

Repentance comes about as the result of conviction, which is the Holy Spirit's making us aware of our sinfulness (Jn. 16:7,8). It is important for us to know the difference between conviction and condemnation. Conviction is a positive experience always accompanied by grace which enables us to change. Condemnation is either a product of the flesh or a direct attack of Satan (the accuser) against us, which in either case leads to negativism and a loss of spiritual power. Read Romans 8:1.

Conviction may come by:

° Reading God's Word or hearing God's Word (preaching, some-one's testimony, etc.).

> *Now when they heard this, they were pierced to the heart, and said to Peter and the rest of the apostles, "Brethren, what shall we do?"*　　　　Acts 2:37

°　The sovereign work of the Holy Spirit.

> *"For I am not come to call the righteous, but sinners to repentance."*　　　　Matt. 9:13b KJV

°　Judgment that has come upon us because of wrong attitudes, the way we are living, etc. In other words, the bitter fruit of our lives causes us to turn to God.

°　The revelation of God's goodness that leads to repentance.

> *Or do you think lightly of the riches of His kindness and forbearance and patience, not knowing that the kindness of God leads you to repentance?*
> 　　　　Rom. 2:4

°　God's use of reproof and chastening to move us to repentance.

> *"Those whom I love, I reprove and discipline; be zealous therefore, and repent."*　　　　Rev. 3:19

## 5. HOW DO WE REPENT?

We repent by:

°　Responding to conviction. This means we must be able to admit that our works are dead, and then exercise our **wills** to change.

# "The Repentance Road"

1. Respond to conviction
2. Confess sin to God
3. Forsake sin

° Confessing our sin to God.

> *I acknowledged my sin to Thee, and my iniquity I did not hide; I said, "I will confess my transgressions to the Lord"; and Thou didst forgive the guilt of my sin.*
>
> Ps. 32:5

° Forsaking that sin.

> *He who conceals his transgressions will not prosper, but he who **confesses** and **forsakes** them will find compassion.* Prov. 28:13

> *Let the wicked **forsake** his way, and the unrighteous man his thoughts; and let him return to the Lord, and He will have compassion on him; and to our God, for He will abundantly pardon.* Isa. 55:7

## 6. HOW CAN WE KNOW THAT OUR REPENTANCE EXPERIENCE WAS REAL AND NOT JUST WORLDLY SORROW?

There is a scriptural principle that a matter can be rightly judged by the fruit that it brings forth. If we have truly repented, then the "fruits of repentance" will follow.

> *"Therefore bring forth fruit in keeping with repentance."* Matt. 3:8

> *"I [Paul] . . . kept declaring both to those of Damascus first, and also at Jerusalem and then throughout all the region of Judea, and even to the Gentiles, that they should repent and turn to God, performing deeds appropriate to repentance."* Acts 26:20

> *"Remember therefore from where you have fallen, and repent and do the deeds you did at first."* Rev. 2:5a

We can also know that our repentance experience is real because the Holy Spirit gives us the assurance that our sins have been forgiven. The Bible tells us that, when "we confess our sins, He is faithful and righteous to forgive us our sins **and** to cleanse us from all unrighteousness" (1 Jn. 1:9).

*"It is Thou who hast kept my soul from the pit of nothingness, for Thou hast cast all my sins behind Thy back."*                                        Isa. 38:17b

*"I, even I, am the one who wipes out your transgressions for My own sake; and I will not remember your sins."*
                                                        Isa. 43:25

*He will again have compassion on us; He will tread our iniquities under foot. Yes, Thou wilt cast all their sins into the depths of the sea.*                                       Mic. 7:19

## 7. IT IS CLEAR THAT A SINNER MUST REPENT IF HE IS TO TURN TO GOD. HOW DOES REPENTANCE CONTINUE TO WORK AS A FOUNDATION STONE IN THE LIFE OF A CHRISTIAN?

a.  Wherever there is sin, there must be repentance.

> *For I am afraid that perhaps when I [Paul] come I may find you to be not what I wish and may be found by you to be not what you wish; that perhaps there may be strife, jealousy, angry tempers, disputes, slanders, gossip, arrogance, disturbances; I am afraid that when I come again my God may humiliate me before you, and I may mourn over many of those who have sinned in the past and **not repented** of the impurity, immorality and sensuality which they have practiced.*
>                                               2 Cor. 12:20,21

b.  There are also attitudes and acts of omission that can only be changed through repentance (Rev. 2:5,16; 3:3,19). Our spirits are renewed by the indwelling of the Holy Spirit (Tit. 3:5). This renewal is meant eventually to reach and be manifested through the body and the soul as well (1 Thess. 5:23; 1 Cor. 6:20). Especially important is the renewing of the mind (Rom. 12:2; Eph. 4:20-24). Repentance is essential to the working of all these things.

## 8. MUST REPENTANCE BE ACCOMPANIED BY A DISPLAY OF EMOTION?

We are all acquainted with the stereotyped repentant sinner falling tearfully on his face before the Lord and crying out for mercy and forgiveness. Although this does frequently happen, and may have even been the case with you, we must keep in mind that everyone is different and repentance can be just as real without an extreme display of emotion. Emotions are good and their proper release is healthy for us. However, the most important part of repentance is the **exercise of our wills** and not the emotional release that may or may not accompany it.

## 9. WHAT HAPPENS WHEN WE REPENT?

We have already established that repentance is the key that unlocks the saving grace of God to sinner and saint alike. Once we have repented of our sin and have confessed it to God, complete forgiveness is ours, and the blood of Jesus cleanses us from all unrighteousness.

> *If we say that we have fellowship with Him and yet walk in the darkness, we lie and do not practice the truth; but if we walk in the light as He Himself is in the light, we have fellowship with one another, and the blood of Jesus His Son cleanses us from all sin. If we say that we have no sin, we are deceiving ourselves, and the truth is not in us. If we confess our sins, He is faithful and righteous to forgive us our sins and to cleanse us from all unrighteousness.*
>
> 1 Jn. 1:6-9

Once our sin is confessed and covered over by the blood of Jesus, it is completely stricken from the record and cast into the sea of God's forgetfulness, and it will never be brought against us, now or at the judgment seat of Christ.

> *"My transgression is sealed up in a bag, and Thou dost wrap up my iniquity."*                    Job 14:17

> *As far as the east is from the west, so far has He removed our transgressions from us.*                    Ps. 103:12

> *Who is a God like Thee, who pardons iniquity and passes over the rebellious act of the remnant of His possession? He does not retain His anger forever, because He delights in unchanging love. He will again have compassion on us; He will tread our iniquities under foot. Yes, Thou wilt cast all their sins into the depths of the sea.*                    Mic. 7:18,19

## HOME STUDY QUESTIONS:  CHAPTER 3

1.  How is repentance different from worldly sorrow?

2.  List five means God uses to bring man to repentance.

3.  Where Scripture references only are given, look them up, and read the passages in their entirety.

# REDEMPTION

**Chapter 4**

**A Supplement to the Chapter on
Repentance From Dead Works**

Redemption (from the Hebrew word meaning "to tear loose" and the Greek word meaning "to ransom" or "to buy back") was originally not a religious term at all, but one which was used to describe marketplace activities and certain other commercial enterprises such as slavery. Old Testament redemption was often concerned with the buying back into the family of land which had been lost through debt, or the release of members of the family who had been sold as slaves. This "buying back" was the right of the nearest of kin.

The New Testament doctrine of redemption, therefore, draws its meaning from these associations and is primarily concerned with the idea of our deliverance from sin and death, with the price of that deliverance being the blood of Jesus Christ.

## 1. WHAT WAS THE OLD TESTAMENT CONCEPT OF REDEMPTION?

a.  The Old Testament concept of redemption was primarily limited to the release and buying back of animals, persons, property, or land.

(1) The firstborn of both man and beast among the Israelites belonged to the Lord but could be redeemed by (1) the substitution of the life of another animal—a lamb (Ex. 13:1-16; 34:18-20), or (2) money (Num. 3:40-51; 18:15-17).

(2) In Hebrew society, any land which had been forfeited through economic distress could be redeemed by the nearest of kin. For the laws concerning redemption of property or land see Leviticus 25:24-34; 27:19,20; Jeremiah 32:7.

(3) Persons who had been sold into slavery could be redeemed (that is, bought out of slavery) by a blood relative (Lev. 25:35-55).

b.  Although Old Testament redemption was concerned mainly with the buying back of persons, animals, and property in a legal-commercial sense, the Israelites also understood its deeper implications concerning their lives:

> *"And I also established My covenant with them, to give them the land of Canaan, the land in which they sojourned. And furthermore I have heard the groaning of the sons of Israel, because the Egyptians are holding them in bondage; and I have remembered My covenant. Say, therefore, to the sons of Israel, 'I am the Lord, and I will bring you out from under the burdens of the Egyptians, and I will deliver you from their bondage. I will also redeem you with an outstretched arm and with great judgments. Then I will take you for My people, and I will be your God; and you shall know that I am the Lord your God, who brought you out from under the burdens of the Egyptians. And I will bring you to the land which I swore to give to Abraham, Isaac, and Jacob, and I will give it to you for a possession; I am the Lord.'"*        Ex. 6:4-8

and even their souls:

> *He has sent **redemption** to His people; He has ordained His covenant forever; holy and awesome is His name.*        Ps. 111:9

*O Israel, hope in the Lord; for with the Lord there is*
*lovingkindness, and with Him is **abundant redemption.** And*
*He will **redeem Israel from all his iniquities.***

Ps. 130:7,8

## 2. WHAT DOES THE OLD TESTAMENT CONCEPT OF REDEMPTION TEACH US?

The Old Testament concept of redemption was given to us by the Lord to serve as a type of the redemption which is ours under the provisions of the New Covenant. Paul wrote to the Galatians, "Therefore the Law has become our tutor ["schoolmaster," KJV] to lead us to Christ, that we may be justified by faith" (Gal. 3:24). The Old Covenant was based on the blood of bulls and goats which could never take away sin (Heb. 10:4); the New Covenant is also a covenant of blood, but a better one (Heb. 8:6), containing one sacrifice for sin for all time (Heb. 10:10-18). By these types and shadows, the Lord has provided clear and abundant instruction for us.

No doubt, the best single example of blood redemption contained in the Old Testament is Israel's deliverance from the slavery of Egypt, having been purchased with the blood of the sacrificial lambs (Ex. 12 and 13).

## 3. WHAT IS THE NEW TESTAMENT DOCTRINE OF REDEMPTION?

When God created Adam, He gave him dominion over the earth and all creation. When Adam sinned, he forfeited to Satan not only the title to himself, but also the title to the world. Thus, mankind became slaves to sin, being part of this world system, with Satan as the "god of this world" (2 Cor. 4:4). **Redemption is the process whereby we are bought out of the slave market of sin to serve the Lord God and to live a new life by and through Him.**

The New Testament doctrine of redemption contains all the elements of Old Testament redemption and is their fulfillment. As such, it declares our deliverance from the enslavement of sin and the accompanying bondage of death, and our release to a new freedom of the Spirit of life by the substitutionary sacrifice of our Redeemer, Jesus Christ—His blood being the redemptive price.

° Both concepts of deliverance and ransom (that is, the price of that deliverance) are contained in Romans 3:23,24:

> *For all have sinned and fall short of the glory of God, being justified as a gift by His grace through the redemption which is in Christ Jesus.*

See also John 3:17; Matthew 20:28; 1 Timothy 2:6.

° The concept of redemption as being "bought with a price" is contained in 1 Corinthians 6:20:

> *For you have been bought with a price: therefore glorify God in your body.*

° The concept of substitutionary sacrifice is contained in Galatians 3:13:

> *Christ redeemed us from the curse of the Law, having become a curse for us—for it is written, "Cursed is everyone who hangs on a tree."*

and 2 Corinthians 5:21:

> *He made Him who knew no sin to be sin on our behalf, that we might become the righteousness of God in Him.*

See also John 11:50; Romans 5:6,8; 2 Corinthians 5:14,15; Mark 10:45.

° Redemption by blood is contained in Ephesians 1:7:

> *In Him we have redemption through His blood, the forgiveness of our trespasses, according to the riches of His grace.*

and 1 Peter 1:18,19:

> *. . . knowing that you were not redeemed with perishable things like silver or gold . . . but with precious blood, as of a lamb unblemished and spotless, the blood of Christ.*

See also Revelation 5:9; Acts 20:28.

° The concept of new ownership (transference of the title to life or property to the kinsman who redeemed it) is contained in 1 Corinthians 6:19,20:

> *Or do you not know that your body is a temple of the Holy Spirit who is in you, whom you have from God, and that you are not your own? For you have been bought with a price: therefore glorify God in your body.*

See also Acts 20:28; 1 Corinthians 7:23; Romans 6:15-23; 2 Peter 2:1.


## 4. WHAT ARE THE BENEFITS OF REDEMPTION?

a. Redemption is the basis for our obtaining forgiveness of sin.

> *In Him we have redemption through His blood, the forgiveness of our trespasses, according to the riches of His grace.*     Eph. 1:7

*For He delivered us from the domain of darkness,
and transferred us to the kingdom of His beloved Son, in
whom we have redemption, the forgiveness of sins.*

Col. 1:13,14

b. Redemption, therefore, implements our justification since the
deliverance achieved through redemption establishes man in a
restored position of favor before God.

c. We are redeemed from the Law and from death, which is the
penalty of the Law.

*But now we have been released from the Law, having
died to that by which we were bound, so that we serve in
newness of the Spirit and not in oldness of the letter.*

Rom. 7:6

*Now if we have died with Christ, we believe that we
shall also live with Him, knowing that Christ, having
been raised from the dead, is never to die again; death
no longer is master over Him. For the death that He
died, He died to sin, once for all; but the life that He
lives, He lives to God. Even so consider yourselves to be
dead to sin, but alive to God in Christ Jesus.*

Rom. 6:8-11

d. We are redeemed from the power of Satan and, subsequently,
from all evil.

*Since then the children share in flesh and blood, He
Himself likewise also partook of the same, that through
death He might render powerless him who had the power
of death, that is, the devil; and might deliver those who
through fear of death were subject to slavery all their
lives.* Heb. 2:14,15

...Christ is our deliverance from the enslavement
of sin and the bondage of death...

e.   We have been redeemed to a new freedom from sin.

> *But thanks be to God that though you were slaves of
> sin, you became obedient from the heart to that form of
> teaching to which you were committed, and having been
> freed from sin, you became slaves of righteousness.*
> *But now having been freed from sin and enslaved to
> God, you derive your benefit, resulting in sanctification,
> and the outcome, eternal life.*          Rom. 6:17,18,22

> *For the law of the Spirit of life in Christ Jesus has set
> you free from the law of sin and of death.*
>
> Rom. 8:2

f.   We have been redeemed to a new life in Christ, having been joined with Him in His death and raised up with Him in the power of His resurrection.

> *Therefore we have been buried with Him through baptism into death, in order that as Christ was raised from the dead through the glory of the Father, so we too might walk in newness of life.'*                    Rom. 6:4

> *Therefore if any man is in Christ, he is a new creature; the old things passed away; behold, new things have come.*                    2 Cor. 5:17

## HOME STUDY QUESTIONS:  CHAPTER 4

1.   Explain the meaning of redemption in your own words.

2.   What is the basis for the New Testament doctrine of redemption?

3.   List three benefits of redemption and explain how they work in your life.

4.   Where Scripture references only are given, look them up, and read the passages in their entirety.

# FAITH TOWARD GOD

**Chapter 5**

Faith toward God is the second of the foundation principles mentioned in Hebrews 6:1,2. If it were possible to classify these principles by their degree of importance, perhaps faith would be first, because all other things work by faith. Hebrews 11:6 says, "Without faith it is impossible to please Him, for he who comes to God must believe that He is, and that He is a rewarder of those who seek Him." Certainly without faith, our entire foundation would be without life and meaning.

## 1. WHAT IS THE MEANING OF THE WORD FAITH?

Volumes have been written and volumes more have been spoken regarding this indefinable something called *faith,* and yet in the final analysis we actually know so little of the subject.

Faith is that quality or power by which the things desired become the things possessed. This is the nearest to a definition of faith attempted by the inspired Word of God.

One of the most common errors we make in this regard is to confuse faith with presumption.

There are many who mix the ingredients of their own mental attitude with a little confidence, a pinch of trust, and a generous handful of religious egotism. They proceed to add some belief, along with many other ingredients, and mixing it in a spiritual apothecary's crucible, they label the total result *faith.* Actually, the consequence of this heterogeneous mixture is more likely to be presumption than faith.

Faith is more than belief; it is more than confidence; it is more than trust.

47

Faith is a gift of God or a fruit of the Spirit; and whether it be gift or fruit, the source and the origin of faith remain the same. It comes from God and is a gift of God.

If faith is powerless, it is not faith. You cannot have faith without results any more than you can have motion without movement.[1]

## 2. HOW DOES THE BIBLE DEFINE FAITH?

*Now faith is the assurance of things hoped for, the conviction of things not seen.* Heb. 11:1

*Now faith is the assurance (the confirmation, **the title-deed**) of the things [we] hope for, being the proof of things [we] do not see and the conviction of their **reality**—faith perceiving as real fact what is not revealed to the senses.* Heb. 11:1 AMP

° Jesus does not require us to understand, but to **believe** (Mk. 16:16; Jn. 11:25,26).

° There are things around us which we do not understand but use in faith every day—electricity, radios, etc. We accept them because (1) they are there, and (2) they work. This is basically what Hebrews 11:6 means: (1) God **is there,** and (2) He **works!!**

## 3. HOW IMPORTANT IS FAITH?

We all know that faith is absolutely necessary in order to be saved (Eph. 2:8; Rom. 5:1), but we often forget that our continuing relationship with God depends upon that same faith. Faith is a foundation stone that, once laid, continues to be a working part of our Christian experience.

*Therefore, do not throw away your confidence, which*
*has a great reward. For you have need of endurance, so that*
*when you have done the will of God, you may receive what*
*was promised. For yet in a very little while, He who is*
*coming will come, and will not delay. But My righteous one*
*shall live by faith; and if he shrinks back, My soul has no*
*pleasure in him. But we are not of those who shrink back to*
*destruction, but of those who have faith to the preserving of*
*the soul.*                                          Heb. 10:35-39

Many of the problems we have in our walk and relationship with the
Lord come under this heading. We often do not have the right attitude
toward God—really trusting the Lord, believing that He always has
our best interest at heart. Sometimes we seem to have the idea He
enjoys playing with our lives, often leading us down a certain corridor
only to slam the door in our faces at the last moment. Remember,
"without faith it is impossible to please Him, for he who comes to
God must believe that He is, and that He is a **rewarder** of those who
seek Him" (Heb. 11:6).

Read also Matthew 7:10,11 and Luke 12:22-32.


## 4.  WHAT IS THE SOURCE OF OUR FAITH?

As we have already read in our definition of faith, it is both a gift of
God and a fruit of the Spirit.

*"And on the basis of faith in His name, it is the name of*
*Jesus which has strengthened this man whom you see and*
*know; and the faith **which comes through Him** has given*
*him this perfect health in the presence of you all."*
                                                   Acts 3:16


*. . . to another* [is given] *faith **by the same Spirit,** and to*
*another gifts of healing by the one Spirit.*       1 Cor. 12:9

49

*For by grace you have been saved through faith; and that not of yourselves, **it is the gift of God.*** Eph. 2:8

*. . . fixing our eyes on Jesus, the author and perfecter of faith, . . .* Heb. 12:2

## 5.  HOW DO WE RECEIVE FAITH?

Faith is a gift of God which we receive upon hearing from God or hearing about Him from His Word or through the testimony of others.

The difference between faith and presumption is that faith rests upon the reality of God's Word. It is possible to have faith in something we do not understand, but it is not possible to have faith in something of which we have no knowledge.

*For "Whoever will call upon the name of the Lord will be saved." How then shall they call upon Him in whom they have not believed? And how shall they believe in Him whom they have not heard?*
*So faith comes from hearing, and hearing by the word of Christ.* Rom. 10:13,14a,17

Knowledge of the Lord and His Word may come to us in many ways; for instance:

°    Hearing the Word through preaching or someone's witness.

*But what does it say? "The word is near you, in your mouth and in your heart"—that is, the word of faith which we are preaching.* Rom. 10:8

# Faith...

# ...A GIFT FROM GOD

*Therefore, those who had been scattered went about preaching the word.*

*But when they believed Philip preaching the good news about the kingdom of God and the name of Jesus Christ, they were being baptized, men and women alike.*
Acts 8:4,12

°    Reading the Word of God or other Christian literature.

*. . . and that from childhood you have known the sacred writings which are able to give you the wisdom that leads to salvation through faith which is in Christ Jesus.*
2 Tim. 3:15

°    Sovereignly through the direct enlightening of the Holy Spirit.

*For I would have you know, brethren, that the gospel which was preached by me is not according to man. For I neither received it from man, nor was I taught it, but I received it through a revelation of Jesus Christ.*
Gal. 1:11,12

## 6.  SINCE FAITH IS A GIFT OF GOD, WHAT IS OUR RESPONSIBILITY CONCERNING IT?

Our responsibility concerning faith is to increase the measure given to us (see Question 10) and to guard the working of faith within us.

*But the goal of our instruction is love from a pure heart and a good conscience and a sincere faith.*    1 Tim. 1:5

*Fight the good fight of faith; take hold of the eternal life to which you were called, and you made the good confession in the presence of many witnesses.*    1 Tim. 6:12

*I have fought the good fight, I have finished the course, I have kept the faith.*                    2 Tim 4:7

## 7.  IN WHAT SHOULD WE PLACE OUR FAITH?

We should have faith in the entire purpose of God as revealed to us in His Word.  Here are some specific things, however, in which we are required to place our faith:

a.  In God:  Heb. 6:1; 1 Pet. 1:21; 1 Tim. 4:10.

b.  In the power of God:  1 Cor. 2:5; 1 Pet. 1:5.

c.  In the working of God:  Col. 2:12; Phil. 2:12,13.

d.  In His name:  Acts 3:16.

e.  In the Word of God:  1 Thess. 2:13.

f.  In the ministries:  2 Chr. 20:20.

g.  **Most particularly in Jesus:**  Jn. 14:1;  Rom. 10:9;  Eph. 3:17; 2 Tim. 3:15; 1 Jn. 3:23.

8.  **WHAT ARE SOME OF THE THINGS THAT ACCOMPANY FAITH (WHAT ARE THE RESULTS OF THE WORKING OF FAITH)?**

a.  Safety:  2 Sam. 22:31; Ps. 9:9,10; 33:18,19; Prov. 30:5; Jer. 39:18; Nah. 1:7;  Eph. 6:16.

b.  Joy:  Ps. 5:11; 64:10; Rom. 15:13.

c.  Mercy (lovingkindness):  Ps. 32:10.

d.  Being blessed:  Ps. 34:8; 40:4; 84:5,12.

e.  Being delivered from fear:  Ps. 112:7,8; Heb. 13:5,6 (Heb. 2:14,15; 1 Jn. 4:18).

f.  Steadfastness:  Ps. 125:1; Col. 1:9-11.

g.  Prosperity:  Isa. 57:13; Jer. 17:7,8.

h.  Peace:  Isa. 26:3; Rom. 15:13.

i.  Healing:  Matt. 9:22; Lk. 8:48; Acts 3:16.

j.  Ability to change circumstances:  Matt. 21:21; Mk. 9:23,24.

k.  Salvation and eternal life:  Jn. 11:25; Acts 13:48; Rom. 1:16; Eph. 2:8; 1 Pet. 1:5-9.

l.  Hope:  Rom. 15:13.

m. Inheriting the promises: Heb. 6:12.

n. Ability to overcome: 1 Jn. 5:4.

## 9. DOES EVERY CHRISTIAN HAVE THE SAME AMOUNT OF FAITH?

Not necessarily. The Bible assures us that each Christian does have a measure of faith—not the same measure, perhaps, but each one receives a portion according to the wisdom of God.

> *For through the grace given to me I say to every man among you not to think more highly of himself than he ought to think; but to think so as to have sound judgment, as God has allotted to each a measure of faith.*　　Rom. 12:3

## 10. CAN WE INCREASE OUR FAITH?

Yes, just as we can increase any of the abilities given to us by the Lord. First of all, we can increase our faith simply by using the measure that has been given to us. It is in this sense that every Christian has faith as a foundation stone of his experience. As we continue to stand upon and build upon the faith given to us, our trust in God's Word and our confidence in His Spirit grow and become stronger by experience.

Secondly, we can increase our measure of faith by praying in the Spirit and maintaining a close relationship with God through His Word.

> *But you, beloved, building yourselves up on your most holy faith; praying in the Holy Spirit; . . . .*　　Jude 20

Read also Mark 9:24; Luke 17:5; 1 Timothy 6:11.

## 11. WHAT IS THE PROPER RELATIONSHIP OF WORKS TO FAITH?

Christians often seem to be divided as to which is more important, works or faith. Those who overemphasize works frequently tend to be legalistic in their approach to the Christian life and walk, while those who place faith as being preeminent often seem to "have their heads in the clouds." It has been said of such Christians that they are "so heaven bound they are no earthly good!"

What is the answer? Obviously, faith and works are both essential to a sound Christian experience. Therefore, the answer lies in having the proper balance of these two elements, each in its own order. By this we mean that faith comes first (we are not saved by works), and then faith is established and proven by what we do (the works that follow).

Here are some scriptural examples using the order we have already established: faith first (Rom. 4:1-5; 11:6; Eph. 2:8; 2 Tim. 1:9); then works (Acts 26:20; 2 Thess. 2:16,17; Tit. 3:14; and especially Jas. 2:14-26).

Here is a good balance of both principles, taken from Romans 10:9,10:

> *That if you confess with your mouth Jesus as Lord, and believe in your heart that God raised Him from the dead, you shall be saved; for **with the heart man believes,** resulting in righteousness, and **with the mouth he confesses,** resulting in salvation.*

## 12. WHAT IS THE DIFFERENCE BETWEEN FAITH AS A FOUNDATION STONE AND THE GIFT OF FAITH MENTIONED IN 1 CORINTHIANS 12:9?

We have already discussed faith as a foundation stone in the life of every Christian. This is the kind of "rock-bottom" faith that assures us, for instance, that, regardless of the outcome of many of the particulars of our day-to-day life, everything will turn out all right in the end.

The gift of faith is given by the Holy Spirit, not to all members of the body, but only to certain individuals according to His will. This gift of the Holy Spirit supplies faith for particular circumstances such as a special answer to prayer or a need for a healing.

A good scriptural illustration of this may be found in Matthew 8:23-27 (q.v.), which relates to us the crossing of the lake by Jesus and His disciples during a storm. Foundational faith would have assured them that, regardless of the raging storm, they would eventually reach the other shore in safety. The gift of faith, had it been working through one of them, would have brought about a change in the particular circumstances surrounding their crossing, such as a calming of the storm.

Notice that this is exactly what Jesus, who has the Spirit without measure, did.

## NOTES

[1] From Kathryn Kuhlman's *I Believe in Miracles* (Englewood Cliffs, N.J.: Prentice-Hall, Inc., 1962), pp. 200-202. Used by permission.

## HOME STUDY QUESTION: CHAPTER 5

1. Where Scripture references only are given, look them up, and read the passages in their entirety.

# THE DOCTRINE OF BAPTISMS: WATER BAPTISM

**Chapter 6**

Water baptism is one of the most misunderstood, and therefore controversial, aspects of the Christian experience in our day. There are those who are of the opinion that it is not necessary to baptize at all; then there are those who believe baptism is necessary but are divided as to the proper mode (that is, by immersion versus by sprinkling) and the correct formula (that is, in the name of the Father, Son, and Holy Ghost versus in the name of the Lord Jesus Christ). The controversy goes on and on. It is only logical to assume that God's Word would not be silent on such an important subject. If Christians would look there for direction instead of to their own ideas or religious traditions, all controversy would be forever settled. After all, Ephesians 4:5,6 says:

> . . . one Lord, one faith, one baptism, one God and Father of all who is over all and through all and in all.

Satan is familiar with the Word of God, too, and knows that, as long as he can keep the church of Jesus Christ divided over such issues, the church will never mature and become a vital threat to him and his kingdom of darkness. Remember, it is not the Lord who is the author of confusion.

It is time for all of God's people to band themselves together on the side of truth instead of aiding the enemy in his campaign of confusion and division.

> For God is not a God of confusion but of peace, as in all the churches of the saints.                    1 Cor. 14:33

In the next few pages we will be studying water baptism as it is presented in the Scriptures. May we all be willing to set aside our preconceived ideas and open ourselves up to the teaching ministry of the Holy Spirit.

## 1. WHAT IS WATER BAPTISM?

Water baptism (from the Anglicized form of the Greek word *baptizo,* meaning "to dip under, immerse, or submerge") is the actual, physical immersion in water of a believer. In the waters of baptism, through faith in the Word of God and by the operation of the Holy Spirit, the believer is baptized into Christ, experiencing **death to sin** and **a new birth to righteousness.**

> *"He who has believed and has been baptized shall be saved; but he who has disbelieved shall be condemned."*
> Mk. 16:16

> *Therefore we have been buried with Him through baptism into* [His] *death, in order that as Christ was raised from the dead through the glory of the Father, so we too might walk in newness of life. For if we have become united with Him in the likeness of his death, certainly we shall be also in the likeness of His resurrection.* Rom. 6:4,5

## 2. WHAT IS THE ORIGIN OF CHRISTIAN BAPTISM?

The record of water baptism begins in the New Testament with the baptism of John, who called the Jews of his day to repent of their sins against the Law of the Old Covenant.

> *John the Baptist appeared in the wilderness preaching a baptism of repentance for the forgiveness of sins. And all the country of Judea was going out to him, and all the people of Jerusalem; and they were being baptized by him in the Jordan River, confessing their sins.* Mk. 1:4,5

a.  Was it necessary for them to receive John's baptism? Yes, according to the testimony of Jesus Himself:

> *"I say to you, among those born of women, there is no one greater than John; yet he who is least in the kingdom of God is greater than he." And when all the people and the tax-gatherers heard this, they acknowledged God's justice, having been baptized with the baptism of John. But the Pharisees and the lawyers **rejected God's purpose for themselves,** not having been baptized by John.*                Lk. 7:28-30

b.  Why was John's baptism necessary?

1.  John's message was the same as the message of Jesus.

> *"Repent, for the kingdom of heaven is at hand."*
> Matt. 3:2; 4:17

Repentance and baptism were the necessary preparations for entering the kingdom.

2.  John required the people to demonstrate their repentance of heart by being baptized.

> *"Therefore bring forth fruits in keeping with repentance, and do not begin to say to yourselves, 'We have Abraham for our father,' for I say to you that God is able from these stones to raise up children to Abraham. And also the axe is already laid at the root of the trees; every tree therefore that does not bear good fruit is cut down and thrown into the fire."*                Lk. 3:8,9

61

3.  John's baptism was in itself a public confession of their sin and the need for repentance.

    *John the Baptist appeared in the wilderness preaching a baptism of repentance for the forgiveness of sins. And all the country of Judea was going out to him, and all the people of Jerusalem; and they were being baptized by him in the Jordan River, confessing their sins.*                                    Mk. 1:4,5

4.  John's baptism was absolutely necessary because without this experience the Jews would not have been able to perceive Jesus as the Christ, just as we cannot see the kingdom without being born again of water and the Spirit (Jn. 3:1-8).

    *"And I did not recognize Him, but in order that He might be manifested to Israel, I came baptizing in water."*                                             Jn. 1:31

c.  Why was water baptism the only vehicle for this experience? The Jews understood baptism as being related to and representative of the cleansing that the priests had to receive before they could minister before the Lord. (See Exodus 29:1-7.) When Jesus was baptized by John, He said that He was fulfilling all righteousness. Jesus, our High Priest and the firstborn among many brethren, was being cleansed in preparation for His office of Prophet, Priest, and King. He Himself did not need the cleansing, but He was giving us a pattern that each one of us, as New Testament priests, would have to follow. (The disciples of Jesus baptized also: John 4:1,2.)

# 3. WHAT DID JESUS TEACH ABOUT WATER BAPTISM?

Jesus provided the link between John's baptism and New Covenant baptism when He commissioned the church before His ascension to:

> *"Go therefore and make disciples of all the nations, baptizing them in the name of the Father and the Son and the Holy Spirit."*                          Matt. 28:19

and:

> *"Go into all the world and preach the gospel to all creation. He who has believed and has been baptized shall be saved."*                          Mk. 16:15,16a

# 4. WHAT DID THE APOSTLES TEACH ABOUT WATER BAPTISM?

a.   Jesus commanded us to be baptized (Matt. 28:19; Mk. 16:16a) and so did the apostles (Acts 2:37,38).

When God visited Cornelius and his household, Peter "commanded ["ordered," NASB] them to be baptized in the name of the Lord" (Acts 10:48 KJV). Water baptism is not an option; it is necessary to our complete born-again experience, because the Bible clearly teaches us that there are three things which testify to a completed work: the blood of Jesus, water baptism, and the baptism of the Holy Spirit (Matt. 26:28; Heb. 9:22; Acts 2:38; Jn. 3:1-7; Tit. 3:5; 1 Pet. 3:18-21; 1 Jn. 5:6-8).

b.   Submission to water baptism is the believer's first act of obedience, thus testifying to a genuine repentance (from dead works) and to a true faith (toward God).

> *"Repent, and let each of you be baptized in the name of Jesus Christ."*
> *So then, those who had received his word were baptized.*                          Acts 2:38a,41

c.  Water baptism has to do with the forgiveness (remission) of sin.

> *And Peter answered them, Repent—change your views, and purpose to accept the will of God in your inner selves instead of rejecting it—and be baptized every one of you in the name of Jesus Christ for the forgiveness of and release from your sins.*
>
> Acts 2:38 AMP

When Adam sinned by breaking the commandment of God, two things happened: (1) sin alienated him (and us) from the life of God, thereby bringing upon all mankind the penalty of death; and (2) sin wrought a basic change in the heart of man, marring the godly image in which he had been created.

Jesus Christ shed His blood on Calvary to redeem man from the bondage of sin and the curse of death. His blood is the legal basis for the forgiveness of sin and man's reconciliation to God. Those who are justified by faith in His blood become partakers of His death and experientially claim for themselves all the work of redemption by being "buried with Him through baptism into death, in order that as Christ was raised from the dead through the glory of the Father, so we too might walk in newness of life" (Rom. 6:4). It is in this way that the working of sin is reversed and the godly image is restored through new birth (Jn. 3:3-5; 2 Cor. 5:17). The indwelling of the Holy Spirit, also a necessary part of our new-birth experience, will be discussed in the next chapter.

d.  Baptism in water has to do with cleansing.

> *"And now why do you delay? Arise, and be baptized, and wash away your sins, calling on His name."*
>
> Acts 22:16

> *. . . Christ also loved the church and gave Himself up for her; that He might sanctify her, having cleansed her by the washing of water with the word.*
>
> Eph. 5:25b,26

e.  We are baptized into Jesus Christ.

> *For all of you who were baptized into Christ have clothed yourselves with Christ.*          Gal. 3:27

> *Or do you not know that all of us who have been baptized into Christ Jesus have been baptized into His death?*          Rom. 6:3

Water baptism and the baptism of the Holy Spirit work together to bring about regeneration.

> *He saved us, not on the basis of deeds which we have done in righteousness, but according to His mercy, by the washing of regeneration and renewing by the Holy Spirit.*          Tit. 3:5

There is, therefore, no discrepancy between the above verses and 1 Corinthians 12:13 with Ephesians 4:5.

f.  We are baptized into the Lordship of Christ.

First Corinthians 10:1,2 declares that all Israel was **"baptized into Moses** in the cloud and in the sea," meaning that they were sealed into him and into his ministry of leadership. If they were to reach the promised land at all, it would be **only by Him!**

Moses is a type of Christ and the same principle applies to us. As we are born again of the water and the Spirit, we enter the kingdom of Jesus Christ and are sealed to His Lordship!

g.   Water baptism has to do with the circumcision of heart.

> *In Him also you were circumcised with a circum-*
> *cision not made with hands, but in a [spiritual] circum-*
> *cision [performed by] Christ by stripping off the body of*
> *the flesh [the whole corrupt, carnal nature with its*
> *passions and lusts]. [Thus you were circumcised when]*
> *you were buried with Him in [your] baptism, in which*
> *you were also raised with Him [to a new life] through*
> *[your] faith in the working of God [as displayed] when*
> *He raised Him up from the dead.*
>
> Col. 2:11,12 AMP

h.   Baptism is therefore the seal upon our New Covenant experience just as circumcision in the flesh was the seal upon the Old Covenant.

> *For he is not a Jew who is one outwardly; neither is*
> *circumcision that which is outward in the flesh. But he is*
> *a Jew who is one inwardly; and circumcision is that*
> *which is of the heart, by the Spirit, not by the letter; and*
> *his praise is not from men, but from God.*
>
> Rom. 2:28,29

## 5.   WHEN WAS CHRISTIAN BAPTISM FIRST PRACTICED?

Christian baptism was first practiced on the day of Pentecost. This is the day the church was born, and this is the gospel which was preached from the beginning.

> *"Therefore let all the house of Israel know for certain*
> *that God has made Him both Lord and Christ—this Jesus*
> *whom you crucified." Now when they heard this, they were*
> *pierced to the heart, and said to Peter and the rest of the*
> *apostles, "Brethren, what shall we do?" And Peter said to*
> *them, "Repent, and let each of you be baptized in the name*

66

*of Jesus Christ for the forgiveness of your sins; and you shall
receive the gift of the Holy Spirit. For the promise is for you
and your children, and for all who are far off, as many as the
Lord our God shall call to Himself."*

*So then, those who had received his word were baptized;
and there were added that day about three thousand souls.*

Acts 2:36-39,41

## 6. WHY IS THIS SPIRITUAL WORK OF GRACE, WROUGHT IN OUR HEARTS IN THE WATERS OF BAPTISM, CALLED *CIRCUMCISION OF HEART?*

a. The word *circumcision* means "the cutting around." When
spoken of as a physical rite in the Bible, it refers to the cutting off
or around of the foreskin in males. God instituted it as a token of
the covenant between Himself and Abraham.

> *"This is My covenant, which you shall keep, between
> Me and you and your descendants after you: every male
> among you shall be circumcised. And you shall be cir-
> cumcised in the flesh of your foreskin; and it shall be the
> sign of the covenant between Me and you."*

Gen. 17:10,11

Abraham was called by God and brought into right-standing with
God when he was seventy-five years old. Abraham walked in that
relationship with God for almost twenty-five years and was called
the "friend of God." When Abraham was ninety-nine years old,
however, God returned to him and confirmed the covenant with
him by the sign of the circumcision as we have read above. Even
though Abraham had been the friend of God, he had to receive
the circumcision of the flesh or else be cut off from God.

> *"But an uncircumcised male who is not circumcised
> in the flesh of his foreskin, that person shall be cut off
> from his people; he has broken My covenant."*

Gen. 17:14

b.  Centuries after the covenant of circumcision had been delivered to Abraham, the Lord revealed to Moses that, although circumcision was still required as a sign of the covenant, it was not an end in itself but pointed to a greater inner need.

> *"And now, Israel, what does the Lord your God require from you, but to fear the Lord your God, to walk in all His ways and love Him, and to serve the Lord your God with all your heart and with all your soul, and to keep the Lord's commandments and His statutes which I am commanding you today for your good?*
> *"Circumcise then your heart, and stiffen your neck no more."*                    Deut. 10:12,13,16

See also Leviticus 26:40,41; Deuteronomy 4:29; 5:29; 6:5.

c.  As we can see in these verses, the Lord required His people to love Him with **all** their heart and with **all** their soul, and yet, this was the one thing they were unable to do. How, then, could this be accomplished? The answer may be found in Deuteronomy 30:1-6.

> *"Moreover the Lord your God will circumcise your heart and the heart of your descendants, to love the Lord your God with all your heart and with **all** your soul, in order that you may live."*                    Deut. 30:6

d.  This revelation and promise of circumcision of heart continues to be unfolded all through the Old Testament: Jeremiah 3:17; 4:1-4; 9:23-26; 24:5-7; 31:31-34; 32:36-41; Ezekiel 11:19,20; 36:22-29; 44:6-9.

In these last verses of Ezekiel especially, the Lord revealed that, even though this "new heart" was not possible under the Old Covenant, there would come a day when no one would be able to enter His kingdom without a heart that had been circumcised.

See also Acts 7:51; Romans 2:28,29.

e.  Although on the day of Pentecost Peter mentioned nothing of the circumcision of heart when he exhorted the people to be baptized, it soon became evident that, for the first time in history, God had formed for Himself a people who were of one heart and one mind, not only toward Him, but also toward one another.

> *And they were continually devoting themselves to the apostles' teaching and to fellowship, to the breaking of bread and to prayer.*
> *And all those who had believed were together, and had all things in common; and they began selling their property and possessions, and were sharing them with all, as anyone might have need. And day by day continuing* **with one mind** *in the temple, and breaking bread from house to house, they were taking their meals* **together with gladness and sincerity of heart,** *praising God, and having favor with all the people.*
> Acts 2:42,44-47a

> *And the congregation of those who believed* **were of one heart and soul.**  Acts 4:32a

f.  Much later, it was revealed to Paul by the Holy Spirit that this marvelous oneness of heart and purpose of God's people was in fact the fulfillment of all the Old Testament prophecies. The Lord had indeed circumcised the hearts of His people (read Colossians 2:11,12).

> *For he is not a Jew who is one outwardly; neither is circumcision that which is outward in the flesh. But he is a Jew who is one inwardly; and circumcision is that which is of the heart, by the Spirit, not by the letter.*
> Rom. 2:28,29

*For we are the true circumcision, who worship in the Spirit of God and glory in Christ Jesus and put no confidence in the flesh.*                              Phil. 3:3

## 7. WHAT DOES CIRCUMCISION OF HEART WORK WITHIN US?

As we have already said, it is in the waters of baptism that we are buried with Him in the "likeness of His death," "knowing this, that our old self was crucified with Him, that our body of sin might be done away with, that we should no longer be slaves to sin" (Rom. 6:1-6).

In dying to sin, our hearts are circumcised—that is, the old self is robbed of its power and effectiveness over us, thus freeing us to be recreated in His image by the Holy Spirit.

*Lay aside the old self, which is being corrupted in accordance with the lusts of deceit.*
*And put on the new self, which in the likeness of God has been created in righteousness and holiness of the truth.*
                              Eph. 4:22b,24

*Do not lie to one another, since you laid aside the old self with its evil practices, and have put on the new self who is being renewed to a true knowledge according to the image of the One who created him.*                              Col. 3:9,10

## 8. WHAT IS THE SCRIPTURAL PATTERN FOR WATER BAPTISM?

The scriptural pattern for water baptism specifies that it must be:

a. Preceded by repentance.

> *And Peter said to them, "Repent, and let each of you be baptized in the name of Jesus Christ for the forgiveness of your sins; and you shall receive the gift of the Holy Spirit."* Acts 2:38

b. By immersion (remember, this is the meaning of the word *baptize*).

> *And they were being baptized by him in the Jordan River, as they confessed their sins.* Matt. 3:6

> *And after being baptized, Jesus went up immediately from the water; and behold, the heavens were opened, and He saw the Spirit of God descending as a dove, and coming upon Him.* Matt. 3:16

> *And John also was baptizing in Aenon near Salim, because there was much water there; and they were coming and were being baptized.* Jn. 3:23

> *And as they went along the road they came to some water; and the eunuch said, "Look! Water! What prevents me from being baptized?"*
> *And he ordered the chariot to stop; and they both went down into the water, Philip as well as the eunuch; and he baptized him. And when they came up out of the water, the Spirit of the Lord snatched Philip away; and the eunuch saw him no more, but went on his way rejoicing.* Acts 8:36,38,39

c.  In the name of the Lord Jesus Christ.

> *And Peter said to them, "Repent, and let each of you be baptized **in the name of Jesus Christ** for the forgiveness of your sins; and you shall receive the gift of the Holy Spirit. "*                                      Acts 2:38

> *But when they believed Philip preaching the good news about the kingdom of God and **the name of Jesus Christ,** they were being baptized, men and women alike.*
> *For He had not yet fallen upon any of them; they had simply been baptized **in the name of the Lord Jesus.***
>                                              Acts 8:12,16

> *While Peter was still speaking these words, the Holy Spirit fell upon all those who were listening to the message. And all the circumcised believers who had come with Peter were amazed, because the gift of the Holy Spirit had been poured out upon the Gentiles also. For they were hearing them speaking with tongues and exalting God. Then Peter answered, "Surely no one can refuse the water for these to be baptized who have received the Holy Spirit just as we did, can he?" And he ordered them to be baptized **in the name of Jesus Christ.** Then they asked him to stay on for a few days.*
>                                              Acts 10:44-48

> *And when they heard this, they were baptized **in the name of the Lord Jesus.***                              Acts 19:5

d.  Administered by one having covenant and kingdom authority.

> *And they came to John and said to him, "Rabbi, He who was with you beyond the Jordan, to whom you have borne witness, behold, He is baptizing, and all are coming to Him." John answered and said, "A man can*

*receive nothing, unless it has been given him from heaven."*          Jn. 3:26,27

The kingdom cannot be ministered by someone who is not in it himself!

## 9. WHY DID THE APOSTLES BAPTIZE IN THE NAME OF THE LORD JESUS CHRIST?

Jesus commissioned His disciples to baptize "in the name of the Father and the Son and the Holy Spirit" (Matt. 28:19), yet all through the record of early church baptism, believers were baptized "in the name of Jesus Christ." Not once do we find anyone being baptized in the name of the Father, Son, and Holy Spirit. We obviously cannot dismiss this as being either a mistake or a misunderstanding; neither can we say that it is unimportant. After all, the fact that the apostles used a different formula when they baptized than that which seems to be contained within Matthew 28:19 means that either (1) they understood perfectly well what they were doing and knew that by baptizing in the name of the Lord Jesus Christ they were fulfilling the requirements laid down by Jesus; or (2) they were, at best, totally ignorant of the truth or, at worst, completely disobedient. If we are to maintain our confidence in the apostolic teachings of the New Testament, we cannot accept this latter statement. Therefore, we must look for the truth of the matter within the Scriptures themselves. Remember our first rule for Bible students:

> Search out all the Scriptures on a given topic. This gives you a balance of doctrine on the entire subject. You will not be lopsided or on a tangent. A doctrine is never built on a single Scripture but is developed out of comparing all that the Bible has to say on the given topic.

When Jesus said to His disciples, "I have many more things to say to you" (Jn. 16:12), He made it clear that more complete revelation would follow the coming of the Helper, the Holy Spirit. In Matthew

28:19, Jesus told them to baptize in the "name"—not "names"—of the Father, the Son, and the Holy Spirit. The disciples understood, as we should be able to do, that Father, Son, and Holy Spirit are not, in themselves, names at all, but descriptive titles referring to the separate functions and manifestations of the Triune Godhead.

The apostles also knew, by revelation, what many religious leaders today fail to recognize:

° That the **fulness of the Godhead** dwells in the bodily form of Jesus.

> *For in Him all the fulness of Deity dwells in bodily form.* Col. 2:9

° That the name of the Son is Jesus.

> *"And she will bear a Son; and you shall call His name Jesus, for it is He who will save His people from their sins."* Matt. 1:21

° That the Son came in the Father's name.

> *"I have come in My Father's name, and you do not receive Me; if another shall come in his own name, you will receive him."* Jn. 5:43

° That the Father had given His name to the Son.

> *"I manifested Thy name to the men whom Thou gavest Me out of the world; Thine they were, and Thou gavest them to Me, and they have kept Thy word.*
> *"And I am no more in the world; and yet they themselves are in the world, and I come to Thee. Holy Father, keep them in Thy name, **the name which Thou hast given Me,** that they may be one, even as We are. While I was with them, I was keeping them in **Thy name***

*which Thou hast given Me; and I guarded them, and not one of them perished but the son of perdition, that the Scripture might be fulfilled."*      Jn. 17:6,11,12

*"And in that day you will ask Me no question. Truly, truly, I say to you, if you shall ask the Father for anything, He will give it to you in My name. Until now you have asked for nothing in My name; ask, and you will receive, that your joy may be made full. These things I have spoken to you in figurative language; an hour is coming when I will speak no more to you in figurative language, but will tell you plainly of the Father. In that day you will ask in My name, and I do not say to you that I will request the Father on your behalf."*      Jn. 16:23-26

NOTE: The Old Testament name of God is Jehovah—I AM THAT I AM! The name Jesus is the Greek form of the Hebrew name Jehoshua, meaning, "The Lord (Jehovah) is salvation." Jesus Himself claimed to be the Jehovah of the Old Testament, and the Jews tried to stone Him for blaspheming.

*"Your father Abraham rejoiced to see My day; and he saw it, and was glad." The Jews therefore said to Him, "You are not yet fifty years old, and have You seen Abraham?" Jesus said to them, "Truly, truly, I say to you, before Abraham was born, I am." Therefore they picked up stones to throw at Him; but Jesus hid Himself, and went out of the temple.*      Jn. 8:56-59

See also John 8:24,28.

° The apostles also knew that the Holy Spirit **is the Spirit of Christ** and that He had come in Jesus' name.

> *. . . seeking to know what person or time the Spirit of Christ within them was indicating as He predicted the sufferings of Christ and the glories to follow.*
>
> 1 Pet. 1:11

> *"But the Helper, the Holy Spirit, whom the Father will send in My name, He will teach you all things, and bring to your remembrance all that I said to you."*
>
> Jn. 14:26

Read also John 1:1-5,14,18; 1 Timothy 6:14-16; John 6:46; Colossians 1:15-19; Hebrews 1:1-3; Acts 4:12.


## 10. IS IT POSSIBLE TO BE SAVED WITHOUT WATER BAPTISM?

The gospel was never meant to be divided into three separate experiences of repentance, water baptism, and the baptism of the Holy Spirit. These three works of grace act as one to bring us by "new birth" into the kingdom of God. It is possible, however, to experience repentance alone, thus effecting a right-standing with God, referred to in the Scriptures as "justification." The experience, while not establishing a covenant, kingdom relationship with God, does save from the wrath of God and an eternity in hell. Many Christians apply the term "saved" to one who has merely taken the first step toward salvation; that is, he has repented of sin and received right-standing with God.

The reason there is often so much confusion when it comes to the subject of new birth is because of a common misuse of Bible language. Regeneration and new birth are the same thing, but are different from justification. The Greek word for regeneration is *palingenesia* (pa-lin-ge-ne-see-a) and is a combination of two words meaning "again" and "birth."

Although this particular word occurs only twice in the New Testament, there are other words and phrases used throughout which mean the same thing. They all refer to the process of spiritual change which transfers us out of the kingdom of sin and darkness and into the kingdom of Jesus Christ, where we are made actual partakers of His holiness and receive as our inheritance eternal life.

Justification, on the other hand, is merely a part of that total process of deliverance from sin, being God's legal declaration of our right-standing, based upon our acceptance of the atonement provided for us by the shed blood of Jesus Christ.

Salvation is actually that larger, more inclusive word of the gospel which carries with it the ideas of deliverance, safety, preservation, and healing unto perfect soundness, and gathers into itself the works of justification, sanctification, and glorification. It is that work of God—Father, Son, and Holy Spirit—whereby one who believes in the Lord Jesus Christ is redeemed from the curse of the Law and is justified, kept, set free from the dominion of sin, sanctified, and finally perfected in the image of his Lord. It therefore falls far short of its scriptural meaning when it is applied strictly to the repentance experience.

## 11. IS IT POSSIBLE TO BE BAPTIZED AND NOT RECEIVE A CIRCUMCISED HEART?

A valid baptism will always bring about a heart that has been circumcised. When a believer's heart has been prepared by the Holy Spirit so that there is faith to be "born again" as well as a desire to be submitted to the Lordship of Jesus Christ, a spiritual circumcision "without hands" will invariably take place. Otherwise, the result will be merely the performance of a dead ritual and not a true spiritual experience.

## 12. HOW CAN WE BE SURE THAT OUR BAPTISM WAS VALID?

Although God will always honor faith, even when some people have acted without true knowledge, the only way to be absolutely sure is to be baptized according to the scriptural pattern, making sure that it is administered by someone having authority in the things pertaining to the kingdom of God.

If there is any doubt that such has been the case, then that person should be baptized. Water baptism is an extremely important foundation stone, and every Christian needs the assurance that he is building firmly upon it.


## 13. CAN INFANTS BE BAPTIZED?

No, it is not possible for an infant to be baptized because he cannot experience faith nor repentance, **both** of which are absolutely necessary for water baptism to be valid.

> *"He who **has believed** and has been baptized shall be saved."*　　　　　　　　　　　　　　　Mk. 16:16a

> *"**Repent,** and let each of you be baptized."*
> 　　　　　　　　　　　　　　　　Acts 2:38

## HOME STUDY QUESTIONS: CHAPTER 6

1. What is the Greek word from which our word *baptism* originated, and what does it mean?

2. Give two reasons why John's baptism was necessary.

3. What would your answer be to a believer who was of the opinion that water baptism is not a necessary experience?

4. What is the work called which is wrought in our hearts by the Holy Spirit as a result of our being water baptized?

5. Explain this work in your own words.

# THE DOCTRINE OF BAPTISMS:
# THE BAPTISM OF THE HOLY SPIRIT

**Chapter 7**

When the subject of Holy Spirit baptism is mentioned, speaking in tongues is usually the most obvious issue associated with it—so much so, that many people are unable to think of the baptism of the Holy Spirit as anything more than a tongues-speaking experience.

This is not a chapter on speaking in tongues, although tongues are discussed as being the evidence of receiving the Holy Spirit baptism; it is a chapter devoted to the study of the entire work of the Holy Spirit within us.

## 1. WHO IS THE HOLY SPIRIT?

We live in a day which is experience-oriented; that is, not only are experiences eagerly sought after, but the quality of one's life is too often measured by the number and types of things experienced. Because of this, Christians are prone to think of the Holy Spirit in terms of "gifts" and "manifestations." Certainly the Holy Spirit is a Giver of gifts and is therefore a great influence upon our lives, but He should not be regarded merely as an influence. He is a Person, the third Person of the Trinity, as much a person as God the Father and God the Son. The Father has given all authority to the Son (Matt. 28:18), but to the Holy Spirit has been committed the responsibility for executing all the designs of heaven with regard to man.

The primary design of the Godhead concerning mankind is that every man, woman, and child should hear the gospel, repent of sin, and as a result of faith in the Lord Jesus Christ, receive a second birth, thus being made a new creature. This is the special sphere of the Holy Spirit, for He is the Agent of our new birth (Jn. 3:8). He does this by coming personally to take up residence in the heart of one who has ventured upon his faith in Christ. This residence is not temporary—the Holy Spirit comes to abide there forever: "And I will ask the Father, and He will give you another Helper, that **He may be with you forever**" (Jn. 14:16).

The Holy Spirit, as the third Person of the Triune Godhead, is:

a. The Helper (from the Greek *paracletos,* meaning "one called alongside to help").

> *"And I will ask the Father, and He will give you another Helper, that He may be with you forever.*
> *"But the Helper, the Holy Spirit, whom the Father will send in My name, He will teach you all things, and bring to your remembrance all that I said to you."*
>
> Jn. 14:16,26

b. The Spirit of truth.

> *"And I will ask the Father, and He will give you another Helper . . . ; that is the Spirit of truth."*
>
> Jn. 14:16,17a

See also John 16:13.

c. The Spirit of Christ.

> *But if anyone does not have the Spirit of Christ, he does not belong to Him.* Rom. 8:9

> *And because you are sons, God has sent forth the Spirit of His Son into our hearts, crying, "Abba! Father!"* Gal. 4:6

82

*For I know that this shall turn out for my deliverance through your prayers and the provision of the Spirit of Jesus Christ.* Phil. 1:19

*As to this salvation, the prophets who prophesied of the grace that would come to you made careful search and inquiry, seeking to know what person or time the Spirit of Christ within them was indicating as He predicted the sufferings of Christ and the glories to follow.* 1 Pet. 1:10,11

See also Acts 16:7.

The Holy Spirit proceeds from the Father (Jn. 14:16), is given by Christ (Jn. 15:26; Lk. 24:49), and comes in the name of Christ (Jn. 14:26).

## 2. WHAT IS THE WORK OF THE HOLY SPIRIT?

The work of the Holy Spirit is extensive, encompassing, and inclusive of all the redemptive processes made possible by the blood of our Lord and Savior Jesus Christ. We could never completely cover here all that the Holy Spirit accomplishes on our behalf, but we will attempt to discuss that which is most obvious.

a.  He quickens us and makes us spiritually alive.

*Jesus answered and said to him, "Truly, truly, I say to you, unless one is born again, he cannot see the kingdom of God." Nicodemus said to Him, "How can a man be born when he is old? He cannot enter a second time into his mother's womb and be born, can he?" Jesus answered, "Truly, truly, I say to you, unless one is born of water and the Spirit, he cannot enter into the kingdom of God. That which is born of the flesh is flesh; and that which is born of the Spirit is spirit."* Jn. 3:3-6

# What is the work of the Holy Spirit?

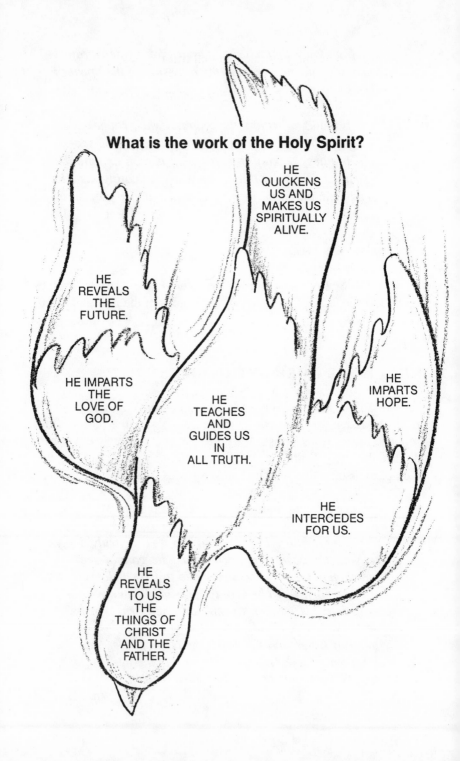

HE QUICKENS US AND MAKES US SPIRITUALLY ALIVE.

HE REVEALS THE FUTURE.

HE IMPARTS THE LOVE OF GOD.

HE TEACHES AND GUIDES US IN ALL TRUTH.

HE IMPARTS HOPE.

HE INTERCEDES FOR US.

HE REVEALS TO US THE THINGS OF CHRIST AND THE FATHER.

b.  He teaches us and guides us into all truth.

> But you have an anointing from the Holy One, and
> you all know.
> And as for you, the anointing which you received
> from Him abides in you, and you have no need for
> anyone to teach you; but as His anointing teaches you
> about all things, and is true and is not a lie, and just as
> it has taught you, you abide in Him.      1 Jn. 2:20,27

See also John 14:26; 16:13.

c.  He reveals to us the things of Christ:

> "He shall glorify Me; for He shall take of Mine, and
> shall disclose it to you."                          Jn. 16:14

and of the Father:

> For to us God revealed them through the Spirit; for
> the Spirit searches all things, even the depths of God.
> For who among men knows the thoughts of a man except
> the spirit of the man, which is in him? Even so the
> thoughts of God no one knows except the Spirit of God.
> Now we have received, not the spirit of the world, but the
> Spirit who is from God, that we might know the things
> freely given to us by God.            1 Cor. 2:10-12

d.  He reveals the future.

> "And He will disclose to you what is to come."
>                                                      Jn. 16:13b

See also Luke 2:26; Acts 21:11.

e.   He imparts the love of God.

> *The love of God has been poured out **within our***
> ***hearts** through the Holy Spirit who was given to us.*
> Rom. 5:5

f.   He imparts hope.

> *Now may the God of hope fill you with all joy and*
> *peace in believing; that you may abound in hope by the*
> *power of the Holy Spirit.*          Rom. 15:13

See also Galatians 5:5.

g.   He intercedes for us.

> *But the Spirit Himself intercedes for us with*
> *groanings too deep for words.*          Rom. 8:26


## 3.   WHAT IS THE BAPTISM OF THE HOLY SPIRIT?

The baptism of the Holy Spirit is our ultimate—the fullest and most complete—experience in the Holy Spirit, making all other spiritual experiences possible. The Spirit of the Lord Jesus Christ, that is, the Holy Spirit, comes into the believer to dwell, thus causing his body to become a temple of the Holy Spirit and initiating within him the "law of the Spirit of life in Christ Jesus" and eventually setting him free "from the law of sin and of death" (Rom. 8:2).

°   John the Baptist spoke of it.

> *"He who sent me to baptize in water said to me, 'He*
> *upon whom you see the Spirit descending and remaining*
> *upon Him, this is the one who baptizes in the Holy*
> *Spirit.'"*          Jn. 1:33

° Jesus referred to it.

> *Now on the last day, the great day of the feast, Jesus stood and cried out, saying, "If any man is thirsty, let him come to Me and drink. He who believes in Me, as the Scripture said, 'From his innermost being shall flow rivers of living water.'" But this He spoke of the Spirit, whom those who believed in Him were to receive; for the Spirit was not yet given, because Jesus was not yet glorified.*     Jn. 7:37-39

> *And gathering them together, He commanded them not to leave Jerusalem, but to wait for what the Father had promised, "Which," He said, "you heard of from Me; for John baptized with water, but you shall be baptized with the Holy Spirit not many days from now."*
>     Acts 1:4,5

## 4. IS THERE A DIFFERENCE BETWEEN HAVING THE SPIRIT, BEING FILLED WITH THE SPIRIT, AND BEING BAPTIZED INTO THE SPIRIT?

Yes! It is true that every person who has experienced justification has the Spirit of the Lord with him. Jesus said the Holy Spirit came into the world to convict the world of sin, and through His work, we are brought to repentance. "But if anyone does not have the Spirit of Christ, he does not belong to Him" (Rom. 8:9b). The Scriptures indicate that this is not the same experience as the baptism of the Holy Spirit. Jesus also said:

> *"That is the Spirit of truth, whom the world cannot receive, because it does not behold Him or know Him, but you know Him because He abides **with** you, and will be **in** you."*     Jn. 14:17

There are many ways of illustrating this (such as a glass filled with water being then entirely immersed in a tub of water, the glass thus being completely full **and** surrounded with water), but it is so plainly set forth for us in Scripture that it should be easy enough for us to grasp without having to rely upon such things.

5. **HOW CAN WE ACHIEVE A MORE COMPLETE UNDERSTANDING OF THESE DIFFERING LEVELS OF EXPERIENCE IN THE HOLY SPIRIT?**

We can achieve a more complete understanding of these differing levels of experience in the Holy Spirit (having the Spirit, being filled with the Spirit, and being baptized with the Spirit) by closely studying the teachings of the whole Word of God concerning the Holy Spirit.

First of all the Old Testament contains many examples of the Spirit of the Lord being placed **upon** men; for instance:

° When Moses was no longer able to bear the burden of judging the people of Israel alone, the Lord took of the Spirit which was "upon" Moses and placed it upon the seventy elders, thus causing them to prophesy as well as enabling them to share in the government of Israel.

> *"Then I will come down and speak with you there, and I will take of the Spirit who is **upon** you, and will put Him **upon** them; and they shall bear the burden of the people with you, so that you shall not bear it all alone."*
> *Then the Lord came down in the cloud and spoke to him; and He took of the Spirit who was **upon** him and placed Him **upon** the seventy elders. And it came about that when the Spirit rested **upon** them, they prophesied. But they did not do it again. But two men had remained in the camp . . . . And the Spirit rested **upon** them . . . , and they prophesied in the camp.*

> *But Moses said to him, "Are you jealous for my sake? Would that all the Lord's people were prophets, that the Lord would put His Spirit **upon** them!"*
> Num. 11:17,25,26,29

°   When Saul was chosen and anointed to be king over Israel, the Lord caused His Spirit to rest "upon" him and he prophesied.

> *"Then the Spirit of the Lord will come **upon** you mightily, and you shall prophesy with them and be changed into another man."*
> *When they came to the hill there, behold, a group of prophets met him; and the Spirit of God came **upon** him mightily, so that he prophesied among them.*
> 1 Sam. 10:6,10

°   Because of Saul's self-will and disobedience, David was chosen in his place to rule over Israel. The Spirit of the Lord "departed from Saul" and "came . . . **upon** David from that day forward" (1 Sam. 16:13,14).

NOTE:  See also the ministries of Samson, Elijah, and Elisha.

Secondly, the Bible tells us that the New Testament is a "better covenant" (Heb. 8:6). It is right, then, that the New Covenant should offer a fuller experience in the Holy Spirit. Following are some of the examples of being "filled" with the Spirit:

°   John the Baptist was filled with the Holy Spirit from his mother's womb (Lk. 1:15).

°   Elizabeth, the mother of John the Baptist, was also filled with the Holy Spirit (Lk. 1:41).

°   Zacharias, the father of John the Baptist, was filled with the Holy Spirit and prophesied (Lk. 1:67).

° Jesus Himself gave the Holy Spirit to His disciples before His ascension into heaven.

> *Jesus therefore said to them again, "Peace be with you; as the Father has sent Me, I also send you." And when He had said this, He breathed on them, and said to them, "Receive the Holy Spirit."* Jn. 20:21,22

So far, we have examined the scriptural experiences of having the Holy Spirit and being filled with the Holy Spirit. That neither one of these is the same as the baptism of the Holy Spirit is made evident by the following two statements of Jesus which we have recorded for us—one in the Gospel of John, the other in the book of Acts:

> *Now on the last day, the great day of the feast, Jesus stood and cried out, saying, "If any man is thirsty, let him come to Me and drink. He who believes in Me, as the Scripture said, 'From his innermost being shall flow rivers of living water.'" But this He spoke of the Spirit, whom those who believed in Him were to receive; for the Spirit was **not yet given,** because Jesus was **not yet glorified.*** Jn. 7:37-39

> *And gathering them together, He commanded them not to leave Jerusalem, but to wait for what the Father had promised, "Which," He said, "you heard of from Me; for John baptized with water, but you shall be **baptized with the Holy Spirit not many days from now."*** Acts 1:4,5

Jesus Himself had breathed upon the disciples and had imparted unto them the Holy Spirit. A few days later, however, He told the same group of men to wait for their final experience in the Holy Spirit—the **baptism** with the Holy Spirit!

## 6. WHEN DID THE DISCIPLES RECEIVE THE BAPTISM OF THE HOLY SPIRIT?

The disciples received their baptism of the Holy Spirit on the day of Pentecost as they were assembled in the upper room in Jerusalem.

> *And when the day of Pentecost had come, they were all together in one place. And suddenly there came from heaven a noise like a violent, rushing wind, and it filled the whole house where they were sitting. And there appeared to them tongues as of fire distributing themselves, and they rested on each one of them. And they were all filled with the Holy Spirit and began to speak with other tongues, as the Spirit was giving them utterance.* Acts 2:1-4

## 7. WHAT WAS PROVEN BY THIS OUTPOURING OF THE HOLY SPIRIT ON THE DAY OF PENTECOST?

The outpouring of the Holy Spirit on the day of Pentecost was proof to the disciples that Jesus had indeed been accepted by the Father and that atonement had been made for the sins of mankind by the shedding of His blood. Jesus promised that He would send the Holy Spirit, the Helper, and He did. (This was the glorification of Jesus which had been spoken of in John 7:39.)

> *"Therefore having been exalted to the right hand of God, and having received from the Father the promise of the Holy Spirit, He has poured forth this which you both see and hear."* Acts 2:33

The baptism of the Holy Spirit not only is the church's corporate assurance of the reality of the indwelling Christ and His redemptive work on its behalf, but also is the assurance that each individual believer may have. The indwelling of the Holy Spirit is our assurance that we are "sealed for the day of redemption" (Eph. 4:30).

## 8. SHOULD EVERY BELIEVER BE BAPTIZED WITH THE HOLY SPIRIT?

Yes! Every believer should be baptized with the Holy Spirit because it is the commandment of the Lord Jesus Christ and is the gospel of our salvation.

> *And gathering them together, He commanded them not to leave Jerusalem, but to wait for what the Father had promised . . .* ***"But you shall be baptized with the Holy Spirit not many days from now."***
> Acts 1:4,5

> *And Peter said to them, "Repent, and let each of you be baptized in the name of Jesus Christ for the forgiveness of your sins; and you shall receive the **gift of the Holy Spirit**. For the promise is for **you** and **your children**, and for **all who are far off**, as many as the Lord our God shall call to Himself."*
> Acts 2:38,39

## 9. WHAT SPIRITUAL BLESSINGS AND ENABLEMENTS ARE OURS THROUGH THE BAPTISM OF THE HOLY SPIRIT?

a. We are sealed by the Spirit.

> *In Him, you also, after listening to the message of truth, the gospel of your salvation—having also believed, you were sealed in Him with the Holy Spirit of promise.*
> Eph. 1:13

> *And do not grieve the Holy Spirit of God, by whom you were sealed for the day of redemption.*
> Eph. 4:30

b.  We are given the ability to pray in the Spirit.

> *For if I pray in a tongue, my spirit prays, but my mind is unfruitful. What is the outcome then? I shall pray with the spirit and I shall pray with the mind also; I shall sing with the spirit and I shall sing with the mind also.*
> 1 Cor. 14:14,15

> *But you, beloved, building yourselves up on your most holy faith; praying in the Holy Spirit.*
> Jude 20

c.  We are given the ability to praise God in the Spirit.

> *I shall sing with the spirit and I shall sing with the mind also.*          1 Cor. 14:15b

> *"I will proclaim Thy name to My brethren, in the midst of the congregation I will sing Thy praise."*
> Heb. 2:12

d.  We are made eligible for the gifts of the Spirit.

> *But to each one is given the manifestation of the Spirit for the common good.*          1 Cor. 12:7

> *But one and the same Spirit works all these things, distributing to each one individually just as He wills.*
> 1 Cor. 12:11

e.  We are given the power (authority) to become the sons of God. As we walk in the Spirit, not fulfilling the lusts of the flesh, we are changed (transformed) by the Holy Spirit into the image of Christ.

> *But as many as received Him, to them He gave the right to become children of God, even to those who believe in His name.*          Jn. 1:12

93

*But I say, walk by the Spirit, and you will not carry out the desire of the flesh.* Gal. 5:16

*For all who are being led by the Spirit of God, these are sons of God.* Rom. 8:14

*Now the Lord is the Spirit; and where the Spirit of the Lord is, there is liberty. But we all, with unveiled face beholding as in a mirror the glory of the Lord, are being transformed into the same image from glory to glory, just as from the Lord, the Spirit.* 2 Cor. 3:17,18

# What Spiritual Blessings and Enablements are ours through the Baptism of the Holy Spirit?

WE ARE SEALED BY THE SPIRIT.

WE ARE ENABLED TO PRAY IN THE SPIRIT.

WE ARE MADE ELIGIBLE FOR THE GIFTS OF THE SPIRIT.

WE ARE GIVEN THE POWER TO BECOME THE SONS OF GOD.

WE CAN PRAISE GOD IN THE SPIRIT.

## 10.  HOW DO WE RECEIVE THIS HOLY SPIRIT BAPTISM?

a.  We receive the Holy Spirit baptism as we obey the gospel of our salvation by (1) repenting, (2) being baptized in the name of Jesus Christ for the forgiveness of our sins, and (3) receiving the gift of the Holy Spirit by asking for it.

> *"And I say to you, ask* ["keep on asking," AMP], *and it shall be given to you; seek* ["keep on seeking," AMP], *and you shall find; knock* ["keep on knocking," AMP], *and it shall be opened to you. For everyone who asks, receives; and he who seeks, finds; and to him who knocks, it shall be opened. Now suppose one of you fathers is asked by his son for a fish; he will not give him a snake instead of a fish, will he? Or if he is asked for an egg, he will not give him a scorpion, will he? If you then, being evil, know how to give good gifts to your children, how much more shall your heavenly Father give the Holy Spirit to those who ask Him?"*          Lk. 11:9-13

b.  Although many valid methods are employed to aid believers in receiving the baptism of the Holy Spirit, there are certain elements or principles to which attention should always be given.

1.  The "baptism" as an experience is not what is to be sought. The believer is to pray for the indwelling of the third Person of the Godhead—the Holy Spirit.

2.  The believer must open himself up to the Holy Spirit in an atmosphere of praise and worship. The Holy Spirit cannot enter a closed vessel.

3.  Timing is an important element, especially when the laying on of hands is involved. No one should be pressured into receiving the Holy Spirit. If it becomes obvious at any time during an attempt to minister the baptism of the Holy Spirit that the candidate is overly anxious, nervous, self-conscious,

etc., and a moderate amount of compassionate counseling fails to alleviate the situation, then it should be put off to another time when the candidate is either better informed or more relaxed.

4. The candidate should be counseled beforehand to know what to expect. For instance, since the evidence of the baptism of the Holy Spirit is speaking in tongues, some explanation of how this takes place should be given to the candidate. Both the length and depth of this counseling will vary from time to time, depending upon such things as the openness of the candidate and the strength of the anointing.

5. No one should ever attempt to minister the baptism of the Holy Spirit by requiring the candidate to repeat certain words or phrases in order to induce speaking in tongues. A free-flowing praise which lifts up the name of Jesus and seeks His presence and anointing is a sufficient doorway for the entrance of the Holy Spirit.

6. The candidate, once having received the baptism of the Holy Spirit, should be exhorted to continue to pray daily in the Spirit, thus developing a fluency in the heavenly language.

## 11. WHAT METHODS ARE EMPLOYED BY THE LORD TO IMPART THE HOLY SPIRIT TO US?

The Lord employs either of the following two methods to impart the Holy Spirit to us:

a. The sovereign act of God.

> *While Peter was still speaking these words, the Holy Spirit fell upon all those who were listening to the message. And all the circumcised believers who had come with Peter were amazed, because the gift of the Holy Spirit had been poured out upon the Gentiles also.*

*For they were hearing them speaking with tongues and
exalting God.* Acts 10:44-46

b.   The laying on of hands.

*Now when the apostles in Jerusalem heard that
Samaria had received the word of God, they sent them
Peter and John, who came down and prayed for them,
that they might receive the Holy Spirit. For He had **not
yet fallen** upon any of them; they had simply been
baptized in the name of the Lord Jesus. Then they began
**laying their hands on them,** and they were receiving the
Holy Spirit. Now when Simon saw that the Spirit was
bestowed through the laying on of the apostles' hands,
he offered them money, saying, "Give **this authority** to
me as well, so that everyone on whom **I lay my hands
may receive the Holy Spirit.**"* Acts 8:14-19

## 12.   MUST SPEAKING WITH TONGUES ALWAYS ACCOMPANY THE BAPTISM OF THE HOLY SPIRIT?

The experience of speaking in tongues will never be refused by a
believer who is acquainted with the Word and has a genuine love for
the truth. The New Testament clearly teaches us that speaking in
tongues is an integral part of the experience of the baptism of the Holy
Spirit. Jesus purchased a full salvation for us, and we **must not** take
it upon ourselves to decide what is necessary and what is expendable
with regard to our experience in Christ.

## 13.   DO WE CONTINUE SPEAKING IN TONGUES AFTER WE HAVE BEEN BAPTIZED WITH THE HOLY SPIRIT?

Definitely!  Speaking in tongues (also referred to as praying in the
Spirit) will always be an important part of our prayer life. By praying
in the Spirit, we allow the Holy Spirit to build us up in our faith,

intercede for us before the throne of God, and reveal the things of God to us. Because of this, we should pray in the Spirit **daily!**

*One who speaks in a tongue edifies himself.*

1 Cor. 14:4

Read also Jude 20; Romans 8:26,27; 1 Corinthians 2:9-11.

## 14. IS THERE A DIFFERENCE BETWEEN THE SPEAKING IN TONGUES THAT BELONGS TO EVERY BELIEVER WHO IS BAPTIZED IN THE HOLY SPIRIT AND THE GIFT OF TONGUES?

Yes. As we have already seen, every believer receives the ability to pray in the Spirit by speaking in tongues when he is baptized in the Holy Spirit. In Chapter 12 of 1 Corinthians, however, Paul describes the special endowments of the Holy Spirit referred to as "various kinds of tongues" (v. 10) and "the interpretation of tongues." In the 14th chapter of 1 Corinthians, he tells us that this gift of tongues, when accompanied by the gift of the interpretation of tongues, not only edifies the church (v. 5), but is also a sign to the unbeliever (v. 22). It is in this sense that Paul makes the statement that not everyone speaks in tongues (1 Cor. 12:30), nor does everyone interpret.

## 15. IS IT TRUE THAT ALL BELIEVERS AUTOMATICALLY RECEIVE THE BAPTISM OF THE HOLY SPIRIT (UPON BELIEVING) AND THAT SPEAKING IN TONGUES DOES NOT NECESSARILY ACCOMPANY THIS EXPERIENCE?

The New Testament Scriptures, especially those of the book of Acts, make it very clear that believers do not always immediately receive the baptism of the Holy Spirit. When this does occur, it is accompanied by the evidence of speaking in tongues (Acts 2:4,33; 10:44-47; 11:15-17). In no way, however, can it be said to be an automatic experience, regardless of any outward manifestation. There are two portions of Scripture that we shall consider here by way of supporting this statement.

Acts 8:5,12-18:

> *And Philip went down to the city of Samaria and began proclaiming Christ to them.*
> *But when they believed Philip preaching the good news about the kingdom of God and the name of Jesus Christ, they were being baptized, men and women alike. And even Simon himself believed; and after being baptized, he continued on with Philip; and as he observed signs and great miracles taking place, he was constantly amazed. Now when the apostles in Jerusalem heard that Samaria had received the word of God, they sent them Peter and John, who came down and prayed for them, **that they might receive the Holy Spirit.** For **He had not yet fallen upon any of them;** they had simply been baptized in the name of the Lord Jesus. Then they began laying their hands on them, and **they were receiving the Holy Spirit.** Now when Simon **saw** that the Spirit was bestowed through the laying on of the apostles' hands, he offered them money.*

First of all, notice that Philip preached Christ to them, and as a result of this preaching, the people of Samaria believed and were water baptized in the name of the Lord Jesus. Although they were baptized believers, however, they had not yet received the Holy Spirit. This they received when the apostles came down from Jerusalem, laid their hands on them, and prayed for them. It does not mention specifically that the Samaritan Christians then spoke in tongues; but Simon "saw" an outward physical manifestation at the time hands were laid on the believers (v. 18), and it was a powerful enough experience that he offered the apostles money in order that he might obtain that same authority. Compare this with Peter's statement in Acts 2:33 where he referred to the pouring forth of the Holy Spirit as being that "which you both see and hear."

Acts 19:1-6:

> *And it came about that while Apollos was at Corinth, Paul having passed through the upper country came to Ephesus, and found some disciples, and he said to them, "Did you receive the Holy Spirit when you believed?" And they said to him, "No, we have not even heard whether there is a Holy Spirit." And he said, "Into what then were you baptized?" And they said, "Into John's baptism." And Paul said, "John baptized with the baptism of repentance, telling the people to believe in Him who was coming after him, that is, in Jesus." And when they heard this, they were baptized in the name of the Lord Jesus. And when Paul had laid his hands upon them, the Holy Spirit came on them, and they began speaking with tongues and prophesying.*

Here is an instance of men who were believers in Jesus Christ, having submitted to the baptism of John. We know that they must have been believers in Jesus, and not merely disciples of John, because the whole point of John's ministry was to turn people not to himself but to Jesus. Compare verse 4 above with John 1:31. It would have been highly improbable that these men could have been contemporaries of John, having been baptized by him, without also having been contemporaries of Jesus and acquainted with Him.

When Paul came to Ephesus and met these disciples, he noticed that something was lacking in their spiritual experience. If it were true that the baptism of the Holy Spirit is an "automatic" experience, Paul would never have asked them whether or not they had received it. Once again, after they had heard Paul's words, they were baptized in water in the name of the Lord Jesus and received the Holy Spirit with the evidence of speaking in tongues as well as prophesying.

## 16. A FREQUENT OBJECTION THAT IS VOICED AGAINST SPEAKING IN TONGUES IS THAT IT CANNOT BE UNDERSTOOD. IS THERE A SCRIPTURAL ANSWER TO THIS OBJECTION?

Yes, God's Word has an answer to every one of our needs. First of all, the ability to speak in tongues, an experience that every believer may and should receive when he is baptized in the Holy Spirit, is not meant for the understanding of men, but it is an avenue of spiritual communication with God. First Corinthians 14:2 declares, "For one who speaks in a tongue does not speak to men, but to God; **for no one understands,** but in his spirit he speaks mysteries."

This problem of man objecting to that which God has provided is nothing new. The prophet Isaiah referred to this very thing.

> *Indeed, He will speak to this people through stammering lips and a foreign tongue, He who said to them, "Here is rest, give rest to the weary," and, "Here is repose," **but they would not listen.*** Isa. 28:11,12

Paul, by the inspiration of the Holy Spirit, reached back into the Old Testament and brought these verses into the immediate context of New Testament experience and speaking in tongues, as he wrote to the Corinthian church.

> *Brethren, do not be children in your thinking; yet in evil be babes, but in your thinking be mature. In the Law it is written, **"By men of strange tongues and by the lips of strangers I will speak to this people, and even so they will not listen to Me,"** says the Lord. So then tongues are for a sign.* 1 Cor. 14:20-22a

When we pray in the Spirit (1 Cor. 14:14,15), our understanding may be unfruitful, but our spirits are rested and strengthened. Man has proven himself to be very capable of finding ways to edify his intellect and his soul. Praise God that He has provided a way to edify our spirit!

## 17. WHAT ARE THE BENEFITS OF SPEAKING IN TONGUES?

In addition to that which we have already discussed in this chapter, the benefits of speaking in tongues are:

a. Spiritual rest and refreshing (Isa. 28:12).

b. More effective prayer—the Holy Spirit prays through us according to the will of God (Rom. 8:26,27).

c. Warring by prayer in the Spirit (Eph. 6:18).

d. Building up our faith (Jude 20).

e. A sharing of secrets and mysteries with no one else but God (1 Cor. 14:2).

f. Self-edification (1 Cor. 14:4).

g. Edification of the spirit (1 Cor. 14:14,15).

h. Edification of the body of Christ when accompanied by the gift of interpretation (1 Cor. 14:5).

i. A sign of the power and presence of the Holy Spirit to the unbeliever (1 Cor. 14:22).

## HOME STUDY QUESTIONS: CHAPTER 7

1.  In your opinion, what is the most important work of the Holy Spirit?

2.  What would your answer be to one who claimed to have received the baptism of the Holy Spirit but had never spoken in tongues and did not want to?

3.  Where Scripture references only are given, look them up, and read the passages in their entirety.

# THE DOCTRINE OF BAPTISMS:
# THE BAPTISM OF FIRE

**Chapter 8**

The baptism of fire is the third aspect of the total work of the Holy Spirit which is included in the foundation stone of the Doctrine of Baptisms. We have already studied the baptism of the Holy Spirit, which has to do with our receiving the **life** of God, and water baptism, which has to do with **cleansing.** We will now consider the baptism of fire, which has to do with the **quality of life** within us.

## 1. WHAT IS THE DOCTRINE OF THE BAPTISM OF FIRE?

The baptism of fire is the process of sanctification (through such things as testings, tribulations, afflictions, and persecution) by which God brings us to maturity. It begins with the baptism of the Holy Spirit and ends with our being separated to Him and set apart for His service.

> *John answered and said to them all, "As for me, I baptize you with water; but One is coming who is mightier than I, and I am not fit to untie the thong of His sandals; He will baptize you with the Holy Spirit and fire. And His winnowing fork is in His hand to thoroughly clear His threshing floor, and to gather the wheat into His barn; but He will burn up the chaff with unquenchable fire."*
> Lk. 3:16,17

> *"I have come to cast fire upon the earth; and how I wish it were already kindled! But I have a baptism to undergo, and how distressed I am until it is accomplished!"*
> Lk. 12:49,50

*. . . strengthening the souls of the disciples, encouraging them to continue in the faith, and saying, "Through many tribulations we must enter the kingdom of God."*

Acts 14:22

## 2. WHY IS IT CALLED THE BAPTISM OF FIRE?

Fire is a symbol of the Holy Spirit and also a symbol of the purifying judgment of God.

*And there appeared to them tongues as of fire distributing themselves, and they rested on each one of them.*

Acts 2:3

*Each man's work will become evident; for the day will show it, because it is to be revealed with fire; and the fire itself will test the quality of each man's work.*

1 Cor. 3:13

God not only wants to burn the chaff out of our lives **now** (Lk. 3:17), but He also wants to purify (or chasten) for Himself a people in whom He can dwell and through whom He can reveal Himself to the world.

*"If you do not listen, and if you do not take it to heart to give honor to My name," says the Lord of hosts, "then I will send the curse upon you, and I will curse your blessings; and indeed, I have cursed them already, because you are not taking it to heart. Behold, I am going to rebuke your offspring, and I will spread refuse on your faces, the refuse of your feasts; and you will be taken away with it."*

Mal. 2:2,3

*. . . who gave Himself for us, that He might redeem us from every lawless deed and purify for Himself a people for His own possession, zealous for good deeds.*     Tit. 2:14

Both Jesus and John the Baptist referred to this separating, purifying, chastening work of the Holy Spirit as the baptism of fire.

> *John answered and said to them all, "As for me, I baptize you with water; but One is coming who is mightier than I, and I am not fit to untie the thong of His sandals; He will baptize you with the Holy Spirit and fire."*
>
> Lk. 3:16

> *"I have come to cast fire upon the earth; and how I wish it were already kindled! But I have a baptism to undergo, and how distressed I am until it is accomplished!"*
>
> Lk. 12:49,50

## 3.  WHAT IS CHASTENING?

Chastening is that work of the Holy Spirit by which the Lord reveals to us through trials, tribulations, and suffering those areas of our character which are weak.

> *"But He knows the way I take; when He has tried me, I shall come forth as gold."*          Job 23:10

> *"Behold, I have refined you, but not as silver; I have tested you in the furnace of affliction."*          Isa. 48:10

With chastening comes the grace to change, and through chastening we are perfected and drawn closer to Him. Read the following from Hebrews 12:12 (read also Hebrews 12:4-11):

> *Therefore, strengthen the hands that are weak and the knees that are feeble.*

## 4. IS CHASTENING THE SAME AS PUNISHMENT?

No. Chastening is that loving work of God our Father towards us, His children, whereby He seeks to correct us and lead us into maturity.

> *And you have forgotten the exhortation which is addressed to you as sons, "My son, do not regard lightly the discipline of the Lord, nor faint when you are reproved by Him; for those whom the Lord loves He disciplines, and He scourges every son whom He receives." It is for discipline that you endure; God deals with you as with sons; for what son is there whom his father does not discipline? But if you are without discipline, of which all have become partakers, then you are illegitimate children and not sons. Furthermore, we had earthly fathers to discipline us, and we respected them; shall we not much rather be subject to the Father of spirits, and live? For they disciplined us for a short time as seemed best to them, but He disciplines us for our good, that we may share His holiness.* Heb. 12:5-10

> *"Every branch in Me that does not bear fruit, He takes away; and every branch that bears fruit, He prunes it, that it may bear more fruit."* Jn. 15:2

Punishment may indeed come, but only if we resist His loving correction now.

> *For if we go on sinning willfully after receiving the knowledge of the truth, there no longer remains a sacrifice for sins, but a certain terrifying expectation of judgment, and* **the fury of a fire** *which will consume the adversaries.* Heb. 10:26,27

## 5.  WHAT IS THE RESULT OF CHASTENING?

Sanctification is the result of chastening.  When we are chastened by God, we learn the difference between His way and our way, His will and our will. When we lovingly and trustingly accept His correction, we are then separated (that is, sanctified) from those fleshly attitudes and works which hinder us from being perfected in Christ. True sanctification is impossible without water baptism, by which we are legally separated from the dominion of sin and self, and the baptism of the Holy Spirit, through which we are indwelt by the Spirit of God, thus becoming "holy temples of God."

> *Do you not know that you are a temple of God, and that the Spirit of God dwells in you? If any man destroys the temple of God, God will destroy him, for the temple of God is holy, and that is what you are.*              1 Cor. 3:16,17

> *"Therefore you are to be perfect, as your heavenly Father is perfect."*              Matt. 5:48

> *"Thus you are to be holy to Me, for I the Lord am holy; and I have set you apart from the peoples to be Mine."*
> Lev. 20:26

## 6.  IS SANCTIFICATION PROGRESSIVE OR INSTANTANE-OUS?

a.  Sanctification is instantaneous in that holiness is imputed or reckoned to us by God when we are indwelt by His Holy Spirit and receive circumcision of heart in the waters of baptism. This is necessary for the cutting away of the "old man of sin," thus obtaining our release from the dominion of sin and self.

> *Therefore we have been buried with Him through baptism into death, in order that as Christ was raised from the dead through the glory of the Father, so we too might walk in newness of life. For if we have become united with Him in the likeness of His death, certainly we shall be also in the likeness of His resurrection, knowing this, that our old self was crucified with Him, that our body of sin might be done away with, that we should no longer be slaves to sin; for he who has died is freed from sin.*
> Rom. 6:4-7

b. Sanctification is progressive in the sense that we must continue to appropriate that which we have thus received freely by the grace of God. We must "walk it out" daily as we go on in God, that is, decisively choosing to put aside "our way," thereby allowing His will to become our will.

> *Even so consider yourselves to be dead to sin, but alive to God in Christ Jesus. Therefore do not let sin reign in your mortal body that you should obey its lusts, and do not go on presenting the members of your body to sin as instruments of unrighteousness; but present yourselves to God as those alive from the dead, and your members as instruments of righteousness to God.*
> *I am speaking in human terms because of the weakness of your flesh. For just as you presented your members as slaves to impurity and to lawlessness, resulting in further lawlessness, so now present your members as slaves to righteousness, resulting in sanctification.*
> *But now having been freed from sin and enslaved to God, you derive your benefit, resulting in sanctification, and the outcome, eternal life.*
> Rom. 6:11-13,19,22

Although holiness (or sanctification) is freely imputed to us by the Spirit of God, our part is to perfect it by the way we live our lives, cooperating with His grace.

*Therefore, having these promises, beloved, let us cleanse*
*ourselves from all defilement of flesh and spirit, perfecting*
*holiness in the fear of God.* 2 Cor. 7:1

## 7. WHY MUST WE BE CHASTENED?

Unless God corrects and disciplines us, we will never partake of His
holiness; consequently, we would never see Him nor behold His glory.

*For they disciplined us for a short time as seemed best to*
*them, but He disciplines us for our good, that we may share*
*His holiness.*
*Pursue peace with all men, and the sanctification without*
*which no one will see the Lord.* Heb. 12:10,14

## 8. IS IT POSSIBLE FOR US TO ATTAIN TO SANCTIFICATION AND HOLINESS?

Yes. God would never require of us something which we could never
achieve. Sanctification enables us to live in accordance with the will
of God.

*"Thus you are to be holy to Me, for I the Lord am holy;*
*and I have set you apart from the peoples to be Mine."*
Lev. 20:26

*But you are a chosen race, a royal priesthood, a holy*
*nation, a people for God's own possession, that you may*
*proclaim the excellencies of Him who has called you out of*
*darkness into His marvelous light; for you once were not a*
*people, but now you are the people of God; you had not*
*received mercy, but now you have received mercy.*
1 Pet. 2:9,10

9. **WHAT IS THE FINAL OUTCOME OF THE SANCTIFYING WORK OF THE LORD IN OUR LIVES?**

Becoming His mature sons! Read again Hebrews 12:5-13 and Romans 8:18-23.

## HOME STUDY QUESTIONS: CHAPTER 8

1. What is the baptism of fire?

2. Why is it called the baptism of fire?

3. What is the difference between chastening and punishment?

4. What is sanctification?

5. Is sanctification instantaneous or progressive? Explain.

# THE LAYING ON OF HANDS

## Chapter 9

Our consideration in all these lessons is our study of the foundation stones of our Christian experience so that we can know and build upon that which the Lord has restored to us. The strength of the early church rested upon these experiences; that is why, even after the life of the Holy Spirit had all but been replaced with the "genius" and organization of man, the church retained the empty forms of these life-giving truths.

Today, we have a very different problem facing us. The Lord is pouring out His Spirit in an unprecedented way upon all who will accept Him. Once again, the people of the Lord have the life which He has always intended for them to have. However, the tendency among many is to divorce this new life from some or all of the traditions of the church. Previously we had a form with no life; now the danger is in having life with no form to contain and channel it. **To discard valid tradition because of the lack of life in the past is just as wrong as holding on to traditions for their own sake once the life has gone out of them.**

Let us also keep in mind the phenomenon we shall refer to as the "pendulum principle." When the Lord makes us to know that we need to change from a particular principle to which we have always adhered, whether in matters of doctrine or practice, we usually overreact, often swinging like a pendulum and taking a position almost totally opposed to our previous stand. For instance, Christians from a heavily traditional or liturgical background may find themselves desiring a loosely associated group of fellow believers, having little or no form of commitment or worship. Also, those from a legalistic background may disdain any type of standard or discipline, as being opposed to their "new-found grace." Fortunately, however, the Holy Spirit in time brings us back to a position that is, we hope, closer to true center.

The laying on of hands has been restored to the church in all its power. Many have not yet recognized this—many have employed it irresponsibly. This chapter is written in the hope that it will help to adjust the pendulum swing of your experience. We must always keep in mind that the Christian experience should be a balanced one, being firmly founded upon the Word **and** the Spirit!

## 1.  WHAT WAS ACCOMPLISHED IN THE OLD TESTAMENT BY THE LAYING ON OF HANDS?

a.  The laying on of hands was a means of imparting blessing.

    1.  Isaac laid his hands upon Jacob and imparted to him a blessing.

> *Then his father Isaac said to him* [Jacob], . . .
> *"Now may God give you of the dew of heaven, and of the fatness of the earth, and an abundance of grain and new wine; may peoples serve you, and nations bow down to you; be master of your brothers, and may your mother's sons bow down to you. Cursed be those who curse you, and blessed be those who bless you."*　　Gen. 27:26a,28,29

It is evident from the verses that follow this portion of the Scripture that the occurrence of a mere formality is not being related to us, but the actual bestowing of a blessing. Although Isaac had been tricked into blessing Jacob instead of Esau, it was not possible for him then to transfer the blessing back to Esau. (Read Genesis 27:30-37.)

2. Jacob laid his hands upon his grandchildren and blessed them.

> *And Joseph took them both, Ephraim with his right hand toward Israel's left, and Manasseh with his left hand toward Israel's right, and brought them close to him. But Israel stretched out his right hand and laid it on the head of Ephraim, who was the younger, and his left hand on Manasseh's head, crossing* [literally, "consciously directing"] *his hands, although Manasseh was the first-born.*
> *(Then Israel said,) "The angel who has redeemed me from all evil, bless the lads."*
>
> Gen. 48:13,14,16a

Although the primary blessing belonged to Manasseh as the firstborn, Israel (whose name was Jacob) knew by revelation from the Lord that Ephraim had been chosen first. Verses 17-20 of the same chapter teach us once again that this was not a ritual but a prophetic impartation of blessing.

> *When Joseph saw that his father laid his right hand on Ephraim's head, it displeased him; and he grasped his father's hand to remove it from Ephraim's head to Manasseh's head. And Joseph said to his father, "Not so, my father, for this one is the first-born. Place your right hand on his head." But his father refused and said, "I know, my son, I know; he also shall become a people and he also shall be great. However, his younger brother shall be greater than he, and his descendants shall become a multitude of nations." And he blessed them that day, saying, "By you Israel shall pronounce blessing, saying, 'May God make you like Ephraim and Manasseh!'"* **Thus he put Ephraim before Manasseh.**
>
> Gen. 48:17-20

b.  The laying on of hands was a means of imparting authority.

1.  Moses, at the direction of the Lord, laid his hands upon Joshua in the sight of the congregation of Israel, thus confirming, or ordaining, that the Lord had indeed called Joshua to lead the people.

> *Then Moses spoke to the Lord, saying, "May the Lord, the God of the spirits of all flesh, appoint a man over the congregation, who will go out and come in before them, and who will lead them out and bring them in, that the congregation of the Lord may not be like sheep which have no shepherd." So the Lord said to Moses, "Take Joshua the son of Nun, a man in whom is the Spirit, and lay your hand on him; and have him stand before Eleazar the priest and before all the congregation; and commission him in their sight. **And you shall put some of your authority on him,** in order that all the congregation of the sons of Israel may obey him."*
> *Then he laid his hands on him and commissioned him.*                              Num. 27:15-20,23a

2.  Was this laying on of hands for the impartation of authority effective?

> *Now Joshua the son of Nun was filled with the spirit of wisdom, **for Moses had laid his hands on him;** and the sons of Israel listened to him and did as the Lord had commanded Moses.*
>
>                              Deut. 34:9

For additional examples of the laying on of hands for impartation, see Leviticus 1:4; 3:2; 16:21 (the sacrificial offering); and Numbers 8:10 (the children of Israel and the Levites).

## 2. WHAT IS ACCOMPLISHED THROUGH THE LAYING ON OF HANDS IN THE NEW TESTAMENT?

The New Testament doctrine of the laying on of hands is concerned not only with the impartation of blessing and authority as in the Old Testament, but also in a much fuller sense with the impartation also of healing, miracles, the Holy Spirit, the gifts of the Spirit, and ministries.

a. The laying on of hands was used by Jesus as a basis for healing.

1. He laid on His hands as He ministered to the needs of the people.

> *He laid His hands upon a few sick people and healed them.* Mk. 6:5

> *And while the sun was setting, all who had any sick with various diseases brought them to Him; and laying His hands on every one of them, He was healing them.* Lk. 4:40

> *And He laid His hands upon her; and immediately she was made erect again, and began glorifying God.* Lk. 13:13

2. He passed on this authority to "those who have believed."

> *And He said to them, "Go into all the world and preach the gospel to all creation. He who has believed and has been baptized shall be saved; but he who has disbelieved shall be condemned. And these signs will accompany those who have believed: in My name they will cast out demons, they will speak with new tongues; they will pick up serpents, and if they drink any deadly poison, it shall not hurt them; they will lay hands on the sick, and they will recover."* Mk. 16:15-18

b. The laying on of hands was used by the disciples and apostles to minister healing and miracles through the authority given them by Jesus.

> *And at the hands of the apostles many signs and wonders were taking place among the people.*
>
> Acts 5:12a

> *And Ananias departed and entered the house, and after laying his hands on him said, "Brother Saul, the Lord Jesus, who appeared to you on the road by which you were coming, has sent me so that you may regain your sight, and be filled with the Holy Spirit."*
>
> Acts 9:17

Read also Acts 14:3; 19:11; 28:8.

NOTE: Chapter 10—"Divine Healing," which follows, is a supplement to this chapter and further develops the New Testament doctrine of healing.

c. Laying on of hands is one of the two methods employed by the Lord to impart the baptism of the Holy Spirit.

> *Then they began laying their hands on them, and they were receiving the Holy Spirit. Now when Simon saw that the Spirit was bestowed through the laying on of the apostles' hands, he offered them money, saying, "Give this authority to me as well, so that everyone on whom I lay my hands may receive the Holy Spirit."*
>
> Acts 8:17-19

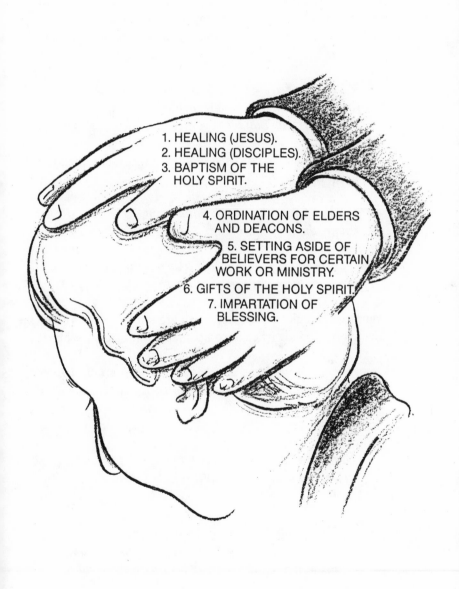

1. HEALING (JESUS).
2. HEALING (DISCIPLES).
3. BAPTISM OF THE
   HOLY SPIRIT.

4. ORDINATION OF ELDERS
   AND DEACONS.
5. SETTING ASIDE OF
   BELIEVERS FOR CERTAIN
   WORK OR MINISTRY.
6. GIFTS OF THE HOLY SPIRIT.
7. IMPARTATION OF
   BLESSING.

d. The laying on of hands is used in the appointment (or ordination) of elders and deacons.

> *And these* [the seven men of good reputation, full of the Spirit and of wisdom] *they brought before the apostles; and after praying, they laid their hands on them.*
> Acts 6:6

> *For this reason I* [Paul] *left you* [Titus] *in Crete, that you might set in order what remains, and appoint elders in every city as I directed you.*
> Tit. 1:5

e. Laying on of hands is also used in the setting aside of believers to a specific work or ministry.

> *And while they were ministering to the Lord and fasting, the Holy Spirit said, "Set apart for Me Barnabas and Saul for the work to which I have called them." Then, when they had fasted and prayed and laid their hands on them, they sent them away.*
> Acts 13:2,3

f. Ministries and gifts of the Holy Spirit are also administered by the laying on of hands when accompanied by directive prophecy.

> *Do not neglect the spiritual gift within you, which was bestowed upon you through prophetic utterance with the laying on of hands by the presbytery.*
> 1 Tim. 4:14

> *And for this reason I remind you to kindle afresh the gift of God which is in you through the laying on of my hands.*
> 2 Tim. 1:6

> *This command I entrust to you, Timothy, my son, in accordance with the prophecies previously made concerning you, that by them you may fight the good fight.*
> 1 Tim. 1:18

We have already said that the laying on of hands in the New Testament is practiced in much the same way as in the Old Testament, but in a fuller measure. Notice the similarity between the above verses which describe for us the setting aside of Timothy to his ministry and the parallel instance in Numbers 27:15-23 of the ordaining of Joshua. These points are identical in both cases: (1) each was initiated by the Lord; (2) each involved the laying on of hands by a presbytery as well as by one who was in a place of higher responsibility (Moses and Paul); (3) prophetic direction accompanied each (Urim and Thummim for Joshua, prophecy for Timothy); and (4) spiritual gifts were bestowed.

g. Laying on of hands is also a means of imparting blessings.

> *And they were bringing children to Him so that He might touch them; and the disciples rebuked them.*
> *And He took them in His arms and began blessing them, laying His hands upon them.*
>
> Mk. 10:13,16

## 3. WHAT DOES THE BIBLE ADMONISH US CONCERNING THE LAYING ON OF HANDS?

The Bible admonishes us to administer the laying on of hands carefully, with discretion, and only according to the Word of God and the direction of the Holy Spirit. We are to know those who minister to us with the laying on of hands; that is, we are to discern that they are "vessels unto honor" and filled with the Holy Spirit.

> *Do not lay hands upon anyone too hastily and thus share responsibility for the sins of others; keep yourself free from sin.* 1 Tim. 5:22

> *But we request of you, brethren, that you appreciate* [literally, "know"] *those who diligently labor among you, and have charge over you in the Lord and give you instruction.*
>
> 1 Thess. 5:12

# HOME STUDY QUESTIONS:  CHAPTER 9

1.  In your own words, explain the "pendulum principle."

2.  How was the laying on of hands used in the Old Testament? Give one example.

3.  Name three additional usages of the laying on of hands as found in the New Testament.

# DIVINE HEALING

## Chapter 10

## A Supplement to the Chapter on Laying on of Hands

### 1. WHY DO WE HAVE SICKNESS AND DISEASE IN THE WORLD?

Sickness, disease, and all forms of suffering came into the world as a result of sin. Because the devil introduced sin into the world, he—not God—is the author of all affliction and adversity.

> *And the Lord God said to the serpent* [that is, the devil], *"Because you have done this, cursed are you . . . ."*
> *To the woman He said, "I will greatly multiply your pain in childbirth, in pain you shall bring forth children . . . ."*
> *Then to Adam He said, "Because you have listened to the voice of your wife, and have eaten from the tree about which I commanded you, saying, 'You shall not eat from it'; cursed is the ground because of you; in toil* ["sorrow," KJV] *you shall eat of it all the days of your life.*
> *"For you are dust, and to dust you shall return."*
> Gen. 3:14,16,17,19b

### 2. HAS GOD MADE A PROVISION FOR OUR HEALING?

Yes! God sent His only-begotten Son Jesus into this world to redeem every man from the curse of sin. The blood of Jesus Christ is not only the propitiation (that is, the acceptable sacrifice) and satisfaction for our sins, but His blood is also the means by which we receive healing for **every** sickness and affliction of the body, the soul, and the spirit.

> *And when evening had come, they brought to Him many who were demon-possessed; and He cast out the spirits with a word, and healed all who were ill in order that what was spoken through Isaiah the prophet might be fulfilled, saying, "He Himself took our infirmities, and carried away our diseases."*
> Matt. 8:16,17

> *But He was pierced through for our transgressions, He was crushed for our iniquities; the chastening for our well-being fell upon Him, and by His scourging we are healed.*
> Isa. 53:5

## 3. WHY, THEN, IS THERE STILL SO MUCH SICKNESS AND DISEASE IN THE WORLD?

Sickness and disease will be in the world as long as sin is in the world. A great majority of the people in the world do not know of the **complete** deliverance from the power of Satan that is theirs because of the death and resurrection of Jesus Christ. Even many Christians are not aware of all that has been purchased for them, and as a result, they suffer needlessly.

> *My people are destroyed for lack of knowledge.*
> Hos. 4:6a

> *You do not have because you do not ask.*     Jas. 4:2b

## 4. CAN EVERYONE BE HEALED?

Everyone who has heard and believed the gospel of their salvation and has personally accepted Jesus Christ as Savior and Lord can experience the healing power of Christ.

*And He Himself bore our sins in His body on the cross,*
*that we might die to sin and live to righteousness; for by His*
*wounds you were healed.* 1 Pet. 2:24

There are instances in the New Testament of nonbelievers being healed, but these were "signs and wonders" granted by the Lord to confirm the preaching of the gospel. (Read Acts 4:29,30; 5:12-16; Hebrews 2:3,4.)

## 5. HOW CAN WE RECEIVE HEALING?

We can receive healing by **believing** the Word of God and exercising **faith** in the name of Jesus Christ.

*"Truly, truly, I say to you, if you shall ask the Father for*
*anything, He will give it to you in My name. Until now you*
*have asked for nothing in My name; ask, and you will*
*receive, that your joy may be made full."*
Jn. 16:23b,24

*But Peter said, "I do not possess silver and gold, but*
*what I do have I give to you: in the name of Jesus Christ the*
*Nazarene—walk!"*
*"And on the basis of faith in His name, it is the name of*
*Jesus which has strengthened this man whom you see and*
*know; and the faith which comes through Him has given him*
*this perfect health in the presence of you all."*
Acts 3:6,16

## 6. WHAT MEANS ARE EMPLOYED BY THE LORD TO ADMINISTER HEALING TO US?

The Bible gives us five means which are employed by the Lord to administer healing. They may be used individually or together, such as the laying on of hands with the gifts of healing.

125

It must be remembered that God is **sovereign** and, as such, is free to move in any way He chooses. This is true with divine healing as well. We must not limit God by setting our own guidelines within which we expect Him to work, but we must ask according to His will and then **believe!**

> *And this is the confidence which we have before Him, that, if we ask anything according to His will, He hears us. And if we know that He hears us in whatever we ask, we know that we have the requests which we have asked from Him.*                    1 Jn. 5:14,15

The five means of administering healing are as follows:

a.   Personal prayer.

> *As an example, brethren, of suffering and patience, take the prophets who spoke in the name of the Lord. Is anyone among you suffering? Let him pray.*
> Jas. 5:10,13a

> *Therefore, confess your sins to one another, and pray for one another, so that you may be healed. The effective prayer of a righteous man can accomplish much.*                    Jas. 5:16

b.   Prayer and anointing by the elders of the church.

> *Is anyone among you sick? Let him call for the elders of the church, and let them pray over him, anointing him with oil in the name of the Lord; and the prayer offered in faith will restore the one who is sick, and the Lord will raise him up, and if he has committed sins, they will be forgiven him.*                    Jas. 5:14,15

c.   The laying on of hands.

> *"And these signs will accompany those who have believed: . . . they will lay hands on the sick, and they will recover."*                    Mk. 16:17a,18b

d.   The gifts of healing.

> *Now concerning spiritual gifts, brethren, I do not want you to be unaware.*
> *For to one is given the word of wisdom through the Spirit, and to another the word of knowledge according to the same Spirit; to another faith by the same Spirit, and to another **gifts of healing by the one Spirit.***
>                                    1 Cor. 12:1,8,9

It is important for us always to keep in mind that, although the gifts of the Holy Spirit are given to us, their working, and therefore their effectiveness, is always **by Him.** One who has been granted the gift of healing or the gift of faith can no more go around healing everyone or working miracles indiscriminately than one having the gift of prophecy can prophesy apart from receiving a word from the Lord. (Read also Acts 14:3; 19:11.)

e.   The sent word.

> *He sent His word and healed them, and delivered them from their destructions.*                    Ps. 107:20

> *But the centurion answered and said, "Lord, I am not worthy for You to come under my roof, but just say the word, and my servant will be healed."*
>                                    Matt. 8:8

**Five Ways the Lord Administers Healing**

Personal Prayer

Prayer and Anointing by the Elders

Gifts of Healing

Laying on of Hands

The Sent Word

## 7. IS IT GOD'S WILL THAT EVERY CHRISTIAN BE HEALED?

Since it is God's will for us to be delivered from the power and the dominion of sin in "this **present** evil age" (Gal. 1:4), it is also His will for us to be free from the effects of sin as they are expressed in our bodies, souls, and spirits. If the Lord had not intended for us to be healed, He would not have provided such abundant means for our deliverance. We must keep in mind, however, that physical healing alone was not the primary reason for Jesus' bearing our sins on the cross.

# 8. WHY, THEN, DO WE NOT ALWAYS RECEIVE HEALING?

There are many reasons why we do not always receive healing when we ask for it, and we must not pretend to have all the answers for this. Divine healing is a spiritual matter and must be "spiritually discerned" (1 Cor. 2:14 KJV). Listed here are only those reasons of which we are presently aware and for which we have a scriptural basis.

a. This life and all the natural frailties that go with it are "a vapor that appears for a little while and then vanishes away" (Jas. 4:14). We will never be completely free from physical infirmity until the day we are released from "the earthly tent which is our house" and that which is mortal is "swallowed up by life" (2 Cor. 5:1,4).

b. God will always honor faith! Even in His earthly ministry, however, Jesus Himself could not work miracles of healing where faith did not exist.

> *And He did not do many miracles there because of their unbelief.*  Matt. 13:58

> *And without faith it is impossible to please Him, for he who comes to God must believe that He is, and that He is a rewarder of those who seek Him.*
> Heb. 11:6

c. If necessary, the Lord will send judgment in the form of sickness or affliction as a means of correcting a Christian who has allowed sin to creep into his life or who has refused to deal with iniquity. **Healing is a covenant blessing and goes hand in hand with covenant obedience!**

> *And He said, "If you will give earnest heed to the voice of the Lord your God, and do what is right in His sight, and give ear to His commandments, and keep all His statutes, I will put none of the diseases on you which I have put on the Egyptians; for I, the Lord, am your healer."*  Ex. 15:26

> *"But you shall serve the Lord your God, and He will bless your bread and your water; and I will remove sickness from your midst."*     Ex. 23:25

There would be no point in going before the Lord for healing with a heart which harbors sin or a neck which has been stiffened against Him.

> *If I regard wickedness in my heart, the Lord will not hear.*     Ps. 66:18

Read also Hebrews 12:5-10.

It should be stressed here that this is not a matter of one Christian judging as to why sickness or some other form of suffering is present in the life of another. No doubt every Job must have his "friends"; but to a Christian who is suffering, it is most disheartening for a fellow believer to imply that there must be some secret sin involved in order for the Lord to judge him so.

d. Timing is always an important element in God's dealings with us. We must keep in mind that our measurement of days, months, and years mean nothing to God—He is an eternal Being and moves in His own seasons. "But do not let this one fact escape your notice, beloved, that with the Lord one day is as a thousand years, and a thousand years as one day" (2 Pet. 3:8).

The Word of God records many instances of this for us. For instance, Jesus and the disciples met a man who had been born blind so that in **due season** he could receive healing from Jesus "in order that the works of God might be displayed in him" (Jn. 9:3). Also, when Lazarus was dying, his sisters sent to Jesus to come and heal their brother. Jesus, however, remained where He was for two days, saying, "This sickness is not unto death, but for the glory of God, that the Son of God may be glorified by it" (Jn. 11:4). Neither the disciples nor the sisters of Lazarus knew nor understood that Jesus delayed answering so that a greater glory might be made manifest.

e.  The Bible tells us that unto us "it has been granted for Christ's sake, not only to believe in Him, but also to suffer for His sake" (Phil. 1:29). Too often, we are concerned with the will of God only as it concerns our well-being, forgetting that it can also be the will of God for us to suffer. Think of the example of Paul, who suffered not only from many beatings, imprisonments, etc., but also from his "thorn in the flesh" (2 Cor. 12:1-10).

> *Moreover—let us also be full of joy now! Let us exult and triumph in our troubles and rejoice in our sufferings, knowing that pressure and affliction and hardship produce patient and unswerving endurance. And endurance (fortitude) develops maturity of character—that is, approved faith and tried integrity. And character [of this sort] produces [the habit of] joyful and confident hope of eternal salvation. Such hope never disappoints or deludes or shames us, for God's love has been poured out in our hearts through the Holy Spirit Who has been given to us.*     Rom. 5:3-5 AMP

Read also Romans 8:17,18; James 1:3; 1 Peter 4:1,19.

f.  Christians can be sick and even die before their time because they have not rightly partaken of the Lord's Supper. The Lord has overlooked many things which have been out of order in this area, because of His mercy. However, the closer we come to understanding the covenant relationship which we have with the Lord God and the body of Christ, the more completely will we be held accountable for wrongdoing.

> *Therefore whoever eats the bread or drinks the cup of the Lord in an unworthy manner, shall be guilty of the body and the blood of the Lord. But let a man examine himself, and so let him eat of the bread and drink of the cup. For he who eats and drinks, eats and drinks judgment to himself, if he does not judge the body rightly. For this reason **many among you are weak and sick, and a number sleep.***     1 Cor. 11:27-30

131

g. Finally, we must simply admit that there are some things we may never fully understand, for "we know in part" (1 Cor. 13:9), and "if anyone supposes that he knows anything, he has not yet known as he ought to know" (1 Cor. 8:2). Paul and Timothy were both men who were mightily used by God. In his first letter to Timothy, Paul gave some medical advice to an ailing Timothy. Instead of upbraiding him for being so "unspiritual" as to be sick (or questioning him as to what secret sin he had to be hiding in order for God to judge him so), he said, "No longer drink water exclusively, but use a little wine for the sake of your stomach **and your frequent ailments**" (1 Tim. 5:23)! In his letter to the Philippian church, Paul mentioned sending Epaphroditus, a "brother and fellow worker and fellow soldier" who had been sick to the "point of death" (Phil. 2:25-28). God had mercy on him and spared him so that he did not die. Paul also tells us of his having to leave Trophimus behind because he was "sick at Miletus" (2 Tim. 4:20).

Isn't that marvelous! They were people just like you and me—with real problems for which they could not always find easy answers. But they were still victorious in the midst of it all. They even seem to have accepted the good and the bad, the highs and the lows, as all being a normal part of what God was doing in them. May we labor to enter into that rest!

9. **IS THERE A DIFFERENCE BETWEEN A HEALING AND A MIRACLE, AND HOW MAY THAT DIFFERENCE BE DESCRIBED?**

A healing may take place instantly or gradually over a period of time, but a miracle is usually instantaneous and always completely supernatural. Frequently, Christians are disappointed because they do not receive an immediate healing. Instead of praying and then waiting in faith for God to answer, they are convinced that their petition has been refused because they do not **feel** healed. Faith cannot gain entrance where negative attitudes prevail.

When Jesus prayed for the man who had been born blind (Jn. 9:6,7), the man had to go and wash in the pool of Siloam before he could receive his sight. Also, when Jesus came to Bethsaida and prayed for a blind man there, He anointed and prayed for him twice before his sight was completely restored (Mk. 8:22-25). In a certain place, Jesus worked a miracle by touching a leper and healing him immediately (Matt. 8:1-3), but in another place, Jesus caused the lepers to be healed as they were on their way to the priests (Lk. 17:12-14).

## HOME STUDY QUESTIONS: CHAPTER 10

1. Who is to blame for sickness and disease being in the world?

2. What means are employed by the Lord to administer healing to us?

3. Give at least three reasons why we do not always receive a healing.

# RESURRECTION OF THE DEAD

## Chapter 11

Resurrection of the dead is the fifth of the six foundation stones of the Christian experience as we have been studying them in Hebrews 6. In order for us to experience fully the resurrection power and newness of life that are ours as a result of the redemptive work of Jesus Christ, we must have a complete commitment of heart and mind to the reality of His resurrection. It is through the resurrection of Christ that we are assured of the resurrection of our own bodies in the future.

## 1. WHAT IS RESURRECTION?

Resurrection is the return to life after death. It is not merely a restoration of life to the soul in an abstract sense, but it is the complete restoration and raising up of the whole man—body, soul, and spirit. Resurrection is the final stage of redemption.

> *For since by a man came death, by a man also came the resurrection of the dead. For as in Adam all die, so also in Christ all shall be made alive.*　　1 Cor. 15:21,22

> *And not only this, but also we ourselves, having the first fruits of the Spirit, even we ourselves groan within ourselves, waiting eagerly for our adoption as sons, the redemption of our body.*　　Rom. 8:23

**This is not what is meant by the Christian Doctrine of the Resurrection of the Dead!**

## 2. IS THE DOCTRINE OF THE RESURRECTION REFERRED TO IN THE OLD TESTAMENT?

Yes, the writers of the Old Testament prophesied of the resurrection of all men in general and of the Holy One, the Messiah, in particular (this latter being only partially understood).

The following four sources are the foremost examples of Old Testament belief in a bodily resurrection:

a.   The book of Job.

> *"If a man dies, will he live again? All the days of my struggle I will wait, until my change comes. Thou wilt call, and I will answer Thee; Thou wilt long for the work of Thy hands."*      Job 14:14,15

> *I know that my Redeemer and Vindicator lives, and at last—the Last One—He will stand upon the earth; and after my skin, even this body, has been destroyed, then from my flesh or without it I shall see God, whom I, even I, shall see for myself and on my side! And my eyes shall behold Him, and not as a stranger! My heart pines away and is consumed within me.*      Job 19:25-27 AMP

b.   The Psalmist:

> *Therefore my heart is glad, and my glory rejoices; my flesh also will dwell securely. For Thou wilt not abandon my soul to Sheol; neither wilt Thou allow Thy Holy One to undergo decay.*      Ps. 16:9,10

> *As for me, I shall behold Thy face in righteousness; I will be satisfied with Thy likeness when I awake.*
> Ps. 17:15

> *But God will redeem my soul from the power of Sheol; for He will receive me.*      Ps. 49:15

137

c.  The prophet Isaiah.

> *He will swallow up death for all time, and the Lord*
> *God will wipe tears away from all faces, and He will*
> *remove the reproach of His people from all the earth; for*
> *the Lord has spoken.*                                 Isa. 25:8

> *Your dead will live; their corpses will rise. You who*
> *lie in the dust, awake and shout for joy, for your dew is*
> *as the dew of the dawn, and the earth will give birth to*
> *the departed spirits.*                               Isa. 26:19

d.  The book of Daniel.

> *"Now at that time Michael, the great prince who*
> *stands guard over the sons of your people, will arise.*
> *And there will be a time of distress such as never*
> *occurred since there was a nation until that time; and at*
> *that time your people, everyone who is found written in*
> *the book, will be rescued. And many of those who sleep*
> *in the dust of the ground will awake, these to everlasting*
> *life, but the others to disgrace and everlasting contempt.*
> *And those who have insight will shine brightly like the*
> *brightness of the expanse of heaven, and those who lead*
> *the many to righteousness, like the stars forever and*
> *ever."*                                             Dan. 12:1-3

## 3.  WHAT DID JESUS TEACH CONCERNING THE RESURRECTION?

Jesus continued the thread of Old Testament revelation.

a.  He taught about the resurrection of all men.

> *And Jesus said to them, "The sons of this age marry*
> *and are given in marriage, but those who are considered*
> *worthy to attain to that age and the resurrection from the*

138

*dead, neither marry, nor are given in marriage; for neither can they die anymore, for they are like angels, and are sons of God, being sons of the resurrection. But that the dead are raised, even Moses showed, in the passage about the burning bush, where he calls the Lord the God of Abraham, and the God of Isaac, and the God of Jacob. Now He is not the God of the dead, but of the living; for all live to Him."*　　　　Lk. 20:34-38

Read also John 5:21,25,28,29; 6:39,40,44; 11:24-26.

b.　He spoke of His own resurrection.

*"For this reason the Father loves Me, because I lay down My life that I may take it again. No one has taken it away from Me, but I lay it down on My own initiative. I have authority to lay it down, and I have authority to take it up again. This commandment I received from My Father."*　　　　Jn. 10:17,18

Read also Matthew 16:21; 17:9,22,23; 20:18,19; 26:61-64; John 2:19-21; 14:19.

## 4.　WHAT DO THE SCRIPTURES TESTIFY CONCERNING THE RESURRECTION OF JESUS?

The Scriptures testify that Jesus did indeed suffer death at the hands of the elders and chief priests of Israel and that He was raised from the dead triumphantly on the third day. (Read Matthew 28:2-10; Mark 16:1-11; Luke 24:1-46; John 20:1-18.)

## 5.　WAS THE RESURRECTION OF JESUS CHRIST MERELY FIGURATIVE AND "SPIRITUAL"?

No, the resurrection of Jesus Christ was the total literal restoration to life of His body, soul, and spirit.

*And while they were telling these things, He Himself stood in their midst. But they were startled and frightened and thought that they were **seeing a spirit**. And He said to them, "Why are you troubled, and why do doubts arise in your hearts? **See My hands and My feet, that it is I Myself; touch Me and see, for a spirit does not have flesh and bones as you see that I have.**"*

*And while they still could not believe it for joy and were marveling, He said to them, "Have you anything here to eat?" And they gave Him a piece of broiled fish; and He took it and ate it before them.*        Lk. 24:36-39,41-43

Read also John 20:26-29.

## 6. WHY IS IT NECESSARY TO BELIEVE IN THE RESURRECTION OF THE LORD JESUS CHRIST?

Belief in the resurrection of the Lord Jesus Christ is essential to our entering into His redemptive work on our behalf and our sharing in the newness of resurrection life.

*Therefore we have been buried with Him through baptism into death, in order that as Christ was raised from the dead through the glory of the Father, so we too might walk in newness of life. For if we have become united with Him in the likeness of His death, certainly we shall be also in the likeness of His resurrection.*        Rom. 6:4,5

*If you confess with your mouth Jesus as Lord, and believe in your heart that God raised Him from the dead, you shall be saved.*        Rom. 10:9

The word *newness*, as it appears in Romans 6:4,5 above, is from the Greek word *kainotes,* meaning a "new quality of life"—a different kind of life. The believer is not just a reformed sinner, but one who has actually died to the old life and has been granted a better quality of life through the Spirit.

Read also Romans 4:24,25; 1 Corinthians 15:1-4,12-19.

## 7. HOW CAN WE KNOW THAT JESUS CHRIST WAS RAISED FROM THE DEAD?

a. We have the witness of the disciples and apostles as recorded in the New Testament.

> *After his suffering he showed himself alive to them in many convincing ways, and appeared to them repeatedly over a period of forty days talking with them about the affairs of the kingdom of God.* Acts 1:3 Phillips

> *For I delivered to you as of first importance what I also received, that Christ died for our sins according to the Scriptures, and that He was buried, and that He was raised on the third day according to the Scriptures, and that He appeared to Cephas, then to the twelve. After that He appeared to more than five hundred brethren at one time, most of whom remain until now, but some have fallen asleep; then He appeared to James, then to all the apostles.* 1 Cor. 15:3-7

b. The indwelling of the Holy Spirit is our personal assurance of the resurrection of Jesus Christ and the truth and reality of His presence in our lives.

> *"And I will ask the Father, and He will give you another Helper, that He may be with you forever; that is the Spirit of truth, whom the world cannot receive, because it does not behold Him or know Him, but you know Him because He abides with you, and will be in you. I will not leave you as orphans; I will come to you."* Jn. 14:16-18

*And gathering them together, He commanded them not to leave Jerusalem, but to wait for what the Father had promised, "Which," He said, "you heard of from Me; for John baptized with water, but you shall be baptized with the Holy Spirit not many days from now."*
Acts 1:4,5

*"This Jesus God raised up again, to which we are all witnesses.*
*"God has made Him both Lord and Christ.*
*"Therefore having been exalted to the right hand of God, and having received from the Father the promise of the Holy Spirit, He has poured forth this which you both see and hear."*
Acts 2:32,36,33

## 8. WHAT ASSURANCE DOES THE RESURRECTION OF JESUS CHRIST BRING TO US?

When Jesus arose from the dead, He assured us:

a. That He is the Son of God.

*Concerning His Son . . . who was declared the Son of God with power by the resurrection from the dead, according to the spirit of holiness, Jesus Christ our Lord.*
Rom. 1:3a,4

b. That He was received and glorified by the Father as He had promised. (Read Question 7, point b. of this same chapter.)

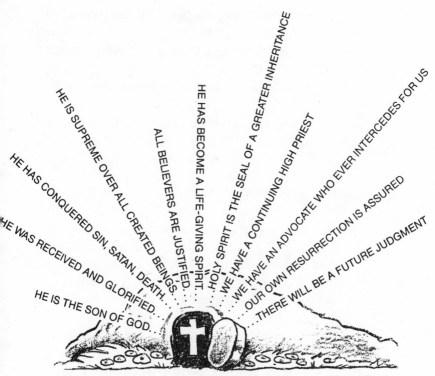

HE IS SUPREME OVER ALL CREATED BEINGS.

ALL BELIEVERS ARE JUSTIFIED.

HE HAS BECOME A LIFE-GIVING SPIRIT.

HE IS THE SEAL OF A GREATER INHERITANCE

HOLY SPIRIT IS THE SEAL OF A GREATER INHERITANCE

WE HAVE A CONTINUING HIGH PRIEST

WE HAVE AN ADVOCATE WHO EVER INTERCEDES FOR US

OUR OWN RESURRECTION IS ASSURED

THERE WILL BE A FUTURE JUDGMENT

HE HAS CONQUERED SIN, SATAN, DEATH.

HE WAS RECEIVED AND GLORIFIED.

HE IS THE SON OF GOD.

**When Jesus rose from the dead, He assured us that:**

c.   That He has conquered sin, Satan, death, and the grave.

> *Since then the children share in flesh and blood, He Himself likewise also partook of the same, that through death He might render powerless him who had the power of death, that is, the devil; and might deliver those who through fear of death were subject to slavery all their lives.*                    Heb. 2:14,15

> *He made you alive together with Him, having forgiven us all our transgressions, having canceled out the certificate of debt consisting of decrees against us and which was hostile to us; and He has taken it out of the way, having nailed it to the cross. When He had*

143

*disarmed the rulers and authorities* [that is, the devil's angels], *He made a public display of them, having triumphed over them through Him.*          Col. 2:13b-15

*"O death, where is your victory? O death, where is your sting?" The sting of death is sin, and the power of sin is the law; but thanks be to God, who gives us the victory through our Lord Jesus Christ.*
                                                1 Cor. 15:55-57

Read also Romans 8:2.

d.    That He is supreme over all created beings.

*And Jesus came up and spoke to them* [after the resurrection], *saying, "All authority has been given to Me in heaven and on earth."*          Matt. 28:18

*That power is the same divine energy which was demonstrated in Christ when he raised him from the dead and gave him the place of supreme honor in heaven—a place that is infinitely superior to any conceivable command, authority, power or control, and which carried with it a name far beyond any name that could ever be used in this world or the world to come. God has placed everything under the power of Christ and has set him up as head of everything for the Church. For the Church is his body; and in that body lives fully the one who fills the whole wide universe.*
                                                Eph. 1:20-23 Phillips

e.    That all believers are justified.

*. . . who* [Jesus our Lord] *was delivered for our offences, and was raised again for our justification.*
                                                Rom. 4:25 KJV

144

f.   That He has become a life-giving Spirit by virtue of His resurrection.

> *So also it is written, "The first man, Adam, became a living soul." The last Adam [Jesus] became a life-giving spirit.*                    1 Cor. 15:45

> *"For just as the Father raises the dead and gives them life, even so the Son also gives life to whom He wishes."*                    Jn. 5:21

g.   That the Holy Spirit is the seal and the earnest (or proof, down payment) of a greater inheritance to come.

> *In Him, you also, after listening to the message of truth, the gospel of your salvation—having also believed, you were sealed in Him with the Holy Spirit of promise, who is given as a pledge of our inheritance, with a view to the redemption of God's own possession, to the praise of His glory.*                    Eph. 1:13,14

> *Now He who establishes us with you in Christ and anointed us is God, who also sealed us and gave us the Spirit in our hearts as a pledge.*                    2 Cor. 1:21,22

h.   That we have a continuing High Priest.

> *He, . . . , because He abides forever, holds His priesthood permanently. Hence, also, He is able to save forever those who draw near to God through Him, since He always lives to make intercession for them.*
>                    Heb. 7:24,25

i. That we have an Advocate who ever lives to make intercession for us.

> *And if anyone sins, we have an Advocate with the Father, Jesus Christ the righteous.* 1 Jn. 2:1b

> *Who will bring a charge against God's elect? God is the one who justifies; who is the one who condemns? Christ Jesus is He who died, yes, rather who was raised, who is at the right hand of God, who also intercedes for us.* Rom. 8:33,34

j. That our own resurrection is assured.

> *"Because I live, you shall live also."* Jn. 14:19b

Read also 1 Corinthians 15:21,22; 1 Thessalonians 4:13-17.

k. That there is going to be a future judgment.

> *"God raised Him up on the third day, and granted that He should become visible, not to all the people, but to witnesses who were chosen beforehand by God, that is, to us, who ate and drank with Him after He arose from the dead. And He ordered us to preach to the people, and solemnly to testify that this is the One who has been appointed by God as Judge of the living and the dead."* Acts 10:40-42

> *Because He has fixed a day when He will judge the world righteously (justly) by a Man Whom He has destined and appointed for that task, and He has made this credible and given conviction and assurance and evidence to everyone by raising Him from the dead.*
> Acts 17:31 AMP

## 9. IN WHAT SENSE ARE CHRISTIANS NOW RISEN?

In John 5:28,29 Jesus spoke of the future resurrection:

> *"Do not marvel at this; for an hour is coming, in which all who are in the tombs shall hear His voice, and shall come forth; those who did the good deeds to a resurrection of life, those who committed the evil deeds to a resurrection of judgment."*

However, in John 5:24,25 He spoke of the **present resurrection** of those who, because they have believed, **have** (now) eternal life and therefore will not come into judgment:

> *"Truly, truly, I say to you, he who hears My word, and believes Him who sent Me, has eternal life, and does not come into judgment, but has passed out of death into life. Truly, truly, I say to you, an hour is coming **and now is,** when the dead shall hear the voice of the Son of God; and those who hear shall live."*

Every believer through regeneration, which is new birth, experiences a death to sin and a quickening to new life in Christ Jesus. As we have already noted in a previous section of this chapter, the conversion experience is not merely a reform of the old life—the turning over of a new leaf—but is an actual dying to sin and a new birth to life!

> *And you were dead in your trespasses and sins . . . .*
> *Even when we were dead in our transgressions, [God] made us alive together with Christ (by grace you have been saved), and raised us up with Him, and seated us with Him in the heavenly places, in Christ Jesus.*     Eph. 2:1,5,6

> *Now if we have died with Christ, we believe that we shall also live with Him.*
> *Even so consider yourselves to be dead to sin, but alive to God in Christ Jesus.*     Rom. 6:8,11

Read also Romans 6:4,5; 2 Corinthians 5:14,15,17; Galatians 2:19,20; Colossians 2:12,13.

## 10. HOW CAN WE KNOW THAT WE HAVE BEEN MADE PARTAKERS OF THE RESURRECTION IN THIS PRESENT LIFE?

Fortunately, the newness of life that is ours as we are made partakers of the resurrection of Jesus Christ does not have to be merely "accepted by faith," but it is made evident in our lives in many ways. The Lord Himself gives us a threefold witness that we are partakers of the resurrection here and now.

a.    We have the Holy Spirit as a witness.

> *But if the Spirit of Him who raised Jesus from the dead dwells in you, He who raised Christ Jesus from the dead will also give life to your mortal bodies through His Spirit who indwells you. So then, brethren, we are under obligation, not to the flesh, to live according to the flesh—for if you are living according to the flesh, you must die; but if by the Spirit you are putting to death the deeds of the body, you will live. For all who are being led by the Spirit of God, these are sons of God. For you have not received a spirit of slavery leading to fear again, but you have received a spirit of adoption as sons by which we cry out, "Abba! Father!" The Spirit Himself bears witness with our spirit that we are children of God.*
> Rom. 8:11-16

> *In Him, you also, after listening to the message of truth, the gospel of your salvation—having also believed, you were sealed in Him with the Holy Spirit of promise, who is given as a pledge of our inheritance, with a view to the redemption of God's own possession, to the praise of His glory.*
> Eph. 1:13,14

> *Now He who establishes us with you in Christ and
> anointed us is God, who also sealed us and gave us the
> Spirit in our hearts as a pledge.*      2 Cor. 1:21,22

b. The Word, which gives us the assurance that our lives have been changed, serves as a second witness.

> *Therefore if any man is in Christ, he is a new
> creature; the old things passed away; behold, new things
> have come.*      2 Cor. 5:17

c. The changed life we experience is our third witness.

> *"For through the Law I died to the Law, that I might
> live to God. I have been crucified with Christ; and it is
> no longer I who live, but Christ lives in me; and the life
> which I now live in the flesh I live by faith in the Son of
> God, who loved me, and delivered Himself up for me."*
>      Gal. 2:19,20

> *But in all these things we overwhelmingly conquer
> through Him who loved us. For I am convinced that
> neither death, nor life, nor angels, nor principalities, nor
> things present, nor things to come, nor powers, nor
> height, nor depth, nor any other created thing, shall be
> able to separate us from the love of God, which is in
> Christ Jesus our Lord.*      Rom. 8:37-39

## 11. WHAT DOES THE BIBLE TEACH CONCERNING THE FUTURE RESURRECTION?

The Bible tells us that a future, bodily resurrection of "all who are in the tombs" as well as those who are alive and on the earth at the second coming of Jesus Christ will take place at the last day.

*Jesus said to her, "Your brother shall rise again."*
*Martha said to Him, "I know that he will rise again in the*
*resurrection on the last day."* Jn. 11:23,24

The Bible further teaches us that there are two future resurrections:
the first being "of life"; the second, "of judgment."

*"Do not marvel at this; for an hour is coming, in which*
*all who are in the tombs shall hear His voice, and shall come*
*forth; those who did the good deeds to a resurrection of life,*
*those who committed the evil deeds to a resurrection of*
*judgment."* Jn. 5:28,29

*"And many of those who sleep in the dust of the ground*
*will awake, these to everlasting life, but the others to*
*disgrace and everlasting contempt."* Dan. 12:2

Read also Revelation 20:1-6.

## 12. WHAT IS THE FIRST RESURRECTION?

The first resurrection is called the resurrection "of life" and is for the
Old Testament righteous dead, all who are believers in the Lord Jesus
Christ (including the "dead in Christ" and those who will be alive at
His second coming), and those who will come to the Lord during the
tribulation period.

*"But immediately after the tribulation of those days the*
*sun will be darkened, and the moon will not give its light,*
*and the stars will fall from the sky, and the powers of the*
*heavens will be shaken, and then the sign of the Son of Man*
*will appear in the sky, and then all the tribes of the earth will*
*mourn, and they will see the Son of Man coming on the*
*clouds of the sky with power and great glory. And He will*
*send forth His angels with a great trumpet and they will*
*gather together His elect from the four winds, from one end*
*of the sky to the other."* Matt. 24:29-31

*For as in Adam all die, so also in Christ all shall be made alive. But each in his own order: Christ the first fruits, after that those who are Christ's at His coming.*

*Behold, I tell you a mystery; we shall not all sleep, but we shall all be changed, in a moment, in the twinkling of an eye, at the last trumpet; for the trumpet will sound, and the dead will be raised imperishable, and we shall be changed.*
1 Cor. 15:22,23,51,52

*But we do not want you to be uninformed, brethren, about those who are asleep, that you may not grieve, as do the rest who have no hope. For if we believe that Jesus died and rose again, even so God will bring with Him those who have fallen asleep in Jesus. For this we say to you by the word of the Lord, that we who are alive, and remain until the coming of the Lord, shall not precede those who have fallen asleep. For the Lord Himself will descend from heaven with a shout, with the voice of the archangel, and with the trumpet of God; and the dead in Christ shall rise first. Then we who are alive and remain shall be caught up together with them in the clouds to meet the Lord in the air, and thus we shall always be with the Lord.* 1 Thess. 4:13-17

*And I saw thrones, and they sat upon them, and judgment was given to them. And I saw the souls of those who had been beheaded because of the testimony of Jesus and because of the word of God, and those who had not worshiped the beast or his image, and had not received the mark upon their forehead and upon their hand; and they came to life and reigned with Christ for a thousand years. The rest of the dead did not come to life until the thousand years were completed. This is the first resurrection. Blessed and holy is the one who has a part in the first resurrection; over these the second death has no power, but they will be priests of God and of Christ and will reign with Him for a thousand years.* Rev. 20:4-6

## 13. WHAT IS THE SECOND RESURRECTION?

The second resurrection is referred to as the one "of judgment" (Jn. 5:29) and takes place at "the end, when He delivers up the kingdom to the God and Father, when He has abolished all rule and all authority and power" (1 Cor. 15:24).

> *The rest of the dead did not come to life until the thousand years were completed.*
> *And when the thousand years are completed, Satan will be released from his prison.*
> *And I saw a great white throne and Him who sat upon it, from whose presence earth and heaven fled away, and no place was found for them. And I saw the dead, the great and the small, standing before the throne, and books were opened; and another book was opened, which is the book of life; and the dead were judged from the things which were written in the books, according to their deeds. And the sea gave up the dead which were in it, and death and Hades gave up the dead which were in them; and they were judged, every one of them according to their deeds. And death and Hades were thrown into the lake of fire. This is the second death, the lake of fire. And if anyone's name was not found written in the book of life, he was thrown into the lake of fire.*
> Rev. 20:5a,7,11-15

## 14. WILL BELIEVERS HAVE TO STAND BEFORE THE "GREAT WHITE THRONE" AND BE JUDGED?

No, the "great white throne" judgment is only for the unbelievers out of every age whose names were "not found written in the book of life" (Rev. 20:15). As Christians, our judgment will take place before the judgment seat of Christ.

*But you, why do you judge your brother? Or you again, why do you regard your brother with contempt? For we shall all stand before the judgment seat of God.*

Rom. 14:10

*. . . on the day when, according to my gospel, God will judge the secrets of men through Christ Jesus.*

Rom. 2:16

**For we must all appear before the judgment seat of Christ,** *that each one may be recompensed for his deeds in the body, according to what he has done, whether good or bad.* 2 Cor. 5:10

The object of our judgment before Christ will not be to determine our eternal status as far as salvation is concerned; that was accomplished and settled the moment we believed.

*"Of Him all the prophets bear witness that through His name everyone who believes in Him receives forgiveness of sins."* Acts 10:43

*For He delivered us from the domain of darkness, and transferred us to the kingdom of His beloved Son.*

Col. 1:13

Our judgment will be for the purpose of judging each man's work in order to determine the extent of his reward in the kingdom of God.

*"For the Son of Man is going to come in the glory of His Father with His angels; and will then recompense every man* ***according to his deeds."*** Matt. 16:27

*Now if any man builds upon the foundation with gold, silver, precious stones, wood, hay, straw, each man's work will become evident; for the day will show it, because it is to be revealed with fire; and the fire itself will test the quality of*

153

*each man's work. If any man's work which he has built upon it remains, **he shall receive a reward.** If any man's work is burned up, **he shall suffer loss;** but he himself shall be saved, yet so as through fire.* 1 Cor. 3:12-15

*Watch yourselves, that you might not lose what we have accomplished, **but that you may receive a full reward.***

2 Jn. 8

## 15. WHAT KIND OF BODIES WILL BELIEVERS HAVE?

The resurrected bodies of believers will be glorious (1 Cor. 15:43), spiritual (1 Cor. 15:44), powerful (1 Cor. 15:43), incorruptible, and immortal (1 Cor. 15:42,50-53)—they will be bodies like that of our risen Lord: "And just as we have borne the image of the earthy, we shall also bear the **image of the heavenly"** (1 Cor. 15:49).

Our mortal bodies are "flesh and blood"—the life of the natural creation being in the blood (Gen. 9:4; Lev. 17:14). Not so with the resurrected body of Jesus. Jesus Himself said, "A spirit does not have flesh and bones as you see that I have" (Lk. 24:39). He had shed His blood (His natural life) at Calvary; the life He now lives does not depend upon the blood, but upon the power of Him who raised Him from the dead, and so it will be with us!

*Beloved, we are [even here and] now God's children; it is not yet disclosed (made clear) what we shall be [hereafter], but we know that when He comes and is manifested we shall [as God's children] **resemble and be like Him,** for we shall see Him just as He [really] is.*

1 Jn. 3:2 AMP

Read also Philippians 3:21.

## 6.  WHAT HAPPENS TO US WHEN WE DIE?

For the believer and the unbeliever alike, death is not endless darkness and oblivion. We do not cease to exist when we die; we are just separated from our bodies—it is our body which dies, not our soul and spirit. When the body returns whence it came (Gen. 3:19), the spirit returns to God who gave it (Eccl. 12:7).

> *As for the days of our life, they contain seventy years, or if due to strength, eighty years, yet their pride is but labor and sorrow; for soon it is gone **and we fly away.***
>
> Ps. 90:10

Luke 16:19-31 (q.v.) gives us a clear picture in Jesus' own words of what happened to the righteous and unrighteous dead under the Old Testament dispensation. Under the provisions of the New Covenant, unbelievers are still consigned to the fires of hell, while believers are taken to be with the Lord.

> *"If anyone serves Me, let him follow Me; and where I am, there shall My servant also be; if anyone serves Me, the Father will honor him."*
>
> Jn. 12:26

> *For we know that if the earthly tent which is our house is torn down, we have a building from God, a house not made with hands, eternal in the heavens. For indeed in this house we groan, longing to be clothed with our dwelling from heaven; inasmuch as we, having put it on, shall not be found naked. For indeed while we are in this tent, we groan, being burdened, because we do not want to be unclothed, but to be clothed, in order that what is mortal may be swallowed up by life. Now He who prepared us for this very purpose is God, who gave to us the Spirit as a pledge. Therefore, being always of good courage, and knowing that while we are at home in the body we are absent from the Lord—for we walk by faith, not by sight—we are of good courage, I say, and prefer rather **to***

*be absent from the body and to be at home with the Lord.*
*Therefore also we have as our ambition, whether at home*
*or absent, to be pleasing to Him.*            2 Cor. 5:1-9

*But I am hard-pressed from both directions, having the*
*desire to depart and be with Christ, for that is very much*
*better.*                                        Phil. 1:23

*. . . who died for us, that whether we are awake or*
*asleep, we may live together with Him.*        1 Thess. 5:10

## 17.   WHAT DOES IT MEAN, THEN, TO SAY THAT THOSE WHO HAVE DIED ARE ASLEEP?

When we say that those who have died are asleep, we do not mean
that they have gone into a state of unconscious rest or some type of
suspended animation until the time of their resurrection. As we
have seen, the Scripture makes it clear that this is not so. This
metaphor was used to describe the appearance of the dead body,
which resembled someone sleeping, rather than the state of the soul
and spirit. Jesus used this term when referring to the death of
Lazarus.

*This He said, and after that He said to them, "Our*
*friend Lazarus has fallen asleep; but I go, that I may*
*awaken him out of sleep." The disciples therefore said to*
*Him, "Lord, if he has fallen asleep, he will recover." Now*
*Jesus had spoken of his death, but they thought that He*
*was speaking of literal sleep. Then Jesus therefore said to*
*them plainly, "Lazarus is dead."*             Jn. 11:11-14

The balance of that chapter makes it clear that Lazarus had indeed
died, that his body had begun to deteriorate, and that he was called
back to life!

## HOME STUDY QUESTIONS: CHAPTER 11

1. Define the word "resurrection."

2. Why is the resurrection of Jesus Christ important to you personally?

3. Who will take part in the first resurrection?

4. Who will take part in the second resurrection?

5. Where Scripture references only are given, look them up, and read the passages in their entirety.

# ETERNAL JUDGMENT

**Chapter 12**

In this chapter, we will study the last of the six foundation stones, the doctrine of eternal judgment. We will consider eternal judgment in three phases, as follows: (1) the **past** judgment of Satan, the world, and man; (2) the **present** judgment of sinners and Christians; and (3) the **future** judgment of all who ever lived, the righteous as well as the unrighteous.

## 1. IN WHAT SENSE IS ETERNAL JUDGMENT A FOUNDATION STONE OF OUR CHRISTIAN EXPERIENCE?

The doctrine of eternal judgment is one of the foundation stones of our Christian experience in that it gives each man and woman, believer and unbeliever alike, the assurance that God is a just God and that all will be required to ultimately give an answer to Him who sits upon the throne of judgment.

In the previous chapter we saw that the Lord will judge the unrighteous at the "great white throne judgment" (Rev. 20:5a,7,11-15) and the righteous before the "judgment seat of Christ" (2 Cor. 5:10). The Bible tells us further that God is a jealous God, "visiting the iniquity of the fathers on the children, on the third and the fourth generations of those who hate [Him], but showing loving-kindness to thousands, to those who love [Him] and keep [His] commandments" (Ex. 20:5,6).

To the Christian, this knowledge should do much to inspire obedience as well as to instill a healthy fear of God.

*For if we go on sinning willfully after receiving the knowledge of the truth, there no longer remains a sacrifice for sins, but a certain **terrifying expectation of judgment, and the fury of a fire which will consume the adversaries.** Anyone who has set aside the Law of Moses dies without mercy on the testimony of two or three witnesses. How much severer punishment do you think he will deserve who has trampled under foot the Son of God, and has regarded as unclean the blood of the covenant by which he was sanctified, and has insulted the Spirit of grace? For we know Him who said, **"Vengeance is mine, I will repay."** And again, **"The Lord will judge His people."** It is a **terrifying thing to fall into the hands of the living God.***

Heb. 10:26-31

*For it is time for **judgment to begin with the household of God;** and if it begins with us first, what will be the outcome for those **who do not obey the gospel of God?***

1 Pet. 4:17

## 2.  IN WHAT SENSE HAS JUDGMENT ALREADY OCCURRED?

God has already judged Satan, the world, and man in the sense of His having made a determination as to the present condition and position, as well as the future outcome. It remains only for that judgment to be formally announced and carried out at the future day of judgment.

By the death and resurrection of Jesus Christ, sentence has been passed upon:

a.  Satan.

> *"The ruler (prince) of this world [Satan] is judged and condemned and sentence already is passed upon him."*
>
> Jn. 16:11 **AMP**

*[God] disarmed the principalities and powers ranged against us and made a bold display and public example of them, in triumphing over them in Him and in it [the cross].*   Col. 2:15 AMP

b.   The world.

*"Now judgment is upon this world; now the ruler of this world shall be cast out."*   Jn. 12:31

c.   Man.

*"He who believes in Him is not judged; he who does not believe has been judged already, because he has not believed in the name of the only begotten Son of God."*   Jn. 3:18

*"Truly, truly, I say to you, he who hears My word, and believes Him who sent Me, has eternal life, and does not come into judgment, but has passed out of death into life."*   Jn. 5:24

*Therefore, since we are now justified—acquitted, made righteous and brought into right relationship with God—by Christ's blood, how much more [certain is it that] we shall be saved by Him from the indignation and wrath of God.*   Rom. 5:9 AMP

# Past Judgments
## -Satan-

IS JUDGED AND CONDEMNED AND
SENTENCE ALREADY IS PASSED
ON HIM.                    JN. 16:11

## -The World-

JUDGMENT IS UPON THIS WORLD
NOW THE RULER OF THIS WORLD
SHALL BE CAST OUT.         JN. 12:31

## -Man-

HE WHO BELIEVES IN HIM IS NOT
JUDGED; HE WHO DOES NOT BELIEVE
HAS BEEN JUDGED ALREADY,
BECAUSE HE HAS NOT BELIEVED IN
THE NAME OF THE ONLY BEGOTTEN
SON OF GOD.                JN. 3:18

# 3. IN WHAT SENSE IS JUDGMENT OCCURRING NOW IN THIS PRESENT WORLD?

The Holy Spirit, sent by the Father to dwell among men after the death and resurrection of His Son Jesus Christ, reproves the world of sin **and** righteousness, and is the Standard by which sinner and Christian alike are judged.

a.  Concerning the judgment of sinners:

> *For God's [holy] wrath and indignation are revealed from heaven against all ungodliness and unrighteousness of men, who in their wickedness repress and hinder the truth and make it inoperative.*
> Rom. 1:18 AMP

> *"He who has believed and has been baptized shall be saved; but he who has disbelieved shall be condemned."*
> Mk. 16:16

See also Romans 1:19-32.

b.  Concerning the judgment of Christians:

> *For if we searchingly examined ourselves—detecting our shortcomings and recognizing our own condition—we should not be judged and penalty decreed [by the divine judgment]. But when we [fall short and] are judged by the Lord, we are disciplined and chastened so that we may not (finally) be condemned (to eternal punishment) with the world.*
> 1 Cor. 11:31,32 AMP

> *If we were closely to examine ourselves beforehand, we should avoid the judgment of God. But when God does judge us, he disciplines us as his own sons, that we may not be involved in the general condemnation of the world.*
> 1 Cor. 11:31,32 Phillips

# Present Judgment

## -Sinners-

HE WHO HAS BELIEVED AND BEEN BAPTISED SHALL BE SAVED; BUT HE WHO HAS DISBELIEVED SHALL BE CONDEMNED.   MK. 16:16

## -Christians-

IF WE WERE TO CLOSELY EXAMINE OURSELVES BEFOREHAND, WE SHOULD AVOID THE JUDGMENT OF GOD. BUT WHEN GOD DOES JUDGE US, HE DISCIPLINES US AS HIS OWN SONS, THAT WE MAY NOT BE INVOLVED IN THE GENERAL CONDEMNATION OF THE WORLD.
   I COR 11:31-32

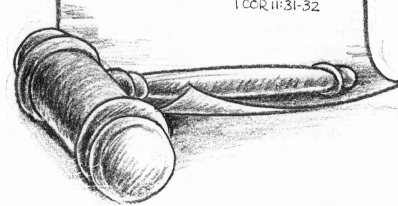

> *For it is time for judgment to begin with the household of God; and if it begins with us first, what will be the outcome for those who do not obey the gospel of God?*
>
> 1 Pet. 4:17

It is primarily in this manner that the foundation stone of eternal judgment operates in our lives today.

## 4. WHAT THEN REMAINS TO BE JUDGED IN THE FUTURE?

Although Satan, this world system, and the unrighteousness of man have all been judged by the death and resurrection of Jesus Christ, God is granting, by His long-suffering and mercy, time for all men to find repentance. He is also allowing the ungodliness and lawlessness in the world to come to their fulness. In due time, a time that is known only to the Father, His judgment will be established and put into effect by the return of Jesus Christ, who will sit upon the throne of David to rule and reign with a rod of iron.

> *"But when the Son of Man comes in His glory, and all the angels with Him, then He will sit on His glorious throne."*
>
> Matt. 25:31

> *. . .when the Lord Jesus shall be revealed from heaven with His mighty angels in flaming fire, dealing out retribution to those who do not know God and to those who do not obey the gospel of our Lord Jesus. And these will pay the penalty of eternal destruction, away from the presence of the Lord and from the glory of His power, when He comes to be glorified in His saints on that day.*
>
> 2 Thess. 1:7b-10a

> *I solemnly charge you in the presence of God and of Christ Jesus, who is to judge the living and the dead, and by His appearing and His kingdom . . . .*
>
> 2 Tim. 4:1

*Behold, the Lord came . . . to execute judgment upon all, and to convict all the ungodly.*                    Jude 14b,15a

## 5. WHAT WILL BE THE DIFFERENCE BETWEEN THE JUDGMENT OF SINNERS AND THE JUDGMENT OF CHRISTIANS?

a. Sinners will appear before the "great white throne" of God, where they will be judged for sin and consigned to punishment.

> *And I saw a great white throne and Him who sat upon it . . . and the dead were judged from the things which were written in the books, according to their deeds.*                    Rev. 20:11a,12b

> *"And the nations were enraged, and Thy wrath came, and the time came for the dead to be judged, and the time to give their reward to Thy bond-servants the prophets and to the saints and to those who fear Thy name, the small and the great, and to destroy those who destroy the earth."*                    Rev. 11:18

> *And if anyone's name was not found written in the book of life, he was thrown into the lake of fire.*                    Rev. 20:15

b. Believers will appear before the "judgment seat of Christ," where they will be judged according to their works and rewarded accordingly.

> *For we must all appear before the judgment seat of Christ, that each one may be recompensed for his deeds in the body, according to what he has done, whether good or bad.*                    2 Cor. 5:10

*We shall all stand before the judgment seat of God.*　　　　　　　　　　　　　Rom. 14:10b

*But if any one builds upon the Foundation, whether it be with gold, silver, precious stones, wood, hay, straw, the work of each [one] will become (plainly, openly) known—shown for what it is; for the day (of Christ) will disclose and declare it, because it will be revealed with fire, and the fire will test and critically appraise the character and the worth of the work each person has done. If the work which any person has built on this Foundation—any product of his efforts whatever—survives (this test),* **he will get his reward.** *But if any person's work is burned up [under the test],* **he will suffer the loss** *(of it all, losing his reward), though* **he himself will be saved,** *but only as [one who has passed] through fire.*　　　　1 Cor. 3:12-15 AMP

NOTE: Hell is the place of future punishment for the wicked. Whatever the different interpretations may be, there can be no doubt that the Scriptures require us to believe in a "place" of punishment, wherever it may be. The Bible refers to this place as being "down." This may or may not be an actual physical direction, but it certainly is, at least, a spiritual direction (even as we say in this life that an individual has gone "downhill"). This same principle may be applied to the fire of hell. It may or may not be fire as we know it, but whatever it is, it is fierce and causes great suffering. It is possible that hell is actually worse than our words have been able to describe it!

There are three words used in the Bible which together describe the place we call "hell":

° *Sheol* is a Hebrew word occurring sixty-five times in the Old Testament, and is translated "grave" thirty-one times, "hell" thirty-one times, and "pit" three times. The general idea is that it is the place of the dead. It is used in reference to both the righteous (Ps. 16:10; 30:3; Isa. 38:10) and the wicked (Num. 16:33; Job 24:19; Ps. 9:17).

Admittedly, these Scriptures are inconclusive in themselves. We must remember that the Old Testament presents a view of many of the teachings of the Bible that is **not incorrect,** but may be **incomplete.** The Old Testament by itself is not God's whole Word; the Old **and** New Testaments must be considered together. Although the New Testament completes the scriptural concept of hell, there are some "hints" in the Old Testament as to the difference between the state of the righteous and the unrighteous dead, as well as the nature of hell itself. (Read Isaiah 33:14; 66:24; Daniel 12:2.)

° *Gehenna* was the valley of Hinnom where the rites of Molech were celebrated during the Jewish apostasy (1 Ki. 11:7). King Josiah used it as a place to burn dead bodies (2 Ki. 23:13,14). The name eventually became symbolic of death and suffering and was used to designate the abode of lost spirits.

The word occurs twelve times in the New Testament and is properly translated "hell" each time (Matt. 5:22,29,30; 10:28; 18:9; 23:15,33; Mk. 9:43,45,47; Lk. 12:5; Jas. 3:6).

° *Hades* is a New Testament Greek word which conveys the same concept as the Hebrew *Sheol.* It refers to the place of the departed, the intermediate state between death and the resurrection. Some of its occurrences are found in Matthew 11:23; 16:18; Luke 16:19-31; Revelation 1:18; 20:13,14.

Until the death of Christ, Hades was the abode of both the righteous and the wicked dead, consisting of Abraham's bosom, as seen in Luke 16:22 (also referred to as "Paradise" in Lk. 23:43), and the place of torment, with a great gulf separating the two (Lk. 16:23-26).

When Jesus died, His spirit descended into the lower parts of the earth (Matt. 12:38-40; Eph. 4:7-10). It was here that He stripped Satan of his power over death and Hades (Rev. 1:18) and preached an eternally condemning word to the wicked (1 Pet. 3:19). His resurrection was also the resurrection of at least some of the Old Testament saints who had been kept in Abraham's bosom (Matt. 27:51-53). When Jesus ascended into heaven, He took all of Paradise with Him (Eph. 4:7-10 with 2 Cor. 12:4). Hades is now the place of torment for the wicked dead only.

The Scripture also refers to a "lake of fire" which is yet to be revealed (Rev.19:19-21; 20:10-15). At the "great white throne" judgment, death (Sheol) and Hades will deliver up their captives to be judged by the Lord God according to all that is "written in the books." All who are condemned to the second death will then be cast into the lake of fire where they will suffer eternally.

**HOME STUDY QUESTION:  CHAPTER 12**

1. Look up all the Scripture references contained within the note above, and study them in their entirety.

# Part Two

## Perfecting the
## Christian Life

# PERFECTING THE CHRISTIAN LIFE

In the previous section of this book, we considered the foundation stones of our Christian experience as set forth in Hebrews 6. These foundation principles are prefaced with the exhortation to "go on unto perfection; not laying again the foundation," but "leaving the principles [that is, the beginnings] of the doctrine of Christ" (Heb. 6:1 KJV). The foundation of any building is not laid for its own sake, but for the purpose of supporting the superstructure that is to follow. So it is in the life of every Christian. Once the spiritual foundation is firmly laid, it is time to "go on unto perfection."

Just as the foundation must be laid according to the Word of God, so also must the building which is to follow be constructed according to God's plan (1 Cor. 3:9-15). This building concept, which has been used by the Lord to illustrate to us the principles involved in beginning our Christian life, and employed a second time in reference to the church, is used to teach us that we are not converted to Christ to live our Christian lives alone, but are to be **"builded together** for an habitation of God through the Spirit" (Eph. 2:22 KJV). Jesus likens our **individual** lives to a building and also compares our **collective** lives to a building, referring to the latter as "**My church.**"

We can only understand this perfecting of our Christian experience as we relate it to the church, which is His body. "For by one Spirit are we all baptized into one body," thus becoming "the body of Christ, and members in particular" (1 Cor. 12:13,27 KJV).

171

# THE CHURCH

**Chapter 13**

From the very beginning, God has desired to have a people for Himself—a nation of people who would love Him and serve Him with their whole being. He began moving toward this end by calling Abraham out of his homeland and out from his people and promising to make of him a new and a great nation of blessed people (Gen. 12:1-3). The Lord soon extended these covenant blessings to the descendants of Abraham (Gen. 17:1-14), thereby succeeding not only in forming a great people, but also in redeeming them **as a nation** out of the bondage of Egypt (Ex. 19:1-6; Deut. 10:15,22), and establishing them in their new homeland, the land which had been promised to them as the heirs of Abraham (Deut. 29:10-13; 30:20).

The pages of the Old Testament contain the failures of Israel in their keeping of the old covenant; they also record for us the Lord's promise of a new covenant which He would one day make with His people, a covenant which would once and for all render their hearts capable of loving and serving only Him.

> *"Moreover the Lord your God will circumcise your heart and the heart of your descendants, to love the Lord your God with all your heart and with all your soul, in order that you may live."*
>
> Deut. 30:6

> *"For I will take you from the nations, gather you from all the lands, and bring you into your own land. Then I will sprinkle clean water on you, and you will be clean; I will cleanse you from all your filthiness and from all your idols. Moreover, I will give you a new heart and put a new spirit within you; and I will remove the heart of stone from your flesh and give you a heart of*

*flesh. And I will put My Spirit within you and cause you to walk in My statutes, and you will be careful to observe My ordinances."*                                      Ezk. 36:24-27

The New Testament is the unfolding of the fulfillment of the Lord's promises. National Israel was rejected for a season because of their unbelief, and the Gentiles, who had formerly not been a people, became the people of God (Rom. 9:22-26) by being grafted into the olive tree—Israel (Rom. 11:1-24)—thus becoming by faith the inheritors of the promises made to Abraham (Rom. 2:28,29; 4:6; 9:6-8; Gal. 3:27-29).

This plan of God which spans the ages is summed up very well by Ephesians 2:11-22:

> *Therefore remember, that formerly you, the Gentiles in the flesh, who are called "Uncircumcision" by the so-called "Circumcision," which is performed in the flesh by human hands—remember that you were at that time separate from Christ, excluded from the commonwealth of Israel, and strangers to the covenants of promise, having no hope and without God in the world. But now in Christ Jesus you who formerly were far off have been brought near by the blood of Christ. For He Himself is our peace, who made both groups into one, and broke down the barrier of the dividing wall, by abolishing in His flesh the enmity, which is the Law of commandments contained in ordinances, that in Himself He might make the two into one new man, thus establishing peace, and might reconcile them both in **one body** to God through the cross, by it having put to death the enmity. And He came and preached peace to you who were far away, and peace to those who were near; for through Him we both have our access in one Spirit to the Father. So then you are no longer **strangers and aliens,** but you are **fellow citizens** with the saints, and are of God's **household,** having been built upon the foundation of the apostles and prophets, Christ Jesus Himself being the corner stone, in whom the whole **building,** being fitted together is growing into a **holy temple** in the Lord; in whom you also **are being built together** into a **dwelling** of God in the Spirit.*

# 1. WHAT CONCEPTS DOES THE BIBLE USE TO TEACH US ABOUT THE NATURE AND FUNCTION OF GOD'S REDEEMED COMMUNITY?

To help us understand more clearly the nature and function of God's redeemed community, the Bible refers to us as being:

a. The Body of Christ, with ourselves as members.

> *For even as the body is one and yet has many members, and all the members of the body, though they are many, are one body, so also is Christ.*
> *But now God has placed the members, each one of them, in the body, just as He desired.*
> *Now you are Christ's body, and individually members of it.*                    1 Cor. 12:12,18,27

> *He is also head of the body, the church.*
>                                                         Col. 1:18a

Read also Ephesians 4:12,16; 5:23; Colossians 2:19.

b. God's building, with ourselves as living stones.

> [You] *having been built upon the foundation of the apostles and prophets, Christ Jesus Himself being the corner stone, in whom the whole building, being fitted together is growing into a holy temple in the Lord; in whom you also are being built together into a dwelling of God in the Spirit.*                    Eph. 2:20-22

175

Being a Christian ("Living Stone") doesn't automatically make us part of the church structure.

"(You)" having been built upon the foundation of the apostles and prophets, Christ Jesus Himself being the cornerstone, in whom the whole building being fitted together is growing into a holy temple in the Lord; in whom also you are being built together into a dwelling of God in the Spirit."

Ephesians 2:20-2?

Many Christians make the mistake of assuming that their being "living stones" automatically makes them a part of the church structure. There are even those who feel that any and every gathering of Christians (home prayer meetings, charismatic "prayer and praise" services, etc.) is a gathering of the local church. This is not only inconsistent with Scripture, but it does not make sense from a natural point of view either. For instance, a load of bricks delivered to a building site does not constitute a house. The bricks must be laid upon a foundation and built together row upon row until the whole structure takes shape and eventually becomes a dwelling. This is the message of the above verses from Ephesians 2. Notice the verb tenses: (1) "having been built upon the foundation" (past tense), (2) "being fitted together" (present tense), and (3) "are being built together" (present tense).

And here is the final purpose of it all:

> *You also, as living stones, are being built up as a spiritual house for a holy priesthood, to offer up spiritual sacrifices acceptable to God through Jesus Christ.*
> 1 Pet. 2:5

You see, each Christian, as a "living stone," must be laid upon a common foundation with other "living stones" and must be built together with them into a spiritual household.

Read also the following Scriptures that pertain to Jesus as the Chief Cornerstone: Isaiah 28:16; 1 Peter 2:4,6; Acts 4:10,11.

NOTE: It would be good for us to take the opportunity here to discuss something that is quite often a matter of confusion and misunderstanding among Christians, that matter being the question of whether or not Peter is the rock upon which the church is founded. The Scripture in question is Matthew 16:13-18, where it is recorded that Jesus asked His disciples, "Who do you say that I am?" To this Peter answered, "Thou art the Christ, the Son of the living God." Jesus then said a curious thing to Peter. He said, "You are Peter." Peter knew that, of course, but Jesus had a reason for speaking that way. In the day that Simon had been introduced to Jesus by his brother Andrew, Jesus had said to him, "Thou art Simon the son of Jona: thou shalt be called Cephas," which is by interpretation, a stone (Jn. 1:41,42 KJV).

Many months after this, we find Jesus reminding Peter of that name which had been given to him. He did this because He wanted Peter to know that he was indeed a part of the foundation of that which Jesus was going to build (*petros*, meaning "a piece of rock, a stone"), but that Jesus Himself was the Rock (*petra*, meaning a "huge rock") upon which the whole structure would rest.

c.  The Bible also refers to us as being God's own nation of "set apart" people (that is, the universal church).

> *But you are a chosen race, a royal priesthood, a holy nation, a people for God's own possession . . . for you once were not a people, but now you are the people of God.*                                                    1 Pet. 2:9a,10a

> [Christ Jesus] *who gave Himself for us, that He might redeem us from every lawless deed and purify for Himself a people for His own possession, zealous for good deeds.*                                                   Tit. 2:14

d.  We are also the congregation or assembly of believers (that is, the local church).

> *And the congregation of those who believed were of one heart and soul; and not one of them claimed that anything belonging to him was his own; but all things were common property to them.*                          Acts 4:32

> *And all those who had believed were together, and had all things in common.*
>
> *And day by day continuing with one mind . . . and breaking bread from house to house.*        Acts 2:44,46

e.   The Bible also calls us the family of God, with God Himself as our Father, Jesus as the first-born among many brethren, and ourselves as brothers and sisters.

> *So then, while we have opportunity, let us do good to all men, and especially to those who are of the household of the faith.*        Gal. 6:10

> *. . . of whom the whole family in heaven and earth is named.*        Eph. 3:15 KJV

Read also 1 Timothy 5:1,2; Romans 8:29; Hebrews 3:6; 2:11-13.

We must stress that the church is a family, not an organization. The concept of family is the same the world over, yet every family is different, just as each individual within the family is different. So it is with the church. The unity of the church is not going to be expressed in the "sameness" of exterior practices and beliefs, but in the inner oneness of mind and Spirit.

f.   We are also the church.

> *"Upon this rock I will build My church; and the gates of Hades shall not overpower it."*
>        Matt. 16:18

## 2.   WHAT DOES THE WORD *CHURCH* MEAN?

In the New Testament, the Greek word *ekklesia,* which has been translated "church," means "that which is called out." This concept of a called-out people does not originate in the New Testament, however, but it also is referred to over seventy times in the Old Testament, being used regularly for the "assembly" or the "congregation" of the people of Israel.

It is obvious from the various applications of the word *church* throughout the entire Bible, but especially in the New Testament, that it refers to **the people** and not to the place or building where they congregate. Neither does it refer to the ecclesiastical organization of any denominational structure.

## 3. WHERE IS THE WORD *CHURCH* FIRST USED IN THE NEW TESTAMENT?

Jesus was the first to speak of the church.

> *"Upon this rock I will build My church; and the gates of Hades shall not overpower it."*      Matt. 16:18

> *"And if he* [your brother] *refuses to listen to them* [the witnesses], *tell it to the church."*      Matt. 18:17

## 4. WHAT DOES THE NEW TESTAMENT USAGE OF THE WORD *CHURCH* SIGNIFY?

The word *church* as it is used in the New Testament signifies two things:

a. The universal church, which is the worldwide body of Christ, consisting of all those who are the called-out from all nations to be a separated people unto His name.

> *But you have come . . . to the general assembly and church of the first-born who are enrolled in heaven.*
>      Heb. 12:22a,23a

Read also Ephesians 1:22,23; 3:10; 1 Corinthians 12:13.

b.  The word *church* is also used to signify the local church, consisting of those who are the called-out in any given area or community, and formed together by the Holy Spirit as a local expression of the body of Christ.

> *And when they had appointed elders for them in every church, having prayed with fasting, they commended them to the Lord.*                Acts 14:23

> *. . . to the church of God which is at Corinth, to those who have been sanctified in Christ Jesus, saints by calling, with all who in every place call upon the name of our Lord Jesus Christ, their Lord and ours . . . .*
>                                        1 Cor. 1:2

> *For you, brethren, became imitators of the churches of God in Christ Jesus that are in Judea.*
>                                        1 Thess. 2:14

Read also Matthew 18:17; 1 Corinthians 4:17; 7:17; 11:18; 14:19,23, 26,28,33-35; 16:1.


## 5.  HOW DO WE BECOME MEMBERS OF THE BODY OF CHRIST, WHICH IS HIS CHURCH?

We become members of the body of Christ by obeying the gospel of our salvation, which includes repentance, water baptism, and the receiving of the gift of the Holy Spirit.

> *And Peter said to them, "Repent, and let each of you be baptized in the name of Jesus Christ for the forgiveness of your sins; and you shall receive the gift of the Holy Spirit."*
> *So then, those who had received his word were baptized; and there were added that day about three thousand souls.*
> *And the Lord was adding to their number day by day those who were being saved.*                Acts 2:38,41,47b

## 6. MUST EVERY BELIEVER BE A FUNCTIONING PART OF A LOCAL BODY?

Spiritual new birth immediately places us in a covenant relationship with God through Jesus Christ and initiates us into the Universal Body of Christ, thus establishing our salvation and eternal future. We have seen, however, that this alone does not sufficiently fulfill God's will for us, but that He has determined that each of us find our place of life and ministry in the local church. We may use the illustration of a child being born into this world: he immediately becomes a member of the human race—definitely a part of mankind—simply by virtue of birth itself. In order to go on and mature properly, however, that child needs to have a home, with parents—thus being a member of a family unit where he can be provided for and raised responsibly.

Since the worldwide body of Christ must express itself locally, all the believers in any given locality are required to submit themselves to the ministries of oversight (Eph. 4:11-16) which are provided by the Lord in that area to watch over them and bring them into maturity.

Once a believer has found that place where the Lord wants him to settle down and be shepherded, a verbal commitment on his part should be made publicly, in the assembly, to the church, and to those in the place of oversight. The pastors then, on behalf of themselves and the entire congregation, accept that commitment and make a like pledge, in return, to watch over him and minister to his needs.

Commitment is indispensable to the proper functioning of the local church. Read Chapter 18 regarding authentic Christian discipleship and commitment.

## 7. WHAT ARE SOME OF THE BASIC, UNCHANGING, AND NECESSARY PRINCIPLES OF THE CHURCH?

a.  Mutual commitment to:

1.  The gospel of Christ.

> *Only conduct yourselves in a manner worthy of the gospel of Christ; so that whether I come and see you or remain absent, I may hear of you that you are standing firm in one spirit, with one mind striving together for the faith of the gospel.*     Phil. 1:27

Read Ephesians 1:13.

2.  One another.

> *Let us therefore, as many as are perfect* [that is, mature], *have this attitude; and if in anything you have a different attitude, God will reveal that also to you; however, let us keep living by that same standard to which we have attained.*     Phil. 3:15,16

b.  Mutual doctrinal foundation (at least within each local church).

> *Teach and preach these principles. If anyone advocates a different doctrine, and does not agree with sound words, those of our Lord Jesus Christ, and with the doctrine conforming to godliness, he is conceited and understands nothing.*     1 Tim. 6:2b-4a

> *Retain the standard of sound words which you have heard from me, in the faith and love which are in Christ Jesus.*     2 Tim. 1:13

Read also Galatians 1:6-10; 2 Corinthians 11:4.

# Principles of the Church

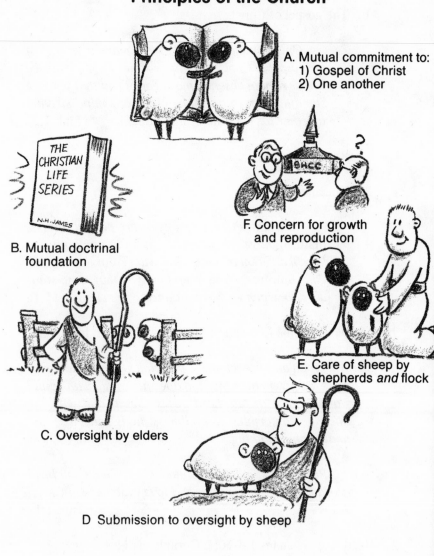

A. Mutual commitment to:
1) Gospel of Christ
2) One another

B. Mutual doctrinal foundation

F. Concern for growth and reproduction

C. Oversight by elders

E. Care of sheep by shepherds *and* flock

D Submission to oversight by sheep

c. Proven and responsible oversight of the church by elders (or shepherds).

> *Therefore, I exhort the elders among you, as your fellow elder and witness of the sufferings of Christ, and a partaker also of the glory that is to be revealed, shepherd the flock of God among you; exercising oversight not under compulsion, but voluntarily, according to the will of God; and not for sordid gain, but with eagerness; nor yet as lording it over those allotted to your charge, but proving to be examples to the flock.*
>
> 1 Pet. 5:1-3

Read also 1 Thessalonians 2:10; 5:12.

NOTE: Refer to Chapter 15, Questions 16, 17, and 18 for further information concerning the ministry of the elder.

d. Submission to the oversight on the part of believers (or sheep).

> *Obey your leaders, and submit to them; for they keep watch over your souls, as those who will give an account. Let them do this with joy and not with grief, for this would be unprofitable for you.*        Heb. 13:17

> *Remember those who led you, who spoke the word of God to you; and considering the result of their conduct* ["manner of life," AMP] *imitate their faith.*
>
> Heb. 13:7

> *You also became imitators of us and of the Lord, having received the word in much tribulation with the joy of the Holy Spirit.*        1 Thess. 1:6

> *But we request of you, brethren, that you appreciate those who diligently labor among you, and have charge over you in the Lord and give you instruction.*
>
> 1 Thess. 5:12

*I exhort you therefore, be imitators of me.*

1 Cor. 4:16

e.  The spiritual and natural care of the sheep, both by the shepherds and by the flock itself.

> *"Be on guard for yourselves and for all the flock, among which the Holy Spirit has made you overseers, to shepherd the church of God which He purchased with His own blood."*
>
> Acts 20:28

> *Let us consider how to stimulate one another to love and good deeds.*
>
> Heb. 10:24

> *And let our people also learn to engage in good deeds to meet pressing needs, that they may not be unfruitful.*
>
> Tit. 3:14

Read also Titus 3:8; 1 Thessalonians 3:12,13.

f.  Concern for healthy growth and reproduction (that is, making disciples).

> *"Go therefore and make disciples of all the nations."*
>
> Matt. 28:19

> *And after they had preached the gospel to that city and had made many disciples, they returned to Lystra and to Iconium and to Antioch.*
>
> Acts 14:21

As was stated in the Preface, the very word *disciple* implies the discipline involved in the process of learning about our new Master and becoming more and more like Him. It is a discipline which includes a systematic impartation of truth as well as a day-to-day sharing of life from one believer to another. The mature, experienced ones are the teachers; the young and inexperienced are the ones who must learn. It is dangerous for any believer to feel that he does not need to be a part of this disciplining process.

## 8. WHAT ARE SOME OF THE PURPOSES OF THE CHURCH?

We have already discussed the importance of the church as the believer's family. Let us now consider some additional purposes of the church.

a.  The church is the instrument ordained by the Lord to manifest His presence to the world.

> *"But you shall receive power when the Holy Spirit has come upon you; and you shall be **My witnesses** . . . even to the remotest part of the earth."*
> Acts 1:8

> *Now all these things are from God, who reconciled us to Himself through Christ, and gave us the ministry of reconciliation, namely, that God was in Christ reconciling the world to Himself, not counting their trespasses against them, and He has committed to us the word of reconciliation. Therefore, we are ambassadors for Christ, as though God were entreating through us; we beg you on behalf of Christ, be reconciled to God.*
> 2 Cor. 5:18-20

b.  The church was created by God to be an expression of His wisdom to all ages.

> *. . . the Gentiles are fellow heirs and fellow members of the body, and fellow partakers of the promise in Christ Jesus through the gospel . . .*
> *. . . and to bring to light what is the administration of the mystery which for ages has been hidden in God, who created all things; in order that the manifold wisdom of*

> *God might now be made known through the church to the rulers and the authorities in the heavenly places.*
> Eph. 3:6,9,10

c. The church is the dwelling place of the Holy Spirit.

> *The whole building, being fitted together is growing into a holy temple in the Lord; in whom you also are being built together into a dwelling of God in the Spirit.*
> Eph. 2:21,22

d. The church is the living body of Christ, indwelt by His presence, and therefore is the residence of the gifts of the Spirit and the ministries which Jesus Christ has given for the edification of each believer.

> *But to each one is given the manifestation of the Spirit for the common good.*
> *Earnestly desire the greater gifts.*
> 1 Cor. 12:7,31a

> *And He gave some as apostles, and some as prophets, and some as evangelists, and some as pastors and teachers, for the equipping of the saints for the work of service, to the building up of the body of Christ; until we all attain to the unity of the faith, and of the knowledge of the Son of God, to a mature man, to the measure of the stature which belongs to the fulness of Christ. As a result, we are no longer to be children, tossed here and there by waves, and carried about by every wind of doctrine, by the trickery of men, by craftiness in deceitful scheming; but speaking the truth in love, we are to grow up in all aspects into Him, who is the head, even Christ, from whom the whole body, being fitted and held together by that which every joint supplies, according to the proper working of each individual part, causes the growth of the body for the building up of itself in love.*
> Eph. 4:11-16

e.   The church is referred to as the "pillar and support of the truth."

> *But in case I am delayed, I write so that you may know how one ought to conduct himself in the household of God, which is the church of the living God, the pillar and support of the truth.*            1 Tim. 3:15

f.   The church is the bride of Christ!

> *Husbands, love your wives, just as Christ also loved the church and gave Himself up for her.*
> *For this cause a man shall leave his father and mother, and shall cleave to his wife; and the two shall become one flesh. This mystery is great; but I am speaking with reference to Christ and the church.*
> Eph. 5:25,31,32

# HOME STUDY QUESTIONS:  CHAPTER 13

1.   What is the meaning of the word *church*?

2.   Name four other concepts used by the Lord to teach us about the nature and function of His redeemed community.

3.   What would your answer be to a Christian who did not feel it was necessary to belong to a local church?

# THE GIFTS OF THE HOLY SPIRIT

**Chapter 14**

In the previous chapter, we discussed the church, which is the body of the Lord Jesus Christ, and each believer's relationship to the church, particularly in its local expression. In the next two chapters, we will study the gifts and ministries placed within the church by the Lord Jesus Christ through the Holy Spirit. A clear understanding of these gifts and ministries is vital to each Christian because they are the means of our being perfected that we may "grow up in all aspects into Him, who is the head, even Christ" (Eph. 4:15).

This chapter is not in any way meant to be a definitive statement concerning the working of the gifts of the Spirit but is an introduction to them and an outline of the Scriptures upon which they are based and which govern their usage.

## 1. WHAT ARE THE GIFTS OF THE SPIRIT?

The gifts of the Spirit are supernatural enablements which are distributed freely by the Holy Spirit to every member of the body according to His will.

> *Now there are varieties of gifts, but the same Spirit. And there are varieties of ministries, and the same Lord. And there are varieties of effects, but the same God who works all things in all persons. But to each one is given the manifestation of the Spirit for the common good.*

*But one and the same Spirit works all these things,
distributing to each one individually just as He wills.*

1 Cor. 12:4-7,11

These gifts, by the very definition of the original Greek word (*charisma*, meaning "gifts of grace"), are distributed to the members of the body solely at the discretion of the Holy Spirit. **They are not given on the basis of merit, nor does a Christian have to have arrived at any particular level of maturity or holiness in order to have a gift of the Spirit manifested through Him.** Perhaps the best example of this may be found in Paul's writings to the church at Corinth. Paul wrote concerning them that they "were enriched in Him [Jesus], in all speech and all knowledge . . . not lacking in **any** gift" (1 Cor. 1:5-7). Yet they were carnal, having allowed divisions (1 Cor. 1:10), immorality (5:1-13), problems concerning marriage and divorce (7:1-40), and especially improper usage and regulation of the spiritual gifts themselves (1 Cor. 12-14).

**It must be remembered that although these gifts are given to the members of the body, their power is derived from, and dependent upon, the Holy Spirit.** A believer having the gift of prophecy, for instance, can only prophesy when the Holy Spirit moves within him, inspiring him to speak. The same principle applies to the gifts of faith, healing, etc.

The Holy Spirit is gentle, never forcing the gifts upon us nor compelling us to manifest them. For this reason, we must earnestly seek the gifts of the Spirit and be careful not to neglect them once we do receive them (1 Tim. 4:14; 2 Tim. 1:6). Many of the questions that we may have concerning the operation of the gifts will be answered by the Spirit Himself as we step out in faith, claiming that which He has given to us.

## 2. HOW MANY GIFTS OF THE SPIRIT ARE THERE?

There are many gifts and enablings given to us by the Holy Spirit. However, those which are usually referred to as "the gifts of the Spirit" are nine in number and are as follows:

a. Three gifts of revelation: the word of wisdom, the word of knowledge, and the discerning of spirits.

b. Three gifts of power: faith, healing, and miracles.

c. Three gifts of utterance: prophecy, tongues, and the interpretation of tongues.

Read 1 Corinthians 12:8-10.


## 3. WHAT ARE SOME OF THE OTHER SPIRITUAL GIFTS OR ENABLEMENTS BESIDES THOSE MENTIONED IN 1 CORINTHIANS 12?

> *And since we have **gifts** that differ according to the grace given to us, let each exercise them accordingly: if **prophecy,** according to the proportion of his faith; if **service,** in his serving; or he who **teaches,** in his teaching; or he who **exhorts,** in his exhortation; he who **gives,** with liberality; he who **leads,** with diligence; he who shows **mercy,** with cheerfulness.* Rom. 12:6-8

> *As each one has received a special gift, employ it in serving one another, as good stewards of the manifold grace of God. Whoever **speaks,** let him speak, as it were, the utterances of God; whoever **serves,** let him do so as by the strength which God supplies; so that in all things God may be glorified through Jesus Christ, to whom belongs the glory and dominion forever and ever. Amen.* 1 Pet. 4:10,11

# 4.  WHAT IS THE GIFT OF THE WORD OF WISDOM?

The word of wisdom is a supernaturally given revelation of God's direction and guidance for a specific situation.  Many times certain problems and situations arise which require an answer that only God can supply. Following are two examples of the word of wisdom working in the early church.

The ministry of deacon was instituted to fulfill a need that had arisen.

> *Now at this time while the disciples were increasing in number, a complaint arose on the part of the Hellenistic Jews against the native Hebrews, because their widows were being overlooked in the daily serving of food. And the twelve summoned the congregation of the disciples and said, "It is not desirable for us to neglect the word of God in order to serve tables. But select from among you, brethren, seven men of good reputation, full of the Spirit and of wisdom, whom we may put in charge of this task. But we will devote ourselves to prayer, and to the ministry of the word." And the statement found approval with the whole congregation.*
>
> Acts 6:1-5a

Paul and Barnabas traveled to Jerusalem because of the dissension that had arisen over the method of accepting Gentile converts into the church. Many of the Jewish Christians believed that the Gentiles should be circumcised in the flesh and made to obey the Mosaic Law. Paul, the apostle to the Gentiles, taught that this was not necessary. It became evident that an answer from the Lord was needed to keep the church from splitting into two camps. Read Acts 15:1-22.

> *And after they* [those who had testified at the conference] *had stopped speaking, James answered, saying, "Brethren, listen to me . . . .*

194

> *"Therefore it is my judgment that we do not trouble those who are turning to God from among the Gentiles, but that we write to them that they abstain from things contaminated by idols and from fornication and from what is strangled and from blood."*
>
> *Then it seemed good to the **apostles** and the **elders,** with the **whole church** . . . .*        Acts 15:13,19,20,22a

In a subsequent letter written to the Gentiles to inform them of the outcome of the conference, the following statement was made concerning the decision that had been reached: "For it **seemed good to the Holy Spirit and to us** to lay upon you no greater burden than these essentials" (Acts 15:28). They evidently recognized that the Holy Spirit had provided them with the solution to a very pressing problem.

Although not every member of the body will be enabled by the Holy Spirit to manifest the gift of a word of wisdom, each member may, and should, possess a certain amount of that wisdom "which comes down from above" (Jas. 3:15). The Bible tells us, that "if any of you lacks wisdom, let him ask of God, who gives to all men generously and without reproach, and it will be given to him" (Jas. 1:5). Read also Ephesians 1:17 and Colossians 1:9; 3:16.


## 5.   WHAT IS THE GIFT OF THE WORD OF KNOWLEDGE?

Through the working of the gift of a word of knowledge, the Holy Spirit reveals to us information that could not have been known by any natural means. One example of this gift may be found in Acts 5, when the Holy Spirit revealed to Peter that Ananias and Sapphira had lied concerning the amount of money they had received for the sale of their property.

Another example of the working of this gift may be found in Acts 14:8-10. While visiting the city of Lystra, Paul came upon a man who had been born lame and had never walked. As Paul "fixed his gaze" upon him, the Holy Spirit made him to know that the man had faith to be healed. The Scriptures say that "[Paul] said with a loud voice, 'Stand upright on your feet.' And he [the lame man] leaped up and began to walk."

## 6. WHAT IS THE GIFT OF DISTINGUISHING OF SPIRITS?

a. The gift of distinguishing of spirits is the supernatural ability to identify the evil spirits in places or persons. The following is an example from the Bible of the working of this gift:

> *And when they* [Barnabas and Saul] *had gone through the whole island as far as Paphos, they found a certain magician, a Jewish false prophet whose name was Bar-Jesus, who was with the proconsul, Sergius Paulus, a man of intelligence. This man summoned Barnabas and Saul and sought to hear the word of God. But Elymas the magician (for thus his name is translated) was opposing them, seeking to turn the proconsul away from the faith. But Saul, who was also known as Paul, filled with the Holy Spirit, fixed his gaze upon him, and said, "You who are full of all deceit and fraud, you son of the devil, you enemy of all righteousness, will you not cease to make crooked the straight ways of the Lord? And now, behold, the hand of the Lord is upon you, and you will be blind and not see the sun for a time." And immediately a mist and a darkness fell upon him, and he went about seeking those who would lead him by the hand. Then the proconsul believed when he saw what had happened, being amazed at the teaching of the Lord.*
> Acts 13:6-12

Anyone would have known that the magician was causing trouble, but the Holy Spirit revealed to Paul that the man was truly in league with the devil. Notice also that the Holy Spirit revealed to Paul not only the real source of opposition, but also the manner in which to deal with it.

The same may be said of Paul in the following, which is another example from the Bible of the working of this gift:

> *And it happened that as we were going to the place of prayer, a certain slave-girl having a spirit of divination met us, who was bringing her masters much profit by fortunetelling. Following after Paul and us, she kept crying out, saying, "These men are bond-servants of the Most High God, who are proclaiming to you the way of salvation." And she continued doing this for many days. But Paul was greatly annoyed, and turned and **said to the spirit,** "I command you in the name of Jesus Christ **to come out of her!**" And it came out at that very moment.* Acts 16:16-18

b. The gift of distinguishing of spirits is also the ability to discern the nature of spirits within men as Jesus did when He rebuked His disciples who wanted to call down fire on Jerusalem, by saying, "You do not know what **kind of spirit you are of**" (Lk. 9:55).


## 7. WHAT IS THE GIFT OF FAITH?

Through the manifestation of the gift of faith, the Holy Spirit supplies us with the complete assurance of God's willingness and ability to act in any given situation. Refer to Chapter 5, Question 12 for the difference between the measure of faith that each Christian receives and the gift of faith that is given only to certain members of the body.

For an example of the working of this gift, let us read from Acts.

*Now Peter and John were going up to the temple at the ninth hour, the hour of prayer. And a certain man who had been lame from his mother's womb was being carried along, whom they used to set down every day at the gate of the temple which is called Beautiful, in order to beg alms of those who were entering the temple. And when he saw Peter and John about to go into the temple, he began asking to receive alms. And Peter, along with John, fixed his gaze upon him and said, "Look at us!" And he began to give them his attention, expecting to receive something from them. But Peter said, "I do not possess silver and gold, but what I do have I give to you: In the name of Jesus Christ the Nazarene—walk!" And seizing him by the right hand, he raised him up; and immediately his feet and his ankles were strengthened. And with a leap, he stood upright and began to walk; and he entered the temple with them, walking and leaping and praising God. And all the people saw him walking and praising God.*

[And Peter said,] *"On the basis of **faith in His name**, it is the name of Jesus which has strengthened this man whom you see and know; and the faith which comes **through Him** has given him this perfect health in the presence of you all."*

Acts 3:1-9,16

## 8. WHAT IS THE GIFT OF HEALING?

The gift of healing is the ability granted to believers by the Holy Spirit to be used as a means of ministering divine healing. There are many Scriptures in the New Testament which bear abundant witness to the working of the gift of healing. We must bear in mind, however, that even though one may manifest the gift of healing, this does not mean that he will be able to minister healing to all who come to him.

Remember that at Capernaum Jesus "did not do many miracles there because of their unbelief" (Matt. 13:58). For additional information, read Chapter 10—"Divine Healing" in Part One of this book.

### 9. WHAT IS THE GIFT OF THE EFFECTING OF MIRACLES?

The gift of the effecting of miracles is the ability to work naturally unexplainable acts by the power of God; for example, Peter raised Tabitha from the dead (Acts 9:36-41), and Paul raised Eutychus from the dead (Acts 20:9-12).

An additional example of the effecting of miracles may be found in Acts 19:11,12 as follows:

> *And God was performing extraordinary miracles by the hands of Paul, so that handkerchiefs or aprons were even carried from his body to the sick, and the diseases left them and the evil spirits went out.*

These two verses are an excellent example because they point out the way in which the various gifts of the Spirit often work together with one another. As a result of the effecting of miracles, many were healed and delivered. These verses also point out something which we have already said—although these gifts are given to members of the body of Christ, their power is derived from, and dependent upon, the Holy Spirit.

### 10. WHAT IS THE GIFT OF PROPHECY?

Prophecy is the utterance, or the speaking forth, of the will and purposes of God under the inspiration of the Holy Spirit in a language which can be understood. There are at least six references to prophets and/or prophecy in the New Testament: Agabus, one of the prophets in the Jerusalem church, prophesied of the famine which was to come to pass in the days of Claudius Caesar (Acts 11:27,28); there were prophets in the church at Antioch (Acts 13:1,2); Judas and Silas were prophets (Acts 15:32); Paul was warned by prophets in the church at Tyre not to return to Jerusalem (Acts 21:4), and he was warned by prophets in other cities of the bonds and afflictions that awaited him there (Acts 20:23); Philip had four daughters who prophesied (Acts 21:8,9); and Agabus visited Caesarea and there signified to Paul by the Spirit the fate that awaited him in Jerusalem (Acts 21:10-13).

The Scriptures of the Old Testament and New Testament alike teach that there is a difference between individuals who may prophesy as the result of an occasional moving of the Holy Spirit upon them and those who are called and established by the Holy Spirit with the prophetic ministry. Paul, who alone established the doctrines which developed and regulated the gift of prophecy, taught specifically that believers need not be satisfied with an occasional prophetic utterance but should especially seek prophecy as a gift of the Spirit (1 Cor. 12:10; 14:1,39). The gift is then to be exercised for the edifying of the church (1 Cor. 14:3-5). At the same time, however, he tempered this exhortation by declaring that not all believers would, in fact, have a prophetic ministry in the body (1 Cor. 12:27-29).

In the fourteenth chapter of his letter to the Corinthian church, which should be read in connection with this question, Paul taught the following concerning the gift of prophecy (read 1 Corinthians 14:1-5,29-32):

° One who prophesies speaks to men for edification (as in Acts 13:1,2), exhortation (as in Acts 11:27,28; 15:32; 21:4), and comfort (1 Cor. 14:3,31).

° Prophecy is for the edification of the church (vv. 4-6,22-26), not for private revelation, and should only be exercised where it can be judged by the others having prophetic ministry (v. 29). This will most normally be done by the eldership, since the gift of prophecy will always be resident within that group of men who share in the oversight of the church.

° All may prophesy in turn (v. 31) and in order (vv. 32,40). There is no reason for anyone to prophesy out of order in an unseemly manner because "the spirits of prophets are **subject** to prophets" (v. 32).

° "Let the women keep silent in the churches . . ." (v. 34) does not pertain to prophetic utterance, because Paul wrote in a previous portion of this same letter (1 Cor. 11:4,5) about the regulating of both the **praying and prophesying of women** (read also Acts 2:17,18; 21:8,9).

NOTE:

*And He gave some as apostles, and some as **prophets**, and some as evangelists, and some as pastors and teachers, for the equipping of the saints for the work of service, to the building up of the body of Christ; until we **all** attain to the **unity of the faith,** and of the knowledge of the Son of God, to a mature man, to the measure of the stature which belongs to the **fulness of Christ.*** Eph. 4:11-13

This is one of the Scriptures which provides us with an answer to those who would say that the ministry of the prophet ended with the book of Revelation. This verse tells us that the ministries mentioned are for the equipping of the saints until the unity of the faith is attained. That this has not yet been achieved should be evident to all. Also, if the ministry of the prophet has been done away with, then we have no authority for the ministry of the evangelist and the pastor.

Another important portion of Scripture to consider in connection with this is 1 Corinthians 13:8-10:

*If there are gifts of prophecy, they will be done away; if there are tongues, they will cease; if there is knowledge, it will be done away. For we know in part, and we prophesy in part* [that is, imperfectly]; *but **when the perfect comes,** the partial will be done away.*

201

Prophecy, tongues, and knowledge, as well as everything else given for the edification of the church, will pass away; but **not** until **that which is perfect comes!** Perfection for the Christian as an individual, and for the Body of Christ as a whole, will not come until Jesus returns. If we are to believe that prophecy and tongues have already passed away, then we have no choice but to believe that knowledge, too, has passed away.

## 11. WHAT IS THE GIFT OF VARIOUS KINDS OF TONGUES?

The gift of various kinds of tongues is the utterance, or the speaking forth, of the will and purposes of God under the inspiration of the Holy Spirit in a language which cannot be understood.

The Scriptures governing the use of this gift are also to be found in 1 Corinthians 14 as follows:

° Tongues is a spiritual gift used for the edification of the church when accompanied by the companion gift of interpretation (v. 5).

° Tongues is a supernatural sign to the unbeliever of the presence and the working of the Holy Spirit (v. 22).

° As with prophecy, any member of the body of Christ may have the gift manifested through him by the Holy Spirit (v. 26) and yet not have the gift as a ministry (1 Cor. 12:30).

° "If anyone speaks in a tongue, it should be by two or at the most three, and each in turn, and let one interpret" (v. 27).

° If it becomes obvious that the interpretation of the message given is not forthcoming, the one speaking in tongues should either pray for the interpretation himself or cease to speak forth in tongues for the duration of that particular meeting (vv. 13,28).

° We are not to forbid or discourage the speaking in tongues in the assembly, but we are to make sure that the gift is being manifested in order and according to Scripture (vv. 39,40).

We should note here that, since prophecy **and** tongues with the interpretation are **both** used to edify the church, the same basic principles governing the use of prophecy also apply to the use of tongues.

## 2.  WHAT IS THE GIFT OF INTERPRETATION OF TONGUES?

The gift of interpretation of tongues is the speaking forth by the inspiration of the Holy Spirit, in a language which can be understood by the assembled worshipers, the meaning of that which has already been given through the manifestation of the gift of tongues. In other words, when the gift of tongues is manifested in a meeting, it is to be followed by the gift of the interpretation of tongues, which means giving in a language which the congregation understands the meaning of the message which has been spoken in tongues.  The gift of interpretation of tongues is the companion gift to the gift of tongues. The two cannot function properly without each other. It must be remembered that this gift is not one of translation, but of interpretation.

## 3.  HOW MAY WE RECEIVE THESE GIFTS OF THE SPIRIT?

We may receive these gifts of the Spirit in the same manner in which we receive the gift of the Holy Spirit Himself: sovereignly as an answer to prayer (1 Cor. 12:11,31), or by impartation by the laying on of hands (1 Tim. 4:14).

## 14. IS IT NECESSARY TO HAVE THESE GIFTS OF THE SPIRIT OPERATING IN THE CHURCH?

Yes, it is absolutely necessary to have these gifts of the Spirit operating in the church. These gifts were given to the church so that it might be molded and perfected, and they are indispensable to the spiritual health and welfare of the body of Christ (1 Cor. 12:7).

## HOME STUDY QUESTIONS: CHAPTER 14

1. What are the nine gifts of the Spirit?

2. Name six other gifts of the Spirit.

3. Are the gifts of the Spirit for everyone in the church or only a certain few?

# THE MINISTRIES WITHIN THE CHURCH

**Chapter 15**

In the previous chapter, we discussed the spiritual gifts which are distributed by the Holy Spirit "to each one individually just as He wills" (1 Cor. 12:11). Since the word *ministry* basically means "place of service," any of the manifestational or motivational gifts may indeed develop as ministries for the members of the church. To this we may also add 1 Corinthians 12:28:

> *And God has appointed in the church, first apostles, second prophets, third teachers, then miracles, then gifts of healings, helps, administrations, various kinds of tongues.*

Having seen the necessity for the members of the body of Christ to be equipped with these spiritual enablements in order to edify one another, we will now study the ministries which are given by Christ to edify the church as a whole.

Let us remember that we are living in days of restoration—days in which the Lord is sending fresh revelation to His church and restoring by the Holy Spirit and the Word of God all that the traditions and precepts of men have eroded. We must not consider what we know about these ministries to be the final word of truth. We are just beginning to see this restoration, and there is much that we have yet to learn.

## 1. WHAT ARE THE FIVEFOLD MINISTRIES GIVEN TO THE CHURCH BY CHRIST?

The fivefold ministries given to the church by Christ are apostles, prophets, evangelists, pastors, and teachers.

*Therefore it says, "When He ascended on high, He led captive a host of captives, and He gave gifts to men."*

*And He gave some as apostles, and some as prophets, and some as evangelists, and some as pastors and teachers.*

Eph. 4:8,11

## Ministries Given to the Church by Christ

## 2. WHY DID CHRIST GIVE THESE MINISTRIES TO THE CHURCH?

These ministries were given to the church by Jesus Christ so that the church might be perfected, edified, and established, but especially that we might be prepared for the work of serving others in the body of Christ.

*[And He gave some] for the equipping of the saints for the work of service, to the building up of the body of Christ; until we all attain to the unity of the faith, and of the knowledge of the Son of God, to a mature man, to the*

*measure of the stature which belongs to the fulness of Christ.*
*As a result, we are no longer to be children, tossed here and*
*there by waves, and carried about by every wind of doctrine,*
*by the trickery of men, by craftiness in deceitful scheming;*
*but speaking the truth in love, we are to grow up in all*
*aspects into Him, who is the head, even Christ.*

Eph. 4:12-15

## 3. WHAT IS AN APOSTLE?

There has been much confusion and misunderstanding among
Christians concerning the ministry of the apostle, primarily for two
reasons. First of all, the apostolic ministry had been largely lost to the
church as a whole until rather recently, when the Lord began to
restore it to its rightful place. Secondly, there has been a general lack
of knowledge of what the Scriptures teach on the subject. A
systematic, objective study of what God's Word says about the
ministry of the apostle would soon straighten out the matter and bring
it into the light of truth for those who want it.

The first thing that we must establish from the Bible is that there were
two groups of apostles. The first group, the preascension apostles, is
variously referred to as "the twelve" and the "apostles of the Lamb";
the second group is referred to as the "postascension apostles." We
will study them in that order.

a. The "twelve apostles of the Lamb":

> *And having summoned His twelve disciples, He gave*
> *them authority over unclean spirits, to cast them out, and*
> *to heal every kind of disease and every kind of sickness.*
> *Now the names of the twelve apostles are these: The first,*
> *Simon, who is called Peter, and Andrew his brother; and*
> *James the son of Zebedee, and John his brother; Philip*
> *and Bartholomew; Thomas and Matthew the tax-*
> *gatherer; James the son of Alphaeus, and Thaddaeus;*

*Simon the Zealot* [or "Cananaean"], *and Judas Iscariot, the one who betrayed Him. These twelve Jesus sent out after instructing them, saying, "Do not go in the way of the Gentiles, and do not enter any city of the Samaritans;* **but rather go to the lost sheep of the house of Israel."**

Matt. 10:1-6

*Then Peter answered and said to Him, "Behold, we have left everything and followed You; what then will there be for us?" And Jesus said to them, "Truly I say to you, that you who have followed Me,* **in the regeneration when the Son of Man will sit on His glorious throne, you also shall sit upon twelve thrones, judging the twelve tribes of Israel."** Matt. 19:27,28

*And at this time Peter stood up in the midst of the brethren (a gathering of about one hundred and twenty persons was there together), and said, "Brethren, the Scripture had to be fulfilled, which the Holy Spirit foretold by the mouth of David concerning Judas, who became a guide to those who arrested Jesus.*

*"For it is written in the book of Psalms, 'Let his homestead be made desolate, and let no man dwell in it'; and, 'his office let another man take.' It is therefore necessary that* **of the men who have accompanied us all the time that the Lord Jesus went in and out among us—beginning with the baptism of John, until the day that He was taken up from us—one of these** *should become a witness with us of His resurrection." And they put forward two men, Joseph called Barsabbas (who was also called Justus), and Matthias.*

Acts 1:15,16,20-23

*And the wall of the city* [the New Jerusalem] *had twelve foundation stones, and on them were the* **twelve names** *of the* **twelve apostles of the Lamb.**

Rev. 21:14

What are the facts which can be gathered from these verses?

1. There were never more than twelve men who formed this first company of apostles. (Although one of them, Judas, was lost, Matthias was chosen to fill the twelfth place.)

2. Jesus gave these twelve men a specific ministry to the lost sheep of the house of Israel. History bears this out. Peter, it seems, is the only one of the twelve who had a ministry to the Gentiles, and no doubt that was because of his having been given the "keys to the kingdom" (Matt. 16:19) by Jesus. It was Peter who symbolically opened the doors of the kingdom to (1) the Jews (Acts 2:14-40), (2) the Samaritans (Acts 8:14), and (3) the Gentiles (Acts 10). The other apostles seem to have had their ministry centered in the Jewish church and indeed, with the exception of James and John, are not even mentioned again in the scriptural account of the development of the church.

3. Jesus promised these twelve a special place of honor in His kingdom where they will "sit upon twelve thrones, judging the **twelve tribes of Israel."**

4. These men are referred to as the twelve apostles of the Lamb because they alone had been with Jesus all the time that He had been before the people "beginning with the baptism of John, until the day that He was taken up." Two men who fit the requirements, Joseph and Matthias, were put forward as possible replacement for Judas, and Matthias was chosen.

There are many who are of the opinion that this choosing of Matthias was not really valid and that the place among the twelve actually belonged to Paul. They claim that this is the meaning of Paul's statement that he had been one "born out of due time" (1 Cor. 15:8 KJV). This, however, is totally inconsistent with the calling, ministry, and purpose of the original twelve. Besides that, we have Paul's own testimony

209

that he did not consider himself to be one of the twelve (1 Cor. 15:5,8).

In 1 Corinthians 15:1-9 Paul is writing about the order of the appearances Jesus made after His resurrection. He appeared to:

° Cephas (Peter);

° Then to the twelve (remember, this was after Judas was no longer one of their number. By the time Paul was writing this to the Corinthian church, Matthias had for many years been recognized as the legitimate replacement to Judas. Paul, therefore, did not consider himself to be one of the twelve, and neither did anyone else.);

° Then to more than five hundred brethren;

° Then He appeared to James;

° Then to **all** the apostles. (It is inconclusive, but possible, that Paul here means that by this time there were apostles other than the original twelve. These would have been numbered among the "postascension" apostles.)

5. These twelve have their names inscribed upon the twelve foundation stones of the New Jerusalem.

b. The "postascension" apostles, among whom were:

1. Paul:

> *Paul, a bond-servant of Christ Jesus, called as an apostle, set apart for the gospel of God.*
> Rom. 1:1

*Am I not free? Am I not an apostle? Have I not
see Jesus our Lord? Are you not my work in the
Lord? If to others I am not an apostle, at least I am
to you; for you are the seal of my apostleship in the
Lord.* 1 Cor. 9:1,2

2. James, the Lord's brother:

*But I did not see any other of the apostles except
James, the Lord's brother.* Gal. 1:19

3. Barnabas:

*And it came about that in Iconium they entered
the synagogue of the Jews together, and spoke in
such a manner that a great multitude believed, both
of Jews and of Greeks. But the Jews who disbelieved
stirred up the minds of the Gentiles, and embittered
them against the brethren. Therefore they spent a
long time there speaking boldly with reliance upon
the Lord, who was bearing witness to the word of His
grace, granting that signs and wonders be done by
their hands. But the multitude of the city was
divided; and some sided with the Jews, and some
with the apostles.*
*But when the apostles, Barnabas and Paul,
heard of it, they tore their robes and rushed out into
the crowd.* Acts 14:1-4,14

*Do we not have a right to take along a believing
wife, even as the rest of the apostles . . . ? Or do only
Barnabas and I not have a right to refrain from
working?* 1 Cor. 9:5,6

4.  Andronicus and Junias:

> *Greet Andronicus and Junias, my kinsmen, and*
> *my fellow prisoners, who are outstanding among the*
> *apostles, who also were in Christ before me.*
>
> Rom. 16:7

5.  It is also probable that Apollos (1 Cor. 3:5) and Silas (Silvanus) (Acts 17:1-10 with 1 Thess. 1:1 and 2:6) were apostles to the early church.

Although the ministry of the "twelve apostles of the Lamb" ended with the death of John, the apostolic ministry itself continued through such men as Paul (who, as we have established, was not one of the twelve), Barnabas, and others. Paul was, no doubt, the most well-known and influential of the early church apostles, and therein lies a problem in itself. Many people are not willing to concede that the ministry of the apostle has been restored to the modern-day church, because they are looking for men of Paul's caliber. No doubt, there will never be another Paul, but the Holy Spirit is calling many men today into the same ministry. Ephesians 4:13 states that the fivefold ministries were given until such time as we "all attain to the **unity of the faith . . .** to a **mature man . . .** to the **fulness of Christ.**" It should be obvious to every sincere Christian that we have not yet attained that level of maturity and unity.

## 4.  WHAT IS THE MINISTRY (OR WORK) OF AN APOSTLE?

An apostle (from the Greek word *apostolos,* meaning "one who is sent forth, a delegate") is a missionary in the truest sense of the word. Apostles are chosen and commissioned by the Lord Himself (1 Cor. 12:28; Eph. 4:11) and represent the most spiritually complete of the ministries to the church. Signs and wonders were an important part of the apostolic ministry in the early church age (2 Cor. 12:12), and still are in those areas of the world today where signs and wonders are required as a means of confirming the preaching of the gospel (Heb. 2:4).

The burden of apostolic preaching is twofold. It is, first of all, a special witness to the reality of the resurrected and living Christ and the reconciliation of a sinful world to God through Him (Acts 4:33; 2 Cor. 5:18-20). Secondly, to the apostle, this reconciling of sinners to God by the preaching of the gospel is synonymous with the establishment and growth of the church, which is the body of Christ. Then the responsibility of the apostle is to minister to these newly founded local churches as an overseer until their own shepherd is raised up and established. In a special sense, the apostle is an elder and shepherd to the whole church, and particularly to those whom he has fathered in the gospel (1 Cor. 4:15). In our day the apostle seems to have a special ministry to establish churches, bringing current truths and New Testament order to them.

How can we know when one is truly an apostle? In the same way we judge any other ministry—by its fruits, and by that we do not mean the "fruit of the Spirit" mentioned in Galatians 5:22,23. For instance, the fruit of the prophetic ministry is sound and accurate prophecy. So also, the fruit of the apostolic ministry is the establishing of believers in a sound local church situation. One is not an apostle simply because he states that he is or because he travels around teaching in various places! (Read 1 Corinthians 9:2 and 2 Corinthians 3:1-4.)

## 5. WHAT IS A PROPHET?

The prophet (from the Greek work *prophetes,* meaning "a forth-teller") is one who speaks forth the message which has been given to him through the inspiration of the Holy Spirit.

The burden of the prophetic ministry is to reveal the will and purposes of God to the church, often warning of things to come (Acts 11:28), occasionally bringing fresh insight to revealed truth (Eph. 3:3-5), but always speaking "unto men to edification, and exhortation, and comfort" (1 Cor. 14:3 KJV).

The ministry of the prophet is one of the more apparent ministries in the New Testament church today. The prophetic ministry, with its roots

213

in the earliest pages of the Old Testament, is certainly not new to the Christian experience. Paul wrote extensively to the Corinthian church concerning this gift of revelation and summarized his teachings on this subject with the exhortation to "covet to prophesy, and forbid not to speak with tongues" (1 Cor. 14:39 KJV).

There is an evident need in the church today for all of God's people, and especially His prophets, to stir themselves out of spiritual slumber and awaken themselves to the increased activity of the Holy Spirit for the purpose of edifying the church. It is written, "The unfolding of Thy words gives light" (Ps. 119:130), and "Faith comes from hearing, and hearing by the word of Christ" (Rom. 10:17).

Our purpose in studying this ministry, as with each of the fivefold ministries, is to bring the church to a greater understanding of it by introducing renewed light and faith by the Word of God. As in any serious study of the doctrines of the Lord, we must begin where He begins and follow His path of revelation as it winds through the pages of the Old Testament and crosses over, by way of the life and ministry of Jesus Christ, into the New Testament.

## 6. WHAT WAS THE OLD TESTAMENT PROPHET?

There are various Hebrew words in the Old Testament which are used to describe the ministry of the prophet and are variously rendered as "a declarer (of the will of God)," "one who sees" ("seer," KJV), and an "interpreter (of the purposes of God)."

Sometimes the prophets were referred to as "shepherds" (Ezk. 34:1-16; Zech. 11:4,5,11,15-17), because to them was entrusted the spiritual care of the flock of Israel. It was in this office that they were commissioned to show the people of God "their transgression, and . . . the house of Jacob their sins" (Isa. 58:1; Ezk. 22:2; 43:10; Mic. 3:8). They also brought to Israel the message of consolation and pardon (Isa. 40:1,2). The prophets were the "watchmen" set upon the walls of Zion to blow the trumpet, bringing timely warning of approaching danger (Isa. 62:6; Jer. 6:17; Ezk. 3:17; 33:2,6,7).

## 7.  WHAT ARE THE TWO ELEMENTS OF OLD TESTAMENT PROPHECY?

Old Testament prophecy contained two elements, the **moral** or **doctrinal** (that is, the declaration of God's will by exposition and application of the Law), and the **predictive.**

It was through the doctrinal element of the prophetic ministry that the prophets taught that man was created by God and shared a common origin (Mal. 2:10); that he has the power of reason (Ezk. 12:2; Isa. 1:18), as well as a capacity for holiness, knowledge, and spiritual progress (Isa. 2:3-5); that he is ruined and cannot save himself (Hos. 13:9; Jer. 2:22; 13:23); that he is a subject of God's moral government and owes entire obedience to His law (Dan. 4:34,35; Ezk. 8:4,5,9; Isa. 1:19,20; 23:11-16); that man is required to worship God and render Him homage (Isa. 60:6,7; Mal. 1:11; 3:10). In addition to these teachings the prophets persistently taught the doctrines of faith and repentance with remarkable clarity (Isa. 26:3,4; 55:7; Ezk. 14:6; 18:30; 36:31).

Concerning the predictive element of prophecy, it must be stressed that prophecy was never intended by God to open the future to idle curiosity, but it was, and is, for the higher purpose of furnishing light to those whose faith needs to be confirmed. The revelation of future events may be necessary in times of discouragement to awaken or sustain hope, to inspire confidence in the midst of general backsliding, and to warn of evil threatening the faithful.[1]

## 8.  WHAT IS THE ORIGIN OF PROPHETIC INSPIRATION?

The Scriptures clearly teach that the Old Testament prophets received their communications by the agency of the Holy Spirit (Num. 11:17,25; 1 Sam. 10:6; 19:20; Jer. 1:5,7; 2 Pet. 1:21), while the false prophets were those who spoke "a vision of their own heart, and not out of the mouth of the Lord" (Jer. 23:16 KJV)—"foolish prophets, that follow their own spirit, and have seen nothing" (Ezk. 13:3 KJV).

The standard for judging prophecy was given to the people of Israel prior to their entry into the Promised Land.

> *"'But the prophet who shall speak a word presumptuously in My name which I have not commanded him to speak, or which he shall speak in the name of other gods, that prophet shall die.' And you may say in your heart, 'How shall we know the word which the Lord has not spoken?' When a prophet speaks in the name of the Lord, if the thing does not come about* **or come true,** *that is the thing* **which the Lord has not spoken.** *The prophet has spoken it presumptuously; you shall not be afraid of him."*
>
> Deut. 18:20-22

We have an instance of this standard being applied by the prophet Jeremiah to the prophecies of Hananiah (Jer. 28:5-9, q.v.).

The many instances of false prophecy in the Old Testament (1 Ki. 22:6-12; Jer. 28:15; 29:21) were occasions of severe rebuke by the Lord (Jer. 23:25-40; Ezk. 13). It is significant that, although it was a serious offense against the Spirit of the Lord to prophesy falsely and was dealt with harshly by the Lord, the people were simply admonished not to be afraid of the false prophet nor to fear his empty words.

## 9. WHAT ARE THE MODES OF PROPHETIC REVELATION IN THE OLD TESTAMENT?

> *He* [the Lord] *said, "Hear now My words: If there is a prophet among you, I, the Lord, shall make Myself known to him in a* **vision.** *I shall speak with him in a* **dream.** *Not so, with My servant Moses, he is faithful in all My household; with him I speak* **mouth to mouth,** *even* **openly,** *and not in dark sayings."*
>
> Num. 12:6-8a

These Scriptures outline for us three modes or methods of communication between God and man for the purpose of revealing the will and mind of God to man. They are: (a) visions, (b) dreams, and (c) apparent revelation.

a. Visions may be defined as supernatural presentations of certain scenery or circumstances to the mind of a person while **awake.** The Lord appeared to Abram in a vision (Gen. 12:7). Balaam's "vision of the Almighty" is described for us in Numbers 24. The prophet Isaiah was given a vision concerning Judah (Isa. 1:1) and a vision of the glory of the Lord (Isa. 6). Ezekiel also received visions of the glory of the Lord (Ezk. 1).

b. Dreams are a supernatural method of communication employed by the Lord during a person's **sleeping hours.** Of the many dreams recorded in the Old Testament, we will make mention of only three: Jacob's dream of the heavenly ladder (Gen. 28:12), Solomon's dream (1 Ki. 3:5), and the dream of Daniel (Dan. 7).

c. The third mode of communication, that of **apparent revelation,** seems to have been reserved for those who had a more specific prophetic ministry. Moses enjoyed this type of communication, as we have already read (Num. 12:7,8), as did Samuel (1 Sam. 3:4,7,21) and Elijah (1 Ki. 19:9). These were not the only ones, however. The Old Testament abounds with instances of the word of the Lord coming directly to His prophets.

It is rather evident that these are not only three methods of prophecy, but levels or, more particularly, measures of fulness of prophecy as well. In keeping with this, we should refer here to another level of prophecy, perhaps the most basic one which was operative in the Old Testament. The seventy elders prophesied when the Spirit rested upon them (Num. 11:25), as did Eldad and Medad (Num. 11:26). Saul prophesied as the Spirit of the Lord came to rest upon him (1 Sam. 10:6,9,10). The messengers of Saul were hindered in their attempt to capture David when the Spirit came upon them and they prophesied (1 Sam. 19:18-24). The Lord used this level of prophecy not so much to communicate with man as to reveal His presence or blessing.

# 10. WHO WERE SOME OF THE OLD TESTAMENT PROPHETS?

The first Old Testament prophet that we have knowledge of is Enoch, in the seventh generation from Adam, although we have to go to the New Testament (Jude 14,15) to find this out. Noah uttered prophetic oracles (Gen. 9:24-27), and Abraham was a prophet as well (Gen. 20:7).

In Numbers 12:1-8 it is suggested that Miriam and Aaron were prophets, but in a lesser sense than was Moses. Moses was a prophet in a special sense (Deut. 34:10) because his prophetic ministry was a type of the Prophet, Jesus Christ (Deut. 18:15-19; Jn. 7:40). Deborah was a prophetess during the time of the judges (Judg. 4:4).

There was a dearth of prophetic vision in the time of Samuel (1 Sam. 3:1). The key to this seems to be given to us in the first nine verses of 1 Samuel 3. Eli knew the voice of the Lord, for he was able to give Samuel instruction, but he had, no doubt, grown lax in this area as well as in the discharge of his priestly duties. Once Samuel became acquainted with the word of the Lord, he continued to grow in his knowledge of the word as well as in the ability to minister it to Israel (1 Sam. 3:19-21 and 4:1a).

It is in this period of Israel's history that we begin to read about the companies of the prophets. These were groups of men who had gathered themselves together to study the word of the Lord. It is possible that established prophets such as Samuel and Elijah schooled them in prophetic principles. It is not clear as to what their spiritual contribution was to the congregation of Israel (1 Sam. 10:5; 19:20; 1 Ki. 20:35; 2 Ki. 2:3,5,7,15-18; 4:38-44; 6:1).

Prophecy continued to be operative in Israel up to and including the ministry of Malachi, the last of the prophets to the restored remnant after the seventy years of captivity. Malachi was followed by a period of prophetic silence lasting almost four hundred years.

**HOW DID THE PROPHETIC MINISTRY MAKE ITS TRANSITION FROM THE OLD TO THE NEW TESTAMENT?**

The prophetic ministry made its transition through John the Baptist and Jesus Christ. The four hundred years of prophetic silence following Malachi, the last of the Old Testament prophets, was finally interrupted by John the Baptist, the "voice of one crying in the wilderness, 'Make ready ("prepare," KJV) the way of the Lord'" (Matt. 3:3). John was called to prepare Israel for the coming Messiah (Lk. 1:13-17; 3:2-18; Jn. 1:31) and to give his witness to the people concerning Jesus that He was the Christ (Jn. 1:6-8,15-34). Jesus in return gave His testimony that John was indeed a prophet, and "more than a prophet" (Lk. 7:24-29).

Jesus, the Christ, the Anointed One of God, had a threefold ministry of prophet (Deut. 18:15; Heb. 1:1,2), priest (Heb. 6:20; 9:11), and king (Matt. 2:2; 1 Tim. 1:17). In His prophetic office He brought the revelation of God's will, not only as it concerned the fulfillment of the Old Testament prophecies relating to the Messiah and the conversion and establishing of Israel, but also as it pointed forward in time to the church (Matt. 16:18), the period of time described by the "mysteries of the kingdom" (Matt. 13), the last days (Matt. 24:3-14), the tribulation (Matt. 24:21,29), His second coming (Matt. 24:27-31), the millennial kingdom (Matt. 19:28), and the judgment of this world (Matt. 25:31).

Jesus laid the foundation for the continuation of the prophetic ministry by declaring that the Holy Spirit would continue to bring revelation after He had returned to the Father (Jn. 14:26; 16:12-15).

**WERE THERE ADDITIONAL OCCURRENCES OF PROPHETIC REVELATION DURING THIS TRANSITIONAL PERIOD?**

Yes, although the main burden of prophecy during this period of time was borne by the ministries of John the Baptist and Jesus, Zacharias and Elizabeth, the parents of John the Baptist, also prophesied (Lk. 1:39-45,67-79)—even though they were not prophets in the sense of having the ministry of prophecy. This fact ranks them in the same category with the seventy elders and Eldad and Medad of Moses' time, and Saul, among others. Simeon, a man who was "righteous and devout, looking for the consolation of Israel," prophesied concerning both Mary and Jesus (Lk. 2:25-35) and belongs to this category as well.

Other than John the Baptist and Jesus, the only prophet mentioned in the gospels is "one Anna, a prophetess, the daughter of Phanuel, of the tribe of Aser: she . . . departed not from the temple, but **served God with fastings and prayers night and day**" (Lk. 2:36,37 KJV).

In addition to this, there are five dreams (Matt. 1:20-24; 2:12,13, 19,22) and three visions (Lk. 1:11-20,26-38; 2:8-14) recorded in the four gospel accounts.

## 13. HOW DID PROPHECY BEGIN TO WORK IN THE EARLY CHURCH?

Strangely enough, the first comment that can be made about prophecy in the early church is in regard to the absence of it in a time of need. While the hundred and twenty disciples were waiting in the upper room for the "promise of the Father," the apostles chose Matthias to replace Judas by drawing lots (Acts 1:15-26). We know by later Scripture that they should have received direction from the Lord through prophecy and the laying on of hands. Since this was prior to the outpouring of the Holy Spirit, however, it was not possible for them to do this. This is a good example of how things are done in the church without the enabling of the Holy Spirit. In most churches today, the appointment of elders and deacons, and even the choosing of pastors, is done by voting instead of by the specific direction of the Lord.

When the church was born on the day of Pentecost, Peter established that the outpouring of the Holy Spirit that had occurred was in direct fulfillment of the prophecy of Joel as recorded in Joel 2:28,29. Notice that Acts 2:17,18 again establishes the three modes of prophetic revelation—**dreams, visions, and direct prophecy** (the apparent word of God):

> *"And it shall be in the last days,"* God says, *"that I will pour forth of My Spirit upon **all** mankind; and your sons and your daughters shall prophesy, and your young men shall see **visions,** and your old men shall dream **dreams;** even upon My bondslaves, both men and women, I will in those days pour forth of My Spirit and they shall **prophesy.**"*

NOTE: It must be remembered that the dream, as is again mentioned here in Acts 2:17,18, is the most elementary (and possibly even the most unreliable) form of communication from God to man. The prophet Jeremiah likened the relationship of dreams to prophecy as being that of straw or chaff to wheat—in other words, vastly inferior and much less useful. "The prophet who has a dream may relate his dream, but let him who has My word speak **My word** in truth. **What does straw [chaff] have in common with grain?**" (Jer. 23:28).

There are no dreams recorded for us in the book of Acts, but there are many visions (Acts 7:55,56; 9:3-6 with 26:13,14; Acts 9:10-12; 10:1-8; 10:9-17; 16:9,10; 18:9; 22:17-21; 23:11; 27:21-25) and at least six references to prophecy (Acts 11:27,28; 13:1,2; 15:32; 21:4; 21:8,9; 21:10-13).

## 14. HOW MAY WE SUMMARIZE PROPHECY AS IT IS IN THE NEW TESTAMENT?

We have already covered in the previous chapter the scriptural regulations concerning the proper working of the gift of prophecy in the New Testament local church. We may summarize dreams, visions, and prophecy, therefore, as follows:

a. Although dreams are a scriptural part of the working of revelation, especially in the Old Testament, it is remarkable and, no doubt, significant that dreams are not dealt with at all in that part of the New Testament from Acts to Revelation. Let us then say, by way of summary concerning dreams, that "we have also a **more sure word of prophecy**" (2 Pet. 1:19 KJV).

b. In the Old Testament, visions were used by God primarily as a means of supplementing and strengthening the apparent word of revelation. The book of Acts contains more recorded instances of visions than any other book of the Bible. Accordingly, we have established by both the Old and New Testaments that visions are a valid means of God's communicating with man.

c. Prophecy has different levels or measures of fulness, as well as varying purposes. The prophet (one who has been called of God and established in the prophetic ministry) fulfills his ministry by:

   ° Revealing the will of God in an immediate sense by prophetic utterance in the assembly.

   ° Revealing, in a fuller measure, the mind or will of God by inspired preaching and teaching.

   ° Consistently being in touch with the knowledge and purposes of God as they concern the body of Christ, or which his ministry is a part.

## 15. WHAT IS AN EVANGELIST?

The evangelist (from the Greek word *euaggelistes,* meaning "one announcing good news") is in a general sense anyone who proclaims the grace and mercy of God as contained in the gospel, the "good news" of our salvation.

The evangelist functions as a part of an apostolic team, being associated with the apostle, and ministering under his authority. As such, the evangelist is sent forth as a missionary preacher of the gospel (Acts 8:39,40; 21:8), a messenger to the churches (1 Cor. 16:10; 2 Cor. 8:23; Phil. 2:19), and a member of the apostolic company (Acts 16; 2 Cor. 1:1,19).

The evangelist may also be sent to certain churches, especially to those newly founded, to "set in order the things that are wanting" (Tit. 1:5 KJV). This may include duties and responsibilities ranging from ordaining elders (Tit. 1:5), preaching the word (2 Tim. 4:2), and guarding the body of truth as delivered by the apostle (1 Cor. 4:17), to always being "an example of the believers, in word, in conversation, in charity, in spirit, in faith, in purity" (1 Tim. 4:12 KJV).

A complete understanding of the ministry of the evangelist may be gained by studying the New Testament account of the relationship between the apostle Paul and Timothy, his own "son in the faith" (1 Tim. 1:2,18). The letters from Paul to Timothy and Titus should be studied in detail as well.

## 6.   WHAT IS THE PASTOR?

There are three words used in the New Testament to describe the ministry of the pastor. First of all, there is the word *pastor* itself (from the Greek word *poimen*, pronounced "poy-mane," meaning "shepherd"), then *elder* (from the Greek word *presbuteros*), and finally, *bishop* (from the Greek word *episkopos*). Traditionally, these three words have come to mean three separate ministries. However, we shall consider them in the above order and show by the Word of God that in the early church it was not so.

Although the Greek word *poimen* has been translated as "pastor" only once, and that in Ephesians 4:11, *poimen* has been translated as "shepherd" seventeen times elsewhere in the New Testament. A pastor, then, is a divinely given shepherd who tends, feeds, and protects God's sheep, the church.

In the book of Acts, we find Paul and Barnabas returning to the bodies of believers they had won to Christ in Lystra, Iconium, and Antioch. It is written that "when they had ordained them **elders** [*presbuteros*] **in every church,** and had prayed with fasting, they commended them to the Lord, on whom they believed" (Acts 14:21-23 KJV). So, in **"every church"** there were **"elders."**

Now let us look at the third word, *bishop,* from the Greek word *episkopos,* meaning **"overseer."** When Paul addressed the Philippian church, he wrote "to all the saints in Christ Jesus which are at Philippi, with the **bishops** and deacons" (Phil. 1:1 KJV). The Amplified Version of Philippians 1:1 reads, "bishops [overseers] and deacons [assistants]." (The ministry of the deacon will be considered later.)

Up to this point we have considered separately the three words which mean **"shepherd," "elder,"** and **"overseer."** Let us now consider them together as we look at Paul's words to the elders of the church at Ephesus with whom he had asked to meet at Miletus. Paul uses these three terms together to define the duties and the responsibilities of the **elders** or **pastors.**

> *And from Miletus he sent to Ephesus and called to him the **elders** [presbuteros] **of the church.***
> [And he said to them,] *"Be on guard for yourselves, and for all the **flock,** among which the Holy Spirit has made you **overseers** [episkopos], to **shepherd** [from poimen; that is, "to tend, feed, and guide," AMP] the church of God which He has purchased with His own blood."*
>
> Acts 20:17,28

From the above verses, we can see that every pastor arises from the group of elders within a church, and not every elder functions as a pastor. The ministry of pastor (senior elder) is one of the fivefold ministries.

17. **WHAT ARE THE QUALIFICATIONS OF THE PASTORS AND ELDERS?**

In 1 Timothy 3:1-7 and Titus 1:5-9, the apostle Paul states the qualifications for a man seeking the eldership. There are twenty-one qualifications given, fifteen of them stated positively, and six negatively.

a. The positive qualifications:

1. He must be above reproach. This means that an elder must be blameless in every area of his life. A good character is indispensable in an elder. This requirement is both the first and the last one noted. Here, it is a matter of being above reproach in the church; later, it involves being of "good report" among non-Christians.

2. He must be the husband of one wife. The meaning of this in the original Greek is a "one-woman man" and obviously prohibits the practice of polygamy. It does not mean, however, that an elder must be married, but that if he is married, he must have only one wife.

3. He must be temperate and sensible. The elder must not be given to excess, but should be moderate, well-balanced, calm, careful, and steady. This pertains to his physical, moral, and mental tastes and habits. The word has also been translated "vigilant," because of a latent meaning that is contained with it—a temperate way of life keeps us alert and vigilant. It is necessary that the "shepherds" of the flock be ever vigilant in keeping away the wolves in sheep's clothing who are always present and just as ready to destroy the flock (Acts 20:28-31).

4. He must be prudent. This means literally "of sound and steady mind." An elder must be a man who can be relied upon. His people should always know what to expect of him.

225

5.  He must be respectable. He must be one who is worthy of respect because of his Christian character.

6.  He must be hospitable. See Titus 1:8 and 1 Peter 4:9. During the time of the early church, Christians on a journey could not resort to the unbelievers nor to the public inns because of the atmosphere for which they were noted. The home and help of any Christian was welcome to the one in need, and the overseer was an example of such hospitality. There needs to be a reawakening of this Christian grace among all of God's people today.

7.  He must be able to teach. These words may be better translated "capable of teaching." This expression represents a variable capacity, for one might be capable of teaching some persons and incapable of teaching others. Since an elder is to be a teacher to a local congregation, it is to the members of the congregation that he must be qualified to teach. Therefore, if he is capable of teaching them, he has met this requirement. His teaching must uphold the Word of God and must be powerful enough to convict "gainsayers."

    > *He must hold fast to the sure and trustworthy Word of God **as he was taught it,** so that he may be able both to give stimulating instruction and encouragement in sound (wholesome) doctrine, and to refute and convince those who contradict and oppose it—showing the wayward their error.*
    >
    > Tit. 1:9 AMP

8.  He must be gentle. The elder should be gentle, patient, and longsuffering with even the weakest member. He should not be too hasty to act or to pass judgment.

9.  He must be able to manage his own household well and keep his children under control with all dignity. If a man does not know how to manage the affairs of his own household, he

cannot possibly manage the household of God. The lessons which an elder learns in his own home are indispensable to his functioning wisely and capably in the church.

10. He must have children who believe. His manner of life and his ability to teach his own children in the things of the Lord will undoubtedly yield fruit in his own household, as his own children come to believe on the Lord.

11. He must be a lover of good. An elder loves all things that are truly good and will not oppose them. This requirement will best profit us when we meditate upon it instead of simply attempting to interpret it.

12. He must be just. A natural sense of justice, or fairness, is essential to an elder, since as an overseer he is frequently called upon to exercise judgment.

13. He must be holy and devout. An elder should be a Christian in the fullest sense of the word—an example to believers and unbelievers alike. His dedication to the Lord should be absolute and unconditional, and his walk with the Lord pure.

14. He must be self-controlled and orderly. An elder must be disciplined in all areas of his life. The Scriptures say, "He that ruleth his spirit [is greater] than he that taketh a city" (Prov. 16:32 KJV) and "Let all things be done decently and in order" (1 Cor. 14:40 KJV). It takes orderly men to carry out this injunction in the church. The orderly man likes to have things well-arranged and planned.

15. He must be able to exhort in sound doctrine and refute those who contradict. "But sanctify Christ as Lord in your hearts, always being ready to make a defense to everyone who asks you to give an account for the hope that is in you, yet with gentleness and reverence; and keep a good conscience so that in the thing in which you are slandered, those who revile your

good behavior in Christ may be put to shame" (1 Pet. 3:15,16). It is a shame when a man can learn a trade in a few months, and yet be unable after years of Christian experience to refute a false doctrine with God's word of truth! This applies to every member of the body of Christ.

b.  The negative qualifications:

1.  He must not be addicted to wine or accused of dissipation. A drinking elder, or one who has anything in excess in his life, is a disgrace to the office and certainly is not above reproach from "within" or "without." Not only the elder, but all Christians, must "abstain from all appearance of evil" (1 Thess. 5:22 KJV).

2.  He must not be pugnacious or contentious. An elder must not be a violent man or one who is always ready for a quarrel. A man who "wears his feelings on his sleeve" or "carries a chip on his shoulder" should not be allowed to become an elder under any circumstances.

3.  He must be free from the love of money. As the Amplified Version states, he must not be "a lover of money—insatiable for wealth and ready to obtain it by questionable means", and he must not be "grasping and greedy for filthy lucre (financial gain)."

4.  He must not be a new convert. The true meaning of the word is one who has been "newly planted." The J. B. Phillips translation says, "He must not be a beginner in the faith."

5.  He must not be self-willed or rebellious. The self-willed and rebellious man is a carnal man. He will look after his own interests and resist authority, and cannot be depended upon to serve the interests of the kingdom of God.

6. He must not be quick-tempered. An elder must not be hot-headed, but self-controlled. "Righteous indignation" is permitted when there are valid reasons, such as, possibly, instances of fidelity to God's Word or disloyalty in Christian living.

## 8. WHAT ARE THE RESPONSIBILITIES OF THE PASTORS AND ELDERS?

The responsibilities of the eldership may be roughly divided into the following three categories:

a. They must take heed unto themselves by—

1. Watching their own lives (1 Tim. 4:15,16; 2 Tim. 2:15).

2. Ruling well their own households (1 Tim. 3:4).

3. Holding fast the teachings of God's Word (2 Tim. 1:13, 2 Tim. 3:14; Tit. 1:9).

4. Being an example to others (1 Tim. 4:12).

b. They must oversee the things relating to the redemption and welfare of the church by maintaining—

1. Worship (Hos. 14:2; 1 Cor. 14:15; Heb. 13:15).

2. Teaching (1 Tim. 4:13; 6:2).

3. Preaching (2 Tim. 4:2).

4. Exhortation (1 Tim. 4:13; 6:17-19; 2 Tim. 2:14).

5. Admonition (or warning: Acts 20:31; 1 Cor. 4:14; 2 Thess. 3:14,15).

c. They must oversee the church by—

1. Seeing that the church is spiritually fed (Acts 20:28; Jn. 21:15).

2. Protecting the church against the enemies of the faith (1 Tim. 1:19,20; 6:20,21).

3. Seeking the wandering ones (Isa. 40:11; Ezk. 34:4,16; Matt. 18:11).

4. Ruling well the church of Christ (Rom. 12:8; 1 Pet. 5:2; 1 Tim. 5:17).

5. Praying for the sick (Jas. 5:14,15).

## 19. WHAT IS THE PRESBYTERY?

The presbytery is that body of elders who share the responsibilities of oversight and government within the local church. The New Testament pattern calls for the local church to be governed by a plurality of equally responsible elders, who function under the direct oversight of the senior pastor. As the church grows, the number of both elders and pastors will grow too, but there will always be just one senior pastor. In addition to this, when a higher ministry, such as an apostle, is resident in the local church, he usually functions as senior pastor. Two examples of this are James in the Jerusalem church (Acts 15:4,13 with Acts 12:17 and Acts 21:17,18) and Timothy in the church at Ephesus (1 Tim. 1:3).

## 20. WHAT IS THE MINISTRY OF THE TEACHER?

There is a separate ministry of teaching within the church, but usually teaching is a necessary part of the ministry of the apostle (Acts 5:42; 1 Cor. 4:17; 2 Tim. 1:11), the evangelist (1 Tim. 4:11; 6:2), and the elder (1 Tim. 3:2). In a more general sense, any member of the body may teach (Col. 3:16; 1 Cor. 14:26). The elder women in particular are exhorted to teach (in the sense of training) the younger women of the church (Tit. 2:4). A teacher who has been called by the Lord into the level of fivefold ministry may minister not only in his own local church, but also among the churches which are under that particular apostolic oversight.

## 21.  WHAT IS THE MINISTRY OF THE DEACON?

Although the ministry of the deacon is not one of the fivefold ministries, we are discussing it here because of its importance and relationship to the other ministries. The word *deacon* means "servant." It is a transliteration of *diakonos,* which means "a serving or waiting man." The office of the deacon affords an excellent opportunity for service in the body of Christ. A man's attitude towards this position is of primary importance—no person should be chosen for the office of deacon who is not willing to **render humble service!**

In Acts Chapter 6, we read of the appointment of seven men to "waiting on tables," which appears to have included everything from seeing that the widows were fed with impartiality, to overseeing the many natural expenditures of the church. These men were not called deacons, but the work they were called to do was, in fact, to "serve tables." Here the word *serve* is translated from the Greek infinitive *diakoneo*. Thus, because the word *diakoneo* is used in Acts 6:2, the idea has been formed that the seven men appointed by the apostles were deacons. These deacons were chosen in response to a definite need. The number of deacons in any church should be governed by the needs of that church—by the amount of work to be done—and can be comprised of both men and women (who have come to be called deaconesses).

## 22. WHAT ARE THE QUALIFICATIONS OF A DEACON?

Following is a list of qualifications (taken from Acts 6:1-6 and 1 Tim. 3:8-13) by which every man and woman aspiring to the office of deacon must be measured. The qualifications are not given in order of their importance, but in the order in which they appear in the Scriptures. None of them are unimportant, and none of them should be overlooked.

A study of these qualifications as they appear in the Scriptures concludes that only the best of men and women be selected as deacons. Stephen, "a man full of faith and of the Holy Spirit," and Philip are excellent examples of the type of men needed for the office. A deacon should be:

a.  Of good reputation (Acts 6:3). A deacon must have a highly regarded character by those both in and out of the church.

b.  Full of the Holy Spirit (Acts 6:3,5). A deacon must possess the fruit of the Spirit: love, joy, peace, patience, kindness, goodness, faithfulness, gentleness, and self-control.

c.  Full of wisdom (Acts 6:3). A deacon must know well how to take care of the temporal needs of the church and should be known for possessing prudence and other practical virtues.

d.  Full of faith (Acts 6:5). Deacons must not be doubters of the power of God, but they must be steadfast and sure of their hope and conviction in God.

e.  Dignified and temperate (1 Tim. 3:8,11). This describes a serious-minded man or woman, who will not make light of the sacred things of God.

f.  Truthful and not double-tongued (1 Tim. 3:8). A deacon's word should always be good with no need of doubting his or her statements.

g.  Not addicted to wine (1 Tim. 3:8). Drinking makes one unfit for business, opens the door to other temptations, and is totally inconsistent with Christian grace.

h.  Not greedy or fond of sordid gain (1 Tim. 3:8). As with the elders, deacons must be willing and eager to fulfill their respective ministries quite apart from any financial gain.

i.  Faithful in all things and holding to the mystery of the faith with a clear conscience (1 Tim. 3:9,11). The deacon must be a sincere, deep-rooted, faithful individual, one who has convictions in the faith and the courage to stand by his convictions.

j.  Tested and approved (1 Tim. 3:10). No ministry should be given indiscriminately, nor should one be assumed until the man or woman is proven worthy, capable, and desirous of continuing in the responsibilities of his ministry, after a satisfactory "trial" period has been accomplished. Many a place of ministry appears glamorous and inviting until the newness wears off and the day-to-day duties and responsibilities become all too real.

k.  Beyond reproach (1 Tim. 3:10). Shame will be brought to the church if a deacon is not blameless and above reproach and of good reputation.

l.  Especially as it applies to women, not a malicious gossip (1 Tim. 3:11). This is in keeping with the dignity she must possess.

m.  The husband of one wife (1 Tim. 3:12). Like the elder, the deacon is to be the husband of only one wife.

n.  A good manager of his own children and household (1 Tim. 3:12). The children of the elders and the deacons are to be nourished and brought up in the faith and disciplined in natural as well as spiritual affairs "with dignity."

## 23. WHAT ARE THE DUTIES OF THE DEACON?

The duties of the deacon are many and varied, but they all come under the heading of "being willing to serve." Deacons will faithfully serve the church by working along with the elders in all matters committed to them.

a. Deacons may be responsible for benevolence, that is, helping members of the church with money, food, or clothing in a time of need; waiting on the sick; administering to members in emergency situations.

b. They may assist in the responsibilities of financial matters, including the related functions of bookkeeping, etc.

c. They may look after the meeting hall and other property owned or rented by the church. This includes seeing that the buildings and grounds are kept in good condition.

### NOTES

[1]   M. F. Unger, *Unger's Bible Dictionary* (Chicago: Moody Press, 1976), pp. 891, 892, used by permission.

## HOME STUDY QUESTION: CHAPTER 15

1. Where Scripture references only are given, look them up and read the passages in their entirety.

# CHURCH DISCIPLINE

## Chapter 16

Through the experience of new birth, those who believe in Jesus Christ become the children of God and, therefore, members of His family—His household. The Bible teaches us, and our experience tells us, that in order for a household to function as it should, peace and harmony are absolutely essential. Among other things, parental authority must be recognized and honored, and the household rules which have been established for the good of every member of the family must be obeyed. When these principles are disregarded, disharmony results, and strict, but loving, parental authority must be exercised to put things right again.

So it is with the church of God, and we have been instructed through the Word as to how we are to conduct ourselves "in the household of God, which is the church of the living God" (1 Tim. 3:15). Psalm 93:5 also tells us, "Holiness befits Thy house, O Lord, forevermore." Because God is holy, there must be holiness in His household, or He cannot indwell it! Disharmony is a sin against the holiness of God; it is also a violation of our love for our fellow brothers and sisters in Christ. We must therefore look to the Word of God and measure ourselves by its instruction so that we can maintain the harmony that is so necessary to God's house.

No one likes to dwell on the unpleasant aspects of disobedience and its resultant disharmony, but neglecting to do so will not render the church a more peaceful and loving place; on the contrary, it will have the opposite effect. When disobedience arises within the home, parents must restore order in the home by dealing with it; when it arises within the church, the leadership of the church must also deal with it according to the Word of God. The main purposes of discipline in the church, therefore, are to train its members in righteousness and to maintain harmony. Church discipline, then, is primarily restorative.

## 1. WHERE IS CHURCH DISCIPLINE FIRST MENTIONED IN THE WORD OF GOD?

Church discipline is first mentioned in Matthew 18:15-35 (q.v.). Although Jesus is primarily referring here to the settling of differences that arise when one member of the church sins against another member, these principles can be rightly applied to dealing with any sin and disharmony in the church. Jesus had already spoken of building His church (Matt. 16:18); here, He gives us instructions as to how we can together maintain its harmonious life.


## 2. WHAT ARE THE STEPS WE MUST FOLLOW IN THE SETTLING OF OUR DIFFERENCES?

a. The first step is for the person who has been wronged to go to the one who is guilty of the offense and attempt to settle it there.

> *"And if your brother sins, go and reprove him in private; if he listens to you, you have won your brother."*
> Matt. 18:15

How much pain and disruption in the body of Christ would be averted if this simple admonition of Jesus would be obeyed! All too often, the injured party feels that he has been hurt too much, or else is too interested in broadcasting the event to the rest of the church, than to seek out the offending member and seek restoration. Honoring and obeying this first step in the settling of personal differences causes each of us to look into our own hearts and discover our motives first, before we go off on a tangent of self-righteous actions.

b. The second step, should the first not be sufficient to bring about restoration between the two parties, is for the one who has been offended to take "two or three witnesses" and go to the sinning member a second time in an attempt to "win" him.

236

> *"But if he does not listen to you, take one or two*
> *more with you, so that by the mouth of two or three*
> *witnesses every fact may be confirmed."*
>
> Matt. 18:16

c.   The third step, if the conflict has not yet been resolved, is for the injured party to bring the matter to the attention of the church.

> *"And if he refuses to listen to them, tell it to the*
> *church."*                                           Matt. 18:17a

We must first of all make sure that the offense is one that is serious enough to require making it public. Step two helps to assure this. Many personal offenses may have to be suffered in love, knowing that the Lord sees everything, judges righteously, and rewards each of us according to our works and the condition of our hearts. If the offense is serious enough that it might affect the harmonious fellowship of the whole church, or at least a large segment of it, then it must be brought to the attention of those in the church who are competent to deal with it. Telling the church, in most cases, means bringing it to the attention of the leadership of the church, so that they can judge the matter. This has always been the way of dealing with personal differences in the household of God (Ex. 18:16,25,26).

d.   The fourth step in the handling of personal differences is the exclusion of the sinning member from the fellowship of the church.

> *"And if he refuses to listen even to the church, let*
> *him be to you as a Gentile and a tax-gatherer."*
>
> Matt. 18:17b

# The Four Steps in Settling our Differences:

1) Go to him and tell him his fault alone.

2) If he won't hear, take two or three more.

3) If he neglects to hear them, tell it to the church.

4) If he neglects to hear the church, he must leave.

No one looks forward to the separation of a brother or sister in Christ from the rest of the body, but there are times when such action can no longer be avoided. Sin in contagious, and it must not be allowed to spread throughout the church! Many local churches have become infected with the sins of rebellion, lust, compromise, etc., because the pastor and elders had too much "love" to deal severely with the sinning member. Such action, or lack of it, is not really love, but weakness, and everybody suffers for it. The church suffers by becoming infected, and the sinning member continues to suffer because he was never really given the chance to become healed of his sin. In extreme situations, disfellowshiping or excommunication may be the only way that the sinning member can be shocked out of his moral error and brought back to the Lord. Matthew 18:18-20 makes it clear that when the church is gathered together in His name, that is, according to the Word and by the anointing of His Spirit, and is acting in obedience to His commands, their decisions (the "binding" and "loosing" of sin) are confirmed in heaven. **The authority of the church** was thus firmly established by Jesus Himself, and the members of His body only bring His judgment upon themselves by disregarding it. When excluding a sinning member of Christ's body has been carried out by the church's leadership according to the Word of God, Jesus Himself will honor it. It is not a light matter, but one with eternal consequences.

In verses 21-35, Jesus exhorts us to extend forgiveness even up to "seventy times seven." Naturally speaking, this is beyond even the most loving of us, even as it was beyond Peter. Only the Holy Spirit and His love, which "has been poured out within our hearts" (Rom. 5:5), can make this possible. We must remember, however, that even the love of God has its limits. God cannot and will not extend His forgiveness to one who has not truly repented, and neither may we. Forgiveness **and** restoration may only be extended to a sinning member when he has both repented and brought forth the fruits of that repentance—**and that takes time!**

## 3. WHAT IS THE PROCEDURE FOR CHURCH DISCIPLINE OTHER THAN THAT OF SETTLING PERSONAL DIFFERENCES?

This is a complex matter, and one that requires a great deal of maturity on the part of the leadership of each local church. There are no pat answers, nor are there any quick solutions. The problem is that there is much within the church that needs to be dealt with by the pastor and the elders through counseling. Some of these matters may never develop into the kind of sin that breeds disharmony. There are times, however, when situations that initially require counseling do develop into occasions of sin, because the counselee will not change, people cannot or will not be reconciled, and so forth. Sometimes these matters are insignificant enough to be left alone; at other times, further steps must be taken. Sometimes bringing these matters before the church only serves to make them worse; at other times, keeping silence allows those sinning members to work their poison in the church. Although there may be no easy answers, the need for church discipline must not be ignored. There is a scriptural pattern, a precedence for dealing with sin in the local church, and we must adhere to it if we expect to find not only harmony but also health in the household of God.

The procedure for church discipline is to follow as closely as possible those steps for settling personal differences as laid down for us by Jesus Himself. We may not be able to adhere to them exactly because of the nature of the sin, the character of the sinning member, or the circumstances which surround the occasion, but we should see in them a pattern, and we should follow it as closely as possible. Every member of every local church should be aware of the scriptural right and responsibility of the local church to exercise church discipline, even to the point of public excommunication, should that become necessary. The leadership of every local church, on the other hand, must recognize and honor the scriptural rights of each believer for whom they have responsibility.

# The Purpose of Church Discipline

1) To cleanse the church and keep it free of those elements which would divide and even destroy it.

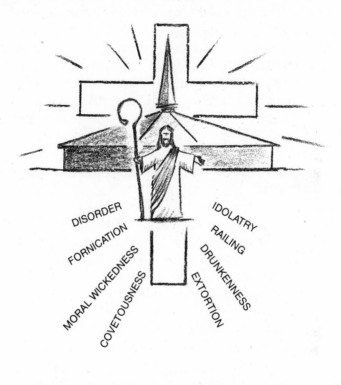

DISORDER  FORNICATION  MORAL WICKEDNESS  COVETOUSNESS  EXTORTION  DRUNKENNESS  RAILING  IDOLATRY

2) To maintain the health and harmony of the local church by restoring sinning members to the Lord.

## 4. WHAT IS THE PURPOSE OF CHURCH DISCIPLINE?

There are at least two goals in the exercising of church discipline: (1) to cleanse the church and keep it free of those elements which would divide and even destroy it, and (2) to maintain the health and harmony of the local church by restoring sinning members to the Lord.

> *Brethren, even if a man is caught in any trespass, you who are spiritual, restore such a one in a spirit of gentleness; each one looking to yourself, lest you too be tempted. Bear one another's burdens, and thus fulfill the law of Christ.*
>
> Gal. 6:1,2

## 5. WHAT ARE THE AREAS WHICH REQUIRE CHURCH DISCIPLINE?

The areas requiring church discipline are twofold: (a) personal sins (those which are contrary to the Christian lifestyle), and (b) public sins (those which disrupt the life and unity of the church).

a.  The **personal sins** the Bible talks about which can require church discipline deal with:

1.  The member who is living a disorderly life (1 Thess. 5:14; 2 Thess. 3:6-15).

> *And we earnestly beseech you, brethren, admonish (warn and seriously advise) those who are out of line—the loafers, the disorderly and the unruly.*
>
> 1 Thess. 5:14 AMP

> *Keep a check upon loafers.*
>
> 1 Thess. 5:14 Weymouth

242

*Now we charge you, brethren, in the name and on the authority of our Lord Jesus Christ, the Messiah, that you withdraw and keep away from every brother (fellow believer) who is **slack in the performance of duty** and is **disorderly, living as a shirker** and **not walking in accord with the traditions** and instructions that you have received from us.*

*Indeed, we hear that some among you are disorderly—that they are **passing their lives in idleness, neglectful of duty**—being **busy with other people's affairs** instead of their own and doing no work.* 2 Thess. 3:6b,11 AMP

Paul has this to say to these idle, undisciplined loafers:

*Now we charge and exhort such persons [as ministers in Him exhorting those] in the Lord Jesus Christ, the Messiah, that they work in quietness and **earn their own food and other necessities.*** 2 Thess. 3:12 AMP

Christianity is not merely a system of beliefs, but it is a way of life—**a walk**—and those who do not walk in accordance with the commandments of Jesus subject themselves to His judgment: (1) the disorderly one is to be admonished, and (2) if he fails to heed that warning, then he is to be "marked" and is not to be associated with.

*And we earnestly beseech you, brethren, admonish (warn and seriously advise) those who are out of line—the loafers, the disorderly and the unruly; encourage the timid and fainthearted, help and give your support to the weak souls [and] be very patient with everybody—always keeping your temper.* 1 Thess. 5:14 AMP

243

> *Now we charge you, brethren, in the name and on the authority of our Lord Jesus Christ, the Messiah, that you **withdraw and keep away from** every brother (fellow believer) who is slack in the performance of duty and is disorderly, living as a shirker and not walking in accord with the traditions and instructions that you have received from us.*
>
> *But if any one [in the church] refuses to obey what we say in this letter, **take note of that person, and do not associate with him,** that he may be ashamed.*
>
> 2 Thess. 3:6,14 AMP

Paul did place limits upon such discipline in that, although the disorderly believer has caused himself to be removed from the life and fellowship of the church, he is not to be treated as an enemy, but rather as a sinning member who may still repent and be restored to the normal life of the church.

> ***Do not regard him as an enemy,*** *but simply admonish and warn him as [being still] a brother.*
>
> 2 Thess. 3:15 AMP

2.  The one who practices moral wickedness (1 Cor. 5).

This area of personal sin, which necessitates church discipline, is typified for us by the occasion of incest which was discovered by Paul to exist in the Corinthian church. Not only was there no question of its existence, but the church actually seemed to be arrogant about it.

> *It is actually reported that there is immorality among you, and immorality of such a kind as does not exist even among the Gentiles, that someone has his father's wife. And you have become arrogant, and have not mourned instead, in order that the one who had done this deed might be removed from your midst.*
>
> 1 Cor. 5:1,2

How could such a thing have happened in a church that was noted for its spiritual gifts and its knowledge (1 Cor. 1:4-7)? It came about because the church had looked to its surrounding social environment (the wicked city of Corinth) for its standard of righteousness rather than to the Word of God. We can be capable of sinning in the same way if we compare ourselves to the worldly society and pride ourselves that we are at least better than they. Moral wickedness (an almost total lack of personal and corporate ethics) has pervaded our society; unfortunately, the same is also true of the church. Unless we have a standard of moral righteousness that is in accordance with the holiness of God and His Word, then we, as many other churches have, shall forfeit the presence of God in our midst.

How do we deal with moral wickedness? If the sinning member has been confronted with his sin, but has refused to repent, then action must be taken immediately. In the Old Testament, the penalty was death; in the New Testament it is, spiritually speaking, no less exacting.

> *For I, on my part, though absent in body but present in spirit, have already judged him who has so committed this, as though I were present. In the name of our Lord Jesus, when you are assembled, and I with you in spirit, with the power of our Lord Jesus, I have decided to deliver such a one to Satan for the destruction of his flesh, that his spirit may be saved in the day of the Lord Jesus. Your boasting is not good. Do you not know that a little leaven leavens the whole lump of dough? Clean out the old leaven, that you may be a new lump, just as you are in fact unleavened. For Christ our Passover also has been sacrificed. Let us therefore celebrate the feast, not with old leaven, nor with the leaven of malice and wickedness, but with the unleavened bread of sincerity and truth.* 1 Cor. 5:3-8

God's ways often seem to be severe to us, especially in this day of moral laxity. When we look at sin from our perspective, which is what the Corinthian Christians did, we are tempted to make excuses for ourselves by justifying our actions. We need to see sin for what it truly is, however, and we can only do that as we see it from God's point of view. Sin is abhorrent; it is a violation of God's holiness. Sin that has not been repented of will bring His judgment upon us, and that judgment may be spiritual death! (Read 1 Corinthians 11:27-30.) We may not understand all that is involved in taking such action as Paul describes here, but the main point is that such sin must be dealt with, and the wicked person expelled from the church.

> *Your boasting is not good. Do you not know that a little leaven leavens the whole lump of dough? Clean out the old leaven, that you may be a new lump, just as you are in fact unleavened. For Christ our Passover also has been sacrificed. Let us therefore celebrate the feast, not with old leaven, nor with the leaven of malice and wickedness, but with the unleavened bread of sincerity and truth. I wrote you in my letter not to associate with immoral people; I did not at all mean with the immoral people of this world, or with the covetous and swindlers, or with idolaters; for then you would have to go out of the world. But actually, I wrote to you not to associate with any so-called brother if he should be an immoral person, or covetous, or an idolater, or a reviler, or a drunkard, or a swindler—not even to eat with such a one. For what have I to do with judging outsiders? Do you not judge those who are within the church? But those who are outside, God judges. Remove the wicked man from among yourselves.*
>
> 1 Cor. 5:6-13

In verse 11 of this fifth chapter of 1 Corinthians, Paul names five other types of moral wickedness other than immorality: covetousness, idolatry, reviling (being abusive), drunkenness, and swindling (living by unlawfully preying on others, or extortion). In every instance, believers are not to associate with those who practice such things—they are **not even to eat with them!**

b. The **public sins** which require church discipline deal with:

1. Those who cause division.

> *I appeal to you, brethren, to be on your guard concerning those who create dissensions and difficulties and cause divisions, in opposition to the doctrine—the teaching—which you have been taught. [I warn you to turn aside from them, to] avoid them. For such persons do not serve our Lord Christ but their own appetites and base desires, and by ingratiating and flattering speech they beguile the hearts of the unsuspecting and simple-minded [people].*　　　Rom. 16:17,18 AMP

Persons such as those described here have always been a distressing threat to the peace and well-being of the church. Because of this, Paul urged the church from the very beginning to "be on the alert."

> *"Be on guard for yourselves and for all the flock, among which the Holy Spirit has made you overseers, to shepherd the church of God which He purchased with His own blood. I know that after my departure savage wolves will come in among you, not sparing the flock; and from among your own selves men will arise, speaking perverse things, to draw away the disciples after them. Therefore be on the alert, remembering that night and day for a*

*period of three years I did not cease to admonish
each one with tears."*                    Acts 20:28-31

Although Paul says plainly of such persons that they do not
serve the Lord Jesus Christ, but their own appetites (Rom.
16:18), they are especially dangerous because they do not
appear to be that way. They use "smooth and flattering
speech" to beguile the "hearts of the unsuspecting" and often
appear to be more "spiritual" than the oversight of the church.
They are the wolves in sheep's clothing that Jesus warned us
about (Matt. 7:15,16):  They look like sheep, sound like
sheep, and smell like sheep, **but they do not act like sheep!**
Sheep do not divide the flock, nor do they devour other
sheep. The shepherds of the flock (pastors and elders) need
to be diligent in the discovery of these "wolves in sheep's
clothing" and quick in separating them from the rest of the
flock. As for the flock itself, it needs to trust the judgment of
the shepherds when this happens. When God judged the
rebellion of Korah (Num. 16) by causing the earth to open up
and swallow him alive along with his co-conspirators and
their families, the people turned against Moses, rather than
being thankful that a great evil had been taken from their
midst. God responded by bringing further judgment against
the whole people of Israel (Num. 16:41-50), and many
thousands died. Let us learn from their examples, **and live!**

2. Rebels:

> *For there are **many rebellious men**, empty talkers and deceivers, especially those of the circumcision.*                                    Tit. 1:10

These may not actually cause division, but by their rebellion, they contradict sound doctrine (Tit. 1:9) and despise authority (2 Pet. 2:10; Jude 8). Sooner or later, such persons spread a cloud of discontent and eventually begin to build a following. There is no doubt that these are vessels of dishonor (2 Tim. 2:20,21) and must be dealt with accordingly.

3. Other categories of people who commit public sin written of by Paul in Titus 1:10, and include:

   ° "The empty talkers." These people have no moral or scriptural base for their thinking and their talking. They are insubordinate troublemakers who are subject neither to God's Word nor to His servants, and are therefore free to work their nonsense in the church.

   ° "Deceivers." The main danger with deceivers is that they are, first of all, deceived themselves. They aren't just people who are telling lies; they have been lying for so long that they have actually come to believe in lies, and that is the reason that they are so convincing. They themselves are convinced of the untruths of which they speak.

   ° "Especially those of the circumcision." In Paul's day, those who were of the circumcision were those who mixed law and grace, not understanding the difference between the two. Legalists have been a thorn in the side of the church from the very beginning and are still causing a great deal of conflict among God's people today.

How should we deal with cancers like these in the body of the church? They **"must be silenced** because they are upsetting whole families, teaching things they should not teach, for the sake of sordid gain" (Tit. 1:11). These warped people work their business behind the scenes of the church, from family to family—subverting whole houses for the sake of what they can get out of it. Whatever the cost, they must be stopped before they cause too much damage to the church and people are lost. As a shepherd lad, David had to fight off the lions and the bears that attacked his father's flock; so must the pastors and the elders do with the flocks of the Lord!

> *He* [the overseer] *must hold fast to the sure and trustworthy Word of God as he was taught it, so that he may be able both to give stimulating instruction and encouragement in sound (wholesome) doctrine, and to refute and convict those who contradict and oppose it—showing the wayward their error. For there are **many disorderly and unruly men who are idle (vain, empty) and misleading talkers and self-deceivers, as well as deceiving others.** [This is true] especially of those [who have come over from Judaism] of the circumcision party. **Their mouths must be stopped, for they are mentally distressing and subverting whole families by teaching what they ought not to teach,** for the purpose of getting base advantage and disreputable gain. One of their [very] number, a prophet of their own, said, Cretans are always liars, hurtful beasts, idle and lazy gluttons. And this account of them is [really] true. Because it is [true], **rebuke them sharply—deal sternly, [even] severely with them**—so that they may be sound in the faith and free from error. [And may show their soundness by] ceasing to give attention to Jewish myths and fables or to rules [laid down] by [mere] men who reject and turn their backs on the Truth.* Tit. 1:9-14 AMP

## 6. WHAT IS THE FINAL STEP IN THE PROCESS OF CHURCH DISCIPLINE?

When the sinning member has repented of his offenses and has brought forth fruits of that repentance, then restoration and harmony are the final results of the discipline process. This is what happened in the case of the young believer in the Corinthian church who had been dealt with so severely by Paul. In his second letter to the Corinthians, Paul actually admonished them to receive the brother back into the fellowship of the church with love (2 Cor. 2:1-8). What a joyous time that must have been for the church!

When repentance has not been manifested, however, the final step in the disciplining process is one of separation. Jesus said, "Let him be to you as a Gentile and a tax-gatherer" (Matt. 18:17). Paul said this:

> *Reject a factious man after a first and second warning, knowing that such a man is perverted and is sinning, being self-condemned.*                    Tit. 3:10,11

## HOME STUDY QUESTIONS:  CHAPTER 16

1. Outline the four steps for settling differences within the church.

2. What is the chief purpose of church discipline?

# NEW TESTAMENT GIVING

**Chapter 17**

The Bible tells us that the ministry of giving played a primary role in the life of the church even in its earliest days. The foremost example of this ministry, no doubt, is that of the church of Jerusalem, concerning whom we read:

> *And all that believed were together, and had all things common; and sold their possessions and goods, and parted them to all men, as every man had need.* Acts 2:44,45 KJV

Although the other churches, especially those of the Gentiles, do not seem to have followed the example of the Jerusalem church, the sharing of material goods and money was an important avenue of communication within each local church as well as from one church to another.

As with most of the teachings of Christ and the apostles, the traditions of men also had their effect upon the ministry of giving. Jesus' words to us on this subject make it very clear that liberal giving of ourselves as well as of material things not only is required of us, but is a means of our inheriting and sharing in the manifold blessings of God. It is therefore of the utmost necessity that the true pattern of giving be restored to the church.

## 1. WHAT IS THE SCRIPTURAL BASIS FOR CHRISTIAN GIVING?

> *"Give, and it will be given to you; good measure, pressed down, shaken together, running over, they will pour into your lap. For **by your standard of measure it will be measured to you in return.**"* Lk. 6:38

253

*Now this I say, he who sows sparingly shall also reap sparingly; and he who sows bountifully shall also reap bountifully. Let each one do just as he has purposed in his heart; not grudgingly or under compulsion; for God loves a **cheerful giver.***                                            2 Cor. 9:6,7

## 2. WHAT ARE THE TWO CATEGORIES INTO WHICH CHRISTIAN GIVING IS DIVIDED?

Christian giving can be divided into two categories: (1) tithes and (2) offerings.

## 3. WHAT IS THE TITHE?

The tithe, from the Old English word *teotha* meaning "tenth," is the tenth portion of our income that belongs to God.

*Bring all the tithes—the **whole tenth** of your income—into the storehouse, that there may be food in My house, and prove Me now by it, says the Lord of hosts, if I will not open the windows of Heaven for you and pour you out a blessing, that there shall not be room enough to receive it.*                                            Mal. 3:10 AMP

## 4. WHAT IS THE ORIGIN OF THE TITHE?

Many people are under the impression that tithing was a requirement of the Law, under the Old Testament dispensation, and is therefore not applicable to us today. A study of the history and development of tithing as it is in the Bible soon disproves this way of thinking.

a. The first mention of tithing in the Bible is almost at the very beginning of the Scriptures, in Genesis 14:17-20, q.v. There we find the patriarch Abraham giving a tithe of the spoils won in battle to Melchizedek, king of Salem. This same incident is also recorded for us in the seventh chapter of Hebrews.

> *For this Melchizedek, king of Salem, priest of the Most High God, who met Abraham as he was returning from the slaughter of the kings and blessed him, to whom also Abraham apportioned a **tenth part of all** the spoils, was first of all, by the translation of his name, king of righteousness, and then also king of Salem, which is king of peace.*
> *Now observe how great this man was to whom Abraham, the patriarch, **gave a tenth** of the **choicest** spoils.*
>
> Heb. 7:1,2,4

b. The second occasion of tithing may be found in the Book of Genesis.

> *Then Jacob made a vow, saying, "If God will be with me and will keep me on this journey that I take, and will give me food to eat and garments to wear, and I return to my father's house in safety, then the Lord will be my God. And this stone, which I have set up as a pillar, will be God's house; and of **all** that Thou dost give me **I will surely give a tenth to Thee.**"* Gen. 28:20-22

c. Tithing was practiced from the earliest times (as was sacrifice), and although we have no record of a command from God to do so, they must have received it in the form of tradition—handed down to them perhaps from Adam himself.

## 5. WHY WAS TITHING, WHICH WAS PRACTICED OVER 400 YEARS BEFORE THE GIVING OF THE LAW, INCORPORATED INTO THE LAW?

Paul tells us that "the Law has become our tutor to **lead us to Christ**" (Gal. 3:24). Tithing was incorporated into the Law because the Lord

255

wanted not only to establish a divine principle which His people had received through their tradition, but to expand the meaning and applications of the tithe in order to bring us into the fulness of the truth of giving as it is in the New Covenant.

## 6. WHAT WAS THE PURPOSE OF TITHING UNDER THE LAW?

Tithing under the Law was a means of giving honor to God, the "Possessor of heaven and earth" (Gen. 14:19,22) and thus the Source of supply for all the needs of man. Tithing has been appointed by God as an antidote for covetousness, as well as a solution to financial difficulties. It is also a test of our faith.

In addition to this, the Lord established the Old Testament tithes (there were three of them) to meet the following needs:

°   The first tithe (Lev. 27:30-33; Num. 18:21-28), called "the Lord's tithe," was given to the priests for their support at the temple.

°   The second tithe (Deut. 14:22-27) consisted of the yearly increase of the land and was eaten by the people in the presence of the Lord with rejoicing.

°   The third tithe (Deut. 14:28,29) consisted of the tenth of every third year's increase, which was to be kept in store. Eventually, this tithe was to be shared by the local Levites, the stranger, the fatherless, and the widow. Read Numbers 18:18-28 and Nehemiah 10:32-39.

## 7. WHAT HAPPENED WHEN THE JEWS NO LONGER GAVE THEIR TITHE IN FAITH TO THE LORD?

*"From the days of your fathers you have turned aside from My statutes, and have not kept them. Return to Me, and*

*I will return to you," says the Lord of hosts. "But you say, 'How shall we return?' Will a man rob God? Yet you are robbing Me! But you say, 'How have we robbed Thee?' In **tithes and offerings.** You are cursed with a curse, for you are robbing Me, the whole nation of you! Bring the whole tithe into the storehouse, so that there may be food in My house, and test Me now in this," says the Lord of hosts, "if I will not open for you the windows of heaven, and pour out for you a blessing until it overflows. Then I will rebuke the devourer for you, so that it may not destroy the fruits of the ground; nor will your vine in the field cast its grapes," says the Lord of hosts. "And all the nations will call you blessed, for you shall be a delightful land," says the Lord of hosts.*

Mal. 3:7-12

## 8. IS THE TITHE A NECESSARY PART OF THE NEW TESTAMENT PATTERN?

Very definitely! Jesus Himself placed His approval upon the tithe in His rebuke to the Pharisees as recorded for us in Matthew 23:23 KJV:

*Woe unto you, scribes and Pharisees, hypocrites! for ye pay tithe of mint and anise and cummin, and have omitted the weightier matters of the law, judgment, mercy, and faith: these ought ye to have done, **and not to leave the other undone.***

Jesus rebuked them for not discerning and fulfilling the weightier matters of the Law, but He did not set aside the tithe. Besides this, the same needs which were met by the Old Testament tithe exist in the church today. We do not have a separate priesthood to support, but the Bible declares in 1 Corinthians 9:14, "So also the Lord directed those who proclaim the gospel to get their living from the gospel." The balance of New Testament teaching makes it plain that the church's ministries are to be supported.

257

## 9. WHY THEN IS TITHING NOT SPECIFICALLY REQUIRED BY NAME IN THE NEW TESTAMENT?

Even a superficial study of the Scriptures makes it readily apparent that the New Testament church did not need to be ministered to about the necessity of tithing. In every way, they far surpassed the tithe, being extremely generous in all that they possessed. This is much to the shame of most Christians today, especially those who do not have enough faith and trust in the Lord to minister to Him and to His body even on the basis of the tithe. The tithe should not be considered the ultimate in Christian giving, but should be regarded as a tutor to bring us into the fulness of the liberality which is ours in Jesus Christ.

## 10. WHY DOES THE LORD ALSO REQUIRE US TO GIVE OFFERINGS?

We are required by the Lord to give offerings in addition to the tithe because of the practical needs that exist. Let us take another look into Malachi 3:8:

> *"Will a man rob God? Yet you are robbing Me! But you say, 'How have we robbed Thee?' In tithes and **offerings**."*

° The tabernacle was built, maintained, and repaired through the offerings of the people (Ex. 30:11-16).

° The temple was built and kept up through the offerings of the people since there was no provision for this need to be met by the tithes (2 Ki. 12:1-16; Ezra 2:68; Neh. 10:32,33; Mk. 12:41,42; Matt. 17:24).

In most churches today, tithes and offerings are taken together; the needs of the building are met first, and then what is left is distributed to the ministries and to those in need. If we are to follow the pattern of the Word of God, it would seem that the tithes should be applied first to support the full-time ministries of the church (this will vary from church to church, depending on the size and needs of each congregation). Offerings then supplement what remains from the tithe and are used to meet building expenses.

## 1. WHERE SHOULD THE TITHE BE PAID?

As we have seen, the Bible tells us very clearly that the tithes and offerings should be brought into the storehouse of the Lord. In the Old Testament this was the temple; in the New Testament, this is the church. Tithes are never to be paid to parachurch ministries (such as Full Gospel Business Men's Fellowship, Women's Aglow, etc.), nor to television "pastors" and "evangelists." Donations or offerings may be sent to worthy and proven ministries outside one's local church, but not in lieu of the tithes and offerings that are, by the Lord's command, to be brought into the church.

## 2. SHOULD THE TITHE BE PAID ON OUR GROSS OR NET INCOME?

The tithe should be calculated and paid based upon our gross income and not on our net income. The Bible tells us to bring "the whole tithe" into the storehouse of the Lord, and the tithe is a tenth of what we make, not what we bring home after taxes. We are to "render to Caesar the things that are Caesar's [that is, taxes], and to God the things that are God's,"— but God always comes first!

## 3. WHAT SHOULD BE OUR RESPONSE IF WE HAVEN'T BEEN GIVING ACCORDING TO THE PATTERN?

As we have seen, the Lord rebuked His people Israel mightily for robbing Him of that which He had required of them from the beginning of time—the tithes and offerings. In Malachi, we find the Lord saying to His people, "From the days of your fathers you have turned aside from My statutes, and have not kept them. **Return to**

**Me, and I will return to you."** Once more the Lord is asking His people to return to Him in that order and pattern which He has established by His Word. Let us be sure that we are not guilty in any way of robbing God. If we have been guilty of doing so, let us repent and obey God in this matter of giving!

For additional information on New Testament giving, read Matthew 5:42; Mark 12:41-44; Luke 6:30,34-38; Acts 2:44-46; 4:32-37; 5:1-4; 11:29; Romans 12:8; 15:25-27; 1 Corinthians 9:1-14; 16:1,2; 2 Corinthians 8:1-15; 9:1-15; Galatians 6:6,7; 1 Timothy 6:6-10,17-19; Titus 3:13,14; 3 John 6-8.

## HOME STUDY QUESTIONS: CHAPTER 17

1. Where did the practice of tithing originate?

2. What should the tithe be primarily used for in the church?

3. What should the offerings be primarily used for in the church?

4. What would your answer be to a Christian who felt that tithing was no longer required?

# DISCIPLESHIP AND COMMITMENT

**Chapter 18**

## 1. WHAT IS DISCIPLESHIP?

Discipleship is that process whereby a "learner" (from the Greek word *mathetes*) becomes a follower of a certain teacher for the purpose of imitating his lifestyle and learning his truth. Discipleship is as old as civilization: the Greek philosophers had disciples, Joshua was a disciple of Moses, Elisha was a disciple of Elijah, the Jewish rabbis had their disciples, John the Baptist had disciples (Matt. 9:14), and Jesus also had His disciples (Matt. 10:1; 20:17; Lk. 10:1; Acts 9:26; 14:20; 21:4; etc.).

Thus, we see that Jesus was not the first teacher to have disciples or "to develop a lifestyle which became an example to a succession of others, who imitated His excellences. The words for *teacher* and *disciple* were already in use, and ready to hand, because already in human experience there had been many teachers, each with his own disciples."[1]

## 2. WHAT IS CHRISTIAN DISCIPLESHIP?

Christian discipleship is that which recognizes Jesus Christ as the ultimate revelation of all truth and the only Way to that truth (Jn. 14:6). He came into this world to "bear witness to the truth" (Jn. 18:37) and is Himself the exact representation of that truth (Heb. 1:1-3; Phil. 2:6; Col. 1:15; Jn. 1:1-17). Christian discipleship recognizes that, in order to become "imitators of God" (Eph. 5:1), we must first become imitators of Christ and be remade by the Holy Spirit into His image.

*"You call Me Teacher and Lord; and you are right, for so I am."* Jn. 13:13

*He is the image of the invisible God.* Col. 1:15a

*And He is . . . the exact representation of His [God's] nature.* Heb. 1:3a

*"It is enough for the disciple that he become as his teacher."* Matt. 10:25a

## 3. WHAT IS THE GOAL OF CHRISTIAN DISCIPLESHIP?

The goal of Christian discipleship is for us, as the disciples of Jesus, to follow after Him, allowing ourselves to be recreated by the Holy Spirit into His image so that we can be like Him.

*For whom He foreknew, He also predestined to become conformed to the image of His Son, that He might be the first-born among many brethren.* Rom. 8:29

*And just as we have borne the image of the earthy, we shall also bear the image of the heavenly.* 1 Cor. 15:49

*But we all, with unveiled face beholding as in a mirror the glory of the Lord, are being transformed into the same image from glory to glory, just as from the Lord, the Spirit.* 2 Cor. 3:18

*Beloved, now we are children of God, and it has not appeared as yet what we shall be. We know that, when He appears, we shall be like Him, because we shall see Him just as He is.* 1 Jn. 3:2

## 4. WHAT IS OUR RESPONSIBILITY REGARDING CHRISTIAN DISCIPLESHIP?

Our responsibility regarding Christian discipleship is twofold.

a.  First, our personal responsibility is to acknowledge the counsel of God as revealed in His Word and to yield ourselves completely to Jesus as Lord of our lives. It is in this way that we become witnesses to Him, living an authentic Jesus-centered lifestyle and proving ourselves to be the "children of God above reproach in the midst of a crooked and perverse generation, among whom [we] appear as lights in the world" (Phil. 2:15). It is in this way that the church is the corporate image of God to the world—"whole communities of disciples whose corporate testimony to Jesus will be more convincing than any one of its members acting on his own." [2]

b.  Secondly, just as the New Testament is not just the gospel of salvation from sins, but is the gospel of the kingdom of God, so also it is our responsibility and our commission, not just to preach the gospel so as to save sinners, but so as to make disciples.

> *And Jesus came up and spoke to them, saying, "All authority has been given to Me in heaven and on earth. Go therefore and **make disciples of all the nations** . . . **teaching them to observe all** that I commanded you."*
> Matt. 28:18-20a

## 5. WHAT IS THE BASIS FOR CHRISTIAN DISCIPLESHIP?

The basis for Christian discipleship is the entire Word of God, especially the four gospels (which contain the gospel of the kingdom and the record of the life and ministry of Jesus Christ) and the balance of apostolic teaching as found in the New Testament epistles.

## 6. WHAT DOES IT MEAN PERSONALLY TO BE A DISCIPLE OF JESUS?

To be a disciple of Jesus means that:

a.  Each of us is **obedient** to the gospel (Acts 6:7; Rom. 1:5; 6:17 15:18; 16:26; 2 Cor. 10:5; etc.).

b.  Each of us is an **imitator** of His word and His example.

> *"You call Me Teacher and Lord; and you are right, for so I am. If I then, the Lord and the Teacher, washed your feet, you also ought to wash one another's feet. For I gave you an example that you also should do as I did to you. Truly, truly, I say to you, a slave is not greater than his master; neither is one who is sent greater than the one who sent him."* Jn. 13:13-16

> *"A disciple is not above his teacher, nor a slave above his master. It is enough for the disciple that he become as his teacher, and the slave as his master. If they have called the head of the house Beelzebul, how much more the members of his household!"* Matt. 10:24,25

c.  Each of us is also a **follower** of Jesus. Jesus said, "I am the way, and the truth, and the life" (Jn. 14:6). To be a follower of Jesus is to walk the way He walked, to live the life that He lived, to proclaim the word that He gave us, and to love with the love with which He loved us so that all men will know that we are His disciples (Jn. 13:35).

> *Now as they observed the confidence of Peter and John, and understood that they were uneducated and untrained men, they were marveling, and began to recognize them as having been with Jesus.* Acts 4:13

To be a Christian, then, means to be a "follower of Jesus," one who "walks in His way." Christianity was first called "the Way" (Acts 9:2; 19:9,23; 22:4; 24:14) because the disciples had more than a belief—they had a lifestyle (a way of living) that was modeled on the words and life of Jesus. The disciples were called **Christ**ians first in Antioch (Acts 11:26) in recognition of their likeness to Christ!

## 7. WHAT IS AUTHENTIC DISCIPLESHIP?

Authentic discipleship is that which is based upon the Word of God. It is Christ-centered and not man-centered.

> . . . *fixing our eyes **on Jesus, the author and perfecter of** **faith.*** Heb. 12:2a

> *But whatever things were gain to me, those things I have counted as loss **for the sake of Christ.** More than that, I count all things to be loss in view of the surpassing value of **knowing Christ Jesus my Lord,** for whom I have suffered the loss of all things, and count them but rubbish in order **that I may gain Christ,** and may be found in Him . . . **that I may know Him.*** Phil. 3:7-10a

Authentic discipleship must begin with an authentic relationship to Jesus Christ as both Savior and Lord, but it does not end there. Jesus is the Head of His body—the church—but He is not the whole body. The many-membered body of Christ is made up of many believers, some of whom are new converts (1 Tim. 3:6), some babes (1 Pet. 2:2), and some mature (Heb. 5:14). It is the job of the older, more mature members of God's family to help train, that is, disciple, the younger members.

> *But as for you, speak the things which are fitting for sound doctrine. Older men are to be temperate, dignified, sensible, sound in faith, in love, in perseverance. Older*

*women likewise are to be reverent in their behavior, not malicious gossips, nor enslaved to much wine, teaching what is good, that they may encourage* [literally, train] *the young women to love their husbands, to love their children, to be sensible, pure, workers at home, kind, being subject to their own husbands, that the word of God may not be dishonored. Likewise urge the young men to be sensible;* **in all things show yourself to be an example** [Greek, *tupos*—**"a die, a pattern"**] *of good deeds, with purity in doctrine, dignified.*

Tit. 2:1-7

*Let no one look down on your youthfulness, but rather in speech, conduct, love, faith and purity, show yourself* **an example** [Greek, *tupos*] *of those who believe.*

1 Tim. 4:12

Here is where we must be extremely careful concerning discipleship. It has always been a temptation for man to substitute his own program for the truth of God's Word. The Jews did it (Mk. 7:6-13), the early church did it (Acts 20:28-31; 2 Cor. 11:1-4; Gal. 1:6-9; Eph. 4:11-15; Jude 1-3; Rev. 2:6,15), the historical church has been doing it for centuries, and many of the Lord's people are in danger of doing the same today. God's Word declares that His people "are destroyed for lack of knowledge" (Hos. 4:6) and that "where there is no vision, the people are unrestrained" (Prov. 29:18). Once we take our eyes off Jesus and His clear words to us, then we become a people who are unrestrained in our imaginations and doing that which seems good to us. We are to be the disciples of Jesus; that is, we are to be like Him. We are also to imitate those among us who have proven themselves to be mature and trustworthy (1 Cor. 4:16; 11:1; 1 Thess. 1:6; Heb. 6:12; 13:7). Churches should even follow the good example set by other churches, imitating their faith (1 Thess. 2:14). But, in all this, we must never allow man to usurp that place in our lives that belongs only to Jesus. Every truth of the Word of God must be kept in careful balance, and the harmony of the "whole purpose of God" (Acts 20:27) must be maintained if we are to continue to walk in truth.

*"If you abide in My word, then you are truly **disciples of Mine;** and you shall know the truth, and the **truth shall make you free.**"*                                Jn. 8:31,32

*Therefore be **imitators of God,** as beloved children; and walk in love, **just as Christ** also loved you.*          Eph. 5:1,2

## 8.  WHAT IS COMMITMENT?

Commitment is our resolve and stated decision to honor and obey Jesus Christ, not only as Savior, but also as Sovereign Lord. It is our recognition of the reality and the validity of His claims upon our lives, especially as they relate to the way we live our lives (our lifestyle) and to our place of service in His body, the church.

## 9.  IS COMMITMENT NECESSARY?

Commitment is necessary because it is part and parcel of the gospel of the kingdom of God. We were not called by God to be private Christians; we were called to be members of Christ's body, His redeemed community, the church.

*For even as the body is one and yet has many members, and all the members of the body, though they are many, are one body, so also is Christ. For by one Spirit we were all baptized into one body, whether Jews or Greeks, whether slaves or free, and we were all made to drink of one Spirit. For the body is not one member, but many.*
*But now God has placed the members, each one of them, in the body, just as He desired.*          1 Cor. 12:12-14,18

## 10. WHAT ARE SOME OF THE PRACTICAL IMPLICATIONS OF OUR TOTAL COMMITMENT TO JESUS AS BOTH SAVIOR AND LORD?

Being totally committed to Jesus Christ as both Savior **and** Lord means that our lives are completely submitted to His Word and His Spirit. It means that we are learning to live His way and not our way.

> Let the wicked forsake his way, and the unrighteous man his thoughts; and let him return to the Lord, and He will have compassion on him; and to our God, for He will abundantly pardon. "For My thoughts are not your thoughts, neither are your ways My ways," declares the Lord. "For as the heavens are higher than the earth, so are My ways higher than your ways, and My thoughts than your thoughts."
>
> Isa. 55:7-9

Therefore, it means that we have adopted a new lifestyle—a new way of living. Remember, Christianity was first called "the Way."

We have the examples of the disciples in the gospels and the example of the early church in Jerusalem. Even though the Jerusalem church was not to be the pattern for the New Testament church, Paul and others preached the same message of commitment and discipleship throughout the New Testament.

Commitment to the Lord Jesus Christ has implications relative to:

° where we live.
° how we live.
° where we worship Him and serve Him—our place in the local church!

## 1. WHAT IS THE SCRIPTURAL BASIS FOR MAKING A COMMITMENT TO A LOCAL CHURCH?

The scriptural basis for making a commitment to a local church may be found in the entirety of the Word of God, in both the Old and the New Testaments. From the very beginning, God has desired a people, not just an assortment of individual believers. We see this reflected throughout the Old Testament, beginning with God calling Israel out of Egypt and forming them into a new nation, through the establishing of that new nation as a kingdom under David. This principle is fulfilled in the New Testament redeemed community, the church.

> *So then you are no longer strangers and aliens, but you are **fellow citizens** with the saints, and are **of God's household**, having been built upon the foundation of the apostles and prophets, Christ Jesus Himself being the corner stone, in whom the **whole building, being fitted together** is growing into a holy temple in the Lord; in whom **you also are being built together** into a dwelling of God in the Spirit.*
>
> Eph. 2:19-22

> *And let us consider how to stimulate one another to love and good deeds, **not forsaking our own assembling together,** as is the habit of some, but encouraging one another; and all the more, as you see the day drawing near.*
>
> Heb. 10:24,25

> *You also, as living stones, **are being built** up as a spiritual house . . . .*
>
> *But you are a chosen **race,** a royal priesthood, a holy **nation, a people for God's own possession** . . . for you once were not a people, but **now you are the people of God.***
>
> 1 Pet. 2:5a,9a,10a

## 12. WHAT ARE SOME OF THE THINGS THAT SHOULD CHARACTERIZE A COMMUNITY OF COMMITTED BELIEVERS?

> *So then, those who had received his word were baptized; and there were added that day about three thousand souls. And they were **continually devoting** themselves to **the apostles' teaching** and to **fellowship**, to the **breaking of bread** and to **prayer**. And everyone kept feeling a **sense of awe**; and many **wonders and signs** were taking place through the apostles. And all those who had believed **were together,** and had all things **in common;** and they began selling their property and possessions, and were **sharing** them with all, as anyone might have need. And day by day continuing with one mind in the temple, and breaking bread from house to house, they were taking their meals together with **gladness** and **sincerity of heart, praising God,** and having favor with all the people. And the Lord was adding to their number day by day those who were being saved.*
>
> Acts 2:41-47

According to these verses in the book of Acts, here are some of those things which should characterize a community of committed believers.

a.  First of all, as we have already pointed out, believers are those who come to the Lord by receiving the Word and walking it out in obedience. Those who have made a true commitment to the Lord and to His gospel of the kingdom continue to receive the Word and obey it.

b.  Believers with true commitment are those who are devoted to the spiritual welfare of the church on a continuing basis. Their devotion to such things as teaching, fellowship, breaking of bread, prayer, and even to one another is not based on feelings, circumstances, or convenience, but is established solidly and continually on the basis of the commitment that they have made to the Lord and to one another.

270

c.   It is thus that believers with true commitment are doers of the Word and not merely hearers (Jas. 1:22). They are not people who "go to church together," but are those who recognize that "they are the church together"—and they act like it. They are not those who occasionally forsake their assembling together (Heb. 10:25); they are devoted, that is, committed from the heart, to one another and to those/things which should characterize the life of the church everywhere.

d.   They are those who reap the good fruits of what they have sown. Because they are devoted doers of the Word, the Lord blesses their assembly, and there is a continuing sense of awe in their midst. When Noah built the ark "as God had commanded" him (Gen. 6:22; 7:5,9), he and those who were committed to him were saved from the flood—they saw the salvation, the power, and the glory of the Lord. When Moses built the tabernacle "just as the Lord commanded him" (Ex. 39:1,5,7,21,26,29,31,32,42,43; 40:16,19,21,23,25,27,29,32), "then the cloud covered the tent of meeting, and the glory of the Lord filled the tabernacle" (Ex. 40:34). When Solomon had built the temple according to the pattern that had been given to his father David by the Holy Spirit (1 Chr. 28:11,19), "then the house, the house of the Lord, was filled with a cloud, so that the priests could not stand to minister because of the cloud, for the glory of the Lord filled the house of God" (2 Chr. 5:13,14). When we build faithfully according to the pattern of all that God has so clearly given us in His Word, then the church, too, will be filled with the glory of the Lord, and there will be a continuing sense of awe in our midst!

e.   Signs and wonders should "accompany those who have believed" (Mk. 16:17). After many centuries, the Lord has restored healing and signs and wonders to His people. So far, these things have been manifested primarily in healing crusades and evangelistic campaigns, rather than in the churches. As the people of God learn to consistently practice true New Testament Christianity, especially as far as church life is concerned, then signs and

271

wonders will characterize and accompany "those who have believed" and who are practicing what they believe!

f.  Those who are truly committed to the Lord and to one another are simply **"together."** Because they are a "congregation of those who believed [and are] of one heart and soul" (Acts 4:32), **they have unity**—not only of beliefs, but also of goals. They are a people who accomplish things for the Lord, and the Lord crowns their labors with growth and prosperity (Acts 2:47; 4:34). And because of their commitment to be of one heart and one mind, they continually work at "being diligent to preserve the unity of the Spirit in the bond of peace," thus believing and demonstrating that "there is one body and one Spirit . . . one hope of your calling; one Lord, one faith, one baptism, one God and Father of all" (Eph. 4:3-6).

g.  To those who share this kind of commitment, **servanthood is a way of life.** Having a commitment to the Lord Jesus Christ means that we are willing, in imitation of Him, to serve one another (Jn. 13:13-15; Mk. 10:43,44). Serving others without any desire for gain or recognition is a true sign of spiritual maturity—and even "greatness"—in the body of Christ. Biblical servanthood is not merely the doing of occasional, convenient good deeds; it is a lifestyle of continuous willingness to lay down one's life for others, being liberated from the bondage of self-centeredness and even selfishness. Serving means giving up the "right" to noninvolvement. Because the body of Christ is only as strong as its individual parts, there should be no such thing as an inactive, or "private," member. This is the kind of radical commitment and practice that is demanded of us as God's kingdom people. Anything else, anything less, may be a "form of godliness," but it will lack the power and the glory!

h.  Commitment not only involves what we do for one another, but it also includes our **giving** to one another: **encouragement** (Acts 14:22; 1 Thess. 5:11; Heb. 10:25); **love** (Jn. 13:34; Rom. 12:10; etc.); **hospitality** (Rom. 12:13; 1 Tim. 3:2); those **gifts of the**

**Spirit** which have been given to us (1 Cor. 12:7,11,20-22; 14:26; Rom. 12:6; Eph. 4:7,16; 1 Pet. 4:10); and even **finances** (Acts 2:44,45; 4:32-37; Rom. 12:13). When Jesus returns, believers will either be rewarded or suffer loss in proportion to the quality of their service and their faithfulness in using what God has given to them (Matt. 25:31-46).

i. Those believers who are truly committed to the Lord will have no problem making a commitment both to others of like faith in the local church and to the oversight of that local church. The Lord not only expects us to be rightly related to delegated authority outside the church (such as those in the home, at work, in governmental capacities, etc.), He also expects, and requires, that each believer will **be rightly related to God's delegated authority in the church.** Pastors are given to the church to feed, lead, provide for, and protect the flock. Every believer needs this pastoral oversight and the accountability that it provides in his life. More than merely accepting it and submitting to it, he should seek it out willingly, knowing that it is the Lord's will and purpose for him (1 Thess. 5:12,13; Heb. 13:17).

j. Finally, for the committed Christian this faithfulness and service is based upon covenant: his **covenant relationship with the Lord,** and his **covenant relationship with his fellow believers.** It has been said that "Christians are an acquired taste," and this is probably true! The church is a fellowship of imperfect people who are learning to live a new life in a new way. This is not accomplished in anyone's life without conflict. The Book of Proverbs tells us, "Iron sharpens iron, so one man sharpens another" (27:17). As submitted and committed members of the body of Christ, we must learn to have the love and patience that we need to deal with conflicts redemptively, and we must keep our hearts free of bitterness, anger, resentment, and unforgiveness. True disciples of Jesus Christ are **loyal** to Him and to one another.

*Love is patient, love is kind, and is not jealous; love does not brag and is not arrogant, does not act unbecomingly; it does not seek its own, is not provoked, does not take into account a wrong suffered, does not rejoice in unrighteousness, but rejoices with the truth; bears all things, believes all things, hopes all things, endures all things. Love never fails.*   1 Cor. 13:4-8a

## 13. WHAT ARE SOME OF THE BENEFITS OF COMMITMENT?

a. By making a commitment to the local church, we become a functioning part of the many-membered body of Christ, putting ourselves in the place of receiving from the various ministries that have been placed there by the Lord.

b. By becoming committed, and therefore, responsible members of the local church, we are then free to exercise the gifts of the Spirit that have been given to us. Gifts and ministries in the local church must operate (1) under oversight, that is, judged, directed, and trained by the leadership of the church; and (2) only after having first been proven. Teaching, preaching, and especially prophecy should not be received from believers who are not committed members, proven, and under the authority of a local church.

c. Commitment brings peace because we know that we have fulfilled the Word of God by obeying the gospel of the kingdom of God. We will have made our personal commitment to Jesus Christ real by submitting ourselves to one another in the fellowship of the saints and to the government of the local church.

*For the kingdom of God is not eating and drinking, but righteousness and peace and joy in the Holy Spirit.*   Rom. 14:17

*. . . being diligent to preserve the unity of the Spirit in the bond of peace.*   Eph. 4:3

d.  Commitment protects us from deceptive teachings and philosophies, winds of doctrine, and wolves in sheep's clothing (Matt. 7:15; Acts 20:27-30; Eph. 4:11-16; 1 Tim. 4:1-3). The church is the pillar and support of the truth (1 Tim. 3:15). Jesus said, "I will build My church; and the gates of Hades shall not overpower it [—the church!]" (Matt. 16:18). Commitment causes us to receive the benefit of oversight and government in many ways.

> *And He gave some as apostles, and some as prophets, and some as evangelists, and some as pastors and teachers, for the equipping of the saints . . . until we all attain to the unity of the faith . . . . As a result, we are no longer to be children, tossed here and there by waves.*
> Eph. 4:11-14a

e.  Commitment to the local church makes it possible for us to be trained for ministry.

> *And He gave some as apostles, and some as prophets, and some as evangelists, and some as pastors and teachers, for the equipping of the saints for the work of service* ["the ministry," KJV].        Eph. 4:11,12a

f.  Commitment to the local church puts us in a place where we can grow up (Eph. 4:14,15) in a family (Eph. 2:19; 3:15; 1 Tim. 5:1,2), learning to give and receive in a life of harmony with one another.

> *To sum up, let all be harmonious, sympathetic, brotherly, kindhearted, and humble in spirit; not returning evil for evil, or insult for insult, but giving a blessing instead; for you were called for the very purpose that you might inherit a blessing.*
> 1 Pet. 3:8,9

## 14. HOW DO WE MAKE A COMMITMENT TO A LOCAL CHURCH?

Commitment to a local church is usually made verbally and publicly. Although there are no specific Scriptures to this effect in the New Testament, common sense dictates that this is the pattern to follow. We also see patterns in many of the Old Testament types that still speak to us and direct our actions today. Such a type and pattern is to be found in the book of Deuteronomy (26:1-11), concerning the offering of the first fruits in the new land.

> *"Then it shall be, when you enter the land which the Lord your God gives you as an inheritance, and you possess it and live in it* [type of finding your place in the local church], *that you shall take some of the first of all the produce of the ground . . . and go to the place where the Lord your God chooses to establish His name* [the church]. *And you shall go to the priest who is in office at that time* [type of the oversight of the church], *and say to him, 'I declare this day to the Lord my God that I have entered the land . . . .' Then the priest shall take the basket from your hand and set it down before the altar of the Lord your God."*
>
> Deut. 26:1-4

Words are powerful instruments which we can use for good or ill. Jesus said, "For by your words you shall be justified, and by your words you shall be condemned" (Matt. 12:37). Pacts and covenants, ranging from business agreements to marriages, are based upon our words. Words establish truths, change relationships (dating/engaged/married), and even have within them the power of life and death (Prov. 18:21). Contracts must be witnessed to become valid and binding; marriage vows are exchanged publicly. For these reasons, our commitment to a local church should be made openly before the congregation to whom we are pledging our support and loyalty.

5. **MUST COMMITMENTS ALWAYS BE EXPRESSED PUBLICLY?**

There are sometimes unusual circumstances, such as extreme shyness on the part of a person making a commitment, when it is possible to have the commitment read by the pastor from the pulpit.

6. **IS COMMITMENT THE SAME FOR EVERYONE?**

Commitment, as we have said, is primarily our resolve and stated decision to honor and obey Jesus Christ as Savior and Lord, recognizing the reality and the validity of His claims upon our lives—especially as they relate to our place of service in His body, the church. Beyond that, each of us is free to walk out our commitment to the local church in direct relationship to the way in which we love the Lord and in proportion to our willingness to love and serve His people.

Everything costs, and we are to calculate those costs before making major decisions (Lk. 14:28). Not everyone is willing to pay the price that complete surrender and commitment demand, and the Lord is merciful enough to receive what we yield to Him. Remember the parable of the sower (Matt. 13:1-23), especially verse 23 where Jesus said, "And the one on whom seed was sown on the good soil, this is the man who hears the word and understands it; who indeed bears fruit, and brings forth, **some a hundredfold, some sixty, and some thirty."** We must keep in mind, though, that we will reap only that which we sow.

> *Do not be deceived, God is not mocked; for whatever a man sows, this he will also reap. For the one who sows to his own flesh shall from the flesh reap corruption, but the one who sows to the Spirit shall from the Spirit reap eternal life. **And let us not lose heart in doing good, for in due time we shall reap if we do not grow weary.** So then, while we have opportunity, let us do good to all men, and especially to those who are of the household of the faith.*
>
> Gal. 6:7-10

17. **DO WE HAVE TO BE IN AGREEMENT WITH EVERY-THING THAT A LOCAL CHURCH DOES IN ORDER TO MAKE OUR COMMITMENT TO IT?**

First of all, each of us must know where the Lord is directing us to serve Him. "But now **God has placed the members, each one** of them, **in the body,** just as He desired" (1 Cor. 12:18). Our choice of a church must not be based upon proximity, family connections, or other such things. Although the Lord does use all of these things in directing us, and each of them has a valid place in our choice, ultimately, we must know that we are making a commitment to a local church because that is the church He has chosen for us. Usually, we will find ourselves in agreement with His choice, but there are those times when we may find the Lord directing us to a church which may not be our choice. In those times, our submission to His Lordship is both tested and proven!

Secondly, the Lord would never lead us to a church whose doctrine was not true to the Word of God, or whose government was not scriptural, or whose people were not loving and moral in their service and conduct. In keeping with this, a believer should not make a commitment to a local church if he cannot be in agreement with it. Christians of various churches, and even the churches themselves, do not have to be in complete doctrinal agreement with one another in order to have fellowship, but it is absolutely imperative that each local church have a common basis for their belief—that they all believe the same things, being of "one heart and soul." Otherwise, not only will they lack integrity, but also there will be an abundance of factions and divisions, and "a house divided against itself shall not stand" (Matt. 12:25).

Thirdly, although it is imperative that each local church be united in its doctrine, it is not necessary that every member of that local church be in agreement with all of its practices. This is especially true of such areas as the way in which offerings are received, the organization of the music ministries, the seating arrangements, the order of services, and so forth.

## 18. IS OUR COMMITMENT TO A LOCAL CHURCH BINDING FOR A LIFETIME?

Our commitment to Jesus Christ as both Savior and Lord should be for a lifetime. Remember, you are not your own; you have been **bought with a price** (1 Cor. 6:19,20). When it comes to our commitment to the local church, our calling and placement there by the Lord is usually a permanent one. We cannot really put down roots if we frequently pull ourselves up and transplant ourselves. There are those times when the Lord will allow us to make moves, but we must be careful to have our lives directed by His Word and His kingdom, and not by the circumstances of this life (such as the condition of the job market, the location where we would rather live, etc.; see Matthew 6:32,33).

In addition to this, the Lord will also require us from time to time to renew, strengthen, and deepen our commitment to Him and to our local church. We can see this principle reflected in the Old Testament practice of piercing the ear of a servant who had been set free but who wanted to stay and serve his master (Deut. 15:12-18).

## NOTES

[1] Michael Griffiths, *The Example of Jesus* (Downers Grove, Ill.: InterVarsity Press, © 1985), p. 15.

[2] *Ibid.*, p. 37.

# HOME STUDY QUESTIONS: CHAPTER 18

1. What is Christian discipleship?

2. What does it mean personally to be a disciple of Jesus Christ?

3. What is authentic discipleship?

4. What is Christian commitment?

5. Why is it necessary for us to make a commitment to a local church?

6. List some of the benefits of making a commitment.

7. What are some of the things that should characterize a community of committed believers?

8. Why is it that everyone does not live out the same level of commitment?

# Part Three

## Understanding the
## Christian Life

# THE BIBLE

## Chapter 19

## 1. WHAT IS THE BIBLE?

The Bible is the divinely inspired Word of God.

*All Scripture is inspired by God.*     2 Tim. 3:16a

It is a collection of 66 books, arranged under two main headings: the Old Testament, containing the first 39 books, and the New Testament, containing the remaining 27 books.

## 2.  WHERE DOES THE WORD *BIBLE* COME FROM?

The word *bible* originally referred to the byblos reed which was used by ancient man for the making of books and scrolls. During Jesus' life on earth, the Greeks referred to their books as *biblios*. Greek Christians soon referred to the books of the Old and New Testaments as *ta biblia*, meaning simply "the books." The English eventually adopted the Greek word, thus referring to this divinely inspired collection of 66 books as the Bible, the "Book of books."

## 3.  WHO WROTE THE BOOKS OF THE BIBLE?

The books of the Bible were written by forty-four different authors over a period of sixteen hundred years. Prophets and priests, such as Moses and Samuel, wrote the books of the Old Testament. Apostles and evangelists, such as Paul and Luke, wrote the books of the New Testament. These holy men did not write according to the dictates of their own intellects or wills, but they were divinely chosen to be God's spokesmen to us.

> *For no prophecy* [of Scripture] *was ever made by an act of human will, but **men moved by the Holy Spirit spoke from God.*** 2 Pet. 1:21

It is because of this divine inspiration and motivation that the Bible is the Word of God, even though written by men.

> *And for this reason we also constantly thank God that when you received from us the word of God's message, you accepted it not as the word of men, but for what it really is, the word of God.* 1 Thess. 2:13

## 4.  WHY DID GOD GIVE US THE BIBLE?

God gave us the Bible as the means of revealing Himself and His will to us, especially as these things are centered in the Person and work of Jesus Christ.

*. . . and that from childhood you have known the sacred writings which are able to give you the wisdom that leads to salvation through faith which is in Christ Jesus.*

2 Tim. 3:15

## 5. HOW DOES THE BIBLE REVEAL CHRIST TO US?

Throughout its pages, the Old Testament foretells the coming of the Messiah. The New Testament contains the fulfillment of these prophetic promises in the life and ministry of Jesus Christ.

*"You search the Scriptures, because you think that in them you have eternal life; and it is these that bear witness of Me."*
Jn. 5:39

## 6. WHAT ARE THE TWO GREAT TEACHINGS OF THE BIBLE?

The two great teachings of the Bible are the Law and the gospel of Grace.

*For the Law was given through Moses; grace and truth were realized through Jesus Christ.*
Jn. 1:17

## 7. WHAT WAS THE LAW?

The Law, which was given by God to Moses, consisted of the judgments, ordinances, and commandments which governed the behavior of the Israelites toward their God. The Law also governed the life they were to live as God's witnesses before all the sinful and unbelieving nations that surrounded them. The keeping of the Law brought blessing; the breaking of it brought judgment. A significant part of the Law contained instructions pertaining to Israel's offering of animal sacrifices to God by faith before they could approach Him for help, strength, and continued blessing and fellowship. Through these sacrifices, God momentarily overlooked the sin which they had inherited from Adam.

## 8. WHY WAS THE LAW GIVEN?

The Law was given to demonstrate beyond any doubt that, although Israel loved God and attempted to serve Him faithfully, the sin which was in them made it impossible for them to do so. Through their repeated breaking of the Law, their hopelessly sinful nature was thus to be fully exposed. Man was incapable of obeying God's command to love Him with the whole heart. This, then, is the message of the Law, even to us! If man was ever to have true and lasting fellowship with God again, He would have to send a provision greater than the Law. Israel—and all mankind—needed a Savior. It is thus that the Law leads us to the inevitability of Christ!

> *Therefore the Law has become our tutor to lead us to Christ, that we may be justified by faith.* Gal. 3:24

> *The old system of Jewish laws gave only a dim foretaste of the good things Christ would do for us. The sacrifices under the old system were repeated again and again, year after year, but even so they could never save those who lived under their rules. If they could have, one offering would have been enough; the worshipers would have been cleansed once for all, and their feeling of guilt would be gone. But just the opposite happened: those yearly sacrifices reminded them of their disobedience and guilt instead of relieving their minds. For it is not possible for the blood of bulls and goats really to take away sins.* Heb. 10:1-4 TLB

## 9. WHAT IS THE MEANING OF THE WORD *GOSPEL*?

The word *gospel* stems from the Anglo-Saxon words *god* (in this case meaning "good") and *spel* (meaning "message" or "word"). The gospel, therefore, is the good message or good news of Jesus Christ.

## 10. WHAT IS THE GOOD NEWS OF JESUS CHRIST?

It is the good news that God Himself has come to us in the Person of His Son Jesus Christ, bringing grace and truth and making them available to every man who believes, thus meeting the rigid demands of the Law and doing for us the very thing that we could not do for ourselves.

> *For Moses gave us only the Law with its rigid demands and merciless justice, while Jesus Christ brought us loving forgiveness* [grace and truth] *as well.*     Jn. 1:17 TLB

> *"For God so loved the world, that He gave His only begotten Son, that whoever believes in Him should not perish, but have eternal life. For God did not send the Son into the world to judge the world, but that the world should be saved through Him."*     Jn. 3:16,17

## 11. WHAT IS THE DIFFERENCE BETWEEN THE LAW OF MOSES UNDER THE OLD TESTAMENT AND THE GRACE OF GOD IN CHRIST UNDER THE NEW TESTAMENT?

Under the provision of the Old Testament, man had to fulfill the requirements of the Law before he could enjoy fellowship with God. As we have seen, sin made this impossible. Even though sacrifices, when offered by faith, caused their sin to be put away for a season (Rom. 3:25 and Heb. 9:15), we know that "by the works of the Law no flesh will be justified in His sight" (Rom. 3:20).

Under the New Testament, God sent Jesus Christ into the world to live a sin-free life under the Law. Jesus, having accomplished all that He was sent to do, then offered up His own sin-free life to God as a once-for-all sacrifice for man's sinfulness. God accepted Christ's sacrifice by raising Him from the dead and now declares all who believe in Christ to be saved from sin and set free from its power. We have thus obtained through the sacrifice of Jesus Christ a new and living way into eternal fellowship with God.

> *This is the fresh, new, life-giving way which Christ has opened up for us by tearing the curtain—His human body—to let us into the holy presence of God.*
>
> Heb. 10:20 TLB

> *Once you were under God's curse, doomed forever for your sins. You went along with the crowd and were just like all the others, full of sin, obeying Satan . . . . We started out bad, being born with evil natures, and were under God's anger just like everyone else. But God is so rich in mercy; he loved us so much that even though we were spiritually dead and doomed by our sins, he gave us back our lives again when he raised Christ from the dead—only by his undeserved favor* **[that is, grace]** *have we ever been saved . . . .*
>
> *Salvation is not a reward for the good we have done* [keeping the Law of Moses], *so none of us can take any credit for it. It is God himself who has made us what we are and given us new lives from Christ Jesus.*
>
> Eph 2:1-5,9-10 TLB

# HOME STUDY QUESTIONS:  CHAPTER 19

1. What is the Bible?

2. Explain why the Bible is the Word of God even though it was written by men.

3. Why did God give us the Bible?

4. What are the two great teachings of the Bible?

5. Explain in your own words the difference between the Law of Moses under the Old Testament and the grace of God in Christ under the New Testament.

# HOW TO USE THE BIBLE

**Chapter 20**

## 1. WHY SHOULD WE READ THE BIBLE?

We should read the Bible because it is God's Word.

> *"Man does not live by bread alone, but man lives by everything that proceeds out of the mouth of the Lord."*
>
> Deut. 8:3

## 2. HOW OFTEN SHOULD WE READ THE BIBLE?

We should read the Bible daily. Moreover, we should not read the Bible merely to gain information, but we should read it prayerfully, with a heart that has been prepared to receive life-giving instruction from the Lord.

> *So faith comes from hearing, and hearing by the word of Christ.*
>
> Rom. 10:17

## 3. WHAT ARE THE BENEFITS OF READING THE BIBLE?

By reading the Bible, which is the Word of God, we receive the knowledge of our salvation and everything else that is available to us through the redemptive merits of Jesus Christ.

> *But these have been written that you may believe that Jesus is the Christ, the Son of God; and that believing you may have life in His name.*
>
> Jn. 20:31

*. . . and that from childhood you have known the sacred writings which are able to give you the wisdom that leads to salvation through faith which is in Christ Jesus. All Scripture is inspired by God and profitable for teaching, for reproof, for correction, for training in righteousness; that the man of God may be adequate, equipped for every good work.*

2 Tim. 3:15-17

## 4. DOES THE BIBLE CONTRADICT ITSELF?

No, the Bible cannot contradict itself since it is the Word of God. If it were contradictory, then God would be contradicting Himself, His word would be unreliable, and we could not trust any of it. There are times when it seems to make contradictory statements because men take it out of context and twist it to support what they want it to say. In every area of doctrine in the Bible there is a key statement of truth which contains the mind of God on that subject. Having that "key" in hand will enable the reader to line up the remaining statements on that subject (even when they seem to be at variance with one another as with the tumblers in a lock) and unlock the word of truth.

*Be diligent to present yourself approved to God as a workman who does not need to be ashamed, **handling accurately the word of truth.***    2 Tim. 2:15

## 5. HOW SHOULD WE STUDY THE BIBLE?

In order to gain the most from our Bible study, we should:

a.  Read it daily.

b.  Read it prayerfully and devotionally.

c.  Read it from beginning (Genesis) to end (Revelation) in order to see the unity and continuity of the Word of God.

d.  Read it and study it a book at a time.

e.  Read it and study it a chapter at a time.

f.  Read it and study it a verse at a time.

g.  Read it topically—that is, according to the various topics it contains (such as creation, redemption, the atonement, God's dealings with Israel, the early church, etc.).

h.  Read it typically—that is, studying the truths of the Word of God as they are revealed in the various types and shadows (for example: Abraham, a type of God the Father; Isaac, a type of Jesus the Son; the Passover lamb, a type of Christ, the Lamb slain from before the foundation of the world, etc.).

i.  Read it biographically—that is, studying the lives of both the Old and New Testament saints for inspiration and hope.

## 6. WHY DO WE HAVE SO MANY ENGLISH TRANSLATIONS OR VERSIONS OF THE BIBLE?

Each new version of the Bible is translated and written by a group of men who attempt to present the truths of the Word of God in the language of their day. Some do this by updating the already existing translation (such as the New King James Version), while others go back to the original Hebrew and Greek.

In each case, the purpose is to make the words of the Bible more understandable by putting them into language the reader will be familiar with. The following example shows how successive translators have presented Hebrews 13:16 to their contemporaries. Which version makes the most sense to you?

> *Beneficense and communication do not forget, for with such hosts God is promerited.*
> *The Douay-Rheims Version,* A.D. 1582

291

*But to do good and to communicate forget not: for with
such sacrifices God is well pleased.*
                                *The King James Version,* A.D. 1611

The King James translation is better than the first example but is still
misleading because of the word "communicate." In the Greek this
word means to "give" or "share," as we see in the following:

*Don't forget to do good and to share what you have with
those in need, for such sacrifices are very pleasing to Him.*
                                *The Living Bible,* A.D. 1971

## 7. WHAT IS THE DIFFERENCE BETWEEN A TRANSLATION AND A PARAPHRASE?

This is a very important difference and should be kept in mind by all
who read the Bible, not just the serious scholars of the Word. A
translation is the rendering from one language **exactly** into another
language. A paraphrased version, however, is simply attempting to
put before the reader the general thought contained within the word.
Paraphrased editions should thus be avoided by those who truly desire
to know the truth and accuracy of God's Word.

## 8. WHY SHOULD WE MEMORIZE THE NAMES OF THE BOOKS OF THE BIBLE?

Aside from the obvious benefit of having the Word of God hidden in
our hearts, knowing the names of the books in the proper order will
help us to locate certain portions of the Scriptures quickly and easily.
Studying the books of the Bible according to the following grouping
will help you to learn them more easily:

# THE OLD TESTAMENT (39 Books)

## Historical Books (17)

| | |
|---|---|
| Genesis | Ruth |
| Exodus | 1 & 2 Samuel |
| Leviticus | 1 & 2 Kings |
| Numbers | 1 & 2 Chronicles |
| Deuteronomy | Ezra |
| Joshua | Nehemiah |
| Judges | Esther |

## Poetical Books (6)

| | |
|---|---|
| Job | Ecclesiastes |
| Psalms | Song of Solomon |
| Proverbs | Lamentations * |

## Prophetical Books (16)

### *The Major Prophets (4)*

| | |
|---|---|
| Isaiah | Ezekiel |
| Jeremiah | Daniel |

### *The Minor Prophets (12)*

| | | |
|---|---|---|
| Hosea | Jonah | Zephaniah |
| Joel | Micah | Haggai |
| Amos | Nahum | Zechariah |
| Obadiah | Habakkuk | Malachi |

---

* Follows Jeremiah in biblical order.

# THE NEW TESTAMENT (27 Books)

## Historical Books (5)

Matthew          John
Mark             Acts
Luke

## Doctrinal Books (Epistles) (21)

### *The Epistles of Paul (13)*

Romans                   Colossians
1 & 2 Corinthians        1 & 2 Thessalonians
Galatians                1 & 2 Timothy
Ephesians                Titus
Philippians              Philemon

### *The Epistle to the Hebrews (1)*

### *The General Epistles (7)*

James                    1, 2, & 3 John
1 & 2 Peter              Jude

## Prophetic Book (1)

Revelation

NOTE: The Bible was not written originally by chapter and verse. Many of the writings of each biblical book were pieced together from ancient manuscripts. Chapters and verses were inserted by scholars and translators of the Hebrew and Greek scrolls to facilitate their work. Having chapters and verses also tends to make the finding of certain Scriptures easier for us. We must be careful, however, that we do not become "chapter-and-verse oriented," thus taking the Word of God out of context and confusing, or losing, the message of the whole.

# HOME STUDY QUESTIONS: CHAPTER 20

1.  Why should you read the Bible?

2.  What happens when you read the Bible?

3.  Read Appendix A. Write out and memorize the Apostles' Creed, the Lord's Prayer, the Ten Commandments, and the Foundation Stones. (NOTE: This assignment may be stretched out over a longer period of time at the discretion of the teacher.)

4.  In order to help you to memorize the books of the Bible, write them out in order. Be prepared to write them from memory.

# THE NATURE OF GOD

**Chapter 21**

## 1. WHY IS IT IMPORTANT THAT WE UNDERSTAND THE TRUE NATURE OF GOD?

We need to know and understand the true nature of God so that we are not guilty of breaking the first and second commandments by making for ourselves a god in our own image. God has revealed Himself to us in the Bible, and we must receive Him and worship Him on that basis alone.

> *"I am the Lord your God . . . .You shall have no other gods before Me. You shall not make for yourself an idol, or any likeness of what is in heaven above or on the earth beneath or in the water under the earth. You shall not worship them or serve them."*      Ex. 20:2-5a

## 2. WHY IS IT IMPORTANT FOR US TO STUDY THE ATTRIBUTES OR CHARACTERISTICS OF GOD?

It is important for us to study the attributes, or characteristics, of God so that we will have a greater knowledge, understanding, and appreciation for who and what God is and is not. Knowing those things which cause God to be uniquely who He is will keep us from mistakenly ascribing His attributes to anyone or anything else—whether it be false gods (that is, anything outside ourselves which we think will be our salvation) or even Satan himself.

## 3.  WHAT IS AN ATTRIBUTE?

An  attribute is an inherent characteristic of someone  or something;
it is a word describing a quality possessed. When speaking of the
attributes of God, we are certainly meaning more than outward or
assumed characteristics. Actually, "it is difficult to clearly distinguish
between the attributes and the nature of God . . . . these qualities of
God which we call attributes are in reality part of His nature and
essence."[1]

## 4.  WHERE DO WE LEARN ABOUT THE TRUE ATTRIBUTES OF GOD?

We learn about the true attributes of God only by reading the Bible.
In the Bible, which is His Word, God speaks to us about Himself and
thus reveals Himself to us.

## 5.  WHAT ARE THE ATTRIBUTES OF GOD?

For ease of study and understanding, the attributes of God are divided
into two categories.

a.   His personal attributes—those having to do with His nature:

1.   God is **spirit.**

He is not limited by a body; thus He is everywhere at all
times.

*"God is spirit."*                              Jn. 4:24a

*"For a spirit does not have flesh and bones."*
                                                Lk. 24:39

*Now to the King eternal, immortal, invisible, the only God, be honor and glory forever and ever.*

1 Tim. 1:17

## 2. He is **eternal** and **preexistent.**

*Lord, Thou hast been our dwelling place in all generations. Before the mountains were born, or Thou didst give birth to the earth and the world, even from everlasting to everlasting, Thou art God.*

Ps. 90:1,2

Simply put, preexistence means that God existed before the universe, the earth, and man were created. You and I and everything that surrounds us are the direct result of something else. You are the result of your parents' love and desire to have a family. A flower is the result of the planted seed. A building is the result of the architect's design and the builder's labor. Yet God has no beginning. He is not the result of some greater being than Himself. He exists in and of Himself and is the cause for all else to be (Isa. 40:12-26). God always was, God always is, and God always will be. Therefore, He is never going to cease being, He will never leave us, and His eternal plans for us will not be changed by another!

*Before the mountains were created, before the earth was formed, you* ***are*** *God without beginning or end.* Ps. 90:2 TLB

*For by Him all things were created, both in the heavens and on earth, visible and invisible, whether thrones or dominions or rulers or authorities—all things have been created by Him and for Him. And He is before all things, and in Him all things hold together.* Col. 1:16,17

300

Read Isaiah 40:12-26 in The Living Bible.

3.  He is **omniscient,** or **all**-knowing.

God's plans are based on complete knowledge, for He knows
what the outcome of something will be before it happens.
God can never be surprised by sudden emergencies or
unlooked-for developments. God sees the truth about all
things. We can hide the truth from one another but not from
the "only wise God" (Rom. 16:27). Nothing can come to
light after we are saved that He did not already know when
He saved us!

> *O Lord, Thou hast searched me and known me.*
> *Thou dost know when I sit down and when I rise up;*
> *Thou dost understand my thought from afar. Thou*
> *dost scrutinize my path and my lying down, and art*
> *intimately acquainted with all my ways. Even before*
> *there is a word on my tongue, behold, O Lord, Thou*
> *dost know it all.* Ps. 139:1-4

Read also Proverbs 5:21; 15:3; 1 John 3:20.

4.  He is **omnipotent**—He is all-powerful: The Bible declares 58
times that God is the Almighty One, or the Almighty, and this
word is used of **no one** but God. Simply stated, God can do
anything He wants to. Revelation 19:6 says, "Hallelujah! For
the Lord our God, the Almighty, reigns!"

> *"I am the Almighty; obey Me and live as you*
> *should."* Gen. 17:1 TLB

> *"I know that Thou canst do all things, and that*
> *no purpose of Thine can be thwarted."* Job 42:2

301

There is no power stronger than His! Read 1 John 4:4; Hebrews 6:13; 1 Peter 1:5.

His strength is made available to us because He indwells us. Read 2 Corinthians 12:9.

Because He is in us, nothing can overcome us, **not even Satan!** Read 1 John 4:4; Romans 8:31,35-39.

It is here that men err in thinking that Satan and the forces of evil are equal with God in power and that both are struggling for supremacy. In the book of Job (1:9-12) we find that Satan must ask for permission to do his work. The Bible teaches, furthermore, that the forces of evil were broken long ago when Satan was cast out of heaven and were forever vanquished when Christ rose from the dead (Col. 2:15). Satan is doomed, awaiting final judgment, and exists at present only to fit into God's divine purpose for man.

5. God is **sovereign.**

The word *sovereign* means "chief, highest, or supreme." God is the Supreme Being in the universe—there is **none other** in that place. This does not mean, however, that He rules the universe as a dictator, because all of God's attributes are harmonious with one another and act in balance: His power is balanced by His love, mercy, and justice. Nothing is out of God's control. His plans do and will triumph!

> . . . *He who is the blessed and only Sovereign, the King of kings and Lord of lords; who alone possesses immortality and dwells in unapproachable light; whom no man has seen or can see. To Him be honor and eternal dominion!*     1 Tim. 6:15b,16

> *"Remember the former things long past, **for I am God, and there is no other; I am God, and there is no one like Me,** declaring the end from the beginning and from ancient times things which have not been done."*                    Isa. 46:9,10

6. He is **omnipresent.**

He is everywhere all the time. His presence fills the universe. God is in heaven (Ps. 11:4; Eccl. 5:2). God is in the person of His Son Jesus Christ, "for in Christ there is all of God in a human body" (Col. 2:9 TLB). God is present everywhere by His Spirit, "over all and through all and in all" (Eph. 4:6).

> *"Am I a God who is near,"* declares the Lord, *"and not a God far off? Can a man hide himself in hiding places, so I do not see him?"* declares the Lord. *"Do I not fill the heavens and the earth?"* declares the Lord.                    Jer. 23:23,24

Nothing escapes Him, and we can hide nothing from Him (Ps. 139:7-12). On the other hand, this means that we always in all places have access to Him—He is always available to us!

7. He is **immutable**—He is unchanging.

God's nature does not change. Being perfect already, God cannot get better, and being perfect, He cannot get worse. God's character does not change—He is not subject to changes in mood. God's truth does not change (Ps. 119:89,152). God's way of doing things does not change, nor do His purposes change. God's plans are based on perfect (complete) knowledge. Unlike man, who often must change his plans due to lack of foresight, God sees all from start to finish and has planned accordingly. Jesus Christ never changes either, because He is the express image of the Father.

*Jesus Christ is the same yesterday, today, and for-*
*ever.* Heb. 13:8 TLB

*"For I, the Lord, do not change."*
Mal. 3:6a

*Every good thing bestowed and every perfect gift*
*is from above, coming down from the Father of lights,*
**with whom there is no variation,** *or shifting shadow.*
Jas. 1:17

b. His moral attributes—those having to do with His relationship with us:

1. God is **holy.**

This certainly means that God is sinless, but it means much more than that. Just as being healthy means more than not being sick, so holiness is more than the absence of sin—it is a positive, healthy state of **being righteous!**

*"I the Lord your God am holy."* Lev. 19:2

*The Lord is upright; . . . and there is no unright-*
*eousness in Him.* Ps. 92:15

*And this is the message we have heard from Him*
*and announce to you, that God is light, and in Him*
**there is no darkness at all.** 1 Jn. 1:5

We are to be, and by redemption can be, holy as He is: "But like the Holy One who called you, be holy yourselves also in all your behavior" (1 Pet. 1:15). Holiness also means "separateness." God has always wanted a people who would separate themselves, making a difference between what they are and what those are who surround them. Whether we like it or not, holiness is the standard by which we shall be judged because He indwells us (1 Cor. 3:16,17; 6:19).

2. He is **just,** or **righteous.**

Holiness principally concerns the character, nature, or essence of God Himself. Justice or righteousness has more to do with the character expressed in His dealings with man. It means that God is equitable—He is no respecter of persons. He has no double standard and judges men according to the truth He has revealed. He does not play favorites, nor can He be influenced to make decisions which are not in keeping with His Word. When we stand before the judgment seat of Christ, we will receive full justice. Our God is impartial! This is both a comfort to those who have been wronged in life and a warning to those who think they have been getting away with something.

> *"His work is perfect, for all His ways are just; a God of faithfulness and without injustice, righteous and upright is He."* Deut. 32:4

3. He is **faithful.**

You can count on God to do everything He said in His Word that He would do. When we take Him at His word, He will never let us down—we will never be sorry or ashamed for putting our trust in Him.

> *If we are faithless, He remains faithful; for He cannot deny Himself.* 2 Tim. 2:13

> *Faithful is He who calls you, and He also will bring it to pass.* 1 Thess. 5:24

4. He is **compassionate.**

Compassion, like mercy, is a sympathetic understanding of one's problems coupled with the desire to solve them. God not only understands our weaknesses but desires to help us overcome them.

> *He has made His wonders to be remembered; the*
> *Lord is gracious and compassionate.*      Ps. 111:4

5.  He is **good.**

    God's motive is only desiring good things for that which He has created.

    > *The Lord is good to all, and His mercies are over*
    > *all His works.*                          Ps. 145:9

    > *"When you call me good you are calling me God,"*
    > *Jesus replied, "for God alone is truly good."*
    >                                       Matt. 19:17 TLB

6.  God is **truth.**

    He is consistent with Himself—with who and what He is by nature.

    > *May it never be! Rather, let God be found true,*
    > *though every man be found a liar.*        Rom. 3:4

    > *. . . in order that by two unchangeable things, in*
    > *which it is impossible for God to lie, we may have*
    > *strong encouragement, we who have fled for refuge*
    > *in laying hold of the hope set before us.*
    >                                             Heb. 6:18

    > *Jesus said to him, "I am the way, and the truth,*
    > *and the life; no one comes to the Father, but through*
    > *Me."*                                         Jn. 14:6

7. God is **love.**

God does not merely **have** love; He **is** love (1 Jn. 4:8), and therein is a great difference. Because all these attributes are part of God's very essence, what may be said of God can be said of each of His attributes. His love is, therefore:

- ° **Omniscient**—Knowing all, He still loves.
- ° **Omnipresent**—He is with us everywhere.
- ° **Omnipotent**—There is nothing His love cannot overcome.
- ° **Sovereign**—Nothing can separate us from His love.
- ° **Eternal**—It will never end.
- ° **Immutable**—It will never change and it has always been fully developed, etc.

## NOTES

[1]    William Evans, *The Great Doctrines of the Bible* (Chicago: Moody Press, © 1974), p. 28.

## HOME STUDY QUESTIONS:  CHAPTER 21

1. Why is it important for us to be aware of and familiar with the attributes of God?

2. List the attributes of God.

3. With each attribute write a short statement showing the implications of that attribute in your day-to-day life.

# THE MYSTERY OF THE TRIUNE GOD

**Chapter 22**

## 1. WHAT DOES THE BIBLE TEACH US CONCERNING THE MYSTERY OF THE TRIUNE GOD?

The Bible gives us the revelation that there are three persons in one God (Deut. 6:4)—one divine nature and Being—but there are three distinct personalities: the Father, the Son, and the Holy Spirit, all sharing equally in the same nature and majesty of the Godhead.

> *"Hear, O Israel! The Lord is our God, the Lord is one!"*
> Deut. 6:4

> *And Jesus came up and spoke to them, saying, "All authority has been given to Me in heaven and on earth. Go therefore and make disciples of all the nations, baptizing them in the name of the Father and the Son and the Holy Spirit."*
> Matt. 28:18,19

> *"I and the Father are one."*
> Jn. 10:30

> *". . . that they may be one, just as We are one."*
> Jn. 17:22b

> *There is one body and one Spirit, just as also you were called in one hope of your calling; one Lord, one faith, one baptism, one God and Father of all who is over all and through all and in all.*
> Eph. 4:4-6

Read also John 14:7-26 and 17:1-26.

## 2. WHY DO WE REFER TO THIS AS A MYSTERY?

The dictionary defines the word *mystery* as "something not understood, something beyond understanding." This divine revelation of the Triune God—being at the same time God the Father, high **above us** in majesty and glory; God the Son **with us** in the person of Jesus Christ; and God the Holy Spirit dwelling **in us** who believe in Christ—is indeed a mystery to us. It is a mystery not because of some desire on the part of God to purposefully withhold information from us, but because man, with his limited knowledge and experience, is unable to grasp it. It is actually **beyond** his natural ability to understand.

> *"For My thoughts are not your thoughts, neither are your ways My ways," declares the Lord. "For as the heavens are higher than the earth, so are My ways higher than your ways, and My thoughts than your thoughts."*
>
> Isa. 55:8,9

> *. . . which doeth great things past finding out; yea, and wonders without number.* Job 9:10 KJV

God has revealed the fact of His triune nature to us not so much that we might define it and completely understand it, but that we might accept it and enjoy this wonderful revelation of Himself by faith.

> *Now to Him who is able to establish you according to my gospel and the preaching of Jesus Christ, according to the revelation of the mystery which has been kept secret for long ages past, but now is manifested, and by the Scriptures of the prophets, according to the commandment of the eternal God, has been made known to all the nations, leading to obedience of faith.* Rom. 16:25,26

# 3. WHAT ARE THE WORKS THAT DISTINGUISH THE THREE PERSONS IN ONE GOD?

a. God the Father is credited primarily with the work of creation.

> *In the beginning God created the heavens and the earth.* Gen. 1:1

b. God the Son is credited primarily with the work of redemption.

> *But when the fulness of the time came, God sent forth His Son, born of a woman, born under the Law, in order that He might redeem those who were under the Law, that we might receive the adoption as sons.*
> Gal. 4:4,5

NOTE: Jesus Christ, the second person of the Triune Godhead, was preexistent with the Father before all time. Christ existed as the eternal "Word" (Jn. 1:1-5, q.v.) but took on flesh (the doctrine of the incarnation, Jn. 1:14) and was named Jesus (Lk. 1:30-35). This doctrine of the preexistence of Christ is essential and indispensable to the Christian faith!

c. God the Holy Spirit is credited primarily with the work of sanctification.

> *. . . according to the foreknowledge of God the Father, by the sanctifying work of the Spirit.*
> 1 Pet. 1:2

# 4. HOW THEN CAN WE SAY THAT THESE THREE DISTINCT PERSONS ARE ONE?

We can say this because it is a revealed truth which we must accept by faith.

*"Hear, O Israel! The Lord is our God, the Lord is one!"*
Deut. 6:4

*There is one body and one Spirit, just as also you were called in one hope of your calling; one Lord, one faith, one baptism, one God and Father of all who is over all and through all and in all.*
Eph. 4:4-6

God has revealed Himself to us through Jesus Christ and the Holy Spirit.

*Yet for us there is but one God, the Father, from whom are all things, and we exist for Him; and one Lord, Jesus Christ, by whom are all things, and we exist through Him.*
1 Cor. 8:6


## 5.  HAS ANYONE EVER SEEN GOD?

No, apart from the purely spiritual manifestations (or visions) in the Old Testament, man has never seen God. God is Spirit and is therefore invisible to us. God has revealed His divine nature to us in the person of His Son Jesus Christ.

*. . . who alone possesses immortality and dwells in unapproachable light; whom no man has seen or can see.*
1 Tim. 6:16a

*No man has seen God at any time; the only begotten God, who is in the bosom of the Father, He has explained Him.*
Jn. 1:18

*And He is the radiance of His glory and the exact representation of His nature, and upholds all things by the word of His power.*
Heb. 1:3a

NOTE: There are many other mysteries mentioned in the Word of God. These are the mysteries of:

° The kingdom of God (Mk. 4:11).
° The hardness of Israel until the time of the fulness of the Gentiles (Rom. 11:25).
° The revelation of Jesus Christ through the gospel (Rom. 16:25; 1 Cor. 2:7; Eph. 1:9; Col. 4:3; Rev. 10:7).
° The immortalization of the saints (1 Cor. 15:51).
° The Gentiles as being fellow heirs and fellow members of the body of Christ (Eph. 3:3-6).
° The church (Eph. 3:9,10).
° The relationship of Christ to the church (Eph. 5:32).
° Christ in us, our hope of glory (Col. 1:26,27).
° Christ Himself (Col. 2:2).
° Iniquity (2 Thess. 2:7).
° The faith (1 Tim. 3:9).
° The revelation of God (1 Tim. 3:16).
° The seven stars and lampstands (Rev. 1:20).
° Babylon the great, mother of harlots (Rev. 17:5).

## HOME STUDY QUESTIONS: CHAPTER 22

1. What is the mystery of the Triune God?

2. What does the Bible mean when it uses the term *mystery*?

3. Choose one of the other mysteries listed at the end of the chapter, and briefly explain it in your own words.

# HEAVEN: GOD'S ABODE

**Chapter 23**

## This is NOT what heaven is like!

## 1. WHAT DOES THE BIBLE TELL US ABOUT HEAVEN?

a.  The Old Testament tells us that:

1.  God created the heavens.

> *In the beginning God created the heavens and the earth.*　　　　Gen. 1:1

2. They are a testimony to His glory.

> *The heavens are telling of the glory of God.*
>
> Ps. 19:1

3. The Lord traverses the heavens.

> *. . . to Him who rides upon the highest heavens, which are from ancient times.* Ps. 68:33

4. The heavens are His throne.

> *He who sits in the heavens laughs.* Ps. 2:4

> *The Lord is in His holy temple; the Lord's throne is in heaven.* Ps. 11:4

> *"Heaven is My throne, and the earth is My footstool."* Isa. 66:1

5. The Lord hears and answers from heaven.

> *Then David built an altar to the Lord there, and offered burnt offerings and peace offerings. And he called to the Lord and He answered him with fire from heaven on the altar of burnt offering.*
>
> 1 Chr. 21:26

> *Then the Levitical priests arose and blessed the people; and their voice was heard and their prayer came to His holy dwelling place, to heaven.*
>
> 2 Chr. 30:27

b. The New Testament record confirms and establishes the Old.

1. Heaven is God's habitation.

316

> *"But I say to you, make no oath at all, either by heaven, for it is the throne of God."*   Matt. 5:34

> *"Our Father who art in heaven . . . ."*
>   Matt. 6:9

> *"I will also confess him before My Father who is in heaven."*   Matt. 10:32

2.  It is His place of enthronement.

> *"The Most High does not dwell in houses made by human hands; as the prophet says: 'Heaven is My throne, and earth is the footstool of My feet.'"*
>   Acts 7:48,49

> *We have such a high priest, who has taken His seat at the right hand of the throne of the Majesty in the heavens.*   Heb. 8:1

3.  It is the place from which He hears and responds.

> *And this is the confidence which we have before Him, that, if we ask anything according to His will, He hears us. And if we know that He hears us in whatever we ask, we know that we have the requests which we have asked from Him.*   1 Jn. 5:14,15

## 2.  WHERE IS HEAVEN?

The Lord's dwelling place is undoubtedly **up.**

> *And Elijah went **up** by a whirlwind to heaven.*
>   2 Ki. 2:11

> *He was received **up** into heaven.*   Mk. 16:19

*"Men of Galilee, why do you stand looking into the sky? This Jesus, who has been taken up from you into heaven...."*                                    Acts 1:11

Read also Acts 1:2; 1:22; 7:55,56; 2 Corinthians 12:4; Ephesians 4:8; Hebrews 7:26.

## 3.  HOW MANY HEAVENS ARE THERE?

a.  In a general sense, the Scriptures indicate there is more than one heaven.

> *For the **heavens** and the **highest heavens** cannot contain Him.*                                    2 Chr. 2:6

> *Since then we have a great high priest who has passed **through the heavens,** Jesus the Son of God, let us hold fast our confession.*                                    Heb. 4:14

b.  More specifically, there are at least three heavens, because the third heaven is mentioned in 2 Corinthians 12:2, ". . . such a man was caught up to the **third heaven."** The "first heaven" may be our atmosphere; the "second heaven," space; and the "third heaven," God's abode.

c.  Finally, Jesus, when He ascended to the Father, was caught up "far above **all the heavens"** (Eph. 4:10).

## 4.  WHO DWELLS IN HEAVEN?

Before the resurrection of Jesus Christ, heaven was the abode of:

°   God.

°   His angels.

318

° The glorified saints of the Old Testament who had been translated bodily: Enoch (Gen. 5:21-24) and Elijah (2 Ki. 2:11).

° The rest of the Old Testament righteous dead who dwelt in Abraham's Bosom (Lk. 16:19-31). Read also Chapter 11—"The Resurrection of the Dead" from Part One.

With His own resurrection, Jesus fulfilled all that had been foretold and thus opened the "gates of heaven" for all the righteous, including the saints of the Old Testament.

> *And Jesus cried out again with a loud voice, and yielded up His spirit. And behold, the veil of the temple was torn in two from top to bottom, and the earth shook; and the rocks were split, and the tombs were opened; and many bodies of the saints who had fallen asleep **were raised;** and coming out of the tombs after His resurrection **they entered the holy city and appeared to many.*** Matt. 27:50-53

> *Therefore it says, "When He ascended on high, **He led captive a host of captives,** and He gave gifts to men." (Now this expression, "He ascended," what does it mean except that **He also had descended into the lower parts of the earth?** He who descended is Himself also He who ascended far above all the heavens, that He might fill all things.)* Eph. 4:8-10

## 5. WHO INHABITS HEAVEN NOW?

a. God, His angels, and the glorified (translated) saints of the Old Testament.

b. Jesus, who ascended to the Father as He said.

c. The Old Testament saints who had been released from Abraham's Bosom by Jesus and taken up with Him at His ascension. This includes those who were resurrected (that is, reunited with their bodily forms) at the death of Jesus as mentioned in Matthew 27:50-53 above.

d. The New Testament saints who have died from the days of the early church to now. To this number will be added all those New Testament saints who will die and go to be with the Lord from now until Jesus comes (2 Cor. 5:1-4,8; Phil. 1:23; Heb. 12:22,23), including the martyred dead of the Tribulation (Rev. 6:9-11; 14:13).

## 6. WHAT IS THE BELIEVER'S RELATIONSHIP TO HEAVEN NOW?

a. Jesus came from heaven (Lk. 1:26-35; Jn. 1:1,2,11,14; 17:1,5,8, 11-13,16,18).

b. Jesus returned to heaven (Mk. 16:19; Jn. 14:27,28; Acts 1:9; 2:32-36; 7:55; Col. 3:1).

c. Jesus made it possible for us to be there with Him (Jn. 14:2,3; 17:24):

1. **Now,** in the realm of the Spirit.

> *But God, being rich in mercy, because of His great love with which He loved us, even when we were dead in our transgressions, made us alive together with Christ (by grace you have been saved), and raised us up with Him, **and seated us with Him in the heavenly places,** in Christ Jesus.*
>
> Eph. 2:4-6

See also Isaiah 57:15; Colossians 3:1; Ephesians 1:3.

The believer is a heavenly person, citizen of another country, member of a kingdom whose King is enthroned on high, and a stranger and pilgrim on earth.

> *For our citizenship is in heaven, from which also we eagerly wait for a Savior, the Lord Jesus Christ; who will transform the body of our humble state into conformity with the body of His glory.*
>
> Phil. 3:20,21

See also Hebrews 3:1; 1 Peter 2:11; Ephesians 2:19; Colossians 1:13.

2.  And in the **future,** should the time of our death precede the second coming of the Lord Jesus Christ.

As we have already seen, to be absent from the body is to be present with the Lord (2 Cor. 5:1-4,8; etc.). We need to keep in mind, however, that, just as heaven is not to be the permanent abode of the Lord Jesus (He is going to return to the earth to rule and reign!), so it is not to be our permanent abode. When Jesus returns, we, too, shall return to rule and reign with Him! And whether or not it will be any of us, there will be some saints who will not die and go to heaven but will be alive when the "immortalization of the saints" takes place!

> *But we do not want you to be uninformed, brethren, about those who are asleep, that you may not grieve, as do the rest who have no hope. For if we believe that Jesus died and rose again, even so God will **bring with Him those who have fallen asleep in Jesus.** For this we say to you by the word of the Lord, that we who are alive, and remain until the coming of the Lord, shall not precede those who have fallen asleep. For the Lord Himself will descend from heaven with a shout, with the voice of the archangel, and with the trumpet of God; and the*

*dead in Christ shall rise first. Then we who are alive and remain shall be caught up together with them in the clouds to meet the Lord in the air, and thus **we shall always be with the Lord.***

1 Thess. 4:13-17

## 7. WHAT IS THE FUTURE OF HEAVEN?

a. During the 1,000-year reign, Jesus will have returned to earth and many of the saints will come with Him (Zech. 14:4-11; Matt. 19:28; 24:28-31; Jude 14,15; Rev. 19:11-14).

b. After the 1,000 year reign, God will create a **new heaven** and a **new earth,** eliminating the barriers of time and flesh between the two realms and making them one.

*And I saw a new heaven and a new earth; for the first heaven and the first earth passed away, and there is no longer any sea. And I saw the holy city, new Jerusalem, coming down out of heaven from God, made ready as a bride adorned for her husband. And I heard a loud voice from the throne, saying, **"Behold, the tabernacle of God is among men, and He shall dwell among them, and they shall be His people, and God Himself shall be among them."*** Rev. 21:1-3

# HOME STUDY QUESTIONS: CHAPTER 23

1. What is heaven?

2. How many heavens are there? Be specific.

3. Who inhabited heaven before Jesus' resurrection?

4. Who inhabits heaven now?

5. What will heaven's future be?

# ANGELS

**Chapter 24**

## 1. DO ANGELS REALLY EXIST?

Yes, they exist because God's Word says they do!

a.  Jesus clearly taught the existence of angels.

> *"For I say to you, that their angels in heaven continually behold the face of My Father who is in heaven."*
> Matt. 18:10

> *"But of that day or hour no one knows, not even the angels in heaven."*      Mk. 13:32

> *"For whoever is ashamed of Me and My words in this adulterous and sinful generation, the Son of Man will also be ashamed of him when He comes in the glory of His Father with the holy angels."*      Mk. 8:38

> *Now an angel from heaven appeared to Him, strengthening Him.*      Lk. 22:43

> *And He said to him, "Truly, truly, I say to you, you shall see the heavens opened, and the angels of God ascending and descending on the Son of Man."*
> Jn. 1:51

b. Paul and the other apostles also taught the existence of angels.

   1.  Paul:

       . . . *and to give relief to you who are afflicted and to us as well when the Lord Jesus shall be revealed from heaven with His mighty angels in flaming fire.*                      2 Thess. 1:7

   2.  John:

       *And I looked, and I heard the voice of many angels around the throne and the living creatures and the elders; and the number of them was myriads of myriads, and thousands of thousands.*
                                       Rev. 5:11

   3.  Peter:

       . . . *who is at the right hand of God, having gone into heaven, after angels and authorities and powers had been subjected to Him.*          1 Pet. 3:22

   4.  Jude:

       *But Michael the archangel, when he disputed with the devil and argued about the body of Moses, did not dare pronounce against him a railing judgment, but said, "The Lord rebuke you."*
                                       Jude 9

   5.  The writer of Hebrews:

       *But you have come to Mount Zion and to the city of the living God, the heavenly Jerusalem, and to myriads of angels.*                Heb. 12:22

## 2. WHAT ARE ANGELS?

Angels are spirit beings created by God. They are God's messengers (both the Hebrew and Greek words for angel mean "messenger") whose chief business it is to carry out His orders in the world. He has given them an ambassadorial charge. He has designated and empowered them as holy deputies to perform works of righteousness.

> *Are they not all ministering spirits, sent out to render service for the sake of those who will inherit salvation?*
> Heb. 1:14

## 3. WHAT IS THEIR NATURE?

a. They are created beings, not spirits of the departed, nor glorified human beings, nor visitors from outer space.

> *For by Him all things were created, both in the heavens and on earth, visible and invisible, whether thrones or dominions or rulers or authorities* [angelic orders]—*all things have been created by Him and for Him.*
> Col. 1:16

Read also Nehemiah 9:6 and Hebrews 12:22,23.

b. Because they are created, **not begotten** (see Hebrews 1:4-14 for the difference), they are completely dependent upon God for their continued existence. **They are not independent beings.** This is **especially** important for us to keep in mind when studying Chapter 25—"The Creation of the World and the Fall of Lucifer and His Angels."

c. They are spiritual beings.

> *. . . who maketh His angels spirits; His ministers a flaming fire.*
> Ps. 104:4 KJV

327

As such, they are essentially **invisible** (Col. 1:16). This does not mean, however, that they are imperceptible or physically undetectable. Air and sound are both also invisible, yet we see the effects of their presence all around us.

Although angels are invisible spirit beings, they often become visible (2 Ki. 6:17; Matt. 1:20; Lk. 1:26; Jn. 20:12), even appearing in human form (Gen. 18; 19:1-22; Dan. 8:15,16; Dan. 10:16,18; Acts 12:7-11). On those occasions when they do appear in the bodily form of men, those corporeal forms are merely "assumed bodies," that is, bodies that are not truly organic.

## 4. WHAT ARE THE CHARACTERISTICS OF ANGELS?

a. They speak to God, to one another, and to man. Indeed, they have their own language (1 Cor. 13:1; 2 Cor. 12:4).

b. They have emotions (Lk. 15:7,10).

c. They are higher than man and therefore more intelligent, but they are **not** omniscient (1 Pet. 1:12; Matt. 24:36). They are more powerful (2 Pet. 2:11; Ps. 103:20; Isa. 37:36), but they are **not** omnipotent (Dan. 10:12,13); rather, their power is delegated. They are the angels of **His** might (2 Thess. 1:7), the ministers through whom God's might is manifested.

d. They sing (Job 38:1-7).

e. They are often portrayed as being surrounded with dazzling light, thus signifying their heavenly origin and their great spirituality.

f. They have wills and, therefore, the ability to make decisions. They have the freedom to obey or disobey God (for example, Lucifer and the "fallen" angels).

g.   They are neither male nor female; they do not marry nor procreate (Matt. 22:30).

h.   They are organized, having ranks and orders. Though some see the ranking of celestial powers as conjectural, it seems to follow this pattern: archangels, angels, seraphim, cherubim, principalities, authorities, powers, thrones, mights and dominions (Col. 1:16; Rom. 8:38; 1 Pet. 3:22).

NOTE: The **only** archangel mentioned in the Scripture is Michael, whose name means "Who is like God?" In Daniel 12:1, he is referred to as a great prince. He is also mentioned by name in Jude 9 and Revelation 12:7 and in general terms in 1 Thessalonians 4:16. Although the Apocryphal books name seven archangels, including Michael, Gabriel (Gabriel is mentioned in Luke 1:11-19,26 as an angel sent from God to Zacharias and Mary, but he is not said to be an archangel), Raphael, Uriel, and Jermiel, these books are not a part of the scriptural canon and therefore cannot be accepted as authoritative.

## 5.   HOW MANY ANGELS ARE THERE?

Moses spoke of 10,000 in Deuteronomy 33:2, and Psalm 68:17 tells us that they are "myriads, thousands upon thousands" (literally, twice 10,000). Jesus, in Matthew 26:53, stated that He could summon twelve legions (12 times 6,000) and more to come to His rescue immediately. There are a number of Scriptures which simply refer to their plurality (Matt. 4:11; 13:36-42,49; 16:27; 18:10; 24:31; 25:31; Lk. 2:13—to name just a few), and Hebrews 12:22 KJV refers to an "innumerable company" of angels.

## 6.  WHAT DO ANGELS DO?

Angels have both a heavenly ministry and an earthly ministry.

a.  Concerning their heavenly ministry:

1.  They witnessed the creation of the world (Job 38:1-7).

2.  They praise and worship God (Ps. 103:20; 148:2; Isa. 6:2,3; Rev. 5:11,12; 7:11).

3.  They serve God, as is apparent in the many references to the "angel of the Lord" and the numerous instances of angels working in cooperation with and on behalf of the Lord.

b.  Concerning their earthly ministry:

1.  They bring the word of the Lord (Gen. 16:7-13;  Dan. 8:16; 9:21,22; Acts 8:26; 10:3-7,22; 11:13; 27:23,24).

2.  They minister to the righteous (Gen. 24:7,40; Ex. 32:34;  Acts 5:19; 12:7-10). They ministered to Jesus (Matt. 4:11; Lk. 22:43).

3.  They guard the elect dead and usher them safely to their destination (Lk. 16:22). Just as they guarded Christ's tomb (Jn. 20:11,12), and as Michael guarded the body of Moses (Jude 9), and as the angels of the Lord safely ushered Lazarus to the bosom of Abraham (Lk. 16:22), so, too, will an angel of the Lord see us safely through to the presence of the Lord at our time of departure. This should be particularly reassuring to us when we stop to realize that Satan is the "prince of the power of the air" and his demonic forces are set to hinder the progress of the saints, even at their death.

4. They are involved in the administration of the judgments of God against the unrighteous, especially in the last days (Read Matthew 13:36-42,49; 16:27; Mark 8:38; 13:27; Luke 9:26; 2 Thessalonians 1:7; Acts 12:23; Revelation 5:2; 7:1,2; etc., throughout Revelation.)

5. They are witnesses to the wisdom and glory of God as it is manifested in and through the church.

> . . . *in order that the manifold wisdom of God might now be made known through the church to the rulers and the authorities in the heavenly places.*
>
> Eph. 3:10

6. They will accompany Christ at His second coming (Matt. 25:31; 2 Thess. 1:7,8).

Generally speaking, to the angels has been committed the administration of the affairs that are material to the senses, such as, showing Hagar the fountain; releasing Peter from the chains and opening the prison doors; and feeding, strengthening, and defending the children of God throughout the Old and New Testaments alike. To the Holy Spirit more particularly has been committed the task of imparting truth concerning spiritual matters.

## 7. ARE THERE GUARDIAN ANGELS?

It is not perfectly clear from the teachings of the Scriptures whether or not there are angels who are specifically charged with the care of individuals. It certainly seems to be implied in such Scriptures as "He will give His angels charge concerning you, to guard you in all your ways" (Ps. 91:11); and "their angels in heaven continually behold the face of My Father who is in heaven" (Matt. 18:10). At any rate, it is definitely in keeping with their overall purpose and ministry, and it has long been believed by the church to be so.

## 8. HOW SHOULD WE REACT TO ANGELS?

a.  We should first of all believe in them, because their reality is so clearly set forth in the Word of God and their ministry is needed as much today as it ever was.

b.  We should not be afraid of them (Matt. 28:1,5; Lk. 1:13,30).

c.  We should respect and, when it is required, obey them (Matt. 1:20,24; 2:13-15,19-21; Lk. 1:13,63; 2:10,11,15,21; Acts 5:19-21; 8:26,27; 10:3,5,7,8; 12:8,9).

d.  However, we are not to worship them (Col. 2:18; Rev. 22:8,9).

## HOME STUDY QUESTIONS: CHAPTER 24

1.  What are angels?

2.  What are the characteristics of angels?

3.  Describe in your own words the ministry of angels.

4.  Go back through the chapter, and where Scripture references only are given, read those portions in your Bible thoroughly.

# THE CREATION OF THE WORLD AND
# THE FALL OF LUCIFER AND HIS ANGELS

**Chapter 25**

## 1. WHEN DID GOD CREATE THE HEAVENS AND THE EARTH?

Genesis 1:1 tells us that "in the beginning God created the heavens and the earth." We are not told anywhere in the Bible just when this "beginning" was, but there are many scientific estimates available to us, should we care to avail ourselves of them, and almost any one of them could be right. We are not concerned here with the technical aspects of the creation of the world and the universe, but only with the fact of their having been brought into being by an Almighty Creator.

## 2. HOW WERE THE HEAVENS AND EARTH CREATED?

The heavens and the earth were created (according to the record of Gen. 1:1 to 2:4) by the spoken Word of God. The creation and organization of the heavens and the creation of the earth begin with the utterance of the words, **"Then God said, 'let there be . . . . '"**

*Then God said, "Let there be light"; and there was light.*
Gen. 1:3

*Then God said, "Let there be an expanse in the midst of the waters, and let it separate the waters from the waters."*
Gen. 1:6

> *Then God said, "Let the waters below the heavens be gathered into one place, and let the dry land appear"; and it was so.*　　　　　　　　　　　　　　　　Gen. 1:9

## 3. HOW LONG DID THE CREATION OF THE EARTH TAKE?

It took God six days to create the earth.

> *And God saw all that He had made, and behold, it was very good. And there was evening and there was morning, the sixth day. Thus the heavens and the earth were completed, and all their hosts. And by the seventh day God completed His work which He had done; and He rested on the seventh day from all His work which He had done.*
> 　　　　　　　　　　　　　　　　Gen. 1:31-2:2

## 4. WHY DID GOD CREATE THE EARTH?

God created the earth for the sake of those who would inhabit it.

> *Then God said, "Let Us make man in Our image, according to Our likeness; and let them rule over the fish of the sea and over the birds of the sky and over the cattle and over all the earth . . . ." And God created man in His own image, in the image of God He created him; male and female He created them. And God blessed them; and God said to them, "Be fruitful and multiply, and fill the earth, and subdue it; and rule over the fish of the sea and over the birds of the sky, and over every living thing that moves on the earth."*
> 　　　　　　　　　　　　　　　　Gen. 1:26-28

## 5. WHAT WAS THE EARTH LIKE?

This original creative work of God which brought the heavens and the earth into being was a completed and finished work. The prophet Isaiah gives us a further glimpse of this pristine creation.

> *For thus says the Lord Who created the heavens, God Himself Who formed the earth and made it, Who established it and **created it not a worthless waste;** He formed it **to be inhabited** . . . .*                    Isa. 45:18 AMP

Thus the earth was originally created as a beautiful, well-ordered home for those who were to inhabit it. Although as Christians we must reject out of hand any concept at all of prehistoric man (this will be discussed further in the next chapter), we do have the fossil records of dinosaurs and other fascinatingly beautiful inhabitants of this first world.

## 6. WHO WAS LUCIFER?

Lucifer, who is referred to by that name in Isaiah 14:12 KJV, was the most beautiful of all heaven's angelic host. The Bible refers to him as "the anointed cherub who covers" because God had anointed him to be over the other angels and to lead them in their worship and adoration of God.

> *"You were the anointed cherub who covers, and I placed you there. You were on the holy mountain of God; you walked in the midst of the stones of fire."*                    Ezk. 28:14

## 7. WHAT WAS LUCIFER'S APPEARANCE?

Apparently, Lucifer was a magnificent creation. Although Lucifer was an angel and therefore a spirit being, the Bible employs this graphically beautiful illustration of his appearance:

335

*"You had the seal of perfection, full of wisdom and perfect in beauty. You were in Eden, the garden of God; every precious stone was your covering: the ruby, the topaz, and the diamond; the beryl, the onyx, and the jasper; the lapis lazuli, the turquoise, and the emerald; and the gold, the workmanship of your settings and sockets, was in you. On the day that you were created they were prepared."*

Ezk. 28:12,13

## 8. WAS LUCIFER FAITHFUL TO GOD?

No. Although the Bible tells us that he was "blameless in [his] ways from the day [he] was created" (Ezk. 28:15), there came a day when Lucifer began to covet the adoration that was ascending up to God from the angelic host. In Isaiah 14:13,14 we see the five rebellious "I Wills" of Lucifer:

*"But you said in your heart, 'I will ascend to heaven; I will raise my throne above the stars of God, and I will sit on the mount of assembly in the recesses of the north. I will ascend above the heights of the clouds; I will make myself like the Most High.'"*

## 9. WHAT WAS THE RESULT OF LUCIFER'S PRIDE AND REBELLION?

Because of Lucifer's pride and rebellion, he was cast out of the heaven of God's presence and into the realm of the lower heavens and the earth. It is for this reason that he is referred to as the "prince of the power of the air" (Eph. 2:2) and the "god of this world" (2 Cor. 4:4).

*"You were blameless in your ways from the day you were created, until unrighteousness was found in you. By the abundance of your trade you were internally filled with violence, and you sinned; therefore I have cast you as profane*

*from the mountain of God. And I have destroyed you, O covering cherub, from the midst of the stones of fire. Your heart was lifted up because of your beauty; you corrupted your wisdom by reason of your splendor. I cast you to the ground; I put you before kings, that they may see you. By the multitude of your iniquities, in the unrighteousness of your trade, you profaned your sanctuaries. Therefore I have brought fire from the midst of you; it has consumed you, and I have turned you to ashes on the earth."* Ezk. 28:15-18

*How art thou fallen from heaven, O Lucifer, son of the morning! how art thou cut down to the ground.*
Isa. 14:12 KJV

## 10. WHO FELL FROM HEAVEN WITH LUCIFER?

When Lucifer was cast out of heaven, he took with him many thousands of angels (perhaps as many as a third of all the angels in heaven—Rev. 12:4), all those whom he had persuaded to join him in his rebellion. These fallen angels are referred to in the Bible as demons.

*Put on the full armor of God, that you may be able to stand firm against the schemes of the devil. For our struggle is not against flesh and blood, but against the rulers, against the powers, against the world forces of this darkness, against the spiritual forces of wickedness in the heavenly places.*
Eph. 6:11,12

*And angels who did not keep their own domain, but abandoned their proper abode, He has kept in eternal bonds under darkness for the judgment of the great day.* Jude 6

*"And these signs will accompany those who have believed: in My name they will cast out demons, they will speak with new tongues."* Mk. 16:17

337

## 11. WHERE IS LUCIFER NOW?

Lucifer, or Satan, and his demons have been given, for a period of time, authority over the earth (especially the world system) and its atmosphere.

> . . . in whose case the **god of this world** has blinded the minds of the unbelieving. 2 Cor. 4:4a

> . . . in which you formerly walked according to the course of this world, according to the **prince of the power of the air, of the spirit** that is now working in the sons of disobedience.
> Eph. 2:2

It is even possible for Satan and his demonic host to make an appearance before the presence of God to accuse the saints (Job 1:6-12; 2:1-7; Rev. 12:10).

## 12. WHAT DO LUCIFER AND HIS DEMONS DO?

a. They rule over the world system (Matt. 4:8,9; 2 Cor. 4:4).

> . . . in which you formerly walked according to the **course of this world,** according to the prince of the power of the air, of the spirit that is now working in the sons of disobedience.
> Eph. 2:2

b. They rule the earth's atmosphere in the sense of hindering the spiritual life and progress of the saints. It was in this way that the angel of the Lord was hindered from reaching Daniel for twenty-one days, finally breaking through only due to the intervention of the archangel Michael. The "prince of the kingdom of Persia" referred to in Daniel 10:13 is the ruling demon of that country.

c. They wage spiritual warfare against the saints (2 Cor. 10:4,5 and Chapter 35—"Spiritual Warfare").

> *Put on the full armor of God, that you may be able
> to stand firm against the schemes of the devil. For our
> struggle is not against flesh and blood, but against the
> rulers, against the powers, against the world forces of this
> darkness, against the spiritual forces of wickedness in the
> heavenly places.* Eph. 6:11,12

d. They cause the church to be infiltrated with deception and demonic doctrines.

> *But the Spirit explicitly says that in later times some
> will fall away from the faith, paying attention to deceitful
> spirits and doctrines of demons.* 1 Tim. 4:1

e. They disguise themselves as the servants and ministers of righteousness, thus beguiling the unstable souls who are not equipped with the truth of the Word of God.

> *For such men are false apostles, deceitful workers,
> disguising themselves as apostles of Christ. And no
> wonder, for even Satan disguises himself as an angel of
> light. Therefore it is not surprising if his servants also
> disguise themselves as servants of righteousness; whose
> end shall be according to their deeds.*
> 2 Cor. 11:13-15

f. Remember, these fallen creatures were once angels of light and, as such, possessed all the characteristics and faculties of that order. They are stronger than men, they have higher intellects than men, and they, too, are organized, with Satan at their head. Just as angels delight in doing the will of the heavenly Father in ministering to the needs of the saints, so, too, demons delight in doing the will of their "father the devil" in hindering the way of the saints.

## 13. IS LUCIFER, THEN, AS STRONG AND POWERFUL AS GOD?

No! We must remember that Lucifer was created to be the "anointed cherub who covers," and is therefore a created being, dependent upon God, just as is the rest of creation. It was ancient Greek philosophy that began to present Satan as being the "dark side of God"—an equal, but malevolent force. This is not true! Satan and his kingdom of darkness are completely under God's authority. A good example is found in Job, Chapters 1 and 2, where Satan had to ask God's permission before testing Job.

Satan has already been judged by the death and resurrection of Jesus Christ, and every time we stand upon that reality, Satan loses.

> *And the seventy returned with joy, saying, "Lord, even the demons are subject to us in Your name." And He said to them, "I was watching Satan fall from heaven like lightning."*
> Lk. 10:17,18

Remember:

> *You are from God, little children, and have overcome them; because **greater is He who is in you** than he who is in the world.*
> 1 Jn. 4:4

## 14. WHAT WILL BE LUCIFER'S END?

As we have already seen, Satan and his demon forces have been defeated by the power of the cross of Jesus Christ—His shed blood—and the power of His Holy Spirit. Revelation 12, however, tells us of a time yet to come when Michael the archangel and his angels will wage a final warfare with Satan and his angels, forever driving them out of even the lowest of the heavens. At this time, the "accuser of the brethren" will be at last cast from the heavenlies down to the earth, where he will go about "having great wrath, knowing that he has only a short time" left before the final judgment of God renders him powerless (Rev. 12:7-12).

At Jesus' return, Satan will be bound and thrown into a "bottomless pit," where he will be kept until after the 1,000-year reign of Christ is fulfilled. At that time he will be released for a season, but at the "great white throne" judgment, he will be condemned eternally to "the lake of fire" (Rev. 20:1-3,7-15).

## HOME STUDY QUESTIONS:  CHAPTER 25

1.  What was the earth like in its original creation?

2.  What event probably caused that original creation to be so dramatically changed?

3.  Who is Lucifer?

4.  Describe briefly in your own words the nature of Lucifer's sin and its disastrous effects.

5.  Where is Lucifer now?

6.  When will Lucifer's final judgment take place?

# THE CREATION AND MAN

**Chapter 26**

## 1. HOW DID GOD CREATE ANIMAL LIFE?

All types of animal life were formed from the dust of the ground.

> *And out of the ground the Lord God formed every beast of the field and every bird of the sky.*　　　Gen. 2:19

## 2. WHAT IS THE THEORY OF EVOLUTION?

It is the **theory** that life on earth was a matter of chance, not of divine will; that animals and man just developed, rather than having been created with a specific purpose in mind; and that this development took place over centuries of time and was the result of various mixtures of energy and matter. Furthermore, these developmental changes, or mutations, in the species are the result of coincidental circumstances thus having brought about our present world.

## 3. IS THE THEORY OF EVOLUTION COMPATIBLE WITH GOD'S WORD?

Absolutely not. Evolution is not only still a theory, but it is an unprovable hypothesis! The Bible contains a record of truth inspired by God. This is what the Word of God has to say:

° In the beginning God created all things: matter and energy, things visible and invisible.

> *For by Him **all things were created,** both in the heavens and on earth, visible and invisible . . . **all things have been created** by Him and for Him.*   Col. 1:16

° Out of this created energy and matter, God Himself created both plant and animal life.

> *And out of the ground the **Lord God formed every beast** of the field and **every bird** of the sky.*
> Gen. 2:19

° God created each form of animal life after its own kind.

> *Then God said, "Let the earth bring forth living creatures **after their kind:** cattle and creeping things and beasts of the earth **after their kind"**; and it was so. And God made the beasts of the earth **after their kind,** and the cattle **after their kind,** and everything that creeps on the ground **after its kind;** and God saw that it was good.*
> Gen. 1:24,25

° Man is not in any way an evolutionary development of some part of the animal family. Just as each form of animal life was created **after its own kind,** so also was man created **after his kind: God!**

> *Then* [after having created all the above] *God said, "Let Us make man in **Our image,** according to **Our likeness** . . . ." And God created man **in His own image,** in the image of God He created him; male and female **He created them.***
> Gen. 1:26,27

# 4. HOW WAS MAN CREATED?

Man was created in the image and likeness of God.

> Then God said, "Let **Us** make man in **Our** image, according to **Our likeness;** and let them rule over the fish of the sea and over the birds of the sky and over the cattle and over all the earth . . ." And God created man in His own image, in the image of God He created him; male and female He created them.                                Gen. 1:26,27

> For in the image of God He made man.        Gen. 9:6b

# 5. WHAT DOES IT MEAN TO SAY THAT MAN WAS CREATED IN THE IMAGE OF GOD?

That man was made in the image and likeness of God is fundamental in all God's dealings with man (1 Cor. 11:7; Eph. 4:21-24; Col. 3:10; Jas. 3:9). Here are some of the implications of that doctrine:

a. The image of God does not denote physical likeness. God is Spirit; He does not have physical parts and passions as a man does. What this does mean, therefore, is that man, unlike the animals, was given, in addition to a body and a soul, a spirit (1 Thess. 5:23), which was his link to God. Because God is Spirit, the breath of life which God breathed into Adam's nostrils in the day He created him was spirit life, thus creating within man a spirit which would be capable of communion and fellowship with God. This union with God **in spirit** was the glory of man. It was his means of power over all created things. Man, by means of this life-giving communion with God, could live forever.

> Then the Lord God formed man of dust from the ground, and breathed into his nostrils the breath of life; and man became a living being.        Gen. 2:7

> *It is the spirit in a man, the breath of the Almighty*
> *which makes him intelligent.* Job 32:8 TLB

b. The original man was endowed with intellectual faculties. He had sufficient intelligence to give names to the animals as they were brought before him (Gen. 2:19,20). Adam had not only the power of speech, but the power of thought and reasoning as well, so that he could put thoughts and words together. What a different picture from that which the evolutionists would have us to believe. This is no undeveloped savage groping his way towards articulate speech by imitating the sounds of animals!

c. The original man possessed moral and spiritual faculties. Adam had power to resist evil and choose good in the moral test found in Genesis 3. Sin was something he could choose or reject—it was a volitional matter. Again, we can see from this that man's original state was not one of savagery. As a matter of fact, it is much more probable that man has actually been degraded because of sin.

## 6. HOW WAS WOMAN CREATED?

Woman was created from one of Adam's ribs which God took from his side.

> *So the Lord God caused a deep sleep to fall upon the*
> *man, and he slept; then He took one of his ribs, and closed*
> *up the flesh at that place. And the Lord God fashioned into*
> *a woman the rib which He had taken from the man, and*
> *brought her to the man.* Gen. 2:21,22

## 7. WHY WAS WOMAN CREATED?

a. Man alone is not the complete representation of the Godhead. Man and woman together completely express all that is to be found in the nature of God.

b.   It was not good for man to be alone.

> *But for Adam there was not found a **helper suitable**
> **for him.***          Gen. 2:20

> *Then the Lord God said, "It is not good for the man
> to be alone; I will make him a **helper suitable for him.**"*
>          Gen. 2:18

> *And the man [Adam] said, "This is now bone of my
> bones, and flesh of my flesh; she shall be called Woman,
> because she was taken out of Man."*          Gen. 2:23

## 8.   WHERE DID ADAM AND EVE LIVE?

They lived in the garden of Eden.

> *And the Lord God planted a garden toward the east, in
> Eden; and there He placed the man whom He had formed.
> And out of the ground the Lord God caused to grow every
> tree that is pleasing to the sight and good for food; the tree
> of life also in the midst of the garden, and the tree of the
> knowledge of good and evil.*          Gen. 2:8,9

## 9.   WHAT WERE THEY TO DO IN THE GARDEN OF EDEN?

a.   They were to enjoy the presence of God.

> *And they heard the sound of the Lord God walking
> in the garden in the cool of the day . . . . Then the Lord
> God called to the man, and said to him, "Where are
> you?"*          Gen. 3:8a,9

347

b.  They were to enjoy His abundant provision for them.

> *Then God said, "Behold, I have given you every plant yielding seed that is on the surface of all the earth, and every tree which has fruit yielding seed; it shall be food for you."*  Gen. 1:29

> *And out of the ground the Lord God caused to grow every tree that is pleasing to the sight and good for food; the tree of life also in the midst of the garden, and the tree of the knowledge of good and evil.*  Gen. 2:9

c.  They were to cultivate the garden.

> *Then the Lord God took the man and put him into the garden of Eden to cultivate it and keep it.*
> Gen. 2:15

d.  They were to rule over God's creation.

> *Then God said, "Let Us make man in Our image, according to Our likeness; and **let them rule** over the fish of the sea and over the birds of the sky and over the cattle and over **all the earth . . . ."** And God created man in His own image, in the image of God He created him; male and female He created them.*  Gen. 1:26,27

e.  Adam was to name all the animals.

> *And out of the ground the Lord God formed every beast of the field and every bird of the sky, and brought them to the man to see what he would call them; and whatever the man called a living creature, that was its name.*  Gen. 2:19

f. They were to live together happily, enjoying one another and obeying God's command to be fruitful and to multiply.

> *And God blessed them; and God said to them, "Be fruitful and multiply, and fill the earth, and subdue it."*
>
> Gen. 1:28a

> *For this cause a man shall leave his father and his mother, and shall cleave to his wife; and they shall become one flesh. And the man and his wife were both naked and were not ashamed.*          Gen. 2:24,25

## WHAT CAUSED THIS IDYLLIC SITUATION TO CHANGE?

> *Now the serpent was more crafty than any beast of the field which the Lord God had made. And he said to the woman, "Indeed, has God said, 'You shall not eat from any tree of the garden'?" And the woman said to the serpent, "From the fruit of the trees of the garden we may eat; but from the fruit of the tree which is in the middle of the garden, God has said, 'You shall not eat from it or touch it, lest you die.'" And the serpent said to the woman, "You surely shall not die! For God knows that in the day you eat from it your eyes will be opened, and you will be like God, knowing good and evil." When the woman saw that the tree was good for food, and that it was a delight to the eyes, and that the tree was desirable to make one wise, she took from its fruit and ate; and she gave also to her husband with her, and he ate. Then the eyes of both of them were opened, and they knew that they were naked; and they sewed fig leaves together and made themselves loin coverings.*          Gen. 3:1-7

Once again, Satan entered the picture. It was with great concern that he witnessed the restoration of the heavens and the earth, the setting of the stage for someone who would take his place in doing the will of the Father and glorifying God alone. The entrance of man was a threat to Satan, but when he saw that man had also been given a freedom of choice to obey or disobey God, then he began to plot man's downfall. He would entice man into committing a sin like his own sin of rebellion against God. He accomplished this by deceiving the woman and thereby causing her to rebel against the commandment of God. She, in turn, caused Adam to sin, and as a result, death spread to all men. But in the midst of defeat, when Adam had been outdone by the craftiness of Satan, God revealed His plan to redeem man, promising to send a Redeemer (Gen. 3:15) who would once and for all crush Satan, his sin, and the death it spread (Heb. 2:14-17).

It is no wonder, then, that all of Satan's energies are devoted to blinding us to the glorious gospel of Jesus Christ and the abundant life He can and will give us today and forever.

> *And even if our gospel is veiled, it is veiled to those who are perishing, in whose case the god of this world has blinded the minds of the unbelieving, that they might not see the light of the gospel of the glory of Christ, who is the image of God.*　　　　　2 Cor. 4:3,4

## 11.　WHAT WAS THE RESULT OF ADAM'S SIN?

a.　The results of the Fall concerning our first parents, Adam and Eve, are as follows:

　　1.　The ground was cursed, so that henceforth it would not yield its fruits willingly (Gen. 3:17).

　　2.　Sorrow and pain to the woman in childbearing, and subjection of the woman to the man (Gen. 3:16).

　　3.　Exhausting physical labor in order to subsist (Gen. 3:19). Work is not the curse of sin—Adam and Eve cultivated and kept the garden before their sin. Rather, vanity and exhausting toil and labor are the fruits of sin.

4. Physical and spiritual death (Gen. 3:19,22; 5:5; Rom. 5:12).

5. In addition to all this, they became afraid of God and felt great shame because of their sin. Finally, they were expelled from the garden (Gen. 3:8-11,22-24).

b. Concerning the rest of mankind:

1. All men, regardless of class or condition, are sinners. There may be a difference in the degree of sin, but not in the fact of sin. Both Jew and Gentile have missed the mark, and all men have failed to attain to God's standard of righteousness (Ps. 14; Isa. 53:6).

> *What then? Are we better than they? Not at all; for we have already charged that both Jews and Greeks are all under sin . . . .*
> *. . . for all have sinned and fall short of the glory of God.* Rom. 3:9,23

2. This universal sinful condition is because of the sin of Adam.

> *Therefore, just as through one man sin entered into the world, and death through sin, and so death spread to all men, because all sinned . . . .*
> *For if by the transgression of the one, death reigned through the one, much more those who receive the abundance of grace and of the gift of righteousness will reign in life through the One, Jesus Christ.* Rom. 5:12,17

3. The entire world is under condemnation, curse, and the wrath of God (Gal. 3:10; Eph. 2:3).

> *. . . that every mouth may be stopped, and all the world may become guilty before God.*
> Rom. 3:19 KJV

4.  Unregenerate men are not the sons of God, but of the devil.

> *"You are of your father the devil, and you want to do the desires of your father."*　　Jn. 8:44

> *And you were dead in your trespasses and sins, in which you formerly walked according to the course of this world, according to the prince of the power of the air, of the spirit that is now working in **the sons of disobedience**. Among them we too . . . were **by nature children of wrath,** even as the rest.*
> 　　　　　　　　　　　　　　　　　Eph. 2:1-3

5.  Therefore, the whole race of men is in helpless captivity to sin and Satan. Read Romans 7; John 8:31-36; Ephesians 2:3.

6.  The entire nature of man—mentally, morally, spiritually, and physically—is sadly affected by sin. The **understanding** is darkened (Eph. 4:18; 1 Cor. 2:14); the **heart** is deceitful and wicked (Jer. 17:9,10); the **mind and conscience** are defiled (Gen. 6:5; Tit. 1:15); the **flesh and spirit** are defiled (2 Cor. 7:1); the **will** is enfeebled (Rom. 7:18); and man is completely destitute of any godlike qualities which meet the requirements of His holiness (Rom. 7:18).

This does not mean that there is a total absence of conscience (Rom. 2:15), nor of all moral qualities (Mk. 10:19-21). Neither does it mean that all men are prone to every kind of sin. What it does mean, however, is that man is, on his own, completely incapable of offering true love to God which is the all-absorbing commandment of the Law (Jn. 5:42). Furthermore, the natural man has an aversion to God (Rom. 8:7) and is incapable of finding the wherewithal within himself to pull himself out of the ever-deepening spiral of sin (Rom. 7:18,23).

The answer to man's dilemma is to be found in the atoning work of Jesus Christ as accomplished by the shedding of His blood upon the cross. See Part One, Chapters 2, 3, and 4.

## HOME STUDY QUESTIONS: CHAPTER 26

1. Why did God create the earth?

2. In your own words, briefly explain why the "theory" of evolution is a total myth and incompatible with the Christian faith.

3. What was the result of Adam's sin (concerning both Eve and himself and mankind)?

# THE KINGDOM OF GOD

**Chapter 27**

> *"The Law and the Prophets were proclaimed until John;*
> *since then the **gospel of the kingdom of God is preached,** and*
> *everyone is forcing his way into it."*      Lk. 16:16

The gospel of the kingdom of God is one of the most misunderstood and neglected concepts of the Word of God. First of all, there are many, especially among the more traditional, denominational churches, who consider themselves to be Christians, but who have merely adopted the "Christian ethic" as a good way of life. They may be sincere and may even, in some cases, appear to be living more moral lives than many true believers, but they are attempting to follow the teachings of Christ without having truly repented of their sin and without having accepted new life by His Spirit. Secondly, even among many of those who have believed by repenting of their sins and accepting the gift of eternal life from Jesus Christ as Savior, there is a tendency to limit the gospel to that basic work of salvation. Jesus did not come into this world and die upon the cross just to bring man a better ethic by which to live; neither did He come merely to bring us forgiveness of our sins and provide us with the gift of eternal life. The New Testament is more than the gospel of the cross—of salvation by the blood of Christ—it is the **gospel of the kingdom of God!** Jesus came preaching the gospel of the kingdom: His kingdom, with Himself as absolute Lord, and ourselves as His subjects. The entire New Testament is the fulfillment, through the words of Jesus and His apostles, of the Old Testament promise of the kingdom of God.

*For a child will be born to us, a son will be given to us; and the government will rest on His shoulders; and His name will be called Wonderful Counselor, Mighty God, Eternal Father, Prince of Peace. There will be no end to the increase of His government or of peace, on the throne of David and over his kingdom, to establish it and to uphold it with justice and righteousness from then on and forevermore. The zeal of the Lord of hosts will accomplish this.* Isa. 9:6,7

## 1. WHAT IS THE KINGDOM OF GOD?

The kingdom of God (also referred to in the Bible as the kingdom of heaven) is that realm where God, through His Son Jesus Christ, is the absolute King and where His authority alone prevails. Just as any citizen is obliged to obey the laws of his country or else suffer the consequences, so also must we obey the laws of Christ and follow the principles of His kingdom if we are to live in it and eventually inherit our eternal place in it. The kingdom, therefore, consists of those who do the will of the Father—and this, not on the basis of convenience, but on the basis of a total, and unwavering, lifetime of obedience.

> *"Not everyone who says to Me, 'Lord, Lord,' will enter the kingdom of heaven; but he who does the will of My Father who is in heaven."* Matt. 7:21

> *Peter, an apostle of Jesus Christ, to those . . . who are chosen according to the foreknowledge of God the Father, by the sanctifying work of the Spirit, that you may obey Jesus Christ.* 1 Pet. 1:1,2

## 2. WHERE DO WE FIND THE KINGDOM OF GOD AND HOW IS IT MANIFESTED?

We find the kingdom of God as it is manifested in and through His people, the church. God has, from the very beginning, planned to have a people who would be completely His—in body, soul, and spirit. Although the kingdom of God grows by the addition of individual members, the Lord is not concerned merely with the saving of individuals as such. He desires to build a church, a redeemed community, a nation, over which He will exercise complete authority and to whom He will entrust His kingdom love and power as an inheritance.

> ". . . I am sending you, to open their eyes so that they may turn from darkness to light and from the dominion of Satan to [the dominion of] God, in order that they may receive forgiveness of sins and **an inheritance among those who have been sanctified by faith in Me.**"
>
> Acts 26:17b,18

> . . . giving thanks to the Father, who has qualified us to share in the inheritance of the saints in light. For He delivered us from the domain of darkness, and **transferred us to the kingdom of His beloved Son.**          Col. 1:12,13

## 3. IS THERE A DIFFERENCE BETWEEN THE CHURCH AND THE KINGDOM OF HEAVEN?

The church is that body of people who have entered into the kingdom of heaven **now,** and who are living according to its laws and principles, being subject to the King, in this present life.

> "Do not be anxious then, saying, 'What shall we eat?' or 'What shall we drink?' or 'With what shall we clothe ourselves?' For all these things the Gentiles eagerly seek; for your heavenly Father knows that you need all these things. But **seek first His kingdom** and His righteousness; and all these things shall be added to you."          Matt. 6:31-33

The kingdom of God, in its ultimate manifestation, will encompass all of creation.

*Then comes the end, when He delivers up the kingdom to the God and Father, when He has abolished all rule and all authority and power. For He must reign until He has put all His enemies under His feet.*　　　　1 Cor. 15:24,25

*"Thou . . . didst purchase for God with Thy blood men from every tribe and tongue and people and nation. And Thou hast made them to be **a kingdom** and priests to our God; and **they will reign upon the earth.**"*　　　Rev. 5:9,10

## 4.  WHEN WILL THIS ULTIMATE MANIFESTATION OF THE KINGDOM TAKE PLACE?

This ultimate manifestation of the kingdom of God will take place at the return of the Lord Jesus Christ.

*And the seventh angel sounded; and there arose loud voices in heaven, saying, "The kingdom of the world **has become the kingdom of our Lord, and of His Christ;** and He will reign forever and ever."*　　　Rev. 11:15

## 5.  HOW DO WE ENTER THE KINGDOM OF GOD?

We gain entrance into the kingdom of God by being "born again" into it, that is, by repenting of our sins, accepting Jesus Christ as both Savior and Lord, being water baptized into His Name, and receiving the baptism of His Holy Spirit.

*"Truly, truly, I say to you, unless one is born again, he cannot see the kingdom of God.*
*"Truly, truly, I say to you, **unless one is born of water and the Spirit, he cannot enter into the kingdom of God.**"*
Jn. 3:3,5

*"Therefore let all the house of Israel know for certain that God has made Him both Lord **and** Christ—this Jesus whom you crucified." Now when they heard this, they were pierced to the heart, and said to Peter and the rest of the apostles, "Brethren, what shall we do?" And Peter said to them, "**Repent,** and let each of you **be baptized in the name of Jesus Christ** for the forgiveness of your sins; and **you shall receive the gift of the Holy Spirit."***

*And the Lord was adding to their number day by day those who were being saved.*        Acts 2:36-38,47b*

*For He delivered us from the domain of darkness, and **transferred us to the kingdom of His beloved Son,** in whom we have redemption, the forgiveness of sins.*

        Col. 1:13,14

Read also Matthew 5:20; 18:3; 23:13; Mark 10:15; Luke 11:52.

## 6. IS ENTERING THE KINGDOM OF GOD THE SAME AS INHERITING THE KINGDOM OF GOD?

No, it is not. As we have seen, anyone who obeys the gospel can be saved and enter the kingdom of God. Only those who continue to walk in obedience to the Lord Jesus Christ will receive their reward by inheriting their place in His kingdom.

*"Enter by the narrow gate; for the gate is wide, and the way is broad that leads to destruction, and many are those who enter by it. For the gate is small, and **the way is narrow** that leads to life, and few are those who find it."*

        Matt. 7:13,14

Jesus spoke specifically about inheriting our place in the kingdom of God.

*"Not everyone who says to Me, 'Lord, Lord,' will enter the kingdom of heaven; but he who does the will of My Father who is in heaven. Many will say to Me on that day, 'Lord, Lord, did we not prophesy in Your name, and in Your name cast out demons, and in Your name perform many miracles?' And then I will declare to them, 'I never knew you; depart from Me, you who practice lawlessness.'"*

Matt. 7:21-23

Jesus is not talking here about unbelievers; He is talking about believers who have exercised the gifts of the Spirit mightily, but who will miss their place of inheritance in the kingdom of God because they practiced lawlessness. This means that, although they knew Jesus as Savior, they did not acknowledge Him as Lord of their lives. They lived just the way they wanted to, out from under His laws.

Being able to prophesy, speak in tongues, cast out demons, work miracles, etc., is not proof nor guarantee of entrance into the kingdom of God; nor are such things even the main purpose of the kingdom. God has from the very beginning wanted a people to whom He could give rule and dominion and through whom He could rule all of creation. This is the twofold purpose of the kingdom: (1) to create a people for God's own possession (and a bride for Christ!), and (2) to bring into being a nation of kings and priests who would rule and reign with Christ. Being able to exercise gifts of the Spirit is not the criterion for inheriting our place in that kingdom—**obedience is!** Furthermore, it is not enough merely to say, "Lord, Lord"; we must actually **do** the will of the Father. Jesus said in John 14:15, "If you love Me, you will **keep My commandments.**"

Read also Matthew 5:1-12; 19:17; 25:14-30,34; Acts 14:22; 20:32; 26:18; Ephesians 1:1,14,18; Colossians 1:12; 3:24; 1 Peter 1:4; Revelation 1:6; 3:21; 5:9,10.

# 7. IS THERE ANYTHING ELSE OTHER THAN DISOBEDIENCE (OUR WILLFULNESS) THAT CAN KEEP US FROM INHERITING OUR PLACE IN THE KINGDOM OF GOD?

All sin has its roots in our willfulness—in our wanting to have our own way. In this sense, building a life of dead works can cause us to lose the reward of our inheritance.

> *According to the grace of God which was given to me, as a wise master builder I laid a foundation, and another is building upon it. But let each man be careful how he builds upon it. For no man can lay a foundation other than the one which is laid, which is Jesus Christ. Now if any man builds upon the foundation with gold, silver, precious stones, wood, hay, straw, each man's work will become evident; for the day will show it, because it is to be revealed with fire; and the fire itself will test the quality of each man's work. If any man's work which he has built upon it remains, **he shall receive a reward.** If any man's work is burned up, **he shall suffer loss;** but **he himself shall be saved,** yet so as through fire.* 1 Cor. 3:10-15

We must remember that salvation is a gift, not a reward. Paul is not discussing here the loss of one's salvation because of building wrongly on the foundation of Jesus Christ; rather, he is stating the possibility of losing one's reward of inheritance in the kingdom (ruling and reigning with Him). It is possible to be saved and have a place with God for eternity even though the kingdom has been forfeited through lack of submission and obedience to the Lord.

More specifically, there are many types of sin which, when permitted to rule our lives, will cause us to lose our kingdom inheritance.

> *Now the deeds of the flesh are evident, which are: immorality, impurity, sensuality, idolatry, sorcery, enmities, strife, jealousy, outbursts of anger, disputes, dissensions, factions, envying, drunkenness, carousing, and things like*

*these, of which I forewarn you just as I have forewarned you that **those who practice such things shall not inherit the kingdom of God.*** Gal. 5:19-21

Read also Matthew 18:8; 19:23-26; 1 Corinthians 6:9,10; Ephesians 5:5.


8. **WHAT ARE THE PRINCIPLES OF THE KINGDOM OF GOD AND WHERE DO WE FIND THEM?**

The principles of the kingdom of God are to be found in the entirety of the Word of God—Old and New Testaments alike. More specifically, the principles of the kingdom may be found in the New Testament teachings of Jesus in the four gospels and especially in the parables of the kingdom. The writers of the epistles continued the New Testament fulfillment and revelation of the kingdom of God.

The parables of the kingdom may be studied by reading:

° The Sower (Matt. 13:1-23).
° Tares Among Wheat (Matt. 13:24-30 [and 36-43]).
° The Mustard Seed (Matt. 13:31,32).
° The Leaven (Matt. 13:33).
° The Hidden Treasure (Matt. 13:44).
° Pearl of Great Price (Matt. 13:45,46).
° The Dragnet (Matt. 13:47-50).
° The Laborers in the Vineyard (Matt. 20:1-16).
° The Two Sons (Matt. 21:28-32).
° The Owner of the Vineyard (Matt. 21:33-46).
° The Marriage Feast (Matt. 22:1-14 [Lk. 14:16-24]).
° The Fig Tree (His Coming) (Matt. 24:32-51).

# HOME STUDY QUESTIONS:  CHAPTER 27

In your own words, define:

1.  The kingdom of God.

2.  The nature of the kingdom now (how it is manifested in the earth today).

3.  Its ultimate manifestation (the fulness of the kingdom).

# THE GOVERNMENT OF GOD

**Chapter 28**

## 1. WHAT IS GOVERNMENT?

*Webster's Seventh New Collegiate Dictionary* defines government as "authoritative direction or control; the continuous exercise of authority over . . . ."[1] To govern implies the aim of keeping in a straight course or smooth operation for the good of the individual and the whole.

## 2. WHERE DID GOVERNMENT ORIGINATE?

The Bible tells us that **all** power and authority come from God. By the word of His own power He brought the worlds into being and He continues to hold all things together by the word of His power alone.

> *Who has measured the waters in the hollow of His hand, and marked off the heavens by the span, and calculated the dust of the earth by the measure, and weighed the mountains in a balance, and the hills in a pair of scales? Who has directed the Spirit of the Lord, or as His counselor has informed Him? With whom did He consult and who gave Him understanding? And who taught Him in the path of justice and taught Him knowledge, and informed Him of the way of understanding? Behold, the nations are like a drop from a bucket, and are regarded as a speck of dust on the scales; behold, He lifts up the islands like fine dust. Even Lebanon is not enough to burn, nor its beasts enough for a burnt offering. All the nations are as nothing before Him,*

*they are regarded by Him as less than nothing and mean-*
*ingless.*

*To whom then will you liken God? Or what likeness will*
*you compare with Him? As for the idol, a craftsman casts it,*
*a goldsmith plates it with gold, and a silversmith fashions*
*chains of silver. He who is too impoverished for such an*
*offering selects a tree that does not rot; he seeks out for*
*himself a skillful craftsman to prepare an idol that will not*
*totter.*

*Do you not know? Have you not heard? Has it not been*
*declared to you from the beginning? Have you not under-*
*stood from the foundations of the earth? It is He who sits*
*above the vault of the earth, and its inhabitants are like*
*grasshoppers, who stretches out the heavens like a curtain*
*and spreads them out like a tent to dwell in. He it is who*
*reduces rulers to nothing, who makes the judges of the earth*
*meaningless. Scarcely have they been planted, scarcely have*
*they been sown, scarcely has their stock taken root in the*
*earth, but He merely blows on them, and they wither, and the*
*storm carries them away like stubble. "To whom then will*
*you liken Me that I should be his equal?" says the Holy One.*
*Lift up your eyes on high and see who has created these*
*stars, the One who leads forth their host by number, He calls*
*them all by name; because of the greatness of His might and*
*the strength of His power not one of them is missing.*

Isa. 40:12-26

And because God is eternal, His Kingship is also eternal: "And His
kingdom will have no end" (Lk. 1:33). He is "the Alpha and the
Omega, the beginning and the end" (Rev. 21:6). What He has begun,
He will carry through to completion.

*"Thou, Lord, in the beginning didst lay the foundation of*
*the earth, and the heavens are the works of Thy hands; they*
*will perish, but Thou remainest; and they all will become old*
*as a garment, and as a mantle Thou wilt roll them up; as a*

*garment they will also be changed. But Thou art the same,
and Thy years will not come to an end."*     Heb. 1:10-12

Read also Job 38-41; Hebrews 11:3; 2 Peter 3:5-7.

## 3. DOES GOD RULE ALONE?

Although the Lord alone is the Absolute Ruler of all that exists, He
has created man and delegated to **him** the authority to rule over the
works of His hands.

> *Then God said, "Let Us make man in Our image,
> according to Our likeness; and let them rule over the fish of
> the sea and over the birds of the sky and over the cattle and
> over all the earth, and over every creeping thing that creeps
> on the earth."*
> *And God blessed them; and God said to them, "Be
> fruitful and multiply, and fill the earth, and subdue it; and
> rule over the fish of the sea and over the birds of the sky, and
> over every living thing that moves on the earth."*
> Gen. 1:26,28

> *"What is man, that Thou rememberest him? Or the son
> of man, that Thou art concerned about him? Thou hast made
> him for a little while lower than the angels; Thou hast
> crowned him with glory and honor, and hast appointed him
> over the works of Thy hands; Thou hast put all things in
> subjection under his feet." For in subjecting all things to
> him, He left nothing that is not subject to him. But now we
> do not yet see all things subjected to him.*     Heb. 2:6-8

# THE GOVERNMENT OF GOD

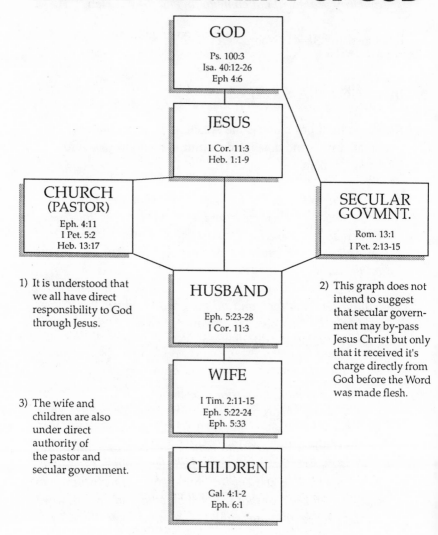

**GOD**

Ps. 100:3
Isa. 40:12-26
Eph 4:6

**JESUS**

I Cor. 11:3
Heb. 1:1-9

**CHURCH (PASTOR)**

Eph. 4:11
I Pet. 5:2
Heb. 13:17

**SECULAR GOVMNT.**

Rom. 13:1
I Pet. 2:13-15

**HUSBAND**

Eph. 5:23-28
I Cor. 11:3

**WIFE**

I Tim. 2:11-15
Eph. 5:22-24
Eph. 5:33

**CHILDREN**

Gal. 4:1-2
Eph. 6:1

1) It is understood that we all have direct responsibility to God through Jesus.

2) This graph does not intend to suggest that secular government may by-pass Jesus Christ but only that it received it's charge directly from God before the Word was made flesh.

3) The wife and children are also under direct authority of the pastor and secular government.

## 4. HOW HAS GOD DISTRIBUTED THIS AUTHORITY HE HAS DELEGATED TO MAN?

We find the pattern for God's distribution of authority plainly set forth in 1 Corinthians 11:3:

> *But I want you to understand that Christ is the head of every man, and the man is the head of a woman, and God is the head of Christ.*

We will discuss this principle as it applies to every area of our lives: the church, the home, and even secular government.

a. **God has first of all invested all power and all authority in His Son Jesus Christ,** who, as the Son of Man, is not only True God, but also True Man, and thus our representative as well as our King!

> *God, after He spoke long ago to the fathers in the prophets in many portions and in many ways, in these last days has spoken to us in His Son, whom He appointed heir of all things, through whom also He made the world. And He is the radiance of His glory and the exact representation of His nature, and upholds all things by the word of His power. When He had made purification of sins, He sat down at the right hand of the Majesty on high; having become as much better than the angels, as He has inherited a more excellent name than they. For to which of the angels did He ever say, "Thou art My Son, today I have begotten Thee"? And again, "I will be a Father to Him, and He shall be a Son to Me"? And when He again brings the first-born into the world, He says, "And let all the angels of God worship Him." And of the angels He says, "Who makes His angels winds, and His ministers a flame of fire." But of the Son He says, "Thy throne, O God, is forever and ever, and the righteous scepter is the scepter of His kingdom. Thou*

369

*hast loved righteousness and hated lawlessness; therefore God, Thy God, hath anointed Thee with the oil of gladness above Thy companions."* Heb. 1:1-9

*Since then the children share in flesh and blood, He Himself likewise also partook of the same, that through death He might render powerless him who had the power of death, that is, the devil; and might deliver those who through fear of death were subject to slavery all their lives.*

*Therefore, He had to be made like His brethren in all things, that He might become a merciful and faithful high priest in things pertaining to God, to make propitiation for the sins of the people.* Heb. 2:14,15,17

b. Christ, who has been appointed by the Father to be the head of all things, is first of all head of the church. **The Son has invested His authority in the church.** Why? Because the government of God, in **every one** of its aspects and manifestations, is a **theocracy** (government by and of God) and not a democracy (government by and of the people). Although God has delegated authority into the hands of man to govern for a season, He has not relinquished it nor given it to man as a permanent right.

*These are in accordance with the working of the strength of His might which He brought about in Christ, when He raised Him from the dead, and seated Him at His right hand in the heavenly places, far above **all** rule and authority and power and dominion, and **every** name that is named, not only in this age, but also in the one to come. And He put **all things in subjection** under His feet, and gave Him as **head** over all things to the **church,** which is His body, the fulness of Him who **fills all in all.***
Eph. 1:19b-23

Furthermore, those who receive Jesus Christ now as Savior, Lord, and King become a part of His kingdom and will rule and reign with Him.

> *For He delivered us from the domain of darkness, and transferred us to the kingdom of His beloved Son, in whom we have redemption, the forgiveness of sins.*
>
> Col. 1:13,14

> *If we endure, we shall also reign with Him.*
>
> 2 Tim. 2:12a

> *"Worthy art Thou to take the book, and to break its seals; for Thou wast slain, and didst purchase for God with Thy blood men from every tribe and tongue and people and nation. And Thou hast made them to be a kingdom and priests to our God; and they will reign upon the earth."*
>
> Rev. 5:9,10

c. As we have already seen, Christ is the head of the church (Col. 1:18). Here, too, however, authority has been delegated to man. Out of the fivefold ministries which Jesus has given to the church to bring it into perfection, **governmental authority is invested in the apostle and in the pastor.**

> *And He gave some as apostles, and some as prophets, and some as evangelists, and some as pastors and teachers, for the equipping of the saints for the work of service, to the building up of the body of Christ.*
>
> Eph. 4:11,12

> *For even if I should boast somewhat further about our authority, which the Lord gave for building you up and not for destroying you, I shall not be put to shame.*
>
> 2 Cor. 10:8

*"Be on guard for yourselves and for all the flock, among which the Holy Spirit has made you overseers, to shepherd the church of God which He purchased with His own blood."*                          Acts 20:28

*Therefore, I exhort the elders among you, as your fellow elder and witness of the sufferings of Christ, and a partaker also of the glory that is to be revealed, shepherd the flock of God among you, exercising oversight not under compulsion, but voluntarily, according to the will of God; and not for sordid gain, but with eagerness; nor yet as lording it over those allotted to your charge, but proving to be examples to the flock.*                          1 Pet. 5:1-3

*He must be one who manages his own household well, keeping his children under control with all dignity (but if a man does not know how to manage his own household, how will he take care of the church of God?).*                          1 Tim. 3:4,5

d.   Concerning the home, Christ is the head of marriage, the home, and the family. He has delegated authority and responsibility for the family **first of all to the man as husband and father.**

*But I want you to understand that Christ is the head of every man, and the man is the head of a woman, and God is the head of Christ.*                          1 Cor. 11:3

*Wives, be subject to your own husbands, as to the Lord. For the husband is the head of the wife, as Christ also is the head of the church, He Himself being the Savior of the body. But as the church is subject to Christ, so also the wives ought to be to their husbands in everything. Husbands, love your wives, just as Christ also loved the church and gave Himself up for her.*

*So husbands ought also to love their own wives as their own bodies. He who loves his own wife loves himself; for no one ever hated his own flesh, but nourishes and cherishes it, just as Christ also does the church.*

*Let each individual among you also love his own wife even as himself; and let the wife see to it that she respect her husband.* Eph. 5:22-25,28,29,33

*And, fathers, do not provoke your children to anger; but bring them up in the discipline and instruction of the Lord.* Eph. 6:4

See also 1 Timothy 3:4,5,12; Colossians 3:18,19,21; Genesis 18:19; Joshua 24:15.

**The father and mother, then, are to rule over the children.**

*Children, obey your parents in the Lord, for this is right. Honor your father and mother (which is the first commandment with a promise), that it may be well with you, and that you may live long on the earth.*
Eph. 6:1-3

*Children, be obedient to your parents in all things, for this is well-pleasing to the Lord.* Col. 3:20

NOTE: The government of God is extended to single men and women as well. The lordship of Christ is required of each of us, single or married, young or old.

e. Concerning secular government, we must remember that **all** authority is from God. For a season, beginning with the creation of man and especially after the Flood, God gave to man the responsibility for governing his society.

*Let every person be in subjection to the governing authorities. For there is no authority except from God, and those which exist are established by God. Therefore he who resists authority has opposed the ordinance of God; and they who have opposed will receive condemnation upon themselves. For rulers are not a cause of fear for good behavior, but for evil. Do you want to have no fear of authority? Do what is good, and you will have praise from the same; for it is a minister of God to you for good. But if you do what is evil, be afraid; for it does not bear the sword for nothing; for it is a minister of God, an avenger who brings wrath upon the one who practices evil. Wherefore it is necessary to be in subjection, not only because of wrath, but also for conscience' sake. For because of this you also pay taxes, for rulers are servants of God, devoting themselves to this very thing. Render to all what is due them: tax to whom tax is due; custom to whom custom; fear to whom fear; honor to whom honor.* Rom. 13:1-7

*First of all, then, I urge that entreaties and prayers, petitions and thanksgivings, be made on behalf of all men, for kings and all who are in authority, in order that we may lead a tranquil and quiet life in all godliness and dignity. This is good and acceptable in the sight of God our Savior, who desires all men to be saved and to come to the knowledge of the truth.* 1 Tim. 2:1-4

Man's government, whether in the church, in the home, or in society, has authority only insofar as it has been delegated to him by God. Therefore, he cannot overstep the boundaries that God has established within which that authority is to operate. Once man, whether in the church, in the home, or in the government of society, attempts to govern beyond those boundaries or else in violation of them, those who are the governed are not bound to obey.

*"Render to Caesar the things that are Caesar's; and to God the things that are God's."* Matt. 22:21b

We find many instances of this in the Word of God. For instance, the Hebrew midwives, because they feared God, did not have to obey the pharaoh's command to kill all the male babies (Ex. 1:15-17).

Much later in the history of Israel, Nebuchadnezzar, king of Babylon, threatened the people with death, ordering them to fall down and worship a golden idol he had constructed. Daniel and his friends, however, did not obey the king because, by doing so, they would have broken the first and second commandments.

No man has the authority to make us disobey God!

## 5. WHAT ARE THE GOVERNING PRINCIPLES OF GOD'S GOVERNMENT?

In a very real sense, the entire Word of God contains His laws and principles of government.

*All Scripture is inspired by God and profitable for teaching, for reproof, for correction, for training in righteousness; that the man of God may be adequate, equipped for every good work.* 2 Tim. 3:16,17

However, the heart of God's law may be found expressed in the Ten Commandments.

. . .He gave Moses the two tablets of the testimony, tablets of stone, written by the finger of God.

**EX. 31:18**

## 6. WHAT ARE THE TEN COMMANDMENTS?

The Ten Commandments are the laws of God, written with His own finger on tables of stone and delivered to Moses (Ex. 19:20; 32:15,16,19; 34:1). Although they were given under the Old Testament dispensation and were the backbone of the Mosaic Law, they still apply to us today. We are indeed no longer under law, but under grace. We are not, however, free from the laws of God. We are not a people of the New Testament only, but also of the Old. Jesus did not come to do away with the Law, but to fulfill it (Matt. 5:17), and He gave us His promise that, under the provisions of the New Covenant, He would write His laws upon our hearts (Jer. 31:33). He also said that He would give us a new heart and a new spirit so that we, too, would be able to fulfill His laws.

*"Moreover, I will give you a new heart and put a new spirit within you; and I will remove the heart of stone from*

*your flesh and give you a heart of flesh. And I will put My
Spirit within you and cause you to walk in My statutes, and
you will be careful to observe My ordinances."*

Ezk. 36:26,27

This is a promise contained in the Old Testament, but it does not
apply to God's Old Testament people; **it applies to us** who are the
inheritors of the New Covenant! And should there be any doubt left,
Jesus said:

*"If you love Me, you will keep My commandments."*

Jn. 14:15

## 7. WHAT IS THE FIRST COMMANDMENT?

*Thou shalt have no other gods before me.*

Ex. 20:3 KJV*

a. What is commanded by the first commandment?

The first commandment tells us **who** must be worshiped. We are
to worship the Lord God and Him alone.

b. What is forbidden by the first commandment?

1. We are forbidden to look to any other creature, object or
   activity either as a focus for our worship or as a means of
   salvation. Man is inherently "religious"—we can be guilty of
   breaking this commandment when we look outside ourselves
   and other than to God for anything that will "save" us from
   the storms and dilemmas of life (such as education, wealth,
   pleasure, health, and physical fitness—even religion itself,
   which is the focusing of our attention on the **way** we worship
   rather than on God, the true object of our worship).

---

* The King James Version will be cited here and throughout the Ten
Commandments for ease of memorization.

2. We are forbidden to believe in or agree with any system which adheres to a "form of godliness, but [which denies] the power thereof" (2 Tim. 3:5), such as liberalism, humanism, or any of the false religions. This also includes any form of the occult, such as astrology, fortune-telling, spiritualism, and the use of charms or spells (Lev. 19:31; 20:6,27; Deut. 18:10,11).

## 8. WHAT IS THE SECOND COMMANDMENT?

*Thou shalt not make unto thee any graven image.*
Ex. 20:4 KJV

a. What is commanded by the second commandment?

The second commandment tells us **how** God is to be worshiped.

*"But an hour is coming, and now is, when the true worshipers shall worship the Father in spirit and truth; for such people the Father seeks to be His worshipers.* ***God is spirit, and those who worship Him must worship in spirit and truth."*** Jn. 4:23,24

b. What are we forbidden by the second commandment?

We are forbidden false ways of worshiping the one true God. We are not to make or venerate images either of God Himself or of anything "religious." In some countries even today, images of false gods are widely and openly worshiped. Most of us, however, would not be guilty of breaking this second commandment in this way. How could we be guilty? In two ways:

1. By worshiping a god other than the One clearly set forth for us in the whole Bible. This could be either an exclusion of

Jesus or a twisting of the true relationship that exists between the Father and the Son (Jn. 5:23). It could even be believing a "different gospel" and preaching "another Jesus" (2 Cor. 11:4; Gal. 1:6). This is often done today, especially by those churches who reject the whole truth of the Word of God. It is in this way that we make for ourselves a god in our own image!

2. By having to form mental pictures or images of God and Jesus in our minds before we can pray. Remember, God is spirit and those who worship Him must do so also in spirit!

This commandment does not forbid us to have sculpture, painting, and other forms of ornamentation in the church. Remember that the bronze serpent in the wilderness was made at the command of the Lord, and both the tabernacle and the temple were profusely ornamented with images of flowers, pomegranates, palm trees, oxen, lions, and cherubim.

## 9. WHAT IS THE THIRD COMMANDMENT?

*Thou shalt not take the name of the Lord thy God in vain.*
Ex. 20:7 KJV

a. What is commanded by the third commandment?

The third commandment tells us to reverence His name and never to use it in a wrong way. This includes much more than the forbidding of profanity.

b. What is forbidden in this commandment?

We are forbidden to use the holy and wonderful name of God or Jesus Christ in a casual or mindless way or to express surprise or anger. This commandment also forbids blasphemy, profanity, empty vows, and lying (he that says, "Lord, Lord" but does not **do**

379

the will of the Father). It also includes using the name of the Lord out of habit or in an attempt to sound "spiritual." See Matthew 5:33-37 and 7:21-23.

## 10. WHAT IS THE FOURTH COMMANDMENT?

*Remember the sabbath day, to keep it holy.*

Ex. 20:8 KJV

a. What is commanded by the fourth commandment?

　1. We are commanded to honor the Lord's day, a day of rest.

　　(a.) What is the sabbath? The Hebrew word *sabbath* means "rest." Because God rested on the seventh day from all His labors of creation, He gave the sabbath as a sign to Israel to be kept by them throughout all their generations (Gen. 2:1-3; Ex. 20:10,11).

　　(b.) Are Christians required to observe the sabbath? No. The sabbath was held on Saturday, the last day of the week, in honor of God's having rested from His labors on that day and, in type, in memorial of God's people resting in Him. From the very beginning, the early Christians worshiped, not on the last day of the week, but on the first day of the week, that is, Sunday, in honor of Christ's resurrection (Matt. 28:1; Mk. 16:2,9; Lk. 24:1; Jn. 20:1,19; Acts 20:7; 1 Cor. 16:2).

　2. Are Christians **commanded** to observe any day as being more special than any other? No. This includes Sundays, festive days, and "holy" days.

　　　*Now accept the one who is weak in faith, but not for the purpose of passing judgment on his opinions. One man has faith that he may eat all things, but he* *who is weak eats vegetables only. Let not him who eats regard with contempt him who does not eat, and let not him who does not eat judge him who eats, for God has accepted him. Who are you to judge the servant of another? To his own master he stands or falls; and stand he will, for the Lord is able to make him stand. One man regards one day above another, another regards every day alike. Let each man be fully convinced in his own mind. He who observes the day, observes it for the Lord, and he who eats, does so for the Lord, for he gives thanks to God; and he who eats not, for the Lord he does not eat, and gives thanks to God.* Rom. 14:1-6*

It is true that we are not commanded to observe special days. Let us not, however, swing legalistically to the other extreme, rejecting festivals and special days of observance out of hand. Remember, God Himself instituted festivals and days of special observance for celebration and rejoicing as well as for other reasons.

3. How then do Christians fulfill this commandment? We fulfill it by ceasing from our own labors and entering into the completed work of Jesus Christ on our behalf.

*Therefore, let us fear lest, while a promise remains of entering His rest, any one of you should seem to have come short of it. For indeed we have had good news preached to us, just as they also; but the word they heard did not profit them, because it was not united by faith in those who heard. For we who have believed enter that rest, just as He has said, "As I swore in My wrath, they shall not enter My rest," although His works were finished from the foundation of the world. For He has thus said somewhere concerning the seventh day, "And God rested on the seventh day from all His works"; and*

*again in this passage, "They shall not enter My*
*rest." Since therefore it remains for some to enter it,*
*and those who formerly had good news preached to*
*them failed to enter because of disobedience, He*
*again fixes a certain day, "Today," saying through*
*David after so long a time just as has been said*
*before, "Today if you hear His voice, do not harden*
*your hearts." For if Joshua had given them rest, He*
*would not have spoken of another day after that.*
*There remains therefore a Sabbath rest for the*
*people of God. For the one who has entered His rest*
*has himself also rested from his works, as God did*
*from His. Let us therefore be diligent to enter that*
*rest, lest anyone fall through following the same*
*example of disobedience.* Heb. 4:1-11

b.  What is forbidden by this commandment?

1.  Even though we are not bound to set aside any special day as
    "The Lord's Day," we must still "not [forsake] the assembling
    of ourselves together" (Heb. 10:25 KJV). Sunday is the most
    convenient day for Christians to gather together to worship.
    Remember, too, that we still need at least one day set apart
    from the others in which we can cease from the normal labors
    of earning a living and enjoy a time of rest.

2.  We also sin against this commandment when we fail to enter
    into the Sabbath rest of Jesus Christ and continue in our own
    strivings to attain godliness.

# 1. WHAT IS THE FIFTH COMMANDMENT?

*Honour thy father and thy mother: that thy days may be long upon the land which the Lord thy God giveth thee.*

Ex. 20:12 KJV

a. What is commanded by the fifth commandment?

This is the first commandment with a promise: "that thy days may be long upon the land . . . ." It is by this promise that the Lord seeks to impress upon us the importance of honoring and obeying not only our parents, but, because they are the representatives of the government of God Himself in our lives, also all those who are "over" us in this life. How do we honor our parents?

°  We honor them by giving them not only love, but also the proper respect and reverence due to them as our parents.

°  We honor them by obeying them and by doing so willingly out of love, not grudgingly, out of compulsion.

°  We honor them by caring for them in their time of need.

b. What are we forbidden by this commandment?

We are forbidden to dishonor, disobey, or neglect not only our parents, but all those who are the legitimate representatives of God's government in our lives: pastors, teachers, those older than we, the government, etc.

## 12. WHAT IS THE SIXTH COMMANDMENT?

*Thou shalt not kill.* *                         Ex. 20:13 KJV

a. What is commanded by the sixth commandment?

We are commanded to take proper care of ourselves, both in spiritual and in natural matters, and to respect the person and rights of our fellow man by not injuring him in any way.

b. What are we forbidden in this commandment?

1. We are, first of all, forbidden to do anything that would jeopardize our own health and welfare: not getting proper rest, not eating proper foods (a balanced diet), taking drugs and medication which might be harmful to our health, smoking (which has now been proven to be cancer-causing and definitely injurious to the smoker, to the nonsmoker who nonetheless must inhale the smoke, and even to the unborn child of a mother who smokes), etc. This also includes suicide!

2. We are forbidden to do anything that would bring harm to others. We are forbidden to injure or kill (that is, murder) another.

3. We are forbidden to say or do anything which would destroy or embitter the life of another. We often forget it, but the Bible tells us that life **and death** are in the power of tongue (Prov. 18:21).

---

*NOTE: This is one instance when the King James Version does not make the meaning of the commandment perfectly clear. The word translated "kill" in the King James Version actually means "murder." Thus the sixth commandment does not forbid us to take up arms for our country in a just cause.

# 3. WHAT IS THE SEVENTH COMMANDMENT?

*Thou shalt not commit adultery.*

Ex. 20:14 KJV

a. What are we commanded by the seventh commandment?

We are commanded to honor, esteem, and protect the marriage covenant. We are commanded to be faithful to each other and to keep our affections set upon that one whom we married.

b. What are we forbidden by the seventh commandment?

1. We are forbidden any adulterous thoughts or actions. What is adultery? It is having sexual relations with someone other than the marriage partner.

2. We are forbidden the breaking of our marriage vows by unfaithfulness or desertion.

3. Inherent in this commandment is the forbidding of all immodesty in words, actions, or looks, either alone or with others (Matt. 15:19; Matt. 5:28; Eph. 5:3,4; Eph. 5:12). We need to be especially wary of the chief dangers to purity which are idleness; immodest dress; bad companions; drinking and drugs; and indecent books, television shows, plays, and movies.

# 4. WHAT IS THE EIGHTH COMMANDMENT?

*Thou shalt not steal.*                   Ex. 20:15 KJV

a. What are we commanded by the eighth commandment?

We are commanded to respect that which belongs to others, to be men and women of our word, to fulfill business agreements and contracts, to pay our debts, and to "provide things honest in the sight of all men" (Rom. 12:17 KJV).

b.  What are we forbidden by the eighth commandment?

1.  Every kind of theft, even if "everybody else does it." One of the biggest losses in most businesses today is employees taking home equipment, sometimes as small as paper and pencils.

2.  Dishonesty in every form: padding the expense account, lying on the tax forms, cheating at school, taking credit that is not our due, neglecting to return something that is not ours, and so forth.

## 15.  WHAT IS THE NINTH COMMANDMENT?

*Thou shalt not bear false witness against thy neighbour.*
Ex. 20:16 KJV

a.  What are we commanded by the ninth commandment?

The ninth commandment is also concerned with truthfulness and honesty, especially as far as it concerns our neighbor, his honor, and his good name.

b.  What are we forbidden by the ninth commandment?

We are forbidden to lie about our neighbor or to slander him in any way or to reveal secrets we have promised to keep. Evil insinuations and dishonest flattery (we are not referring to honest compliments), faultfinding, and unjust criticism are also forbidden by this commandment.

*Behold, Thou dost desire **truth** in the innermost being.*
Ps. 51:6

# 6. WHAT IS THE TENTH COMMANDMENT?

> *Thou shalt not covet thy neighbour's house, thou shalt not covet thy neighbour's wife, nor his manservant, nor his maidservant, nor his ox, nor his ass, nor any thing that is thy neighbour's.* Ex. 20:17 KJV

a. What does the tenth commandment require of us?

This commandment requires that we cultivate a heart that is satisfied with the Lord's portion in life for us. Listen to what the Bible has to say about covetousness:

> *"For from within, out of the heart of men, proceed the evil thoughts, fornications, thefts, murders, adulteries, **deeds of coveting** and wickedness, as well as deceit, sensuality, envy, slander, pride and foolishness. **All these evil things proceed from within and defile the man."***
> Mk. 7:21-23

> *And He said to them, "Beware, and be on your guard against **every form of greed** [covetousness]; for not even when one has an abundance does his life consist of his possessions."*
> Lk. 12:15

> *Or do you not know that the **unrighteous shall not inherit the kingdom of God?** Do not be deceived; neither fornicators, nor idolators, nor adulterers, nor effeminate, nor homosexuals, nor thieves, **nor the covetous,** nor drunkards, nor revilers, nor swindlers, shall inherit the kingdom of God.* 1 Cor. 6:9,10

> *For this you know with certainty, that no immoral or impure person **or covetous man,** who is an idolater, **has an inheritance in the kingdom of Christ and God.***
> Eph. 5:5

b. What does the tenth commandment forbid us?

1. We are not to covet (that is, to desire something so strongly that a feeling of discontentment comes over us) our neighbor's house or possessions. In other words, let us not get eaten up over trying to "keep up with the Joneses"!

2. We are not to covet our neighbor's wife. Of course, this includes the obvious sin of adultery. What is not so obvious is that we can be guilty of breaking this commandment if looking at another man's wife **causes us to be dissatisfied with the one we have.**

3. We are not to covet anything else that is a part of our neighbor's household or his business or the success of his life.

Let us be like Paul, who said:

> *I have learned **to be content** in whatever circumstances I am. I know how to get along with humble means, and I also know how to live in prosperity; in any and every circumstance I **have learned the secret** of being filled and going hungry, both of having abundance and suffering need. **I can do all things through Him who strengthens me.*** Phil. 4:11b-13

## NOTES

[1] *Webster's Seventh New Collegiate Dictionary* (Springfield, Mass.: G. & C. Merriam Company, © 1971).

## HOME STUDY QUESTIONS: CHAPTER 28

1. What is government and where does it originate?

2. Explain the areas of distribution of God's government as He has delegated it to man; include those who are, in each case, in authority.

3. Memorize the Ten Commandments in order.

# Part Four

*Living the
Christian Life*

# THE ORDINANCE OF BAPTISM

## Chapter 29

While water baptism is one of the most important ordinances in our Christian experience, we will not discuss it here since it has been previously covered. See Part One, Chapter 6 for a complete discussion of the subject of water baptism.

# THE LORD'S SUPPER

**Chapter 30**

## 1.  WHAT IS THE LORD'S SUPPER?

The Lord's Supper is the New Testament fulfillment of the Old Testament Passover meal.  Just as the Israelites confirmed their covenant with God through the blood of the Passover lamb and commemorated with the Passover feast their deliverance from the bondage of Egypt, so also do we confirm in the Lord's Supper the New Covenant of the shed blood of Christ (who has become our Passover Lamb) and commemorate our deliverance from the bondage of sin.

> For I received from the Lord that which I also delivered to you, that the Lord Jesus in the night in which He was betrayed took bread; and when He had given thanks, He broke it, and said, "This is My body, which is for you; do this in remembrance of Me."  In the same way He took the cup also, after supper, saying, "This cup is the new covenant in My blood; do this, as often as you drink it, in remembrance of Me."  For as often as you eat this bread and drink the cup, you proclaim the Lord's death until He comes.
>
> 1 Cor. 11:23-26

## 2.  WHAT WAS THE PASSOVER FEAST?

The Passover feast commemorated the Israelites' liberation from the slavery of Egypt.  The Lord, through Moses, instructed each household to sacrifice a lamb (a type of Christ) and smear the blood upon the doorpost and lintel of each and every home (a type of our personal appropriation of Christ's atoning sacrifice). Thus applied, sacrificial blood was the means of their deliverance from God's judgment against Egypt, which was the smiting with death of every firstborn, both of man and beast.

> *"Speak to all the congregation of Israel, saying, 'On the tenth of this month they are each one to take a lamb for themselves, according to their fathers' households, a lamb for each household.*
>
> *"'And you shall keep it until the fourteenth day of the same month, then the whole assembly of the congregation of Israel is to kill it at twilight.*
>
> *"'Now you shall eat it in this manner: with your loins girded, your sandals on your feet, and your staff in your hand; and you shall eat it in haste—it is the Lord's Passover. For I will go through the land of Egypt on that night, and will strike down all the first-born in the land of Egypt, both man and beast; and against all the gods of Egypt I will execute judgments—I am the Lord. And the blood shall be a sign for you on the houses where you live; and when I see the blood I will pass over you, and no plague will befall you to destroy you when I strike the land of Egypt. Now this day will be a memorial to you, and you shall celebrate it as a feast to the Lord; throughout your generations you are to celebrate it as a permanent ordinance.'"*

Ex. 12:3,6,11-14

### 3.  HOW DOES THE LORD'S SUPPER FULFILL THE OLD TESTAMENT PASSOVER?

a.  Jesus fulfilled the Old Testament type of the Passover lamb.

> *The next day he saw Jesus coming to him, and said, "Behold, the Lamb of God who takes away the sin of the world!"*

*And he looked upon Jesus as He walked, and said,*
*"Behold, the Lamb of God!"* Jn. 1:29,36

b. The Passover lamb was set aside for a period of time so that it could be proven to be without blemish (Ex. 12:5,6). Jesus fulfilled this type as He spent thirty years of His life in subjection to His parents and "increasing in wisdom and stature, and in favor with God and men" (Lk. 2:51,52).

c. The Israelites, by households, were commanded to:

1. Slay the lamb (Ex. 12:1-6). Jesus, as the Lamb of God, was slain for our transgressions, thus fulfilling the Old Testament type (Isa. 53:5-7; Rom. 5:6-10).

2. Apply the blood (Ex. 12:7). Each of us fulfills this as we appropriate personally the redemptive work of Calvary (Eph. 1:7; Heb. 13:12).

3. Eat the lamb (Ex. 12:8-10). Jesus fulfilled this when He said:

*"I am the living bread that came down out of heaven; if anyone eats of this bread, he shall live forever; and the bread also which I shall give for the life of the world is My flesh." The Jews therefore began to argue with one another, saying, "How can this man give us His flesh to eat?" Jesus therefore said to them, "Truly, truly, I say to you, unless you eat the flesh of the Son of Man and drink His blood, you have no life in yourselves. He who eats My flesh and drinks My blood has eternal life, and I will raise him up on the last day. For My flesh is true food, and My blood is true drink. He who eats My flesh and drinks My blood abides in Me, and I in him."*
Jn. 6:51-56

We fulfill the Old Testament type by actually partaking of Him by faith. Christianity is not just an intellectual exercise.

d. The blood upon the doorposts of the Israelite houses was their means of deliverance from death. The Passover was thus a remembrance, both of that deliverance from death and of their having been set free from the government of Pharaoh. The Lord's Supper is the remembrance and celebration of our own deliverance from death and from the dominion of the devil and this world.

> *"For the Lord will pass through to smite the Egyptians; and when He sees the blood on the lintel and on the two doorposts, the Lord will pass over the door and will not allow the destroyer to come in to your houses to smite you. And you shall observe this event as an ordinance for you and your children forever. And it will come about when you enter the land which the Lord will give you, as He has promised, that you shall observe this rite. And it will come about when your children will say to you 'What does this rite mean to you?' that you shall say, 'It is a Passover sacrifice to the Lord who passed over the houses of the sons of Israel in Egypt when He smote the Egyptians, but spared our homes.'" And the people bowed low and worshiped.*
> Ex. 12:23-27

> *And you were dead in your trespasses and sins, in which you formerly walked according to the course of this world, according to the prince of the power of the air, of the spirit that is now working in the sons of disobedience.*
> *But God, being rich in mercy, because of His great love with which He loved us, even when we were dead in our transgressions, made us alive together with Christ (by grace you have been saved),*

*and raised us up with Him, and seated us with Him
in the heavenly places, in Christ Jesus.*
Eph. 2:1,2,4-6

e.  The Lord's Supper is our covenant meal by which we
commemorate **all** that has been fulfilled on our behalf in
Christ Jesus.

> *For I received from the Lord that which I also
> delivered to you, that the Lord Jesus in the night in
> which He was betrayed took bread; and when He
> had given thanks, He broke it, and said, "This is My
> body, which is for you; do this in remembrance of
> Me." In the same way He took the cup also, after
> supper, saying, "This cup is the new covenant in My
> blood; do this, as often as you drink it, in
> remembrance of Me." For as often as you eat this
> bread and drink the cup, you proclaim the Lord's
> death until He comes.*     1 Cor. 11:23-26

## 4.  WHY DO WE CALL IT THE LORD'S SUPPER?

We call it the Lord's Supper because that is the name Paul gave to
that last Passover meal that Jesus and His disciples kept in the upper
room.

> *Therefore when you meet together, it is not to eat the
> Lord's Supper.*     1 Cor. 11:20

We also refer to it as Communion:

> *The cup of blessing which we bless, is it not the
> communion of the blood of Christ? The bread which we
> break, is it not the communion of the body of Christ? For we
> being many are one bread, and one body: for we are all
> partakers of that one bread.*     1 Cor. 10:16,17 KJV

and Breaking of Bread:

> *And they were continually devoting themselves to the apostles' teaching and to fellowship, to the breaking of bread and to prayer.*
> *And day by day continuing with one mind in the temple, and breaking bread from house to house, they were taking their meals together with gladness and sincerity of heart.*
>
> Acts 2:42,46

> *And on the first day of the week, when we were gathered together to break bread . . . .*
>
> Acts 20:7

and the Lord's Table:

> *You cannot drink the cup of the Lord and the cup of demons; you cannot partake of the table of the Lord and the table of demons.*
>
> 1 Cor. 10:21

## 5. WHY DO WE CELEBRATE THE LORD'S SUPPER?

We celebrate the Lord's Supper because the Lord Jesus commanded that we do so. It is one of the ordinances of the church instituted by Christ for the spiritual health, strength, and maturity of the church.

> *And when He had given thanks, He broke it, and said, "This is My body, which is for you; do this in remembrance of Me." In the same way He took the cup also, after supper, saying, "This cup is the new covenant in My blood; do this, as often as you drink it, in remembrance of Me."*
>
> 1 Cor. 11:24,25

## 6. WHAT ARE THE VISIBLE ELEMENTS OF THE LORD'S SUPPER?

The visible elements of the Lord's Supper are the bread and cup.

> *For I received from the Lord that which I also delivered to you, that the Lord Jesus in the night in which He was betrayed took bread; and when He had given thanks, He broke it, and said, "This is My body, which is for you; do this in remembrance of Me." In the same way He took the cup also, after supper, saying, "This cup is the new covenant in My blood; do this, as often as you drink it, in remembrance of Me." For as often as you eat this bread and drink the cup, you proclaim the Lord's death until He comes.*
>
> 1 Cor. 11:23-26

In the majority of New Testament local churches today, grape juice is being used in place of wine in deference to the problem of alcoholism. This is perfectly acceptable since grape juice is just unfermented wine.

## 7. WHAT DID JESUS MEAN WHEN HE SAID, "THIS IS MY BODY, THIS IS MY BLOOD"?

When Jesus said these words, He was indicating that the visible elements of the bread and the cup were representative of the sacrifice of His own body and blood which would soon take place. He then instructed us by saying, "Do this **in remembrance** of Me." It would be ludicrous for us to believe that the actual nature and substance of that bread and cup were changed into the body and blood of Christ or that that is what happens again for us every time we partake of it.

This also applies to John 6:51-58:

> *"I am the living bread that came down out of heaven; if anyone eats of this bread, he shall live forever; and the bread also which I shall give for the life of the world is My*

*flesh." The Jews therefore began to argue with one another, saying, "How can this man give us His flesh to eat?" Jesus therefore said to them, "Truly, truly, I say to you, unless you eat the flesh of the Son of Man and drink His blood, you have no life in yourselves. He who eats My flesh and drinks My blood has eternal life, and I will raise him up on the last day. For My flesh is true food, and My blood is true drink. He who eats My flesh and drinks My blood abides in Me, and I in him. As the living Father sent Me, and I live because of the Father, so he who eats Me, he also shall live because of Me. This is the bread which came down out of heaven; not as the fathers ate, and died, he who eats this bread shall live forever."*

Jesus was not implying that it would be necessary for believers actually to "eat" His flesh and "drink" His blood. He was declaring, however, that, if we are to be in real and saving union with Him, we must partake of His very nature, that is, receive Him into ourselves, especially as that nature is revealed in its sacrificial aspects.

> *O taste and see that the Lord is good; how blessed is the man who takes refuge in Him!*                    Ps. 34:8

The effectiveness of the Lord's Supper does not depend upon a super-mystical transformation of elements; neither do we need to look for veiled spiritualities or deep, hidden meanings. Whether you call it "transubstantiation" or "real presence," there is no foundation for it in Scripture.

## 8. WHAT, THEN, IS THE STRENGTH OF THE LORD'S SUPPER?

a.  The strength of the Lord's Supper is, first of all, our confirming every time we partake of it that we are indeed standing on covenant ground with God—that covenant ground being the New Covenant in His blood and by His Spirit. The Lord's Supper is primarily a covenant meal! This is why it should never be partaken by nonbelievers, by believers not on covenant ground, or by covenant believers who have violated their covenant relationship with God either by sin or by neglect.

b.  Secondly, the "communion" aspect of the Lord's Supper means that we are in fellowship and in good standing with one another as fellow members of the body of Christ.

> *Is not the cup of blessing which we bless a sharing in the blood of Christ? Is not the bread which we break a **sharing in the body of Christ?** Since there is one bread, we who are many **are one body;** for **we all partake** of the **one bread.***
> 1 Cor. 10:16,17

## 9.  WHAT DOES IT MEAN TO PARTAKE OF THE LORD'S SUPPER IN AN UNWORTHY MANNER?

> *Therefore whoever eats the bread or drinks the cup of the Lord in an unworthy manner, shall be guilty of the body and the blood of the Lord. But let a man examine himself, and so let him eat of the bread and drink of the cup. For he who eats and drinks, eats and drinks judgment to himself, if he does not judge the body rightly.*     1 Cor. 11:27-29

The "unworthily" of 1 Corinthians 11:27,29 in the King James Version does not mean that we are personally worthy or unworthy to partake of the Lord's Supper. It goes without saying that none of us are worthy of receiving anything from the Lord, and there is no condemnation in the knowledge of that. What Paul is saying here is that the **manner** in which we partake of the Lord's Supper may be unworthy.

Paul, in these verses, is therefore telling us two things:

a.  Because the Lord's Supper is primarily a covenant meal, when we partake of it with known sin in our lives or with something between us and the Lord that should not be there, we are guilty of the body and blood of the Lord (see Hebrews 10:26-29). We are guilty because we are proclaiming to one and all our good standing with the Lord when it is not so. We are living a lie, and we will be judged for it!

b.  The Lord's Supper is also a remembrance and a celebration of the covenant relationship we have with one another as fellow believers and members of the body of Christ. When we partake of it with enmity in our hearts toward our brother, or when there is a break of any kind in our fellowship with one another and there has been no attempt at reconciliation, then we are guilty of not judging the body rightly. We are once again living a lie by breaking bread and proclaiming that we are members in good standing when, in fact, we are not. (See Matthew 5:23,24; read also Malachi 1:6-14.)

10.  **WHAT DOES PAUL MEAN WHEN HE SAYS HE THAT EATS AND DRINKS IN AN UNWORTHY MANNER "EATS AND DRINKS JUDGMENT TO HIMSELF"?**

He means that those who have partaken of the Lord's Supper in such an unworthy manner have sinned against the Lord and against His body, the church. The judgment decreed for such action is spiritual, and it may even result in physical weakness and sickness and, for those deserving of it, even premature death.

> *For he who eats and drinks, eats and drinks judgment to himself, if he does not judge the body rightly. For this reason many among you are weak and sick, and a number sleep.*                    1 Cor. 11:29,30

1. **HOW CAN WE PREVENT THIS FROM HAPPENING?**

Paul tells us to examine ourselves, repent of those things which would block real communion and fellowship both with the Lord Jesus and with our brethren, and then partake. It is thus, as we judge ourselves according to the Word of the Lord and the Spirit of God and are cleansed, that we escape the judgment of the Lord.

> *But let a man examine himself, and so let him eat of the bread and drink of the cup.*
> *But if we judged ourselves rightly, we should not be judged. But when we are judged, we are disciplined by the Lord in order that we may not be condemned along with the world.*                    1 Cor. 11:28,31,32

2. **SHOULD THE LORD'S SUPPER BE CLOSED TO THOSE WHO ARE NOT MEMBERS OF OUR PARTICULAR LOCAL CHURCH?**

No, that would be counterproductive to the whole purpose of the Lord's Supper. The purpose of this covenant meal is not to separate Christians but to bring them together in fellowship and common commitment to the blood of Jesus Christ. The Lord's Supper is serious business and certainly not to be partaken by unbelievers or by those who knowingly are out of fellowship with the Lord and His body. The pastor, or the one presiding over the Lord's Table (should it be one other than the pastor), should announce that the Lord's Supper should not be partaken by those not in right relationship with the Lord. Then we must leave it up to the individual and the Lord. The Lord is merciful, sometimes more merciful than we are; and even when the Lord's Supper is partaken in an unworthy manner, but out of ignorance, the Lord will understand and forgive. Read 2 Chronicles 30:18-20.

### 13. SHOULD CHILDREN PARTICIPATE IN THE LORD'S SUPPER?

Children should participate in the Lord's Supper only if they are in covenant relation with Christ, having been justified by His blood and baptized into Christ for the remission of sin and the circumcision of heart.

## HOME STUDY QUESTIONS: CHAPTER 30

1. What is the Lord's Supper?

2. Explain briefly, but in your own words, how the Lord's Supper relates to the Passover Feast.

3. What are the benefits of partaking of the Lord's Supper?

# THE ORDINANCE OF FOOT WASHING

**Chapter 31**

## 1. WHAT IS FOOT WASHING?

Foot washing is one of the ordinances given to the church by Jesus Christ to provide us with a means of ministering forgiveness, cleansing, and restoration to one another.

> *Then He poured water into the basin, and began to wash the disciples' feet, and to wipe them with the towel with which He was girded. And so He came to Simon Peter. He said to Him, "Lord, do You wash my feet?" Jesus answered and said to him, "What I do you do not realize now, but you shall understand hereafter." Peter said to Him, "Never shall You wash my feet!" Jesus answered him, "If I do not wash you, you have no part with Me." Simon Peter said to Him, "Lord, not my feet only, but also my hands and my head." Jesus said to him, "He who has bathed needs only to wash his feet, but is completely clean; and you are clean, but not all of you." For He knew the one who was betraying Him; for this reason He said, "Not all of you are clean." And so when He had washed their feet, and taken His garments, and reclined at the table again, He said to them, "Do you know what I have done to you? You call Me Teacher and Lord; and you are right, for so I am. If I then, the Lord and the Teacher, washed your feet, you also ought to wash one another's feet. For I gave you an example that you also should do as I did to you."* Jn. 13:5-15

## 2. WHY DO WE NEED THIS CLEANSING AND RESTORATION?

In order to understand fully the ordinance of foot washing and appropriate its work of grace and blessing, we must first understand its Old Testament background and typology.

° The initial cleansing and sanctifying of the priests:

Before the priests (both the high priest and the Levites) could minister before the Lord, they had to experience blood sacrifice, a complete washing with water and anointing with oil, and investiture with the priestly robes.

> *"Now this is what you shall do to them to consecrate them to minister as priests to Me: take one young bull and two rams without blemish . . . .*
> *"Then you shall bring Aaron and his sons to the doorway of the tent of meeting, and wash them with water. And you shall take the garments, and put on Aaron the tunic and the robe of the ephod and the ephod and the breastpiece, and gird him with the skillfully woven band of the ephod . . . .*
> *"Then you shall take the anointing oil, and pour it on his head and anoint him.*
> *"And you shall gird them with sashes, Aaron and his sons, and bind caps on them, and they shall have the priesthood by a perpetual statute. So you shall ordain Aaron and his sons.*
> *"And you shall slaughter the ram, and take some of its blood and put it on the lobe of Aaron's right ear and on the lobes of his sons' right ears and on the thumbs of their right hands and on the big toes of their right feet, and sprinkle the rest of the blood around on the altar."*
> Ex. 29:1,4,5,7,9,20

Read also Exodus 40:12,13; Numbers 8:5-7,20,22.

° Their continuing cleansing:

Not only were the priests commanded to wash themselves prior to serving in the tabernacle, but they were also commanded to keep themselves free from defilement during their course of service. For this purpose, a bronze laver was placed in the tabernacle, to which they resorted from time to time as they had need. Remember, the Mosaic Law was a law of blood sacrifice. As the priests ministered in the tabernacle, their hands and feet would become defiled with that blood. It is interesting to note that the laver was made from the looking-glasses of the Israelite women who donated them for that purpose (Ex. 38:8). The significance of this will become more evident as we go on through this chapter.

> *And the Lord spoke to Moses, saying, "You shall also make a laver of bronze, with its base of bronze, for washing; and you shall put it between the tent of meeting and the altar, and you shall put water in it. And Aaron and his sons shall wash their hands and their feet from it; when they enter the tent of meeting, they shall wash with water, that they may not die; or when they approach the altar to minister, by offering up in smoke a fire sacrifice to the Lord. So they shall wash their hands and their feet, that they may not die; and it shall be a perpetual statute for them, for Aaron and his descendants throughout their generations."*
>
> Ex. 30:17-21

How does this apply to us? We, too, as New Testament believer-priests (1 Pet. 2:5,9), must follow this same pattern of blood sacrifice, initial cleansing from sin in the waters of baptism, and the anointing of the Holy Spirit for life and for service. We, too, receive our robes of righteousness qualifying us for priesthood. We also become defiled as we go about serving the Lord and ministering to one another—defiled not with blood, but with the things of the world, wrong attitudes toward one another and toward serving, and even wrong attitudes toward sin. How do we receive cleansing from these things so that we do not disqualify ourselves from service? Repentance and confession are always necessary, and when they are followed by foot washing, cleansing is assured. Jesus said:

> "He who has bathed needs only to wash his feet, but is completely clean; and you are clean, but not all of you.
> "If I then, the Lord and the Teacher, washed your feet, you also ought to wash one another's feet. For I gave you an example that you also should do as I did to you."
> Jn. 13:10,14,15

## 3. AS NEW TESTAMENT PRIESTS AND FELLOW BELIEVERS, WHAT ARE THE THINGS FROM WHICH WE MOST FREQUENTLY NEED TO BE CLEANSED?

Like Jesus' disciples, we most frequently need to be cleansed from enmity and division, and from the root of these problems, which is **self.** We think too highly of ourselves and desire to be put over others, thus seeking only our own interests. This is exactly what happened the night of the Last Supper. As Jesus and His disciples were gathering together to partake of the Passover meal, the disciples began to argue among themselves as to who was the greatest.

> "But behold, the hand of the one betraying Me is with Me on the table. For indeed, the Son of Man is going as it has been determined; but woe to that man by whom He is betrayed!" And they began to discuss among themselves which one of them it might be who was going to do this thing. And there arose also a dispute among them as to which one of them was regarded to be greatest.
> Lk. 22:21-24

Just as water baptism enables us to conquer the enmity in us against God and makes it possible for us to love Him with our whole hearts, so foot washing removes the enmity in our hearts against our brother, enabling us to love him as we love ourselves.

> *And so when He had washed their feet, and taken His garments, and reclined at the table again, He said to them, "Do you know what I have done to you? You call Me Teacher and Lord; and you are right, for so I am. If I then, the Lord and the Teacher, washed your feet, you also ought to wash one another's feet. For I gave you an example that you also should do as I did to you. Truly, truly, I say to you, a slave is not greater than his master; neither is one who is sent greater than the one who sent him. If you know these things, you are blessed if you do them."*  Jn. 13:12-17

## 4.  WHY DID JESUS WASH THE DISCIPLES' FEET?

Jesus washed the feet of the disciples for three reasons:

a.  To give us a pattern of righteousness.

> *And during supper, the devil having already put into the heart of Judas Iscariot, the son of Simon, to betray Him, Jesus, knowing that the Father had given all things into His hands, and that He had come forth from God, and was going back to God, rose from supper, and laid aside His garments; and taking a towel, He girded Himself about.*  Jn. 13:2-4

b.  To show them that they were not to allow self and the spirit of competition to rule them and disrupt their fellowship. They were to become servants of the Lord by first of all learning to serve one another.

409

> *He called the twelve and said to them, "If anyone wants to be first, he shall be last of all, and servant of all."* Mk. 9:35

> *For you were called to freedom, brethren; only do not turn your freedom into an opportunity for the flesh, but through love serve one another. For the whole Law is fulfilled in one word, in the statement, "You shall love your neighbor as yourself."* Gal. 5:13,14

> *And He said to them, "The kings of the Gentiles lord it over them; and those who have authority over them are called 'Benefactors.' But not so with you, but let him who is the greatest among you become as the youngest, and the leader as the servant. For who is greater, the one who reclines at the table, or the one who serves? Is it not the one who reclines at the table? But I am among you as the one who serves."* Lk. 22:25-27

Jesus did this, not by rebuking them, but by demonstrating with His own example.

> *[Jesus] rose from supper, and laid aside His garments; and taking a towel, He girded Himself about. Then He poured water into the basin, and began to wash the disciples' feet, and to wipe them with the towel with which He was girded.* Jn. 13:4,5

c.  Finally, as an example for us to follow.

> *"If I then, the Lord and the Teacher, washed your feet, you also ought to wash one another's feet. For I gave you an example that you also should do as I did to you."* Jn. 13:14,15

410

## 5. HOW DO WE PREPARE OURSELVES FOR FOOT WASHING?

a. By searching our hearts with the aid of the Holy Spirit and repenting of all the enmity, pride, and self-seeking we find there—toward the Lord, our loved ones, and our fellow believers.

b. By asking the Lord to grant us His love for those whom we have wronged.

c. By realizing that a foot washing is a humbling experience. **It is meant to be!** Look at the trouble Peter had with it:

> *And so He came to Simon Peter. He said to Him, "Lord, do You wash my feet?" Jesus answered and said to him, "What I do you do not realize now, but you shall understand hereafter." Peter said to Him, "Never shall You wash my feet!" Jesus answered him, "If I do not wash you, you have no part with Me."*     Jn. 13:6-8

d. By realizing that, as with the other ordinances of the church, foot washing must be entered into by faith in God's Word and in His provision. What He has promised to do for us, **He will do.**


## 6. HOW OFTEN SHOULD WE HAVE A FOOT WASHING?

A foot washing should be held whenever the members of a local church feel the need for cleansing, especially when it is from enmity and division. Often, it will be a need that the whole church will recognize and to which they will respond. However, most of the time the direction will come from the oversight of the church.

## 7. WHAT IS THE PROCEDURE FOR FOOT WASHING?

We should simply do what Jesus did:

> [Jesus] *rose from supper, and laid aside His garments; and taking a towel, He girded Himself about. Then He poured water into the basin, and began to wash the disciples' feet, and to wipe them with the towel with which He was girded.*
>
> Jn. 13:4,5

In order to have everything done decently and in order (1 Cor. 14:40), the men and women should be separated with each group conducting its own service, the men washing the men's feet and the women washing the women's feet.

## HOME STUDY QUESTIONS: CHAPTER 31

1. What is foot washing?

2. What is the purpose of foot washing?

3. How do we prepare ourselves for foot washing?

# THE ORDINANCE OF CONFIRMATION

**Chapter 32**

Strictly speaking, confirmation is not an ordinance of the church, in one sense, because it was not instituted by Christ. Confirmation is, however, inherent in the doctrine of the laying on of hands and, therefore, should be included here.

Because of the way confirmation is practiced in the more traditional churches (that is, as a rite of the church and not as a confirming of true believers in the Lord Jesus Christ), fundamentalist churches and even most Spirit-filled churches have totally rejected confirmation as a valid Christian experience. This is unfortunate, because not only is it a valid experience, but it is also an extremely important one. It is the purpose of this chapter to show why it is such an important part of the Christian experience. As with other matters of faith, let us not reject truth because we have seen it set aside in error. Rather, let us lift the truth out of that into which it has fallen and restore it to its rightful place.

## 1. WHAT IS CONFIRMATION?

Confirmation is, by inference and inclusion, an ordinance of the church through which Christians are established and strengthened in their faith as it is in the Lord Jesus Christ. This is ministered to the believer by the laying on of hands, by which grace and spiritual strengthening are imparted.

> *And Judas and Silas, also being prophets themselves, encouraged and strengthened* ["confirmed," KJV] *the brethren with a lengthy message.*      Acts 15:32

*But Paul chose Silas and departed, being committed by the brethren to the grace of the Lord. And he was traveling through Syria and Cilicia, strengthening* ["confirming," KJV] *the churches.*                          Acts 15:40,41

*And after they* [Paul and Barnabas] *had preached the gospel to that city and had made many disciples, they returned to Lystra and to Iconium and to Antioch, strengthening* ["confirming," KJV] *the souls of the disciples, encouraging them to continue in the faith, and saying, "Through many tribulations we must enter the kingdom of God."*                          Acts 14:21,22

## 2. WHY DO WE NEED TO BE ESTABLISHED AND STRENGTHENED IN OUR FAITH?

We need to be established and strengthened in our faith because times of testing will come—storms and trials from without, and doubts and fears from within. With the laying on of hands, we receive a divine impartation of grace from the Lord to remain firm and steadfast during such times.

*As you therefore have received Christ Jesus the Lord, so walk in Him, having been firmly rooted and now being built up in Him and established in your faith, just as you were instructed, and overflowing with gratitude.*          Col. 2:6,7

*As a result, we are no longer to be children, tossed here and there by waves, and carried about by every wind of doctrine, by the trickery of men, by craftiness in deceitful scheming; but speaking the truth in love, we are to grow up in all aspects into Him, who is the head, even Christ.*
Eph. 4:14,15

### 3. HOW IS CONFIRMATION ADMINISTERED?

It is administered with the laying on of the hands of the presbytery, that is, the ministers and the elders of the church.

> *Do not neglect the spiritual gift within you, which was bestowed upon you. through prophetic utterance with the laying on of hands by the presbytery.* 1 Tim. 4:14

### 4. WHEN SHOULD WE BE CONFIRMED?

All believers, young and old alike, should be confirmed upon their completion of training in, and experiencing of, the doctrines (teachings) of Christ, as they are referred to in Hebrews 6:1,2, and in the ordinances of the church.

> *As you therefore have received Christ Jesus the Lord, so walk in Him, having been firmly rooted and now being built up in Him and established in your faith, just as you were instructed, and overflowing with gratitude.* Col. 2:6,7

> *This I say therefore, and affirm together with the Lord, that you walk no longer just as the Gentiles also walk, in the futility of their mind, being darkened in their understanding, excluded from the life of God, because of the ignorance that is in them, because of the hardness of their heart.*
> *But you did not learn Christ in this way, if indeed you have heard Him and have been taught in Him, just as truth is in Jesus.* Eph. 4:17,18,20,21

### 5. WHAT ARE THE RESULTS OF CONFIRMATION?

Because of the impartation of grace and spiritual strength through the laying on of hands, the believer is in a much stronger position to withstand the storms of life and the onslaughts of the enemy.

*Therefore, take up the **full armor of God,** that you may be able to resist in the evil day, and having done everything, **to stand firm. Stand firm** therefore, **having girded your loins with truth,** and having put on the breastplate of righteousness, and having **shod your feet** with the **preparation of the gospel of peace.***

*And take the helmet of salvation, and the sword of the Spirit, **which is the word of God.*** Eph. 6:13-15,17

## HOME STUDY QUESTIONS: CHAPTER 32

1. What is confirmation?

2. In your own words, explain briefly why confirmation is necessary.

3. When should a believer be confirmed?

# THE ORDINANCE OF MATRIMONY

**Chapter 33**

## 1. WHAT IS MATRIMONY?

Matrimony is one of the ordinances of the church instituted by God, through which a man and a woman vow to live together as husband and wife "as long as they both shall live." These vows are made to each other in the presence of God and are usually witnessed by family and members of the believing community (the church) of which they are a part. Matrimony, not to be confused with any particular type of wedding ceremony, goes back to the very beginning of time. Society has always recognized the difference between a marriage and an adulterous relationship, even before any type of formal wedding ceremony was practiced or required.

> *For this cause a man shall leave his father and his mother, and shall cleave to his wife; and they shall become one flesh.* Gen. 2:24

Matrimony is God's will for the great majority of His people and should never be disparaged or despised.

> *Then the Lord God said, "It is not good for the man to be alone; I will make him a helper suitable for him."*
> Gen. 2:18

> *Two are better than one because they have a good return for their labor. For if either of them falls, the one will lift up his companion. But woe to the one who falls when there is*

*not another to lift him up. Furthermore, if two lie down together they keep warm, but how can one be warm alone? And if one can overpower him who is alone, two can resist him. A cord of three strands is not quickly torn apart* [the third Person being the Lord!].                        Eccl. 4:9-12

Marriage is often difficult, but for most of us the married life contains that which is God's best and most rewarding. When Jesus was speaking to the disciples about marriage and divorce, the disciples answered by saying, "If the relationship of the man with his wife is like this, **it is better not to marry**" (Matt. 19:10). Jesus cautioned them that only those who had actually been called to a life of singleness (celibacy) could live in such a manner (Matt. 19:11). He went on to say:

> *"For there are eunuchs who were born that way from their mother's womb; and there are eunuchs who were made eunuchs by men; and there are also eunuchs who made themselves eunuchs for the sake of the kingdom of heaven. He who is able to accept this, let him accept it."*
>                                             Matt. 19:12

We must be careful not to interpret Paul's comments about marriage in 1 Corinthians 7 as being against marriage. And we must be especially wary of those who have actually formulated any teachings against marriage and of strange ideas about the need for being single in the last days.

> *But the Spirit explicitly says that in later times some will fall away from the faith, paying attention to deceitful spirits and doctrines of demons*
>   . . . *men who forbid marriage.*          1 Tim. 4:1,3a

The single life can be a very rewarding life for those who are called to it, but even then there will be many struggles: loneliness, unfulfilled sexual desires, etc. Those who feel they are called to the single life must draw very close to the Lord and to their fellow brothers and sisters in the body of Christ. For all of us, even for the singles:

> *Let marriage be held in honor among all.*
>
> Heb. 13:4a

## 2. WHAT IS THE NATURE OF THE MATRIMONIAL AGREEMENT?

In the matrimonial agreement, the husband and the wife agree to become "one flesh" with each other exclusively, in order that they may be joined together in a physical and spiritual union that can be ended only by death.

> *For this cause a man shall leave his father and mother, and shall cleave to his wife; and the two shall become one flesh. This mystery is great; but I am speaking with reference to Christ and the church. Nevertheless let each individual among you also love his own wife even as himself; and let the wife see to it that she respect her husband.*
>
> Eph. 5:31-33

## 3. WHY IS THE SPIRITUAL EMPHASIS UPON THE MATRIMONIAL UNION SO IMPORTANT?

Marriage is first of all a physical union between two people for the establishment of a home. The Word of God requires marriage even for unbelievers. Marriage is the solid basis for every society, and always has been! If, however, the Christian man and woman are not joined in spirit as well, they miss one of the most important purposes of God for matrimony—to make their relationship and love for one another an example of the love that Christ has for the church.

> *So husbands ought also to love their own wives as their own bodies. He who loves his own wife loves himself; for no*

*one ever hated his own flesh, but nourishes and cherishes it, just as Christ also does the church, because we are members of His body. For this cause a man shall leave his father and mother, and shall cleave to his wife; and the two shall become one flesh. This mystery is great; but I am speaking with reference to Christ and the church. Nevertheless let each individual among you also love his own wife even as himself; and let the wife see to it that she respect her husband.*                          Eph. 5:28-33

## 4. WHAT DOES IT MEAN FOR A HUSBAND AND WIFE TO BECOME "ONE [IN SPIRIT AND] FLESH"?

In a sense, the process of a man and a woman becoming "one flesh" is one of the mysteries of God.

> *For this cause a man shall leave his father and mother, and shall cleave to his wife; and the two shall become one flesh. This mystery is great.*                          Eph. 5:31,32a

It is the process of their becoming dependent upon one another and even like one another so that their thoughts, desires, faith, and spirit blend into one harmonious whole with the will of God for their lives. This becoming one in flesh and spirit can only take place where believing couples build a life together based upon the vows they have made to one another in the presence of God.

> *"Consequently they are no longer two, but one flesh. What therefore God has joined together, let no man separate."*                          Matt. 19:6

## 5. SINCE MATRIMONY WAS ACTUALLY INSTITUTED BY GOD, WHAT HAS JESUS DONE FOR CHRISTIAN MARRIAGE?

Jesus came into this world to redeem man from the curse of sin. He not only redeemed the soul and the spirit of man, He also redeemed everything pertaining to this life.   Jesus redeemed the marital relationship from pagan and even Jewish error and restored it to the wonderful and holy relationship that it was meant to be. Through Christ's teachings in the Gospels and the apostles' teachings throughout the balance of the New Testament, the husband/wife relationship and the places of the man and of the woman (and children) as individuals, each with their own responsibilities and rights, have been rescued from worldly concepts and practices and restored to the proper place of true love and dignity.

> *Grace and peace be multiplied to you in the knowledge of God and of Jesus our Lord; seeing that His divine power has granted to us everything pertaining to life and godliness, through the true knowledge of Him who called us by His own glory and excellence. For by these He has granted to us His precious and magnificent promises, in order that by them you might become partakers of the divine nature, having escaped the corruption that is in the world by lust.*
>
> 2 Pet. 1:2-4

## 6. ARE THERE ANY RESTRICTIONS AS TO WHOM A CHRISTIAN MAY MARRY?

Yes.  The following is not to be taken as a comprehensive list, but only as including those restrictions that are the most important.

a.   A Christian is not permitted to marry an unbeliever.

> *Do not be bound together with unbelievers; for what partnership have righteousness and lawlessness, or what*

> *fellowship has light with darkness? Or what harmony has Christ with Belial, or what has a believer in common with an unbeliever?* 2 Cor. 6:14,15

b.  Since married couples are to be "heirs together of the grace of life" (1 Pet. 3:7 KJV), a Christian should not marry another Christian whose life is inconsistent with the holy standard of God's Word.

> *Or do you not know that the unrighteous shall not inherit the kingdom of God? Do not be deceived; neither fornicators, nor idolaters, nor adulterers, nor effeminate, nor homosexuals, nor thieves, nor the covetous, nor drunkards, nor revilers, nor swindlers, shall inherit the kingdom of God.* 1 Cor. 6:9,10

> *But do not let immorality or any impurity or greed even be named among you, as is proper among saints; and there must be no filthiness and silly talk, or coarse jesting, which are not fitting, but rather giving of thanks. For this you know with certainty, that no immoral or impure person or covetous man, who is an idolater, has an inheritance in the kingdom of Christ and God.* Eph. 5:3-5

c.  Christians should not enter into marriage unless they are ready and willing to break the spiritual, emotional, and even financial ties with their respective families as they resort to each other for the establishing of their own home and family ties.

> *For this cause a man shall leave his father and his mother, and shall cleave to his wife; and they shall become one flesh.* Gen. 2:24

d.  A Christian is not permitted to marry one who has been previously married, unless that one has been widowed or has been divorced under conditions which meet the requirements of God's Word.

422

> *For the married woman is bound by law to her husband while he is living; but if her husband dies, she is released from the law concerning the husband. So then if, while her husband is living, she is joined to another man, she shall be called an adulteress; but if her husband dies, she is free from the law, so that she is not an adulteress, though she is joined to another man.*
>
> Rom. 7:2,3

Concerning the matter of divorce and the Christian, see Questions 10 through 16.


## 7. WHAT DOES MARRIAGE REQUIRE OF A WIFE?

Marriage requires the following of a wife:

a. That she realize that her husband and family will require a submission and dedication she once had to give only to the Lord.

> *But I want you to be free from concern. One who is unmarried is concerned about the things of the Lord, how he may please the Lord; but one who is married is concerned about the things of the world, how he may please his wife, and his interests are divided. And the woman who is unmarried, and the virgin, is concerned about the things of the Lord, that she may be holy both in body and spirit; but one who is married is concerned about the things of the world, how she may please her husband.* 1 Cor. 7:32-34

b. That she submit to the headship of her husband as it has been delegated to him by the Lord, and do so willingly and without fear.

> *Wives, be subject to your own husbands, as to the Lord.* Eph. 5:22

> *Thus Sarah obeyed Abraham, calling him lord, and*
> *you have become her children if you do what is right*
> *without being frightened by any fear.*         1 Pet. 3:6

c.  That she trust the Lord and rely on Him to perform His Word,
    while submitting to her husband. She should not berate her
    husband for his failures and shortcomings, but she should live a
    life before him that will demonstrate the grace of God and the
    power of His Word.

> *For this reason I, Paul, the prisoner of Christ Jesus*
> *for the sake of you Gentiles—if indeed you have heard of*
> *the stewardship of God's grace which was given to me*
> *for you . . . .*                              Eph. 3:1,2

> *The king's heart is like channels of water in the hand*
> *of the Lord; He turns it wherever He wishes.*
>                                                Prov. 21:1

d.  That she live in such a way that her life will be a credit to him, for
    the wife is the glory or reflection of her husband. This includes
    her conversation, her behavior, and her dress.

> *In the same way, you wives, be submissive to your*
> *own husbands so that even if any of them are disobedient*
> *to the word, they may be won without a word by the*
> *behavior of their wives, as they observe your chaste and*
> *respectful behavior. And let not your adornment be*
> *merely external—braiding the hair, and wearing gold*
> *jewelry, and putting on dresses; but let it be the hidden*
> *person of the heart, with the imperishable quality of a*
> *gentle and quiet spirit, which is precious in the sight of*
> *God. For in this way in former times the holy women*
> *also, who hoped in God, used to adorn themselves, being*
> *submissive to their own husbands.*         1 Pet. 3:1-5

e.   That she teach the children by her attitude and conduct that the father is the head of the home.

> *Children, obey your parents in the Lord, for this is right.*
> *And, fathers, do not provoke your children to anger; but bring them up in the discipline and instruction of the Lord.*                                            Eph. 6:1,4

f.   That she understand that she does not have exclusive rights over her own body. The sexual relationship between the husband and wife is ordained by God and given by Him not only for procreation, but also for enjoyment. It should never be abused, nor should sex be used by either party to manipulate the other.

> *Let the husband fulfill his duty to his wife, and likewise also the wife to her husband. The wife does not have authority over her own body, but the husband does; and likewise also the husband does not have authority over his own body, but the wife does. Stop depriving one another, except by agreement for a time that you may devote yourselves to prayer, and come together again lest Satan tempt you because of your lack of self-control.*
> 1 Cor. 7:3-5

> *Let marriage be held in honor among all, and let the marriage bed be undefiled; for fornicators and adulterers God will judge.*                                           Heb. 13:4

g.   That she pray earnestly for her husband and children.

> *Finally, all [of you] should be of one and the same mind (united in spirit), sympathizing [with one another], loving [each the others] as brethren (of one household), compassionate and courteous—tenderhearted and humbleminded. Never return evil for evil or insult for insult—scolding, tongue-lashing, berating; but on the*

*contrary blessing—praying for their welfare, happiness and protection, and truly pitying and loving them. For know that to this you have been called, that you may yourselves inherit a blessing [from God]—obtain a blessing as heirs, bringing welfare and happiness and protection.*                                                  1 Pet. 3:8,9 AMP


## 8. IS THE WIFE REQUIRED TO SUBMIT TO HER HUSBAND IN ALL THINGS?

A wife is required to submit to the headship of her husband just as it has been **delegated** to him by the Lord. In other words, the husband has the authority and headship over his wife and children only insofar as he is serving the Lord and fulfilling the Word of God. He does not have the right to hinder their way in the Lord, for instance (even if he is an unbeliever), nor can he rightly require anything of his wife and children that would cause them to sin.


## 9. WHAT DOES MARRIAGE REQUIRE OF A HUSBAND?

Marriage requires the following of a husband:

a.   That he be willing to assume the headship over his wife and children, knowing that the Lord requires him to be the head of his family.

> *But I want you to understand that Christ is the head of every man, and the man is the head of a woman, and God is the head of Christ.*                          1 Cor. 11:3

> *For the husband is the head of the wife, as Christ also is the head of the church, He Himself being the Savior of the body.*                                           Eph. 5:23

426

b.  That he understand that having the headship over his family is not a matter of being "boss" or of being "in charge." Authority certainly entails responsibility, and the ultimate responsibility for his family's welfare rests firmly upon the shoulders of the man. The balancing factor, however, and that which keeps the husband from becoming a "benevolent dictator" (or worse!), is that the Word of God requires the husband to be the husband-redeemer, loving his wife as Christ loved the church, that is, sacrificially.

> *Husbands, love your wives, just as Christ also loved the church and gave Himself up for her; that He might sanctify her, having cleansed her by the washing of water with the word, that He might present to Himself the church in all her glory, having no spot or wrinkle or any such thing; but that she should be holy and blameless. So husbands ought also to love their own wives as their own bodies. He who loves his own wife loves himself; for no one ever hated his own flesh, but nourishes and cherishes it, just as Christ also does the church.*
>
> Eph. 5:25-29

c.  That he respect, honor, and cherish his wife **just as Christ does the church,**

> *So husbands ought also to love their own wives as their own bodies. He who loves his own wife loves himself; for no one ever hated his own flesh, but nourishes and cherishes it, just as Christ also does the church.*
>
> Eph. 5:28,29

recognizing their being heirs together of the grace of life.

> *In the same way you married men should live considerately with [your wives], with an intelligent recognition [of the marriage relation], honoring the woman as [physically] the weaker, but [realizing that you] are joint heirs of the grace (God's unmerited favor)*

427

*of life, in order that your prayers may not be hindered*
*and cut off.—Otherwise you cannot pray effectively.*

1 Pet. 3:7 AMP

d.  That he realize that he is the one responsible for the welfare of his family.

> *But if anyone does not provide for his own, and*
> *especially for those of his household, he has denied the*
> *faith, and is worse than an unbeliever.*        1 Tim. 5:8

e.  That he assume leadership in the home in all things, especially in the things pertaining to the spiritual life of the family. The husband is the "priest" in his home and, as such, is the Lord's direct representative. This does not in any way obviate the responsibility of the wife to pursue her own relationship with the Lord. The spiritual headship of the husband is given to augment that of the Lord in the home, not to replace it.

> *He must be one who manages his own household*
> *well, keeping his children under control with all dignity.*

1 Tim. 3:4

> *"For I have chosen him, in order that he may*
> *command his children and his household after him to*
> *keep the way of the Lord by doing righteousness and*
> *justice."*                                      Gen. 18:19

> *"And if it is disagreeable in your sight to serve the*
> *Lord, choose for yourselves today whom you will serve:*
> *whether the gods which your fathers served which were*
> *beyond the River, or the gods of the Amorites in whose*
> *land you are living; but as for me and my house, we will*
> *serve the Lord."*                              Josh. 24:15

f.  That he understand that his wife and children are not in any way subservient to him. If anything, he is there to serve them. The Christian marriage is based upon the dignity of both partners.

> *And be subject to one another in the fear of Christ.*
> Eph. 5:21

## IS IT EVER PERMISSIBLE TO DISSOLVE A MARRIAGE?

Yes, there are two conditions under which it is permissible to dissolve a marriage.

a.  It is permissable when one of the partners is guilty of fornication (the Greek word *pornea* includes adultery, incest, homosexuality, and all sins of impurity). Jesus said that this sin would warrant a complete dissolution of the marriage covenant.

> *"But I say to you that everyone who divorces his wife, except for the cause of unchastity, makes her commit adultery."*
> Matt. 5:32

b.  It is permissable when the unbeliever departs. The Bible says the other partner is not "under bondage in such cases."

> *But to the rest I say, not the Lord, that if any brother has a wife who is an unbeliever, and she consents to live with him, let him not send her away. And a woman who has an unbelieving husband, and he consents to live with her, let her not send her husband away. For the unbelieving husband is sanctified through his wife, and the unbelieving wife is sanctified through her believing husband; for otherwise your children are unclean, but now they are holy. Yet if the unbelieving one leaves, let him leave; the brother or the sister is not under bondage in such cases, but God has called us to peace. For how do you know, O wife, whether you will save your*

*husband? Or how do you know, O husband, whether you will save your wife?* 1 Cor. 7:12-16

## 11. IS IT WRONG TO SEEK A DIVORCE?

No, it is not wrong to seek a divorce when the requirements of Scripture have been met.

## 12. WHAT SHOULD BE DONE BEFORE SEEKING A DIVORCE?

Before seeking a divorce, steps should be taken by the parties involved who, with the help of the oversight of the church, seek to bring about a reconciliation. Forgiveness, understanding, admonition, exhortation from God's Word, repentance—these and more are required by those involved if the marriage is to be saved. Only after a fervent attempt at reconciliation has failed should a divorce be sought.

## 13. IS REMARRIAGE EVER PERMITTED?

Remarriage is permitted when the oversight of the local church (the pastor and elders) knows that the injured party was innocent and that the marriage in question was beyond restoration.

## 14. WHAT SHOULD BE DONE WHEN ONE HAS SUFFERED DIVORCE FOR WRONG REASONS PRIOR TO BECOMING A CHRISTIAN?

Such a situation often occurs, especially in today's society. Persons who have gone through a divorce **for whatever reasons** prior to becoming a Christian should thank the Lord for new beginnings!

*Therefore if any man is in Christ, he is a new creature;*
*the old things passed away; behold, new things have come.*
2 Cor. 5:17

Often in such cases, it is advisable for the oversight of the local church to establish a period of "probation" for the purpose of making sure that the new convert understands Christian principles and that the same mistakes will not be repeated.

## WHAT SHOULD THE CHURCH'S ATTITUDE BE TOWARD THE DIVORCED?

In the case of a divorce that is scripturally permissible, the church should have acceptance and compassion for the divorced. Restoration, not judgment, is what is needed, especially if the injured party is the woman. Divorced brothers or sisters in the local church are not "second class citizens." They should be accepted and worked with as a normal part of the local body, neither ignored nor patronized.

*But speaking the truth in love, we are to grow up in all aspects into Him, who is the head, even Christ, from whom the whole body, being fitted and held together by that which every joint supplies, according to the proper working of each individual part, causes the growth of the body for the building up of itself in love.*
Eph. 4:15,16

*And do not grieve the Holy Spirit of God, by whom you were sealed for the day of redemption. Let all bitterness and wrath and anger and clamor and slander be put away from you, along with all malice.*
Eph. 4:30,31

## 16. ARE THE DIVORCED PERMITTED TO HAVE A POSITION OF MINISTRY IN THE CHURCH?

This is a difficult question and one requiring much prayer and wisdom. At the present time, it is our position that the scriptural requirement of "the husband of one wife" (1 Tim. 3:2) precludes those involved in a divorce **in most cases** from serving the church in the capacity of pastor, elder, or deacon.

> Now a bishop (superintendent, overseer) must give no grounds for accusation but must be above reproach, the husband of one wife . . . .
> Let deacons be the husbands of but one wife . . . .
> 1 Tim. 3:2,12 AMP

## HOME STUDY QUESTIONS: CHAPTER 33

1. What is matrimony?

2. What does marriage require of the wife?

3. What does marriage require of the husband?

4. What are the scriptural reasons permitting a divorce?

5. What should be the place of the divorced person in the local church?

# THE ORDINANCE OF THE
# DEDICATION OF CHILDREN

**Chapter 34**

The dedication of children is another of the ordinances of the church which, like confirmation, was not specifically instituted by Christ but is inherent in His teachings.

> *But Jesus said, "Let the children alone, and do not hinder them from coming to Me; for the kingdom of heaven belongs to such as these."*                                                    Matt. 19:14

> *And He took them in His arms and began blessing them, laying His hands upon them.*                                                    Mk. 10:16

Jesus also said there were many more things He had yet to teach the church through the disciples, but that they would be revealed later through the ministry of the Holy Spirit.

> *"I have many more things to say to you, but you cannot bear them now. But when He, the Spirit of truth, comes, He will guide you into all the truth; for He will not speak on His own initiative, but whatever He hears, He will speak; and He will disclose to you what is to come. He shall glorify Me; for He shall take of Mine, and shall disclose it to you."*                                                    Jn. 16:12-14

Paul and the other apostles continued to minister the truth of the Word of God as the Holy Spirit brought them further understanding and fresh revelation. They taught authoritatively both by the command of the Lord and by that which seemed good to them (1 Cor. 7:10,25; Acts 15:19,22,28).

## 1. WHAT IS THE DEDICATION OF CHILDREN?

The dedication of children is that ordinance of the church wherein the parents present their children before the Lord, acknowledging Him as the Giver of life and asking Him for His direction and protection in their spiritual life and development.

## 2. WHAT IS ACKNOWLEDGED AND AGREED TO IN THIS ORDINANCE?

a. The parents acknowledge that the lives of their children are neither an accident nor merely the product of their own volition, but are the gift of the Lord, the Giver of all life.

> *Behold, children are a gift of the Lord; the fruit of the womb is a reward. Like arrows in the hand of a warrior, so are the children of one's youth. How blessed is the man whose quiver is full of them; they shall not be ashamed, when they speak with their enemies in the gate.*
> Ps. 127:3-5

b. The parents also acknowledge the Lordship of Christ over their home and especially in the raising of their children. In the dedication of children, parents are reminded that their children are given by God into their hands for a season and that their chief responsibility is to raise those children to serve the Lord.

> *Fathers, do not provoke your children to anger; but bring them up in the discipline and instruction of the Lord.* Eph. 6:4

> *Train up a child in the way he should go, even when he is old he will not depart from it.* Prov. 22:6

Read also Genesis 18:19; Joshua 24:15; 1 Timothy 3:4.

c.  The parents present their children to the Lord as they also call upon Him, agreeing to raise them in the instruction of the Lord and acknowledging **their need** for His provision in enabling them to fulfill their parental responsibilities.

> *O my Lord . . . teach us what we shall do unto the child You have given us to rear for Thee.*
>
> Jud. 13:8 RSV

> *Unless the Lord builds the house, they labor in vain who build it; unless the Lord guards the city, the watchman keeps awake in vain.* Ps. 127:1

> *How blessed is everyone who fears the Lord, who walks in His ways. When you shall eat of the fruit of your hands, you will be happy and it will be well with you. Your wife shall be like a fruitful vine, within your house, your children like olive plants around your table. Behold, for thus shall the man be blessed who fears the Lord. The Lord bless you from Zion, and may you see the prosperity of Jerusalem all the days of your life. Indeed, may you see your children's children. Peace be upon Israel!* Ps. 128

d.  In turn, the Lord gives assurance to the parents through His Word that He will set those children apart unto Himself, keeping them and protecting them until such time as they are mature enough to make their own decision unto salvation.

> *For He will give His angels charge concerning you, to guard you in all your ways. They will bear you up in their hands, lest you strike your foot against a stone.*
>
> Ps. 91:11,12

*"See that you do not despise one of these little ones,*
*for I say to you, that their angels in heaven continually*
*behold the face of My Father who is in heaven."*

Matt. 18:10

This maturing to the place of being able to make one's own decision whether or not to follow the Lord differs from child to child. There are those who, on the basis of Jesus' going into the temple at the age of twelve according to the Jewish custom (Lk. 2:41,42), subscribe to the belief that a child is not responsible for making such a decision until he has reached the "age of accountability," that is, twelve years of age. Our feeling, however, is that children know the difference between right and wrong at a very early age and are capable of making decisions for following the ways of the world long before they reach the age of twelve. Parents should feel it their primary responsibility to lead their children to Christ and should not wait for them to reach a specific age; rather, they should wait upon the Lord for wisdom and the discerning of the proper time to respond to the working of the Word of the Lord in the lives of their children. It is natural for children to want to turn to the Lord, but many have been lost because parents waited for the "age of accountability," only to find out that the spirit of the age had already captured them.

3. **WHAT IS THE SCRIPTURAL BASIS FOR BELIEVING THE LORD WILL SET APART UNTO HIMSELF CHILDREN WHO HAVE BEEN DEDICATED TO HIM?**

The record of the entire Word of God serves to assure the parents that the Lord will indeed establish the house which has been set apart unto Himself (Ps. 127:1). Perhaps the strongest Scripture in support of this may be found in 1 Corinthians 7:14 AMP:

*For the unbelieving husband is set apart (separated, withdrawn from heathen contamination and affiliated with the Christian people) by union with his consecrated*

436

*(set-apart) wife; and the unbelieving wife is set apart and separated through union with her consecrated husband. Otherwise your children would be unclean [unblessed heathen, outside the Christian covenant], but as it is they are prepared for God—pure and clean.*

## 4. WHAT SPECIFIC ASSURANCE IS GIVEN TO PARENTS IN 1 CORINTHIANS 7:14?

A believing parent who is married to an unbeliever is specifically assured that their children are in a special, set-apart place in God's care and protection until those children are capable of making their own decision for the Lord.

## 5. DOES THIS MEAN THAT CHILDREN DEDICATED TO THE LORD ARE SAVED?

No. The Bible teaches very clearly that we are born into this world in sin (Ps. 51:5; Rom. 3:23; Eph. 2:1-3). The only remedy for this lost condition is our repentance and being saved according to the gospel.

> *Jesus answered and said to him, "Truly, truly, I say to you, unless one is born again, he cannot see the kingdom of God.*
> *"Truly, truly, I say to you, unless one is born of water and the Spirit, he cannot enter into the kingdom of God.*
> *"Do not marvel that I said to you, 'You must be born again.'"*                                        Jn. 3:3,5,7

> *"Sirs, what must I do to be saved?" And they said, "Believe in the Lord Jesus, and you shall be saved, you and your household."*                    Acts 16:30b,31

God has given His Word to us that, when we dedicate our children to Him and fulfill our responsibility to raise them in a godly home where they will both see and hear the Word of God, He will accept them as belonging to Himself. Just exactly what that entails, we are not told. The promises of God are powerful enough without our attempting to make them more than they are. What He has spoken, He will fulfill!

> *For I know whom I have believed and I am convinced that He is able to guard what I have entrusted to Him until that day.* 2 Tim. 1:12b

## 6. WHAT HAPPENS TO THE CHILDREN OF BELIEVING PARENTS WHO HAVE BEEN DEDICATED TO THE LORD BUT DIE BEFORE THEY REACH THE AGE OF SPIRITUAL MATURITY?

We simply do not know. This is one of those areas where we must realize that we only "know in part" and "see in a mirror dimly" (1 Cor. 13:12), and we must trust the sovereign and loving will of our heavenly Father. No doubt, when we stand before the Lord and "know fully," and no longer "in part," then we shall be able to praise the Lord for His excellent will in all the affairs of man. If He is God, then He cannot do anything that is contrary to His just nature.

## 7. WHEN BOTH PARENTS ARE UNBELIEVERS, WHAT IS THE CONDITION OF THEIR CHILDREN?

The children of parents who are both unbelievers are considered by the Word of God to be "unclean, unblessed heathen, outside the Christian covenant."

> *For the unbelieving husband is set apart (separated, withdrawn from heathen contamination and affiliated with the Christian people) by union with his consecrated (set-apart) wife; and the unbelieving wife is set apart and separated through union with her consecrated husband. Otherwise your children would be unclean [unblessed heathen, outside the Christian covenant], but as it is they are prepared for God—pure and clean.* 1 Cor. 7:14 AMP

438

## 8. WHAT DOES THE BIBLE HAVE TO SAY ABOUT DISCIPLINING OF CHILDREN?

The Bible clearly teaches, first of all, the need for firm discipline in the sense of training.

> *Train up a child* in the *way he should go,* *even when he is old he will not depart from it.*     Prov. 22:6

Secondly, there is also the need for that training to be followed by correction (punishment) when necessary.

> *Correct your son, and he will give you comfort; he will also delight your soul.*     Prov. 29:17

> *"For those whom the Lord loves He disciplines, and He scourges every son whom He receives."* *It is for discipline that you endure; God deals with you as with sons; for what son is there whom his father does not discipline?*
> *Furthermore, we had earthly fathers to discipline us, and we respected them; shall we not much rather be subject to the Father of spirits, and live? For they disciplined us for a short time as seemed best to them, but He disciplines us for our good, that we may share His holiness. All discipline for the moment seems not to be joyful, but sorrowful; yet to those who have been trained by it, afterwards it yields the peaceful fruit of righteousness.*     Heb. 12:6,7,9-11

The training of children is a twofold necessity and responsibility. Children need to be trained by their parents in the natural disciplines of life (habits, manners, attitudes, schooling, etc.) so that they will grow up to be whole and responsible adults. Parents also need to train their children in the things of the Lord (the Word, life in the Spirit, prayer, holiness, etc.) so that they will grow up to be strong in the Lord.

## 9. WHY IS DISCIPLINE NECESSARY?

Correction is necessary because the inclination of the human heart, by nature, is against the government of God.

> *And you were dead in your trespasses and sins, in which you formerly walked according to the course of this world, according to the prince of the power of the air, of the spirit that is now working in the sons of disobedience. Among them we too all formerly lived in the lusts of our flesh, indulging the desires of the flesh and of the mind, and were by nature children of wrath, even as the rest.*
>
> Eph. 2:1-3

Rebellion and the spirit of disobedience are very evident in "bad" children, but even "good" children are included in this lost, rebellious condition. Parents not only have the responsibility, but they have the privilege and the opportunity of raising their children in a home where they can see the government of God in action through the godly lives of their parents.

> *Now I say, as long as the heir is a child, he does not differ at all from a slave although he is owner of everything, but he is under guardians and managers until the date set by the father.*
>
> Gal. 4:1,2

> *He* [the elder] *must be one who manages* ["ruleth," KJV] *his own household well, keeping his children under control with all dignity.*
>
> 1 Tim. 3:4

## 10. WHAT METHOD OF CORRECTION DOES THE BIBLE SANCTION?

Among such things as verbal correction, etc., the Bible sanctions and recommends that children be spanked by their parents when necessary.

*He who spares his rod hates his son, but he who loves him disciplines him diligently.*  Prov. 13:24

*Discipline your son while there is hope, and do not desire his death.*  Prov. 19:18

*Foolishness is bound up in the heart of a child; the rod of discipline will remove it far from him.*  Prov. 22:15

*Do not hold back discipline from the child, although you beat him with the rod, he will not die. You shall beat him with the rod, and deliver his soul from Sheol.*

Prov. 23:13,14

A spanking should never be administered in a haphazard fashion, that is, inconsistently, out of anger, or merely when the parent's patience has reached "the limit." A spanking, and all forms of correction, should be administered in love and only when the parent is in complete control of himself. Correction administered in anger only stirs up anger in the child being corrected. Discipline administered in a haphazard fashion only serves to confuse the child. Violence or physical abuse should never be used, nor should correction be administered for the purpose of breaking the will of the child, but rather for the purpose of directing the will and bringing it into proper subjection. It is well to pray with a child before correcting him. Frequent, mild, but firm admonition is all part of good child-training and, coupled with prayer, is the best training a child can have.

*Fathers, do not exasperate your children, that they may not lose heart.*  Col. 3:21

*And, fathers, do not provoke your children to anger; but bring them up in the discipline and instruction of the Lord.*

Eph. 6:4

11. **WHAT KIND OF ATTITUDE SHOULD CHILDREN HAVE TOWARD THOSE WHO ARE IN AUTHORITY OVER THEM?**

No one, by nature, likes and appreciates correction and discipline. This applies especially to children. Children, then, should be taught to appreciate discipline by learning to obey, respect, and honor those in authority over them. If this begins in the home and is done properly according to the Word of God, it will extend to teachers, ministers, the elderly, employers, the government and its officials, **and especially to God!**

> *Therefore he who resists authority has opposed the ordinance of God; and they who have opposed will receive condemnation upon themselves.*  Rom. 13:2

See Chapter 28 on the government of God.

## HOME STUDY QUESTIONS: CHAPTER 34

1. What is the ordinance of the dedication of children?

2. What are the responsibilities of parents in this agreement?

3. What has God promised to do as His part of the agreement?

4. Why is discipline necessary?

# SPIRITUAL WARFARE

**Chapter 35**

## 1. WHAT IS SPIRITUAL WARFARE?

Spiritual warfare is that continuing battle that we, as Christians, must wage against our adversary, the devil. Satan, along with his demonic forces, has from the beginning set himself to oppose the authority of God, especially as it resides in the body of Christ—the church.

> *Finally, be strong in the Lord, and in the strength of His might. Put on the full armor of God, that you may be able to stand firm against the schemes of the devil. For our struggle is not against flesh and blood, but against the rulers, against the powers, against the world forces of this darkness, against the spiritual forces of wickedness in the heavenly places.*
>
> Eph. 6:10-12

## 2. WHY IS SATAN SO OPPOSED TO THE CHURCH?

Satan, as "god of this world" (2 Cor. 4:4) and of the kingdom of darkness (Col. 1:13), is the ruler of a system that is diametrically opposed to the kingdom of God and everything for which it stands. Satan has already lost the battle with God Himself (see Chapter 25—"The Creation of the World and the Fall of Lucifer and His Angels") and with Christ (Acts 2:22-24,32-36; Col. 2:15). He is now concentrating all his efforts against the church.

*Be of sober spirit, be on the alert. Your adversary, the devil, prowls about like a roaring lion, seeking someone to devour.*                                                      1 Pet. 5:8

## 3.  WHAT MUST WE DO TO THWART THE PURPOSES OF SATAN?

As members of the body of Christ, we must present ourselves as soldiers to be trained for battle.

*He trains my hands for battle, so that my arms can bend a bow of bronze.*
*For Thou hast girded me with strength for battle; Thou hast subdued under me those who rose up against me.*
                                                             Ps. 18:34,39

*Blessed be the Lord, my rock, who trains my hands for war, and my fingers for battle.*                        Ps. 144:1

*Suffer hardship with me, as a good soldier of Christ Jesus.  No soldier in active service entangles himself in the affairs of everyday life, so that he may please the one who enlisted him as a soldier.*                    2 Tim. 2:3,4

## 4.  WHAT ARE SOME OF THE THINGS AGAINST WHICH WE MUST FIGHT?

We will find ourselves fighting this battle on many fronts. We could not begin to name them all here; however, here are a few of the most important:

a.  The insidiousness of this world system that continually threatens to encroach upon the people of God.

*"I have given them Thy word; and the world has hated them, because they are not of the world, even as I am not of the world. I do not ask Thee to take them out of the world, but to keep them from the evil one. They are not of the world, even as I am not of the world."*

Jn. 17:14-16

*Beloved, do not believe every spirit, but test the spirits to see whether they are from God . . . .*
*You are from God, little children, and have overcome them; because greater is He who is in you than he who is in the world. They are from the world; therefore they speak as from the world, and the world listens to them. We are from God; he who knows God listens to us; he who is not from God does not listen to us. By this we know the spirit of truth and the spirit of error.*

1 Jn. 4:1a,4-6

*We know that we are of God, and the whole world lies in the power of the evil one.*

1 Jn. 5:19

*You adulteresses, do you not know that friendship with the world is hostility toward God? Therefore whoever wishes to be a friend of the world makes himself an enemy of God.*

Jas. 4:4

b. The wisdom of this world.

*But if you have bitter jealousy and selfish ambition in your heart, do not be arrogant and so lie against the truth. This wisdom is not that which comes down from above, but is earthly, natural, demonic. For where jealousy and selfish ambition exist, there is disorder and every evil thing.*

Jas. 3:14-16

c. The vain philosophies of this world and those elementary religious notions of the world that blind people from seeing the truth of the Word of God.

> *See to it that no one takes you captive through philosophy and empty deception, according to the tradition of men, according to the elementary principles of the world, rather than according to Christ.*
>
> Col. 2:8

d. The speculative thinking and reasoning of man that flows from, and is the natural result of, the above.

> *For the weapons of our warfare are not of the flesh, but divinely powerful for the destruction of fortresses. We are destroying speculations and every lofty thing raised up against the knowledge of God, and we are taking every thought captive to the obedience of Christ.*
>
> 2 Cor. 10:4,5

e. Deceitful spirits and the doctrines of demons.

> *But the Spirit explicitly says that in later times some will fall away from the faith, paying attention to deceitful spirits and doctrines of demons, by means of the hypocrisy of liars seared in their own conscience as with a branding iron, men who forbid marriage and advocate abstaining from foods, which God has created to be gratefully shared in by those who believe and know the truth.*
>
> 1 Tim. 4:1-3

Read also 2 Thessalonians 2:3-11; 2 Timothy 3:1-5.

f. False prophets and those who disguise themselves as the ministers of righteousness.

> *"Beware of the false prophets, who come to you in sheep's clothing, but inwardly are ravenous wolves."*
>
> Matt. 7:15

> *For such men are false apostles, deceitful workers, disguising themselves as apostles of Christ. And no wonder, for even Satan disguises himself as an angel of light. Therefore it is not surprising if his servants also disguise themselves as servants of righteousness; whose end shall be according to their deeds.*
>
> 2 Cor. 11:13-15

> *"And from among your own selves men will arise, speaking perverse things, to draw away the disciples after them."*
>
> Acts 20:30

g. Spiritual oppression in the heavenlies that hinders our prayers to God and His answers to us.

> *Then he said to me, "Do not be afraid, Daniel, for from the first day that you set your heart on understanding this and on humbling yourself before your God, your words were heard, and I have come in response to your words. But the prince of the kingdom of Persia was withstanding me for twenty-one days; then behold, Michael, one of the chief princes, came to help me, for I had been left there with the kings of Persia."*
>
> Dan. 10:12,13

h. The false accusations of the enemy against ourselves and other Christians.

> *"Now the salvation, and the power, and the kingdom of our God and the authority of His Christ have come, for the accuser of our brethren has been thrown down, who accuses them before our God day and night."*
>
> Rev. 12:10

i.	The blinding power of the "god of this world" over the minds of unbelievers, hindering them from understanding and accepting the gospel.

> *And even if our gospel is veiled, it is veiled to those who are perishing, in whose case the god of this world has blinded the minds of the unbelieving, that they might not see the light of the gospel of the glory of Christ, who is the image of God.*	2 Cor. 4:3,4

j.	Demonic possession and oppression.

> *And when evening had come, after the sun had set, they began bringing to Him all who were ill and those who were demon-possessed. And the whole city had gathered at the door. And He healed many who were ill with various diseases, and cast out many demons; and He was not permitting the demons to speak, because they knew who He was.*	Mk. 1:32-34

k.	Sickness and illness caused by demonic possession (in the case of unbelievers) and demonic oppression (in the case of believers):

1.	Dumbness (Matt. 9:32,33).

2.	Blindness and dumbness (Matt. 12:22).

3.	Deafness, dumbness, and epilepsy (Matt. 17:14-18; Mk. 9:17-25).

4.	Violent nature (Mk. 5:1-5).

5.	Disruptive nature (Lk. 4:33-35).

6.	Oppression by a spirit of infirmity (Lk. 13:10-16).

Is all sickness, deformity, and mental imbalance caused by demonic possession or oppression? No! Jesus healed many who had been made ill by unclean spirits, but He also healed many who were just "normally" sick. Read Matthew 8:16,17; 10:1; 15:29-31; Mark 1:32,34; etc.

## 5. WHAT IS DEMONIC POSSESSION?

Demonic possession is the actual indwelling of a demonic spirit in a human body. Demons are disembodied spirits who seek to inhabit a living being.

> *"Now when the unclean spirit goes out of a man, it passes through waterless places, seeking rest, and does not find it. Then it says, 'I will return to my house from which I came'; and when it comes, it finds it unoccupied, swept, and put in order. Then it goes, and takes along with it seven other spirits more wicked than itself, and they go in and live there; and the last state of that man becomes worse than the first. That is the way it will also be with this evil generation."* Matt. 12:43-45

> *And when He had come to the other side into the country of the Gadarenes, two men who were demon-possessed met Him as they were coming out of the tombs; they were so exceedingly violent that no one could pass by that road. And behold, they cried out, saying, "What do we have to do with You, Son of God? Have You come here to torment us before the time?" Now there was at a distance from them a herd of many swine feeding. And the demons began to entreat Him, saying, "If You are going to cast us out, send us into the herd of swine." And He said to them, "Begone!" And they came out, and went into the swine, and behold, the whole herd rushed down the steep bank into the sea and perished in the waters.* Matt. 8:28-32

## 6. HOW DOES DEMONIC POSSESSION OCCUR?

Demonic possession usually does not occur all at once. Most of the time it begins as a form of oppression as the unclean spirit gains access to an individual through an unguarded portal (that is, the five senses). Drugs, alcohol, extreme fear, etc., are all contributing factors in one's defenses being down. One of the best examples in the Bible of demonic possession is that of Judas Iscariot. We can follow the progress of his possession through the Word of God:

Step One: Read John 12:1-8. Mary washed the feet of Jesus out of love and in preparation for His burial. Judas found fault with this, ostensibly because he thought the money should have been spent on the poor, but in reality, it was because he was the treasurer and had been stealing money from the bag. Greed had begun to be his downfall.

Step Two: Read Matthew 26:14-16; Mark 14:10,11. Greed led him to bargain with the high priest for thirty pieces of silver for the betrayal of Jesus. No doubt, he justified this to himself by blaming Jesus for being wasteful.

Step Three: Read John 13:2. He was not even afraid of coming into the Passover meal (remember, this is a type of the Lord's Supper!) with this sin, because the devil had already put it into his heart. What had begun as greed and progressed to thievery had by now developed into a complete breakdown of judgment.

Step Four: Read John 13:27. **Satan entered into him!**

## 7. CAN A CHRISTIAN BE DEMON-POSSESSED?

It is possible for one who has become a justified believer, but who has not completed his born-again experience by going into the waters of baptism and receiving the baptism of the Holy Spirit, to be demon-possessed. It is not possible for a Spirit-filled believer to be demon-possessed because the Holy Spirit is the seal upon his spiritual experience (Eph. 1:13). Jesus gave us a principle in Matthew 12:29:

> "Or how can anyone enter the strong man's house and carry off his property, **unless he first binds the strong man?** And then he will plunder his house."

In other words, in order for an unclean spirit to indwell a Spirit-filled believer, it would have to bind the Holy Spirit and cast **Him** out. Common sense tells us that could never happen. And for those who need a little something to prod their common sense, we have the sure promise of 1 John 4:4:

> You are from God, little children, and have overcome them; because **greater is He who is in you** than he who is in the world.

Should there be any argument, let him who is of any other opinion show from the Word of God whether it is possible for a Spirit-filled Christian to be demon-possessed. **It cannot be done!** There is not one single example to be found in the Word of God.

## 8. CAN A CHRISTIAN BE DEMON-OPPRESSED?

Yes, this can happen. Demonic possession is the inhabiting of an unclean spirit in one's life; oppression is demonic influence by overshadowing. Oppression is the most common form of demonic activity we see today, especially in this country where most of the cases of possession have been diagnosed as schizophrenia, etc., and committed to institutions. In most heathen lands, such as India and Africa, cases of demonic possession are still very evident. Here are some scriptural examples of demonic oppression:

- Peter had opened himself up to satanic influence, the result being muddled thinking (Matt. 16:23).

- Satan had a continuing desire to "sift" Simon Peter like wheat (Lk. 22:31).

- Ananias and Sapphira had opened themselves up to the same sin as Judas had—**greed.** It had already oppressed their minds so much that they had not only lied to the Holy Ghost, but were prepared to come into the assembly and lie there, too (Acts 5:3).

NOTE: Spiritual experiences, by their very nature, tend to be subjective. We cannot afford to judge the Word of God by what we feel or think we see. Rather, we must judge what we feel or think we see **by the Word of God.** Many who have gone off into error and the shipwreck of their faith over the present-day deliverance movement would still be healthy and active in the church today if they had used the Word of God as their guide and not their own subjective judgments and experiences.

## 9.  WHAT IS THE REMEDY FOR DEMONIC OPPRESSION?

The power of the enemy must be broken by prayer and anointing with oil in the name of the Lord Jesus Christ, and often by fasting, for both the saved:

> *"Simon, Simon, behold, Satan has demanded permission to sift you like wheat; but I have prayed for you, that your faith may not fail; and you, when once you have turned again, strengthen your brothers."*     Lk. 22:31,32

> *"Is this not the fast which I choose, to loosen the bonds of wickedness, to undo the bands of the yoke, and to let the oppressed go free, and break every yoke?"*     Isa. 58:6

and the unsaved:

> *"You know of Jesus of Nazareth, how God anointed Him with the Holy Spirit and with power, and how He went about doing good, and healing all who were oppressed by the devil; for God was with Him."* Acts 10:38

## WHAT IS THE REMEDY FOR DEMONIC POSSESSION?

In the case of those who have actually become possessed or indwelt by an unclean, evil spirit, casting out of that demon is the only answer.

## WHAT IS OUR AUTHORITY FOR THE CASTING OUT OF DEMONS?

a. Jesus cast out demons. We have already seen many examples of this in the Word of God.

b. He gave this power to the twelve and to the seventy. Read Matthew 10:1; Mark 6:7; Luke 9:49,50.

c. The apostles used this power. Read Acts 16:16-18; etc.

d. He also gave this power to us. Read Mark 16:17.

## WHAT ARE THE STEPS TO BE FOLLOWED IN THE CASTING OUT OF DEMONS?

a. Be spiritually prepared by prayer and fasting (Matt. 17:21; Mk. 9:29); do not take it lightly or presumptuously (Acts 19:13-16; Jude 8,9); seek the anointing (Isa. 61:1).

b.  Establish the identity of the spirit—either by a word of knowledge (Acts 16:16, Paul knew the girl had a spirit of divination) or by asking the spirit to identify itself (Mk. 5:9; Lk. 8:30).

c.  Bind the evil spirit (Matt. 12:29).

d.  Command it to leave (Mk. 5:8; Acts 16:18).

As soon as the unsaved person is delivered from the demonic spirit(s), he should be led to the Lord through repentance, water baptism, and, as soon as possible, the baptism of the Holy Spirit, which is his only protection against being possessed again.

> *"Now when the unclean spirit goes out of a man, it passes through waterless places, seeking rest, and does not find it. Then it says, 'I will return to my house from which I came'; and when it comes, it finds it unoccupied, swept, and put in order. Then it goes, and takes along with it seven other spirits more wicked than itself, and they go in and live there; and the last state of that man becomes worse than the first. That is the way it will also be with this evil generation."* Matt. 12:43-45

> *In Him, you also, after listening to the message of truth, the gospel of your salvation—having also believed, you were sealed in Him with the Holy Spirit of promise.* Eph. 1:13

## 13.  WHAT DO WE MEAN BY THE TERM *BINDING*?

The power of binding and loosing is one of the most powerful spiritual weapons we have been given by the Lord.

> *"I will give you the keys of the kingdom of heaven; and whatever you shall bind on earth shall be bound in heaven, and whatever you shall loose on earth shall be loosed in heaven."* Matt. 16:19

454

> *"Truly I say to you, whatever you shall bind on earth shall be bound in heaven; and whatever you loose on earth shall be loosed in heaven. Again I say to you, that if two of you agree on earth about anything that they may ask, it shall be done for them by My Father who is in heaven. For where two or three have gathered together in My name, there I am in their midst."*　　　　Matt. 18:18-20

Although these verses primarily have to do with the binding and loosing of sin and its guilt (and therefore, by association, have to do with forgiveness), we can also see a basis for binding demonic activity (Matt. 12:29).

## WHAT ARE THE OTHER SPIRITUAL WEAPONS AVAILABLE TO US?

> *For the weapons of our warfare are not of the flesh, but divinely powerful for the destruction of fortresses.*　　　　2 Cor. 10:4

> *. . . in the word of truth, in the power of God; by the weapons of righteousness for the right hand and the left . . . .*　　　　2 Cor. 6:7

a.　The full armor of God comprises the **defensive weapons** that are available to us (Eph. 6:10-18):

1.　Loins girded with truth.

2.　The breastplate of righteousness.

3.　Feet shod with the preparation of the gospel of peace.

4.　The shield of faith.

5.　The helmet of salvation.

6. The sword of the Spirit, which is the Word of God.

7. Prayer in the Spirit.

b. The following **offensive weapons** are divinely powerful to the tearing down of strongholds (2 Cor. 10:4 KJV):

1. The name of Jesus Christ! Read Philippians 2:9-11.

2. The gifts of the Spirit (1 Cor. 12:8-10).

3. The Word of God, which is the sword of the Spirit (Matt. 4:1-11).

4. Prayer (Jas. 5:16b-18).

Read also Psalm 33:16,17; 18:34; 144:1; Philippians 4:7; 1 Peter 1:5; John 10:28,29; 1 Thessalonians 2:18 with Romans 1:13 and 15:22; 1 Thessalonians 5:8; Daniel 10:13,20; 2 Thessalonians 3:3.

# HOME STUDY QUESTIONS: CHAPTER 35

1. In your own words, explain what spiritual warfare is.

2. What is demonic possession? What is the difference between possession and oppression?

3. Explain why a born-again, Spirit-filled Christian cannot be demon-possessed.

4. What are some of the spiritual weapons that are available to us?

# THE MINISTRY OF PRAYER

**Chapter 36**

## 1. WHAT IS PRAYER?

The most basic definition of prayer is that it is communication with God. Just as there are many types and levels of communication among ourselves, so are there types and levels of prayer between ourselves and God. There is mental and oral prayer, and prayer with our understanding and in the Spirit. We can pray while we are standing, walking, sitting, or kneeling; but whatever mode of prayer we choose, we can have the assurance that God will hear us.

> *And this is the confidence which we have before Him, that, if we ask anything according to His will, He hears us. And if we know that He hears us in whatever we ask, we know that we have the requests which we have asked from Him.* 1 Jn. 5:14,15

## 2. IS THERE ANY PARTICULAR MODE OF PRAYER THAT IS MORE ACCEPTABLE TO GOD?

No, all types of prayer are acceptable to God as long as they are:

°   Sincere (prompted by love and commitment to Him and His will).

> *Delight yourself in the Lord; and He will give you the desires of your heart. Commit your way to the Lord, trust also in Him, and He will do it.* Ps. 37:4,5

°    Offered with reverence and godly fear.

> *The Lord is near to all who call upon Him, to all who call upon Him in truth. He will fulfill the desire of **those who fear Him;** He will also hear their cry and will save them.*              Ps. 145:18,19

°    Accompanied by faith, knowing that God always hears our cry and will answer.

> *The eyes of the Lord are toward the righteous, and His ears are open to their cry.*
> *The righteous cry and the Lord hears, and delivers them out of all their troubles.*       Ps. 34:15,17

> *As for me, I shall call upon God, and the Lord will save me.*              Ps. 55:16

## 3.  HOW MANY KINDS OF PRAYER ARE THERE?

There are many kinds of prayer, including:

°    Personal and private prayer (both silent and spoken).

> *"But you, when you pray, go into your inner room, and when you have shut your door, pray to your Father who is in secret, and your Father who sees in secret will repay you."*           Matt. 6:6

> *And after He had sent the multitudes away, He went up to the mountain by Himself to pray; and when it was evening, He was there alone.*       Matt. 14:23

°    Corporate prayer, such as family prayers, gatherings outside the church building (home meetings, etc.) and congregational prayer meetings.

*And when they had been released, they went to their own companions, and reported all that the chief priests and the elders had said to them. And when they [the disciples] heard this, they lifted their voices to God with one accord.*

*And when they had prayed, the place where they had gathered together was shaken, and they were all filled with the Holy Spirit, and began to speak the word of God with boldness.*  Acts 4:23,24,31

All types of both private and corporate prayer include **prayer as praise** (Ex. 15:1-18; 2 Sam. 22; 23:1-7; 1 Ki. 8:22-27; Lk. 1:46-55), **prayer as thanksgiving** (Judg. 5; 1 Sam. 2:1-10), **prayer as repentance** (2 Chr. 7:13,14), and **prayer as a general means of speaking to, and hearing from, God** (Ex. 3; 4:1-17; Jn. 17).

° Supplicatory (general intercessory) prayer.

*I exhort therefore, that, first of all, supplications, prayers, intercessions, and giving of thanks, be made for all men.*  1 Tim. 2:1 KJV

° Prayer as spiritual warfare: travailing (specific intercessory) prayer. Read Ephesians 6:10-17, and especially verse 18.

*With all prayer and petition pray at all times in the Spirit, and with this in view, be on the alert with all perseverance and petition for all the saints.*
Eph. 6:18

*And in the same way the Spirit also helps our weakness; for we do not know how to pray as we should, but the Spirit Himself intercedes for us with groanings too deep for words.*  Rom. 8:26

*The effective* ["effectual fervent," KJV] *prayer of a righteous man can accomplish much.*  Jas. 5:16b

## 4. DID JESUS GIVE US A PATTERN FOR BOTH OUR PERSONAL AND OUR CORPORATE PRAYER?

Yes, Jesus gave us a pattern for prayer in what is usually referred to as "The Lord's Prayer," in Matthew 6:9-13:

> *"Pray, then, in this way:*
> *'Our Father who art in heaven,*
> *Hallowed be Thy name.*
> *'Thy kingdom come.*
> *Thy will be done,*
> *On earth as it is in heaven.*
> *'Give us this day our daily bread.*
> *'And forgive us our debts, as we also have forgiven our debtors.*
> *And do not lead us into temptation, but deliver us from evil.*
> *For Thine is the kingdom, and the power, and the glory, forever.*
> *Amen.'"*

Notice that Jesus did not give us a prayer to pray—He did not say, "Pray this"; rather, He said, "Pray, then, **in this way.**" In this pattern for prayer, we are exhorted:

°   To come into the presence of the Lord with praise and thanksgiving, acknowledging His supreme Lordship.

°   To come before Him in the power of the Spirit, not in our own strength (v. 9, "who art in **heaven**")—God is spirit, and those who approach Him must do so in spirit and in truth (Jn. 4:24).

°   To acknowledge the power and holiness of His name (Ps. 9:10; 105:3; Jn. 14:13; 16:23-26).

°   To come before Him and present our petitions to Him by faith in our kingdom, covenant relationship with Him (Matt. 7:11; Lk. 12:32).

- To not take His availability for granted, but to seek His presence and His favor (1 Chr. 28:9; Jer. 29:12; 33:3), asking Him for all we need (Matt. 7:7-10; 21:22).

- To acknowledge the sovereignty of His will and be willing to receive His answer accordingly (Lk. 22:42; 1 Jn. 5:14,15).

- To receive forgiveness from Him (because we have repented) and, at the same time, to forgive others (Matt. 6:14,15).

- To sum up our petitions by once again acknowledging His sovereignty and giving Him the thanks and the praise that are due His mighty name!

## 5. DOES THE LORD HELP US TO PRAY?

Yes, the Lord does help us to pray. He has first of all given us the pattern for prayer found in Matthew 6:9-13. He has also given us His Holy Spirit, who will teach us to pray and will even pray through us in the language of the Spirit (tongues).

> *And in the same way the Spirit also helps our weakness; for we do not know how to pray as we should, but the Spirit Himself intercedes for us with groanings too deep for words; and He who searches the hearts knows what the mind of the Spirit is, because He intercedes for the saints according to the will of God.*　Rom. 8:26,27

## 6. WHY IS IT NECESSARY FOR US TO PRAY IN TONGUES?

As we have seen, it is necessary for us to pray in tongues because we often do not know how to pray as we ought. The Holy Spirit comes to our assistance at such times, interceding for us and presenting our petitions to God for us. At such times, we can have the assurance that we are praying according to the will of the Father. In addition to this, there are times when demonic powers come against us when we pray. The language of the Spirit is one thing with which the devil and his evil forces cannot interfere (much like the Old Testament example of Daniel, whose prayers were hindered for 21 days by the "prince of Persia"—a satanic force, which was broken by the intervention of Michael the archangel).

> *For one who speaks in a tongue does not speak to men, but to God; for no one understands, but in his spirit he speaks mysteries.* 1 Cor. 14:2

> *Finally, be strong in the Lord, and in the strength of His might. Put on the full armor of God, that you may be able to stand firm against the schemes of the devil. For our struggle is not against flesh and blood, but against the rulers, against the powers, against the world forces of this darkness, against the spiritual forces of wickedness in the heavenly places. Therefore, take up the full armor of God, that you may be able to resist in the evil day, and having done everything, to stand firm.*
> *With all prayer and petition pray at all times in the Spirit, and with this in view, be on the alert with all perseverance and petition for all the saints.* Eph. 6:10-13,18

## 7. HOW DOES PRAYING IN TONGUES BENEFIT US?

In addition to being enabled to pray according to the will of God and being provided with a clear and protected channel of communication to God, praying in the Spirit enables us to be built up in our faith.

> *But you, beloved, building yourselves up on your most holy faith; praying in the Holy Spirit . . . .*　　　Jude 20

> *One who speaks in a tongue edifies himself; but one who prophesies edifies the church.*　　　1 Cor. 14:4

## 8. IS PRAYING IN TONGUES BETTER THAN PRAYING WITH OUR UNDERSTANDING?

Both means of prayer are necessary. There are times when we can express ourselves perfectly to the Lord, using our own words and our understanding. It is also better to pray in this manner when we are participating in corporate prayer so that others will understand us and pray with us. There are other times, however, and especially in personal prayer, when we can release ourselves into praying in the Spirit, experiencing new heights of power and love for God.

> *For if I pray in a tongue, my spirit prays, but my mind is unfruitful. What is the outcome then? I shall pray with the spirit and I shall pray with the mind also; I shall sing with the spirit and I shall sing with the mind also. Otherwise if you bless in the spirit only, how will the one who fills the place of the ungifted say the "Amen" at your giving of thanks, since he does not know what you are saying? For you are giving thanks well enough, but the other man is not edified.*　　　1 Cor. 14:14-17

## 9.  WHAT IS INTERCESSORY PRAYER?

Intercessory prayer is praying for the needs and welfare of others.

> *With all prayer and petition pray at all times in the Spirit, and with this in view, be on the alert with all perseverance and petition for all the saints.*          Eph. 6:18

> *"Moreover, as for me, far be it from me that I should sin against the Lord by ceasing to pray for you; but I will instruct you in the good and right way."*          1 Sam. 12:23


## 10.   WHO MAY PRAY AS AN INTERCESSOR?

Every believer should participate in intercessory prayer because he has been called to be a priest to intercede for others before the Lord.

> *The effective prayer of a righteous man can accomplish much.*          Jas. 5:16

> *But you are a chosen race, a royal priesthood, a holy nation, a people for God's own possession, that you may proclaim the excellencies of Him who has called you out of darkness into His marvelous light.*          1 Pet. 2:9


## 11.   WHAT ARE THE TWO TYPES OF INTERCESSORY PRAYER?

The two types of intercessory prayer are: (1) general, or supplicatory, intercession; and (2) specific, or travailing, intercession.

## 2. WHAT IS TRAVAILING PRAYER?

Travailing prayer is that kind of intercession which is inspired by the Holy Spirit, and in which we travail for our own needs or for the needs of others. It is for the purpose of bringing about change in our lives or circumstances (or in those of another) through divine intervention.

> *Therefore, confess your sins to one another, and pray for one another, so that you may be healed. The effective prayer of a righteous man can accomplish much. Elijah was a man with a nature like ours, and he prayed earnestly that it might not rain; and it did not rain on the earth for three years and six months. And he prayed again, and the sky poured rain and the earth produced its fruit.* Jas. 5:16-18

> *My children, with whom I am again in labor until Christ is formed in you . . . .* Gal. 4:19

> *In the days of His flesh, He offered up both prayers and supplications with loud crying and tears to the One able to save Him from death, and He was heard because of His piety.* Heb. 5:7

## 3. WHAT IS THE PRIMARY DIFFERENCE BETWEEN GENERAL INTERCESSORY PRAYER AND SPECIFIC, OR TRAVAILING, INTERCESSORY PRAYER?

In general intercessory prayer, we come before the Lord to present our petitions to Him on behalf of someone else. Travailing intercessory prayer is more intense, involving spiritual warfare "against the rulers, against the powers, against the world forces of this darkness, against the spiritual forces of wickedness in the heavenly places" (Eph. 6:12).

*For though we walk in the flesh, we do not war according to the flesh, for the weapons of our warfare are not of the flesh, but divinely powerful for the destruction of fortresses. We are destroying speculations and every lofty thing raised up against the knowledge of God, and we are taking every thought captive to the obedience of Christ.*

*2 Cor. 10:3-5*

*Blessed be the Lord, my rock, who trains my hands for war, and my fingers for battle; my lovingkindness and my fortress, my stronghold and my deliverer; my shield and He in whom I take refuge; who subdues my people under me.*

*Ps. 144:1,2*

## 14.  WHAT IS SPIRITUAL WARFARE?

Spiritual warfare is a battle in which the believer is equipped by the Holy Spirit to fight against the devil and his demonic forces.

*Finally, be strong in the Lord, and in the strength of His might. Put on the full armor of God, that you may be able to stand firm against the schemes of the devil. For our struggle is not against flesh and blood, but against the rulers, against the powers, against the world forces of this darkness, against the spiritual forces of wickedness in the heavenly places. Therefore, take up the full armor of God, that you may be able to resist in the evil day, and having done everything, to stand firm. Stand firm therefore, having girded your loins with truth, and having put on the breastplate of righteousness, and having shod your feet with the preparation of the gospel of peace; in addition to all, taking up the shield of faith with which you will be able to extinguish all the flaming missiles of the evil one.*      Eph. 6:10-16

## 5. HOW OFTEN DO WE ENGAGE IN THIS KIND OF TRAVAILING PRAYER?

We engage in travailing prayer as spiritual warfare every time the Holy Spirit initiates it within us. When we sense the Holy Spirit stirring our spirits to come before the Lord, we should yield ourselves to Him and keep praying until we know the victory has been won.

> *With all prayer and petition pray at all times in the Spirit, and with this in view, be on the alert with all perseverance and petition for all the saints.* Eph. 6:18

NOTE: For further study of spiritual warfare, read Chapter 35 in Part Four.

## 6. WHAT SHOULD WE AVOID IN PRAYER?

We should avoid:

a. Meaningless repetitions—saying the same prayers over and over, and mindless repetition of tongues.

> *"And when you are praying, do not use meaningless repetition, as the Gentiles do, for they suppose that they will be heard for their many words."* Matt. 6:7

b. Being led by feelings rather than by the Holy Spirit. This means that we do not avoid prayer because we do not feel like it; neither do we rely upon our feelings to guide us in our prayer. The Word of God and the Spirit of the Lord have been given to us to guide us in all our life and ministry before the Lord.

# HOME STUDY QUESTIONS: CHAPTER 36

1. What is prayer?

2. How many kinds of prayer are there?

3. What is "praying in the Spirit," and how does it benefit us?

4. What are the two types of intercessory prayer? Explain the difference between the two.

# THE MINISTRY OF FASTING

**Chapter 37**

## 1. WHAT IS FASTING?

Fasting is abstaining from food and drink for a period of time during which we seek the Lord's special intervention for our needs or the needs of another.

> *"Is this not the fast which I choose, to loosen the bonds of wickedness, to undo the bands of the yoke, and to let the oppressed go free, and break every yoke?"*  Isa. 58:6

## 2. HOW MANY KINDS OF FASTS ARE THERE?

There are three kinds of fasts:

° The regular, or normal, fast in which we abstain from all food and drink except water for a specified period of time.

> *And after He had fasted forty days and forty nights, He then became hungry.*  Matt. 4:2

° The partial fast, in which we omit either one or two meals each day or else in some way limit the quantity of food and drink which we consume.

> *I did not eat any tasty food, nor did meat or wine enter my mouth, nor did I use any ointment at all, until the entire three weeks were completed.*  Dan. 10:3

    &deg;   The complete fast, in which we abstain from all food and drink. This kind of fast should not be followed for more than three days. We can get along for an extended period of time without food, but water is essential to our health and the normal operation of our bodily functions.

> *And he was three days without sight, and neither ate nor drank.*
>                        Acts 9:9

> *"Go, assemble all the Jews who are found in Susa, and fast for me; do not eat or drink for three days, night or day. I and my maidens also will fast in the same way. And thus I will go in to the king, which is not according to the law; and if I perish, I perish."*
>                        Esth. 4:16

## 3.  WHAT ARE SOME WRONG MOTIVES FOR FASTING?

According to Isaiah 58:1-5 (q.v.), the following are some wrong motives for fasting:

a.   Merely for religious observance.

b.   Fasting for contention and strife.

c.   Trying to get your way with God.

d.   Fasting as a form of asceticism, that is, as a form of fleshly "self-abasement" (read Colossians 2:16-23).

## 4.  WHAT ARE SOME RIGHT MOTIVES FOR FASTING?

According to Isaiah 58:6,7 (q.v.), the following are right motives for fasting:

a.   To loosen the bonds of wickedness.

b. To free oneself or others from bondage.

c. To free the oppressed.

d. To break every yoke of spiritual wickedness.

e. To be able to share food and other provisions with others who are in need.

## 5. WHAT ARE THE BENEFITS OF FASTING?

According to Isaiah 58:8-12 (q.v.), the benefits of fasting (in addition to the above) are:

a. Your health will spring forth; your energies will be renewed.

b. The glory of the Lord will be your portion.

c. The Lord will answer you speedily.

d. All oppression will be banished.

e. The Lord will guide you and satisfy you.

f. Others of your household will share in the blessings.

## 6. WHAT ARE SOME GUIDELINES FOR FASTING?

a. It is first of all important to begin your period of fasting with a positive kind of faith, because it is the only kind of faith that God will honor. Hebrews 11:6 says:

> *And without faith it is impossible to please Him, for he who comes to God must believe that He is, and that He is a rewarder of those who seek* ["diligently seek," KJV] *Him.*

Because of all that the Lord promises to us in His Word concerning fasting, we can expect that He will reward our efforts when we seek Him accordingly.

b. Do not draw attention to yourself by going out of your way to let others know that you are fasting. Avoid the appearance of being "religious." Jesus promised us that when we fast with the right motives, our Father, who sees in secret, will reward us openly (Matt. 6:18 KJV).

c. Sometimes the critical periods of pressing needs of life drive us to times of fasting, but do not wait for such times to come before entering into a fast. Fasting can be a powerful and rewarding part of our normal Christian experience.

d. Remember that it is perfectly acceptable to set various time periods for the duration of your fasting. Initially, it is good to abstain from food for a relatively short period of time, such as omitting only one or two meals. You can then "graduate" to longer periods of time: one or two days without food, or eliminating a meal or two a day for a longer period of time.

e. Be sure to set aside plenty of time for prayer and Bible reading, but also remember to balance these times with normal activity—including spending time with your family and others.

## 7. WHAT ARE SOME PHYSICAL ASPECTS OF FASTING?

a. It is, first of all, important to remember that if you have any special health problems, or if you are on any regular medications, you should check with your doctor before beginning any fast, even a short one. Some medications are not to be taken without food, and some health problems may actually be aggravated by prolonged abstinence from food.

b. During the first day or so of your fasting, you will probably experience some unpleasant physical symptoms, such as nausea, dizziness, and headaches. This is normal and should not deter you from your decision to fast. These unpleasant feelings usually go away after the first day or so.

c. Hunger will be one of the most persistent feelings that you will have to cope with, especially at the outset of your fasting. Since hunger is partly a matter of habit, however, these sensations will become manageable with self-control.

d. Some people drink only water during their fast, while others drink fruit juices, milk, broth, and so forth. Find out what works for you, and stick with it! (NOTE: Do not abstain from liquids for longer than seventy-two hours; more than that can have disastrous physical effects.)

e. Do not break your fast abruptly. Break it gradually and with moderate amounts of mild food.

## 8. WHAT CONCLUSIONS CAN WE DRAW CONCERNING FASTING?

Although the physical aspects of fasting intrigue us and sometimes discourage us, we must never forget that the major work of scriptural fasting is in the realm of the spirit. What goes on spiritually is of much more consequence than what is happening bodily. You will be engaged in spiritual warfare that will necessitate all the weapons of Ephesians 6. One of the most spiritually critical periods is at the close of the physical fast when we have a natural tendency to relax. But not all fasting is a heavy spiritual struggle—fasting can also bring us "righteousness and peace and joy in the Holy Spirit" (Rom. 14:17).

Fasting can bring breakthroughs in the spiritual realm that could never be had in any other way. It is a means of God's grace and blessing that should not be neglected any longer.

## HOME STUDY QUESTIONS: CHAPTER 37

1. Read Isaiah 58 in its entirety.

2. In your own words, explain what fasting is.

3. What are the benefits of fasting?

4. What are some right motives for fasting?

# THE MINISTRY OF PRAISE AND WORSHIP

**Chapter 38**

## 1. WHAT IS THE NEW TESTAMENT MINISTRY OF PRAISE AND WORSHIP?

The New Testament ministry of praise and worship is our giving to God the spiritual offerings and sacrifices which He so richly deserves.

> *You also, as living stones, are being built up as a spiritual house for a holy priesthood, to offer up spiritual sacrifices acceptable to God through Jesus Christ.*
>
> 1 Pet. 2:5

The New Testament reality of praise and worship fulfills all the Old Testament patterns, especially those established by David. The New Testament is a better covenant; therefore, we should have **more, not less!** (Read Hebrews 7:22; 8:6; Haggai 2:9.)

## 2. WHAT ARE SPIRITUAL SACRIFICES?

Spiritual sacrifices are our offerings of praise and thanksgiving to the Lord.

> *I will praise the name of God with song, and shall magnify Him with thanksgiving. And it will please the Lord better than an ox or a young bull with horns and hoofs.*
>
> Ps. 69:30,31

*Take words with you and return to the Lord. Say to Him,
"Take away all iniquity, and receive us graciously, that we
may present the fruit of our lips* ["render the calves of our
lips," KJV]. *"*                                            Hos. 14:2


*" . . . creating the praise* [literally, "fruit"] *of the lips.
Peace, peace to him who is far and to him who is near."*
                                                           Isa. 57:19


## 3. IS THIS MINISTRY OF PRAISE AND WORSHIP REQUIRED OF US?

Yes, the ministry of praise and worship is required of us because:

a.  We are a New Testament priesthood and therefore must have a
    sacrifice to offer when we come into the presence of the Lord.
    (Read Hebrews 8:3 and Acts 13:2.)

b.  We are required to present the sacrifice of praise to the Lord even
    when we do not feel like it and even when, in those rare times that
    befall all of us, we do it only out of a sense of duty. David
    **appointed** and **assigned** those who praised and worshiped
    (1 Chr. 15:16-19; 16:4,7; 25:1-7; read also 2 Chr. 20:21; etc.).
    Such praise is acceptable and, when offered to the Lord with a
    willing spirit, always leads to praise from the heart.


## 4. WHAT ARE THE SPIRITUAL SACRIFICES THAT THE LORD REQUIRES US TO GIVE HIM?

There are three spiritual sacrifices that the Lord requires of us:

a.  Ourselves as living sacrifices.

> *I urge you therefore, brethren, by the mercies of God, to present your bodies a living and holy sacrifice, acceptable to God, which is your spiritual service of worship.* Rom. 12:1

b. Our lips (our praise, our conversation, and our testimony).

> *Through Him then, let us continually offer up a sacrifice of praise to God, that is, the fruit of lips that give thanks to His name.* Heb. 13:15

> *I will bless the Lord at all times; His praise shall continually be in my mouth.* Ps. 34:1

c. Our service and our giving.

> *And do not neglect doing good and sharing; for with such sacrifices God is pleased.* Heb. 13:16

## 5. WHAT IS WORSHIP?

Worship is the proclaiming of His "worth-ship," which we express through the psalms, hymns, and spiritual songs that we sing in His presence.

> *. . . speaking to one another in psalms and hymns and spiritual songs, singing and making melody with your heart to the Lord . . . .* Eph. 5:19

> *Let the word of Christ richly dwell within you, with all wisdom teaching and admonishing one another with psalms and hymns and spiritual songs, singing with thankfulness in your hearts to God.* Col. 3:16

## 6. WHAT ARE THE ESSENTIAL CHARACTERISTICS OF TRUE WORSHIP?

The essential characteristics of true worship are that it is of and by the Spirit of God and also that it is according to the truth of His Word.

> *"But an hour is coming, and now is, when the true worshipers shall worship the Father in spirit and truth; for such people the Father seeks to be His worshipers. God is spirit, and those who worship Him must worship in spirit and truth."*
>
> Jn. 4:23,24

## 7. WHAT IS PRAISE?

a.  Praise is that part of worship which we express solely in and by the Holy Spirit. We sing psalms (choruses) and hymns as an expression of the worship that comes from our hearts, but praise is that expression of love and worship which is only by the Holy Spirit and through the Holy Spirit. It is the spiritual song referred to in the New Testament scriptures.

> *. . . speaking to one another in psalms and hymns and spiritual songs, singing and making melody with your heart to the Lord . . . .*
>
> Eph. 5:19

> *Let the word of Christ richly dwell within you, with all wisdom teaching and admonishing one another with psalms and hymns and spiritual songs, singing with thankfulness in your hearts to God.*
>
> Col. 3:16

b.  Praise is a spiritual song which, although not always expressed in tongues, includes and embraces "singing in the spirit."

*For if I pray in a tongue, my spirit prays, but my mind is unfruitful. What is the outcome then? I shall pray with the spirit and I shall pray with the mind also; I shall **sing with the spirit** and I shall sing with the mind also.*

1 Cor. 14:14,15

Read also Ephesians 5:19 and Colossians 3:16.

c. Praise is the "sound of many waters"—the voice of the Spirit of God in the midst of His people.

*And His feet were like burnished bronze, when it has been caused to glow in a furnace, and **His voice was like the sound of many waters.*** Rev. 1:15

*And I heard, as it were, the voice of a great multitude and **as the sound of many waters** and as the sound of mighty peals of thunder, saying, "Hallelujah! For the Lord our God, the Almighty, reigns."* Rev. 19:6

For this reason, it is important for the congregation to sing in the same key, and with all the voices blending together in harmony.

d. Praise is the "song of the Lord"—Jesus, in the midst of the congregation, singing praise through the people unto the Father.

*For both He who sanctifies and those who are sanctified are all from one Father; for which reason He is not ashamed to call them brethren, saying, "I will proclaim Thy name to My brethren, **in the midst of the congregation I will sing Thy praise."***

Heb. 2:11,12

## 8. HOW DOES WORSHIP IN THE NEW TESTAMENT DIFFER FROM OLD TESTAMENT WORSHIP?

In the Old Testament, Israel worshiped the Lord through patterns and "copies of the things in the heavens" (Heb. 9:1-23). These patterns of worship were given to them, but were meant to be fulfilled in us as New Testament priests by the Holy Spirit. Here are some of the basic differences in worship between the two covenants:

a.   Under the provisions of the Old Covenant, a few men were chosen to be priests (Levites), and one man was chosen to be the high priest. In the New Covenant, every believer is a priest, and our worship is offered to God through the ministry of our High Priest, Jesus Christ.

> You also, as living stones, are being built up as a spiritual house for a **holy priesthood, to offer up spiritual sacrifices** acceptable to God through Jesus Christ.                                    1 Pet. 2:5

> But you are a chosen race, a **royal priesthood,** a holy nation, a people for God's own possession, **that you may proclaim the excellencies of Him** who has called you out of darkness into His marvelous light.
>
>                                    1 Pet. 2:9

b.   In the Old Testament, only the high priest was permitted to enter the holy of holies once a year. In New Testament worship, we all have access into the presence of God any time we come before Him.

> Since therefore, brethren, we have confidence to enter the holy place by the blood of Jesus, by a new and living way which He inaugurated for us through the veil, that is, His flesh, and since we have a great priest over the house of God, let us draw near with a sincere heart.
>
>                                    Heb. 10:19-22

c.  Under the Old Covenant, the blood of animals covered sins for a time, but this sacrifice had to be repeated time and again. Through the provisions of the New Covenant, the blood of Jesus Christ has taken our sin away for all time.

> *But in those sacrifices there is a reminder of sins year by year. For it is impossible for the blood of bulls and goats to take away sins.*
> *And every priest stands daily ministering and offering time after time the same sacrifices, which can never take away sins; but He, having offered **one sacrifice for sins for all time**, sat down at the right hand of God.*
> *For **by one offering He has perfected for all time those who are sanctified.*** Heb. 10:3,4,11,12,14

d.  Under the Old Covenant, worship was confined to the tabernacle and, later, to the temple. In the New Covenant, worship is in the Spirit and is therefore not restricted to special times and special places.

> *"Woman, believe Me, an hour is coming when neither in this mountain, nor in Jerusalem, shall you worship the Father.*
> *"God is spirit, and those who worship Him must worship in spirit and truth."* Jn. 4:21,24

In the Old Testament, worship began in the outer court, moved into the inner court, and found its most complete expression in that which was accomplished in the holy of holies. This is a pattern for New Testament worship, which begins with singing "with the mind" (hymns and choruses), moves into praise, and finally touches the presence of God in worship in the spirit ("spiritual songs and melodies"). Read 1 Chronicles 16:1-7. Worship should, therefore, flow and progress from soul (that is, the singing of hymns and choruses with our understanding) to spirit, which is the singing of our spirits in true, Spirit-activated worship.

## 9. WHAT IS THE FIVEFOLD PURPOSE OF PRAISE AND WORSHIP?

a. Praise is the proclaiming of God's "worth-ship" and the presenting of our thanksgiving to Him.

> *Ascribe to the Lord the glory due His name; bring an offering, and come before Him; worship the Lord in holy array.*                                           1 Chr. 16:29

b. Praise brings pleasure to God.

> *Praise the Lord! Sing to the Lord a new song, and His praise in the congregation of the godly ones.*
> *For* **the Lord takes pleasure** *in His people; He will beautify the afflicted ones with salvation.*
>                                           Ps. 149:1,4

c. Praise makes a place of spiritual enthronement for the presence of God in our midst.

> *"The Lord is my strength and song, and He has become my salvation; this is my God, and* **I will praise Him** *["prepare him a habitation," KJV]; my father's God, and I will extol Him."*                    Ex. 15:2

> *Yet Thou art holy, O Thou who art* **enthroned upon** *["that inhabitest," KJV]* **the praises of Israel.**
>                                           Ps. 22:3

d. Praise is our means of ascent unto the throne of God.

> *When the queen of Sheba perceived all the wisdom of Solomon, the house that he had built, the food of his table, the seating of his servants, the attendance of his waiters and their attire, his cupbearers, and* **his stairway by which he went up to the house of the Lord** *[literally, "his burnt offering which he offered"] there was no more spirit in her.*                                    1 Ki. 10:4,5

Who may ascend? He who has clean hands and a pure heart (Ps. 24:3-5; Ps. 15). Just as worship affects our way of living, so also the way we live affects the quality of our praise. James 3:9-12 tells us that a fountain cannot send forth both sweet and bitter water; so our mouths should not give forth both praise to God and cursing to our brother.

e. Once God is enthroned and we have ministered to Him, He ministers to us. God has ordained praise and worship as an avenue for releasing His blessings to us.

1. Praise leads us to repentance, cleanses us, and keeps us in our place, because we acknowledge His place (Isa. 6:1-7).

2. Praise reveals His glory to us (2 Chr. 5:13,14).

3. Praise motivates and releases the gifts of the Spirit to operate within the congregation (Acts 13:1-3; 4:31; Ps. 73:17).

4. Praise releases the power of God (2 Chr. 20:20-22).

5. Praise brings liberty and release to us (2 Cor. 3:17).

6. Praise releases God's grace (Ps. 123:1-3) and His blessings (Ps. 128:5) to us.

7. Praise brings us the refreshing rain of His presence (Ps. 104:10-13; 68:9).

8. Praise beautifies the people of God (Ps. 33:1; 147:1; 149:1-4).

## 10. HOW DO WE EXPRESS OUR PRAISE?

The Bible tells us that we are to worship the Lord with our whole being, that is, "spirit, soul, and body" (1 Thess. 5:23).

> *Hear, O Israel! The Lord is our God, the Lord is one! And you shall love the Lord your God **with all your heart and with all your soul and with all your might.***
>
> Deut. 6:4,5

We have already discussed what it means to worship God in spirit. Worshiping God with all our heart and soul means that our emotions, too, are involved. There is a difference between worshiping God with our emotions, and "emotionalism." Emotionalism carries with it the connotation that we are ruled by our emotions, and that we are not in control. Worshiping God with our emotions of love, and joy, etc., means simply that we have approached God with our whole heart and have submitted our emotions to Him. The Bible tells us in many places that we are to worship the Lord with joy, gladness, shouts, and even laughter.

> *For I used to go along with the throng and lead them in procession to the house of God, with the voice of joy and thanksgiving, a multitude keeping festival.* Ps. 42:4

> *Her priests also I will clothe with salvation; and her godly ones **will sing aloud for joy.*** Ps. 132:16

Furthermore, by presenting our bodies as a living sacrifice to the Lord, we praise Him "with all our might" by:

a.  Lifting up our hands.

> *Because Thy lovingkindness is better than life, my lips will praise Thee. So I will bless Thee as long as I live; **I will lift up my hands** in Thy name.*
>
> Ps. 63:3,4

484

b.  Clapping our hands.

> *O clap your hands, all peoples; shout to God with the voice of joy.* Ps. 47:1

c.  Singing.

> *Sing to God, sing praises to His name; lift up a song for Him who rides through the deserts, whose name is the Lord, and exult before Him.* Ps. 68:4 RSV

d.  Playing musical instruments.

> *Praise Him with trumpet sound; praise Him with harp and lyre. Praise Him with timbrel and dancing; praise Him with stringed instruments and pipe. Praise Him with loud cymbals; praise Him with resounding cymbals.* Ps. 150:3-5

e.  Dancing.

> *Praise Him with timbrel and **dancing.*** Ps. 150:4

> *Let the sons of Zion rejoice in their King. **Let them praise His name with dancing;** let them sing praises to Him with timbrel and lyre. For the Lord takes pleasure in His people; He will beautify the afflicted ones with salvation.* Ps. 149:2b-4

f.  Shouting.

> *Be glad in the Lord and rejoice you righteous ones, and **shout for joy,** all you who are upright in heart.* Ps. 32:11

## 11. IS IT POSSIBLE TO WORSHIP GOD IN THE SPIRIT WITHOUT THE BAPTISM OF THE HOLY SPIRIT?

No. It is impossible to worship God in the Spirit without the baptism of the Holy Spirit because:

> *"An hour is coming, and now is, when the true worshipers shall worship the Father in spirit and truth; for such people the Father seeks to be His worshipers. God is spirit, and those who worship Him must worship in spirit and truth."*
> Jn. 4:23,24

First Corinthians 2:14 tells us that the natural (unregenerate and immature believer) man cannot receive the things of the Spirit. This, together with 14:13-15, makes it clear that praying and worshiping in the spirit must be by the Holy Spirit and not just our own effort.

## HOME STUDY QUESTIONS: CHAPTER 38

1. What is the New Testament ministry of praise and worship?

2. What is the fivefold purpose of praise and worship?

3. What is singing "in the Spirit"?

# ABOUT THE AUTHOR

Pastor Norman H. James, Sr., is the founding pastor of a New Testament, Spirit-filled church in Bridgeville, Pennsylvania, and has provided its spiritual direction and overall leadership for over thirty years. He also has apostolic oversight for a number of U.S. and international churches located in Pennsylvania, Alabama, Ohio, Hawaii, Japan, England, Jamaica, Brazil, and South Africa.

In addition to having authored *The Christian Life Series,* which is a study of the basic doctrines of the Christian faith, he has also written and developed extensive teaching materials for the training of ministries within the local church.

# APPENDIX A: MEMORY SECTION

## THE BOOKS OF THE BIBLE

66 Books of the Bible—Written by 44 Authors
39 Old Testament Books—27 New Testament Books

### Old Testament

| | | |
|---|---|---|
| Genesis | 2 Chronicles | Daniel |
| Exodus | Ezra | Hosea |
| Leviticus | Nehemiah | Joel |
| Numbers | Esther | Amos |
| Deuteronomy | Job | Obadiah |
| Joshua | Psalms | Jonah |
| Judges | Proverbs | Micah |
| Ruth | Ecclesiastes | Nahum |
| 1 Samuel | Song of Solomon | Habakkuk |
| 2 Samuel | Isaiah | Zephaniah |
| 1 Kings | Jeremiah | Haggai |
| 2 Kings | Lamentations | Zechariah |
| 1 Chronicles | Ezekiel | Malachi |

### New Testament

| | | |
|---|---|---|
| Matthew | Ephesians | Hebrews |
| Mark | Philippians | James |
| Luke | Colossians | 1 Peter |
| John | 1 Thessalonians | 2 Peter |
| Acts | 2 Thessalonians | 1 John |
| Romans | 1 Timothy | 2 John |
| 1 Corinthians | 2 Timothy | 3 John |
| 2 Corinthians | Titus | Jude |
| Galatians | Philemon | Revelation |

# THE TEN COMMANDMENTS
Exodus 20:3-17
(Based on the King James Version)

1. Thou shalt have no other gods before Me.
2. Thou shalt not make unto thee any graven image.
3. Thou shalt not take the name of the Lord thy God in vain.
4. Remember the sabbath day, to keep it holy.
5. Honor thy father and thy mother: that thy days may be long upon the land which the Lord thy God giveth thee.
6. Thou shalt not kill (murder).
7. Thou shalt not commit adultery.
8. Thou shalt not steal.
9. Thou shalt not bear false witness against thy neighbor.
10. Thou shalt not covet thy neighbor's house, thou shalt not covet thy neighbor's wife, nor his manservant, nor his maidservant, nor his ox, nor his donkey, nor anything that is thy neighbor's.

# THE LORD'S PRAYER
Matthew 6:9-13

"Our Father who art in heaven,
Hallowed be Thy name.
Thy kingdom come. Thy will be done,
On earth as it is in heaven.
Give us this day our daily bread.
And forgive us our debts, as we also have forgiven our debtors.
And do not lead us into temptation, but deliver us from evil.
For Thine is the kingdom, and the power, and the glory, forever.
Amen."

# THE SIX FOUNDATION STONES
## Hebrews 6:1,2

The six principles (foundation stones) are the foundations we must personally experience before we can go on to maturity in Christ. They are:

1. Repentance From Dead Works
2. Faith Toward God (Justification)
3. Doctrine of Baptisms
   a. Water Baptism
   b. Baptism of the Holy Spirit
   c. Baptism of Fire
4. Laying on of Hands
5. Resurrection of the Dead
6. Eternal Judgment

# THE APOSTLES' CREED

I believe in God the Father Almighty, Creator of heaven and earth; and in Jesus Christ, His only Son, our Lord; who was conceived by the Holy Ghost, born of the Virgin Mary, suffered under Pontius Pilate, was crucified, died, and was buried. He descended into hell; and on the third day He rose again from the dead; He ascended into heaven, and sitteth at the right hand of God the Father Almighty; from thence He shall come to judge the quick and the dead.

I believe in the Holy Ghost, the holy Christian Church, the communion of saints, the forgiveness of sins, the resurrection of the body, and life everlasting. Amen.